ROCK ATLAS

650 great music locations and the fascinating stories behind them

Written and researched by David Roberts

CLARKSDALE

First Published 2011 by Clarksdale
an imprint of Ovolo Books Ltd

Paperback ISBN: 978 1 905 959 242
E-book ISBN: 978 1 905 959 662

Printed by Finidr Ltd, Cesky Tesin, the Czech Republic
For more information visit: www.clarksdalebooks.co.uk

Front cover photo of Jimi Hendrix: David Magnus/Rex Features

ROCK ATLAS

650 great music locations and the fascinating stories behind them

Written and researched by David Roberts

PLACES TO VISIT

Album cover &
music video locations
Statues, graves,
memorials & plaques
Venues, festivals & places
that influenced songs

Rock Atlas

Being a collector by nature, Rock Atlas began five years ago with an uncoordinated jumble of facts and fascinating back-stories based on British and Irish locations and developed into a huge, slightly more coordinated jumble, once I'd talked publisher Mark Neeter into agreeing to publish it. Maps were poured over, camera batteries charged and notebooks purchased as I set off, often accompanied by my able Rock Atlas lieutenant, Martin Downham, on safari to capture the essence of as many of, close to, 700 eventual entries as we could manage. Emotions can't help but be stirred when the Smiths fan stands on the steps of Salford Lads Club, or the life-long Beatlemaniac enters John Lennon's boyhood Liverpool home bedroom, or the Hendrix devotee stands proudly next to their hero's Isle of Wight statue.

The worthiest entries in the book were simply those exact spots where music fans can get themselves photographed at the setting of a particularly momentous moment in rock history: a plaque, an album cover

Colin Unwin

photo shoot, a statue, or even a gravestone. But, it was the downright quirky stories – the Black Sabbath blacksmith's gates, Ian Dury's musical park bench, Kurt Cobain and the Duchess of York's sofa and Bob Dylan ghost hunting – that really appealed. Fans, photographers, current owners of former rock star homes and even the musicians themselves, have all contributed

Eleanor Rigby's gravestone in the churchyard at St Peter's, Liverpool. You can sit, like Lennon did, and ponder the description 'asleep' which so fascinated the young Beatle

hugely to the wealth of info in these pages.

Not every iconic location included in the book is still standing. Sometimes your imagination has to work overtime to conjure up the excitement generated by a demolished treasure, when all that remains is a door or a plaque to remember it by. Time and the developers have not been kind to The Undertones

ROCK ATLAS **ACKNOWLEDGEMENTS**

This is the part of the book where the author says 'I couldn't a have done it without the help of...' and I'm no exception. Aside from the tireless expert and creative work of publisher Mark Neeter, proof reader Matt White and Herita du Plessis' assistance with page layouts, I really owe a huge debt of gratitude

to my chief enthusiastic supporters, wife Janet and friend Martin Downham. Others who have played big parts in the production include photographers Peter Tarleton, Colin Unwin, Alan Simpkins, Vernon Stokes and Eddie Evans. Expert advice has been on tap whenever I needed it from Brian Southall, Trevor Simpson,

Pete Nash, Michael Heatley, Julie Fielder, Mike Darling, Pete Chambers and Melanie Smith.

Thanks also go to: Jean Allen, Andrew Batt, David Bainbridge, Janet Bateman, Nicola Beard (Stroud Subscription Rooms), David Bedford (Liddypool: Birthplace of The Beatles), Simon

Bell, Colin Bishop, Sarah Blankfield, Andrew Bowell, Jamie Bowman, Michael Bradley (Undertones), Tony Calvert, Andy Clare, Graham Cook, Ron Cooper (Zabadak Magazine), C Debby, Keith Dickens, Drownedinsound. com, Ian Dunlop, Mark Ellen, Dorothy Elliott, Jaki Florek, Pete Frame (Rock Gazetteer/ Rockin' Around Britain)

> ❛ There's a real spiritual connection in being on the very spot where something that has been a really important part of your life took place. ❜

first venue, the Hertfordshire pub where Cliff Richard first made an impression and dozens of iconic spots that are now car parks, shopping centres or, weirdly in several cases, retirement or care homes. Fortunately, there's now a growing willingness to remember milestone events and places associated with British popular music. These are the tourist attractions of the 21st-century. While rock and pop's anti-establishment early participants can never have imagined they would, or perhaps want to, be remembered with plaques and statues, these locations mean just as much to the music fan with decades of fan worship behind them as, Edinburgh Castle or Stonehenge does to the traditional tourist. There's a real spiritual connection to being in the very spot where something that has been a really important part of your life took place.

Rock Atlas isn't a definitive or comprehensive guide, I got far too carried away with the back stories on some entries for that. There's so many more tales to be told, and

The author's quest for the Holy Grail of rock artefacts sees him staring intently for clues at the sculpture in memory of local hero Rory Gallagher in Cork, Ireland

we'd like to hear yours. If you can add to the recollections, memories and pictures of rock locations we'd like to hear from you. If they are used we'll send you a complimentary copy of the edition they appear in. So, please send us your recommendations for new entries to the next Rock Atlas.

David Roberts
clarksdale@ovolobooks.co.uk

James Fraser, Paul Ford (Isle of Man Post Office), Martin Gardiner, Andy Gunton, John Harris (Hail! Hail! Rock 'n' Roll), Pete Harrison, Bill Harry, David Hart (Beatles Belfast), James H Healey, Simon Heptinstall (Devon — the Best of Britain), Chris Hewitt, Chris Hillman, Brian Hinton (Nights in Wight Satin An Illustrated History of The Isle of Wight Pop Festivals), Pete Hopcraft, Mick Jackson, Trevor Jackson, Ewan Jamieson, Ellie Laycock, John Lemon, Tim Johnston (Beatles Belfast), David Jones, Peter Lewry, Spencer Leigh, Martin Lightfoot, Ed McCann (Beatles Belfast), Mrs SJ Marsh, Jakki Maybury, Nick Maybury (aka Gammy Pulex), Kai Monk, Gail Moss, Ruth Mottram, Tom Murphy, Ray O'Brien (There Are Places I'll Remember), Damian O'Neill (Undertones), Dave Okomah, Carl and Georgina Payne, Al Perkins, Jennifer Powell (Bristol Boxing Club), Edna Pritchard, Jill Punter, Stefano Quadrio, Bernie Quayle (Manx Radio), Ben Roberts, Christopher Sandford (McCartney), John Scholes, Andrew Spencer (Leader Times Newspapers), Johnny Stewart (Stroud News and Journal), George Strange, Andy Sykes, Joy Thacker, John Tindell, Paul Trynka (Starman), Peter Wadsworth (Strawberry Studios), Mrs JM Webb, Paul White (California Ballroom), Dave Wood, Andy Worrall, Ian Wright, Jacqueline Wright, Chris M Zangara

ROCK ATLAS

South West England

UK and Ireland Edition

'There are little services here nearly every weekend, ashes sprinkled on the land, some of whom came as kids in the Seventies. This is where they want to be throughout eternity, which is rather nice, isn't it?'

Michael Eavis, rock's most famous farmer and Glastonbury Festival founder

South West of England

CORNWALL

The county of ship wrecks, tin mines, pasties and a staunchly independent people also boasts some of Britain's finest surfing beaches. At least one Beach Boy puts Cornwall on a par with the Big Sur when it comes to inspirational locations. Speaking from his Santa Barbara home to rock paper Melody Maker back in 1974, Mike Love of The Beach Boys waxed lyrical on the subject. "I'm very fond of England and have always thought of leasing an estate in Cornwall, just to be able to write. The whole atmosphere and mood of the countryside as well as the tradition there would lend itself to some serious writing." Fellow Americans Gram Parsons and Blondie also 'adopted' the British west coast for creative inspiration, but it was British folkies Ralph McTell and Donovan that are best associated with the laidback Cornish vibe, honing their developing performing skills as Sixties beachniks.

❛Cliffs, ice-cream, sunshine: it looks like someone's got tiny little Lego homes and thrown them at the cliffs. It's like Hobbit land. ❜

KT Tunstall describes her favourite Cornish location, Polperro

BODELVA A STUNNING MUSIC VENUE AT THE EDEN PROJECT

The world famous giant greenhouse-domed botanical gardens and eco visitor centre attract some of the best names in music to the 6,000-capacity venue at this natural bowl at Bodelva.

LOCATION 001: four miles from St Austell, postcode PL24 2SG

Can there be a more beautiful music venue in Britain? The Kaiser Chiefs rock the 2008 Eden Sessions

INDIAN QUEENS NICK LOWE'S DRIVING SONG STORY

It was the "pretty name" rather than the place itself that inspired Nick Lowe to write 'Indian Queens', a track on his 2001 album The Convincer. Lowe owned a little retreat down in Cornwall for writing and merry-making with his mates. In order to get there he had to drive past the village on the main A30 route down through the county. "I was driving back up to London after one of these bacchanals and I was a bit hung over and I get kind of soulful and the next thing I know I'm pulling up outside my house in West London where I live and I found I'd written this little song."

LOCATION 002: on the main A30 in the centre of Cornwall, postcode TR9 6TF

NEWQUAY THE MAGICAL MYSTERY TOUR HITS TOWN

A rectangular plaque on the grassed area by the sea at Killacourt, Newquay marks the most westerly point of The Beatles' Magical Mystery Tour. The Fab Four and a coach load of passengers arrived in Newquay in September 1967, shooting scenes for the movie that made its debut on BBC TV on Boxing Day that year. Based at the Atlantic Hotel, the group, crew and entourage also filmed a number of other Cornish scenes at Porth, Watergate Bay, Holywell Bay and Tregurrian.

LOCATION 003: on the north Cornwall coast, postcode: TR7 1HR. Further info: www. beatlesnewquay.co.uk

TINTAGEL SETH LAKEMAN'S CAMELOT COVER SHOOT

The mid noughties saw West Country musician Seth Lakeman grab a Mercury Prize nomination and Best Album and Singer trophy at the BBC Radio 2 Folk Awards swiftly followed by Top 10 album status with the release of Poor Man's Heaven. This 2008 rhythm-driven offering was made in Cornwall with the addition of a rugged album cover shot of the wreckers' coast at Tintagel.

❛ The shoot was conceived to reflect the coastal, maritime influence of the music. Seth has strong, definite themes to his albums. He's inspired by his surroundings and the stories he heard as a child, which make this part of Cornwall perfect. It was our intention to shoot the artwork on a stormy day, with

rough seas and hellish-looking skies. But shoot day came and the skies cleared, leaving us with the beautiful scenery you see in the artwork. Tintagel

Andrew Whitton's stunning view of the Cornish coastline taken near Tregatta facing South West

offered us many options, fishing villages, a seafaring cemetery, a stunning coast line and the site of what is thought to be the location of Camelot, home of King Arthur. One thing that strikes you as you wander around is how life for villages like that are built up on folklore. Once you experience this you can really delve into and appreciate the songs of an artist like Seth. For me, it just gave me an exquisite location of meaning and relevance to Seth as an artist and his work. ❜

Photographer Andrew Whitton describes the artistic merits of this maritime location

LOCATION 004: near Tintagel, six miles west of the A39 in North Cornwall, postcode PL34 0AH

ST NEOT ECHO AND THE BUNNYMEN'S FINEST HOUR

The cover for what many consider to be Echo and The Bunnymen's finest album, was shot here in the cathedral-like Carnglaze Caverns near Liskeard. A public tourist attraction that also doubles as a music venue, the caverns were the location for photographer Brian Griffin's picture of the band that accompanies the Ocean Rain album.

LOCATION 005: one mile north of the village of St Neot, postcode PL14 6HQ www.carnglaze.com

Echo chamber: Ocean Rain in Carnglaze Caverns

TRURO A BEGINNING FOR QUEEN

On June 27th June 1970, singer Freddie Mercury, guitarist Brian May and drummer (and local boy) Roger Taylor made their debut as Smile. The venue for this gig was Truro City Hall (later renamed Hall for Cornwall), hired as a fundraiser for The Red Cross by Taylor's mother. On bass guitar that night was Mike Gross. It would be a further 12 months before John Deacon would fill that role on stage and complete the classic Queen line-up.

LOCATION 006: postcode TR1 2LL, accessed via Boscawen Street or Back Quay

South West of England

GOLANT UP THE CREEK AT THE SAWMILLS STUDIO

Oasis in a rowing boat? This could have been a regular sight on the River Fowey near Golant, location of the extraordinary Sawmills studio. Tucked away in its own private tidal creek, the only way to access the secluded recording complex is by dinghy or canoe. "No neighbours make it a great place to make noise and plenty of bands have recorded outside on the lawn by the water," states Studio Manager Ruth Taylor. Oasis, Muse, Terrorvision, Supergrass and The Verve are just some of the visitors that have recorded albums in this beautiful hideaway. The Stone Roses, Robert Plant and The Kooks have also experienced Sawmills' welcoming directions to the 17th century water mill. "Down into the village and past the Fisherman's Arms until you reach a car park and level crossing. This is where we'll meet you with the boat," as the Sawmills website invitingly puts it.

❝We've had lots of boat-related shenanigans.❞
Studio Manager Ruth Taylor

The watery setting provided a Cornish haven while Oasis recorded Definitely Maybe

LOCATION 007: four miles east of the A390 and four miles north of Fowey, postcode PL23 1LW. Status: private property www. sawmills.co.uk

ST IVES DONOVAN'S BOHEMIAN BEACH PARTY

St Ives was a sanctuary for free-spirited young poets, artists and musicians in the early Sixties. A teenage Donovan hitch-hiked there in 1962 from his Hatfield, Hertfordshire home to busk his guitar-accompanied poetry for cash to feed himself and his companion Gypsy Dave. Describing himself as a "beachnik", Donovan supplemented his earnings by waiting table. "I earned my bread by waiting in coffee bars and they fired me because my hair was too long." Resisting the bohemian invasion, some St Ives locals would display signs demanding 'No Undesirables', articulating their distaste for male visitors sporting hair curling over their collar. Good days saw Donovan bed down in an art studio, but when money was scarce he frequently slept the night on the beaches. By 1966, a then internationally famous Donovan returned to St Ives with an ITV film crew to make a documentary about his early days as a musician in the town. Keen to recreate his earlier lifestyle living on Porthminster beach, the crew gathered together his old friends from the town, paying them an extravagant £3 per day as beatnik extras.

LOCATION 008: near the tip of Cornwall, three miles north of the A30, postcode TR26 2

MITCHELL THE FOLK COTTAGE CLUB

The Folk Cottage Club was variously based at Rose, near Perranporth, and later in Truro, but its heyday was when based in an old ramshackle cottage in the village of Mitchell. Resident musician, Monday to Friday, in the summer of 1967 was 22-year-old Ralph McTell, who played the club room above the downstairs coffee and snack bar. Years later McTell, who lived that summer in a rented caravan north of Mitchell, remembered his Cornish folk apprenticeship fondly: "Its unique spirit got to me, a mix of swashbuckling seafarer bravado and Methodist rectitude."

LOCATION 009: formerly at postcode TR8 5AX but sadly no more

TRESCO
BLONDIE'S 'ISLAND OF LOST SOULS'

Blondie found the perfect location to promote their 1982 single 'Island Of Lost Souls' when the second largest of the Scilly Isles was chosen. The video for what turned out to be Blondie's last Top 20 chart hit for almost 17 years was shot amid the tropical plants and statues at the Abbey Garden on the island of Tresco. The band made the crossing for the photo shoot by small boat with Debbie Harry clutching her cellophane-protected collection of outfits and blonde wig to disguise her dark hair.

LOCATION 010: 30 miles from the Cornish coast, postcode TR24 0QQ. www.tresco.co.uk

ST MARTIN GRAM PARSONS' CORNISH HOLIDAY

Country rock pioneer Gram Parsons' visits to England, hanging out with The Rolling Stones, are well documented elsewhere, but in 1971 he also spent extended periods holidaying in Cornwall. The location was the Tregidden Mill home of fellow Flying Burrito Brothers and International Submarine Band member Ian Dunlop near the village of St Martin. Dunlop, still a touring musician to this day, had moved from the American West Coast to England's West Country, where he works as an artist from his Cornish studio – the same place where Gram Parsons visited his friend decades ago. Parsons was so taken with the Lizard Peninsula that he even proposed to girlfriend Gretchen Burrell here before marrying shortly afterwards back in the USA. Remembering that summer well, Dunlop recalls how he and Parsons walked the Kennack, Cadgwith, Lizard and Mullion stretches of the South West Coast Path and visited the local pubs.
"We used to go up for a pint to the Prince of Wales, a mile up the lane in Newtown, or, 3 miles away on the coast, to the Five Pilchards at the (then) fishing cove of Porthallow, near St Keverne." Exactly two years on from his Cornish vacation, Parsons was dead and the subject of sensational reports surrounding his infamous botched cremation in California's Joshua Tree National Park.

Drink The Cup: one of Ian Dunlop's portraits of his friend and sometime Cornish holidaymaker Gram Parsons

LOCATION 011: the Lizard peninsula south Cornwall, postcode TR12 6DS. Status: private property

❛ These images draw from the years I spent with Gram Parsons playing music, being on stage together, sharing an apartment, a similar sense of humour and irony, travelling, on tour, through the music biz and often out of our heads. Using Gram as a subject, an icon and a symbol is something that I have previously shied away from, but recently I have enjoyed 'working' with him again. Once in a very odd while I do have a 'music tourist' knocking on my door asking if Gram did visit here. ❜
Ian Dunlop

Born in Cornwall
Mick Fleetwood, drums, Fleetwood Mac (b. 24 Jun 1947, Redruth)
Andy Mackay, saxophone, Roxy Music (b. 23 Jul 1946, Lostwithiel)

DEVON

Covering a large chunk of the county, even the wild and untamed Dartmoor National Park is not immune from rock music associations. The rocky granite landscape prompted an artistic strop by Rick Wakeman, provided folk legends for Seth Lakeman's gritty ballads and, in its gentler, nearby rolling South Hams, bolt-hole seclusion for rock's glitterati. The archetypal small seaside town of Teignmouth gets a hat-trick of Rock Atlas entries if you include Patrick Wolf's homage 'Teignmouth', from his 2005 album Wind in The Wires. But it's the north coast you need to head for to discover Britain's most expansive and romantic rock location at Saunton Sands. Here, a windswept Robbie Williams filmed his 1997 'Angels' video and Pink Floyd, less romantically, turned the beach into a giant hospital ward and battleground.

SAUNTON SANDS PINK FLOYD'S BEDS ON THE BEACH

More than 700 hospital beds stretch along Saunton Sands on the cover of Pink Floyd's 1987 album A Momentary Lapse Of Reason. Five years earlier the vast expanse of sand and sea also provided the perfect spot for filming World War II troop landing scenes in Pink Floyd's movie The Wall.

In the days before computerised imagery, all these beds were manhandled into place to create this memorable cover

LOCATION 012: nine miles from Barnstaple on Devon's north coast, postcode EX33 1LQ

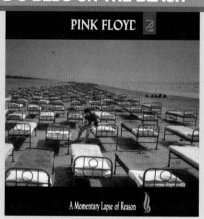

PINK FLOYD

A Momentary Lapse of Reason

SAUNTON SANDS ROBBIE WILLIAMS SHOOTS 'ANGELS'

Miles of flat sands and dunes on Devon's north coast were the location for shooting the video that accompanied Robbie's single 'Angels'. A life-time's Brownie points would surely be secured by any guy selecting this spot to propose to his very own 'Angel'.

LOCATION 013: nine miles from Barnstaple on Devon's north coast, postcode EX33 1LQ

BICKLEIGH BRIDGE THE BRIDGE OVER TROUBLED WATER

Staying at the Fisherman's Cot Inn on the banks of the River Exe, Paul Simon was reported to have drawn inspiration to later write the Simon & Garfunkel classic 'Bridge Over Troubled Water'. Stopping at the Devon hostelry while touring Britain's folk haunts as a performer and observer back in the Sixties, the New Jersey-born singer-songwriter was able to gaze out over the bridge at Bickleigh from in front of his room (No.6). Though the facts are sketchy, the river is susceptible to flood at this point on the Exe and Simon was, according to locals, apparently aware of a reported drowning at nearby Thorverton during his stay, which may have contributed to the maudlin nature of arguably his most famous recording.

LOCATION 014: on the A396 Exeter Road as it crosses the River Exe, postcode EX16 8RW www.marstonsinns.co.uk/ home/hotels/hotel-tiverton/ fishermans-cot

DITTISHAM OLD RECTORY REHEARSALS FOR LED ZEPPELIN

In the early Eighties, Led Zeppelin band member John Paul Jones owned the Old Rectory, a perfect Devonshire retreat for the band to rehearse with its recording studio, swimming pool and nine bedrooms. Rebuilt after a fire in the Seventies almost destroyed it, the house was, until recently, the property of Duran Duran manager Michael Berrow.

LOCATION 015: at the end of Rectory Lane, Dittisham, postcode TQ6 0HD. Status: private house

EAST PRAWLE THE ROCKING PIG'S NOSE

The Pig's Nose Inn is situated in the village of East Prawle and for its eccentricity alone deserves a place in any guide book, let alone one specifically related to rock locations. Chris Farlowe, Paul Young, Wishbone Ash, The Animals, The Yardbirds, The Boomtown Rats and Curiosity Killed The Cat have all played Pigs Nose gigs at the village hall next door. Damon Albarn, who owns a house a few miles north at Beesands, chose the Pig's Nose to launch his new project, The Good, The Bad & The Queen. Band members Albarn, Paul Simonon, Simon Tong and Tony Allen made their collective live debut in front of 150 people there in 2006.

LOCATION 016: opposite the village green at East Prawle, near the southernmost tip of Devon, postcode TQ7 2BY. www.pigsnose.co.uk

TEIGNMOUTH
MUSE COME HOME

"We used to spend all our time hanging out there," revealed Matt Bellamy to the hordes of Muse fans. Bellamy was pointing at the old Teignmouth pier at a huge outdoor homecoming gig, staged for the band who hailed from this genteel seaside town on Devon's south coast. Bellamy and drummer Dominic Howard met for the very first time at The Den, the large grassy area on the seafront that hosted 10,000 fans on two nights in September 2009 for their "Seaside Rendezvous." The trio's bass guitarist, Chris Wolstenholme, still a Teignmouth resident, was even involved in the council meeting that gave the go-ahead to road closures in the town and approval for the band's giant Punch and Judy-styled stage.

LOCATION 017: on the Teignmouth seafront, postcode TQ14 8BD

The Teignmouth Post & Gazette does Muse proud

YES TOR **THE RICK WAKEMAN 'NO!' ALBUM COVER**

The second highest point on Dartmoor, Yes Tor, appears on 1978 Yes album cover Tormato. Designs for the cover did not go down well with the band's keyboard wizard Rick Wakeman. He threw a tomato at the originally titled Yestor album sleeve artwork in disgust, prompting a change of name to Tormato. Wakeman's critical contribution to the design process was adopted on the finished cover. The tenth Yes hit album, Tormato heralded the departure of both Wakeman (for the second time) and vocalist Jon Anderson.

LOCATION 018: grid reference SX580901: about five miles south of the A30 at Okehampton

The Tormato cover, complete with Rick Wakeman's artistic contribution

WISTMAN'S WOOD **LAKEMAN COUNTRY**

Seth Lakeman's 2005 album Kitty Jay features a cover with the Devon-born folk singer kneeling pensively at Wistman's Wood near his Dartmoor home. The title track relates the legend of an 18th century pregnant servant girl who committed suicide and was buried on the moor. Mysteriously, her grave near Hound Tor is still decorated with flowers by unseen visitors to this day.

LOCATION 019: north of Two Bridges and the B3212. Two Bridges postcode: PL20 6SW

WOODCOMBE
KATE BUSH'S AERIAL INSPIRATION

Kate Bush bought her South Hams hideaway in 2004. The 1920s house appealed to the UK's first woman to record a No.1 album due to its remote, beautiful and private position. The 17 acres incorporate a pebble beach, boathouse and two small offshore islands, the perfect inspiration for the maritime themes explored in her 2006 album Aerial.

LOCATION 020: seven miles south-west of Kingsbridge, postcode TQ7 2NJ. Status: private property

Trevor Leighton/EMI

Remote, beautiful and private: Kate Bush settled in the perfect spot for maritime inspiration

TEIGNMOUTH **THE BEATLES' STOP-OVER**

The Beatles stayed in the Royal Hotel in 1967 while filming The Magical Mystery Tour and this was their Newquay to London stop-over.

LOCATION 021: Royal Court Apartments, postcode TQ14 8BR

Born in Devon

David Cross, violin/keyboards, King Crimson (b. 23 Apr 1949, Plymouth)

Beth Gibbons, vocals, Portishead (b. 4 Jan 1965, Exeter)

Dave Hill, guitar, Slade (b. 4 Apr 1946, Holberton)

Seth Lakeman (b. 26 Mar 1977, Buckland Monachorum)

Chris Martin, vocals, Coldplay (b. 2 Mar 1977, Exeter)

Serge Pizzorno, vocals/guitar, Kasabian (b. 15 Dec 1980, Newton Abbot)

Pete Quaife, bass, The Kinks (b. 31 Dec 1943, Tavistock, d. 23 Jun 2010)

Danny Thompson, double bass, (b. 4 Apr 1939, Teignmouth)

South West of England

SOMERSET

This is where it would appear more musical merrymaking goes on outdoors than anywhere else. Early pioneering rock festivals began at Glastonbury, Shepton Mallet and Bath. Somerset was the place to be as the 60s gave way to the 70s. The first UK act to top the US charts, Acker Bilk, was born, bred and lives in the village of Pensford and some familiar pictures of The Beatles were snapped on Somerset's golden sands. The spiritual Somerset landscape comes complete with trip-hop, Wurzels, Peter Gabriel's solo inspiration, a Tudor 'pile' that gave Radiohead the shivers, Kylie singing down the village pub and Anthony Newley's hijacking of the quaintly-named village of Gurney Slade.

GURNEY SLADE
ANTHONY NEWLEY'S WEIRD WORLD

The theme to 1960 weird comedy The Strange World of Gurney Slade by Max Harris provided TV immortality for the village of Gurney Slade. The show's central character was Anthony Newley and the metronomic tune's TV exposure led to a No.11 chart hit.

LOCATION 023: north of Shepton Mallet on the A37, postcode BA3 4TQ

BATH **NASHERS MUSIC STORE**

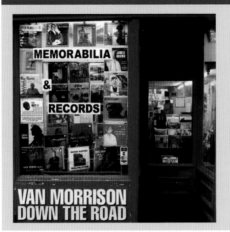

The wonderfully named Nashers independent record shop, with American Dream Comics upstairs for good measure, is the enticing emporium featured on the cover of Van Morrison's 2002 album Down The Road.

LOCATION 022: 72 Walcot Street, Bath, postcode BA1 5BD

Van Morrison's favoured record emporium

BATH **LED ZEPPELIN ROCK THE RECREATION GROUND**

Perhaps the attendance wasn't large by today's standards - MC John Peel even offered the crowd a lift back to London in his camper van - but the Bath Festival of Blues was an important rock milestone back on a barmy summer's day in 1969. Set in the Recreation Ground surrounded by the splendour of Bath's Georgian architecture, this spot was notable for Led Zeppelin's earliest festival appearance. Local opinion was fearful of such a large youth invasion. However, the powers that be were so impressed with the behaviour of the 12,000 festival fans that they offered, those that wished to, an impromptu sleepover.

LOCATION 024: Bordered by Great Pulteney Street and Pulteney Road. Status: now home to Bath Rugby Club. Postcode: BA2 4DS

BECKINGTON
MORRISSEY'S 'MURDER AT THE WOOL HALL'

In 1987, The Smiths recorded their final studio album Strangeways, Here We Come at Bath's Wool Hall. A single taken from the album, 'I Started Something I Couldn't Finish', carried an etching in the vinyl by Morrissey that namechecked The Wool Hall and a pseudonym the singer used before he became a Smith in a fake movie title. 'MURDER AT THE WOOL HALL (X) STARRING SHERIDAN WHITESIDE' was etched into the 7-inch and 12-inch singles on release at the same time Morrissey had returned to The Wool Hall to create his first solo offering, Viva Hate. Other notable working visitors to the studios down the years include Joni Mitchell, Paul Weller and Stereophonics. Van Morrison recorded so frequently there that he bought the place in 1994.

LOCATION 025: The Wool Hall is up Church Street from the centre of Beckington village, postcode BA3 6TA

Actress Avril Angers: cover star on 'I Started Something I Couldn't Finish'

COMPTON MARTIN KYLIE PLAYS THE RING O' BELLS

A seven-month-long secret kept by pub landlord and landlady Reuben and Lauren Goddard ended on August 19th 2010 when Kylie Minogue performed at the Ring O' Bells pub in this tiny north Somerset village. Locals assumed the pub's blackboard advertising "For One Night Only! – Kylie Minogue" was either a hoax or a tribute performer night but were shocked when they realised their pub had been selected for a Parlophone company outing to witness the label's artists Kylie, Tinie Tempah, Eliza Doolittle and Morning Parade in action.

> **Everyone was sworn to secrecy, even the staff didn't know about it.**
> Ring O' Bells landlady Lauren Goddard talking to the BBC

Yes, it really is Kylie Minogue performing among the beams, horsebrasses and a few lucky pub regulars at the Ring O' Bells

Laura Goddard

LOCATION 026: on the A368 Bath to Weston-Super-Mare road, postcode BS40 6JE. Website: www.ringobells compton-butcombe..com

BATH
EDDIE COCHRAN'S MEMORIAL

In 1960, Eddie Cochran died from the injuries suffered in a car crash in Chippenham at St Martin's Hospital in Bath. Prominently displaying the words 'Three Steps To Heaven', a large marble memorial to the American rock 'n' roll star is situated in the hospital's meditation garden. Cochran's body was returned to California, where he is buried at Forest Lawn Cemetery, Cypress.

LOCATION 027: situated on Clara Cross Lane off the B3110, postcode BA2 5RP

FROME
VINYL HEAVEN

Music lovers in this small market town are spoilt with not one but two record shops. Raves From The Grave's owner had so much stock he opened a second shop next door selling only vinyl and accurately named it Vinyl Heaven.

LOCATION 028: 18a and 20 Cheap Street, Frome, BA11 1BN. www.ravesfromthegrave.com

South West of England

PILTON THE GLASTONBURY EXPERIENCE

Jason Bryant

❝There are little services here nearly every weekend, ashes sprinkled on the land, some of whom came as kids in the 70s. This is where they want to be throughout eternity, which is rather nice, isn't it?❞

Michael Eavis, rock's most famous farmer

These days, Glastonbury is a true British institution in the same league as the Henley Regatta, the Chelsea Flower Show and Wimbledon fortnight. Alright, Glastonbury hasn't yet got a Royal enclosure, but our best-loved rock festival's creator Michael Eavis has probably pondered over whether it should have. It's been an incredible journey for the man who started it all from his Worthy Farm back in 1970. Excited by the possibilities thrown-up by the nearby 1970 Bath Blues Festival, Eavis set about creating an outdoor festival of his own in a money-making bid to rid himself of a £5,000 overdraft. The early festivals did not go down well with all of his neighbours. Some Somerset locals took exception to the invasion of hippies, whose cause was not helped by a lunatic fringe who would wander the nearby villages under the influence of LSD, naked but for top hats and Wellington boots. Established as the elder statesman of rock festivals, Glastonbury now produces £100 million annually in tourism and trade for the south-west of England. The 900-acre farm, with its 30 permanent festival staff, attracts 137,000 music fans and support staff numbering an additional 40,000. Despite the very greenest of profiles, festival fans still regularly leave behind 1,650 tonnes of waste to be cleaned-up.

Jason Bryant

Jason Bryant

Above:
A performer's
view of the crowd:
Glastonbury 2009

Right: Rock's
biggest campsite:
Glastonbury 2008

LOCATION 029:
the festival site is
actually at Pilton
not Glastonbury,
postcode BA4 4BY.
www.glastonbury
festivals.co.uk

South West of England

SHEPTON MALLET BRITAIN'S VERY OWN WOODSTOCK

With an artists' taxi service provided by Hells Angels, dodgy weather conditions that halted proceedings and traffic chaos, the Bath Festival of Blues & Progressive Music in 1970 was the closest thing to Woodstock that Britain could muster. Promoter Freddie Bannister's ambitious project drew a 150,000 attendance, prompting the first use of viewing screens for the benefit of fans some way from the action. Bannister also cleverly tapped into the huge surge in popularity of American groups. The Byrds, Frank Zappa, Johnny Winter, Steppenwolf and Jefferson Airplane, plus Woodstock 'veterans' Santana, Canned Heat and Country Joe, joined forces with top homegrown rock favourites Pink Floyd and Led Zeppelin for what many now

consider to be the finest British festival bill of all time.

❛I'm going to warm up my hands on the amplifier, they're totally numb.❜
Frank Zappa at Shepton Mallet

LOCATION 030: Royal Bath & West Showground, 2 miles south of Shepton Mallet, postcode BA4 6QN

GLASTONBURY
THE WATERBOYS' SPIRITUAL AWAKENING

Turned on by the mythical literature he read in the early Eighties, Waterboys singer-songwriter Mike Scott was a frequent visitor to Glastonbury the place, not just the festival. This "awakening", as he puts it, filtered through to the lyrics of a spiritual journey on the band's 1993 hit single 'Glastonbury Song'. A much more 'mud and music' Glastonbury song was recorded by Nizlopi a decade later.

LOCATION 031: Glastonbury Tor sits atop its green hill east of the town of Glastonbury, just north of the A361. Postcode for nearby Wellhouse Lane is BA6 8BL. Owned by the National Trust and free to visit

ST CATHERINE THE HOUSE THAT GAVE RADIOHEAD THE SHIVERS

More than half of Radiohead's first chart-topping album OK Computer was recorded in the isolated splendour of St Catherine's Court, which has also attracted the likes of New Order and The Cure. Thom Yorke reportedly found the 16th-century haunted house rented out to Radiohead by owner and actress Jane Seymour distinctly unsettling.

LOCATION 032: east of the A46, north of Bath. St Catherine's Court is a private home rented out for weddings, events and recordings in the hamlet of St Catherine

PORTISHEAD TRIP-HOP TOWN

The small town on the banks of the River Severn is now most famous as the name of the Mercury Prize-winning band who cornered the market in the darker side of 90s trip-hop. Although based in nearby Bristol, Portishead were named by band member Geoff Barrow, who grew up in the town and was referred to as "that bloke from Portishead" so frequently that the phrase stuck when creating the band name.

LOCATION 033: at the end of the A369, west of Bristol

NAILSEA
WURZEL COUNTRY

The Royal Oak pub in Nailsea is the place responsible for fermenting a folk sound synonymous with the Somerset accent. It was here in 1966 that those legendary cider drinkers The Wurzels recorded a live album that would set them on the road to international fame. The band were formed by folk singer Adge Cutler, who lived in the nearby village of Tickenham. Cutler was killed in a car crash in 1974 and is buried in the Christ Church graveyard in Nailsea.

LOCATION 034: High Street, Nailsea, postcode BS48 1AS

YATTON
STACKRIDGE HQ

Yatton is the epicentre of folk-rock band Stackridge's world. Their crowd pleaser, 'Purple Spaceships Over Yatton', also features as the title of the 2006 Best Of album for a group whose appreciation enjoyed something of a reawakening in the Noughties, four decades on from their omnipresence on the early 70s festival scene.

LOCATION 035: approximately three miles east of the M5 on the B3133, north of Congresbury

GD Smith

WESTON-SUPER-MARE BEATLES AND OASIS PHOTO-SHOOTS

The Beatles are visually linked with this traditional seaside resort courtesy of photographer Dezo Hoffmann's 1963 shots of John, Paul, George and Ringo pictured in Victorian stripy swim suits and straw boaters. Hoffmann also captured the group donkey riding on the beach at Brean Down, go-karting and suited and booted back at their Royal Pier Hotel during a week of concerts at Weston-super-Mare's Odeon cinema. Beatles fans Oasis used the Weston-super-Mare Grand Pier (devastated by fire in 2008 but reopened two years later) as the backdrop to the group photo on their 1995 single 'Roll With It'.

LOCATION 036: Royal Pier Hotel, postcode BS23 2EJ, Brean Down beach TA8 2RS, Grand Pier BS23 1

Above left: The Beatles, snapped by local Weston-super-Mare photographer G D Smith

Above right: Oasis visit a famous Beatles photoshoot location for one of their own

SOLSBURY HILL
PETER GABRIEL'S INSPIRATION

The ancient hill fort was a favourite place for jogger and walker Peter Gabriel and immortalised in his 1977 hit single 'Solsbury Hill'. An obvious spiritual source of strength to Gabriel, the hill offers excellent views of Bath and the surrounding countryside from its summit. 'Solsbury Hill' is a symbol of Gabriel's career turning-point from Genesis band member to solo musician.

LOCATION 037: east of the A46 near the village of Batheaston, postcode BA1 7RA

Born in Somerset

Geoff Barrow, Portishead (b. 9 Dec 1971, Walton-in-Gordano)
Acker Bilk, clarinet (b. 28 Jan 1929, Pensford)
Ritchie Blackmore (b. 14 Apr 1945, Weston-super-Mare)
Adge Cutler, The Wurzels (b. 19 Nov 1931, Portishead, d. 5 May 1974)

Debbie Googe, bass, My Bloody Valentine (b. 24 Oct 1962, Yeovil)
PJ Harvey (b. 9 Oct 1969, Yeovil)
John Parish, musician, PJ Harvey (b. 1959, Yeovil)
Peter Salisbury, drums, The Verve (b. 24 Sep 1971, Bath)
Curt Smith, vocals/bass, Tears For Fears (b. 24 Jun 1961, Bath)

South West of England

BRISTOL

UK hip-hop, and more specifically trip-hop, was responsible for a 'Bristol sound' in the city famous for its historical tobacco and slave trade links. Massive Attack, Tricky and Portishead all evolved from late 80s collective The Wild Bunch to do their bit in putting Bristol on rock's atlas in the 90s and Tricky even named an album after his birthplace, 2008's Knowle West Boy. At the beginning of the decade, music papers eager for the next new sound descended on Bristol. The Face even likened Bristol's Massive Attack to "Pink Floyd with bigger bass sounds and better drum patterns" to underline the new order of things. Towards the end of the Nineties, fellow Bristolian Roni Size brought yet more critical acclaim to the city when pioneering drum 'n' bass and bagging the 1997 Mercury prize for debut album New Forms. Fan forums still argue about the first place The New Yardbirds called themselves Led Zeppelin, but Bristol has a pretty claim for nailing that one, and sadly there's no doubt at all about where American Eddie Cochran played his last gig before ascending his own stairway to heaven.

Left: Colston Hall has staged 140 years of music concerts. Above: Bob Dylan and Fiona Flanagan filming a scene from Hearts Of Fire on the Colston Hall stage

BRISTOL ROCK 'N' ROLL'S COLSTON HALL OF FAME

A glittering list of rock's finest have played Bristol's premier rock venue down the decades. Jimi Hendrix, The Stones, Bowie, Roxy Music, Elton, Thin Lizzy, Lou Reed and Bob Marley all played the hall in their heyday. At the end of their 1964 UK tour, The Beatles sportingly played, despite being the victims of a stunt that saw them showered in flour from the lighting gantry by four students. Two decades later Bob Dylan, with supporting roles for Ronnie Wood, Ian Dury and Richie Havens, played in front of 1,000 extras hired for the filming of scenes for his Hearts of Fire movie.

LOCATION 038: the city centre at 13 Colston Street, postcode BS1 5AR

BRISTOL GENE PARSONS AND THE BRISTOL BLUES

When The Byrds flew in to England to appear at the 1971 Lincoln Festival, they took the opportunity to book into the CBS studio in London's Bond Street, recording tracks for the Farther Along LP released later that same year. Among the album's UK recordings was a bluegrass track written by the band's Gene Parsons and Clarence White. An enthusiast for such things, the California-born Parsons had frustratingly missed the Bristol Steam Convention on his previous two visits to England with the band due to unkind scheduling. The instrumental track was a result of his disappointment and was duly titled 'The Bristol Steam Convention Blues'.

BRISTOL EDDIE COCHRAN'S FINAL SHOW

The Bristol Hippodrome was Eddie Cochran's final stop on his UK tour before returning to America in 1960. Cochran never made the plane home, dying as a result of a car crash on the A40 heading east for Heathrow Airport. Aside from a plaque in Cirencester and a memorial in Bath, Cochran is also remembered here by a small framed presentation plaque located in the Hippodrome Cast Bar. These days the Hippodrome majors in musicals.

Above: Cochran's last stand was at the Hippodrome

LOCATION 039: 10 St Augustine's Parade in the city centre, postcode BS1 4UZ

The framed tribute presented to the Hippodrome by Cochran fan Gwen Hale, who attended Eddie's final show

BRISTOL LED ZEPPELIN ROUGHED-UP AT THE BOXING CLUB

Although they made a few earlier performances as The Yardbirds and The New Yardbirds, Led Zeppelin's first appearance advertised under that name was on October 26th 1968 at Bristol Boxing Club. Supported by The Deviants, both bands suffered a torrid time. A beer glass throwing incident started by a member of The Deviants quickly led to fire extinguishers, buckets and bricks being hurled on stage by local hooligans, which threatened to end Led Zeppelin's career before it had barely started. Boxing club location unknown.

Born in Bristol

Julie Burchill, writer/ columnist (b. 3 Jul 1959)
Russ Conway (b. 2 Sep 1925, d. 16 Nov 2000)
Roger Cook, songwriter (b. 19 Aug 1940)
Sara Dallin, vocals, Bananarama (b. 17 Dec 1961)
Rob Ellis, drums, P J Harvey (b. 13 Feb 1962)
Roger Greenaway, songwriter (b. 23 Aug 1938)
Abi Harding, saxophone, The Zutons (b. 1982)
Nellee Hooper, producer (b. 1963)
Wayne Hussey, vocals, The Mission (b. 26 May 1958)
Nik Kershaw (b. 1 Mar 1958)
Grantley Marshall (Daddy G), vocals, Massive Attack (b. 18 Dec 1959)
Roni Size, DJ/producer (b. 29 Oct 1969)
Tricky (b. 27 Jan 1968)
Andrew Vowles (Mushroom), keyboards, Massive attack (b. 10 Nov 1967)
Keren Woodward, vocals, Bananarama (b. 2 Apr 1961)
Robert Wyatt (b. 28 Jan 1945)

South West of England

GLOUCESTERSHIRE

While not quite conjuring up images of a Severn delta steeped in roots music, the county dominated by the wide and often muddy river throws up its own rock ghosts. Pictured famously in the estuary's open landscape are Bob Dylan and Echo and The Bunnymen, while the unsolved mystery of Manic Street Preacher Richey Edwards and the early death of blues rock pioneer Brian Jones are reminders of how heavy a price was paid for rock immortality by the county's two most influential young musicians. The Gloucestershire gloom is lifted by the enthusiastic folk of Stroud who welcomed The Beatles to their town for the Fab Four's first proper UK gig outside their native north west. Slade performing in a nuclear power station? Heavy rock recordings at Clearwell Castle? A Mott The Hoople punch-up in Coleford? Gloucestershire has the lot...

AUST FERRY TERMINAL DYLAN CROSSES THE SEVERN

One of the most iconic photographs taken of Bob Dylan was snapped here by Barry Feinstein. The picture appears on DVD and CD covers for the Martin Scorsese movie No Direction Home and portrays an inscrutable Dylan waiting for the next Aust Ferry en-route to a concert in Cardiff. His mode of transport, an Austin Princess loaned by The Rolling Stones, waits patiently at the end of a slipway terminal closed for business shortly after the picture was taken on May 11th 1966. The times were certainly a-changing, as can be seen by the new Severn Bridge nearing completion in the background, which rendered the quaint old Aust Ferry redundant. All

Barry Feinstein's No Direction Home cover shot shows Dylan about to cross the Severn in 1966 Bottom left: a fan left this delicately created graffiti on what remains of the Aust Ferry terminal site (inset)

that remains today are the overgrown weed-infested platform and ruins of the terminal building, turnstile and slipway stretching out into the muddy banks of the Severn Estuary.

LOCATION 040: leave the A403, join Passage Road and head for the banks of the River Severn

CHELTENHAM THE BLUE MOON AND THE NIGHT OWL

Currently The Night Owl Club, this high street venue began its pop venue life as a milk bar called Egg & Bacon in the 60s. By the end of the decade as The Blue Moon club, it attracted The Rolling Stones, Mott The Hoople, Cream and Jimi Hendrix. A reputation built on a

mod audience saw Rod Stewart's early incarnation with The Steampacket. Happily, the venue has survived down the decades and into the 21st century attracting the likes of Stereophonics and Feeder despite changing names from The Night Owl, Misty's, The Attic and

back to The Night Owl again. Perhaps the club's biggest claim to fame came as The Blue Moon in the Sixties when The Four Tops made their UK debut there.

LOCATION 041: 170 High Street, postcode GL50 1EP

CHELTENHAM BRIAN JONES' HOME CITY

In the unlikely setting of a sunken tropical garden in the Beechwood Shopping Centre you can find the bust of Brian Jones. The founder member of The Rolling Stones was a key figure in the development of the British blues and R&B movements. His childhood home near the centre of Cheltenham still stands largely unchanged since the 1950s in the quaintly named 17 Eldorado Road. The guitarist's gravestone can be located in Prestbury Cemetery, a short distance to the north of the city.

LOCATION 042: Beechwood Shopping Centre is at 123 High Street, postcode GL50 1DQ. Brian Jones' childhood home is located at 17 Eldorado Road, postcode GL50 2PU. Prestbury Cemetery can be found by taking the B4632 north-east out of Cheltenham city centre

The original Rolling Stone: the city centre bust of Brian Jones

CLEARWELL CASTLE A HEAVY ROCK REHEARSAL HAVEN

The dungeons at Clearwell Castle proved an inspirational rehearsal and recording location for the cream of British heavy rock in the 1970s. Black Sabbath's Sabbath Bloody Sabbath and Deep Purple's Burn albums were written there. Work by Led Zeppelin on In Through The Out Door also owed much to the atmosphere at the mock Gothic mansion, where the band composed and rehearsed new material for the album in 1978. Looked after royally by Clearwell's owner's son Bernie Yeates and using Ronnie Lane's mobile recording unit, Bad

Lords of the manor: Deep Purple pose in the grounds of Clearwell Castle

Company were typical of groups eschewing the London studios at the time in favour of a live recording vibe. Hawkwind and The Sweet were also visitors to this heavy haven, now a popular venue for weddings.

❛We're looked after very well. Bernie and his wife cook us breakfast at 5 p.m. and then we're into the rehearsal room recording until six in the morning.❜
Mick Ralphs, Bad Company

LOCATION 043: a mile west of the B4228 south of Coleford, postcode GL16 8LG

COLEFORD MOTT THE HOOPLE ESCAPE THE ANGRY MOB

The band who once caused a temporary rock music ban at London's Royal Albert Hall after damage caused to the venue during one of their typically high-energy shows caused a less well reported riot in the village of Coleford. A pub gig turned nasty when Mott The Hoople organist Verden Allen was set upon by a group of local yobs. The band beat

a hasty retreat in a van, but only after vocalist Ian Hunter had leapt from the stage attacking the offenders with his microphone stand.

LOCATION 044: Coleford, in the administrative centre for the Forest of Dean, is situated less than a mile south of the A4136

STROUD THE BEATLES LEAVE THEIR NATIVE NORTH WEST

Stroud, March 31st 1962: an important place and time in Beatles history as the Subscription Rooms saw the first UK performance of the group outside their native north-west in front of a paying audience. John, Paul, George and Pete Best (Ringo was yet to join) were still seven months shy of their UK chart debut, but significantly were just three months into new manager Brian Epstein's tenure. The Shadows, Helen Shapiro and Roy Orbison were the top three chart acts that week, but the beat group era was about to begin.

Local 20-year-old apprentice George Strange recalls how he met The Beatles in the Post Office Inn at 17 George Street, now an estate agent.

We were all dressed-up and used to go for a drink in the old Post Office dead opposite the Sub Rooms. In walk these four very scruffy lads who we end up playing darts with. I remember they commented on our accents, and of course we did the same back at them. It was only once they'd slipped away and we'd crossed over the road to see the concert that we realised who we'd been chatting to. There they were up on stage. I don't think they could have been that good as the local paper reported the next week that local Teds [Teddy Boys] were throwing pennies at them!

The dance hall at the Subscription Rooms was a sprung floor which those present say bounced up and down with the group's sound. The venue would quite often attract queues to get in on a Saturday with a likely crowd of about 150–200 attending the night the Beatles first came to town.

Joy Thacker, who was a 16-year-old schoolgirl, witnessed her first concert that day

My Mum did the half-time refreshments downstairs at the Subscription Rooms and her usual helper wasn't around so I was persuaded to help. I even remember what I was wearing: blackwatch tartan top and a short pleated navy blue skirt. Later, I was led up the staircase by my friend to see The Beatles perform and what I mostly remember was how really dark, noisy and crowded it was. To be honest I can't say they were any different from the other groups I'd then go and see twice a week from that point. They hadn't their mop tops then. With their quiffs they looked much more like the local and Gloucester Teddy Boys that used to cause trouble outside.

The Beatles returned for a second concert on September 1st later that year. Maybe it was to once again sample the delights of the Subscription Rooms' bread and butter pudding (a speciality of Joy's Mum's catering according to Joy) or the local beer in the Post Office pub. By this time they were just two short months from experiencing their first UK chart entry when 'Love Me Do' crept into the Top 40 at No.32 in the first week of November.

Roger Weyman (17) also saw The Beatles in Stroud that year:

They certainly weren't the best Mersey beat group we saw down here. The Big Three were the group I thought was best.

Ben Roberts

Above: The Beatles first proper gig outside their north-west of England and Hamburg comfort zone

Above left: Little changed since it hosted The Beatles: the late Regency splendour of the Subscription Rooms

According to Roger, local man "Ganger" Powell was responsible for booking John, Paul, George and Pete for a £30 fee. At least one establishment turned away the four-piece – the town's Laurels hotel felt they were way too scruffy and Roger recall's that one Beatle had connections with someone who lived in Chapel Street where the band spent the night.

Sixteen-year-old farm hand Bob Gardiner spotted their potential:

❛ I saw The Beatles on both of their visits to Stroud. There are reports down the years of The Beatles not getting a good reception. In my view the opposite was true, although at first some of the crowd were laughing at Paul because of his way of appearing to swallow the microphone when he sang. It was clear to me that I was watching a very special and talented band. Up to that night I had never heard a band sing three-part harmony. I remember vividly The Beatles doing a version of the Bruce Channel hit 'Hey! Baby'. John played harmonica on this number and it was well received by the audience, as were their Buddy Holly covers.❜

LOCATION 045: The Subscription Rooms, George Street, postcode GL5 1AE. Website www.stroud.gov.uk/subrooms

SEVERN VIEW SERVICES
THE UNSOLVED RICHEY EDWARDS MYSTERY

Richey Edwards disappeared on the day he and Manic Street Preachers lead vocalist James Dean Bradfield were due to fly to the States on a promotional tour. This Gloucestershire spot marks the location where the guitarist effectively vanished: in what has become British rock's most famous tragic mystery. Here at Severn View services on February 15th 1995 his silver Vauxhall Cavalier was found abandoned just a short distance from the Severn Bridge. With no further sign of him, Edwards was officially declared missing and "presumed dead" in 2008.

LOCATION 046: at the Moto service station on the M48, which replaced the original Aust Services, in existence when Richey Edwards vanished. Postcode: BS35 4BH

SEVERN ESTUARY
SEVERN HEAVEN FOR
ECHO AND THE BUNNYMEN

Difficult to locate precisely, but the south bank of the River Severn was the setting for the cover shoot for Echo and The Bunnymen's first Top 10 album Heaven Up Here.

LOCATION XXX: postcode BS35 1RQ

The cover image was shot on a day off from recording at Rockfield Studios in Wales

OLDBURY NAITE
NUCLEAR POWER
PERFORMANCE BY SLADE

A nuclear power station must surely be a contender for the craziest venue Slade has ever played. When the BBC wanted to crank up the excitement for a performance by Noddy Holder and co for a 70s edition of Top Of The Pops, they came up with the idea of the band delivering smash hit 'Gudbuy T' Jane' from Oldbury power station on the banks of the Severn Estuary. Their dramatic appearance wasn't just *at* the place, it was very much *in* it. Sadly, no footage remains of the band playing inside the reactor on one of the fuelling machines atop the pilecap!

LOCATION 047: postcode BS35 1RQ

Born in Gloucestershire

James Atkin, vocals, EMF (b. 28 Mar 1969, Cinderford)
Derry Brownson, keyboards, EMF (b. 10 Nov 1970, Gloucester)
Dominic Chad, guitar, Mansun (b. 5 Jun 1972, Cheltenham)
Jaz Coleman, vocals, Killing Joke (b. 26 Feb 1960, Cheltenham)
Mark Decloedt, drums, EMF (b. 26 Jun 1969, Gloucester)
Ian Dench, guitar, EMF (b. 7 Aug 1964, Cheltenham)

Zachary Foley, bass, EMF (b. 9 Dec 1970, Gloucester, d. 3 Jan 2002)
Brian Jones, The Rolling Stones (b. 28 Feb 1942, Cheltenham, d. 3 Jul 1969)
Alex Kapranos, vocals/guitar, Franz Ferdinand (b. 20 Mar 1972, Almondsbury)
Joe Meek, producer (b. 5 Apr 1929, Newent, d. 3 Feb 1967)
Tom Smith, Editors (29 Apr 1981, Stroud)

South West of England

WILTSHIRE

Wiltshire should be prefaced with the adjective wild! Long before the wild lions and tigers were introduced to Longleat's park land, The Rolling Stones, Heinz and The Wild Boys and Billy J Kramer and The Dakotas all played al fresco dates at the stately home. Wilder still, scenes of mayhem ensued during a riotous Kinks gig at Salisbury's City Hall in 1965. And, so incendiary was the band's Neeld Hall, Chippenham, appearance that same year, that the 900-strong audience chased all four Kinks off the stage to grab a piece of them, fuelled on nothing stronger than Coca-Cola, according to one eye-witness. Less chaotically there follow Wiltshire stories surrounding The Beatles filming Help!, ghostly goings-on for The Feeling, Peter Gabriel on Solsbury Hill, Eddie Cochran's tragic death, Buddy Holly in Woolworths, XTC's motoring nightmare, a Sting album cover and the arrival of Radiohead. The county has been blessed with a rich heritage of medium and small-sized venues. The Devizes Corn Exchange was the place to encounter the best of British prog and glam rock in the 70s, while Swindon's Oasis was said to have been where Liam Gallagher got the idea for his band's name and the town's tiny Affair club once played host to The Clash when their original venue, the nearby Central Hall, caught fire!

AMESBURY
THE BEATLES' HIDEAWAY HOTEL

While filming scenes on Salisbury Plain for their second movie Help!, The Beatles stayed at the Antrobus Arms Hotel, checking in on May 2nd and out on May 6th, 1965. Each day the four most famous pop stars on earth were ferried to and fro in a black Austin Princess, which was ransacked overnight in the hotel garage by fans searching for cigarette ends and any other 'souvenirs' the band may have left behind in the car.

LOCATION 048: Church Street, Amesbury, SP4 7EU, website: www.antrobusarmshotel.co.uk

BOX
PETER GABRIEL'S REAL WORLD

Real World is the world music label and studio complex created by Peter Gabriel. The residential recording studio has played host to a varied client list including Robbie Williams, the late Amy Winehouse, Paul Simon, Paolo Nutini, A-ha and Deep Purple.

LOCATION 049: Box Mill, Mill Lane, Box, SN13 8PL, midway between Chippenham and Bath on the A4. Status: private property: www.realworldstudios.com

KNIGHTON DOWN THE BEATLES STAY MAINLY ON THE PLAIN

Knighton Down is the wild and windswept spot on Salisbury Plain where The Beatles filmed sequences for their second movie Help! The script demanded a remote location where The Beatles could record their latest tunes while protecting Ringo from a bunch of baddies pursuing him, intent on removing his sacred ring. Used by the army to practice manoeuvres, Salisbury Plain provided not only some dismally cold spring weather but, owing to the generosity of the Royal Artillery, tanks for the storyline and real protection from over-enthusiastic fans on the days of filming.

LOCATION 050: Knighton Down is near Larkhill army Base. From the A303, head north on the A345, turning left to Larkhill. Knighton Down is a short ramble north-west of the army base

MAIDEN BRADLEY WITH YARNFIELD STATELY HOME FOLLOW-UP FOR THE FEELING

When The Feeling were looking for the perfect place to create a follow-up to their No.1 debut album Twelve Stops And Home', they hit upon the 300-year-old stately home of the Dukes of Somerset, Bradley House. Recordings and rehearsals were completed in a fun "follow your nose" type of fashion, according to the band's Dan Gillespie Sells. The enjoyable stay was enhanced by guitarist Kevin Jeremiah discovering he was sleeping in a bed once occupied by Henry VIII, and his brother, keyboard player Ciaran, claiming he had seen a ghost. Their work done, Join With Us provided The Feeling with their second chart-topping album, in 2008.

❝It was the biggest, most impressive house I've ever been in in my entire life. Surprisingly, it was a budget option; a week there cost less than two days in a big traditional studio.❞
Ciaran Jeremiah, The Feeling

LOCATION 051: a venue for hire, Bradley House is on Kingston Lane, Maiden Bradley, north of the A303 at Mere. Postcode: BA12 7HL. Website: www.bradleyhouse.org

CHIPPENHAM
EDDIE COCHRAN'S
ROADSIDE PLAQUE

A plaque beside the old Bristol to London main A40 marks the place where influential rock 'n' roller Eddie Cochran was fatally injured in a car accident on April 16th 1960. The star had completed the final date of his British tour at the Bristol Hippodrome and the taxi driving him was heading east to London Heathrow Airport for his flight home to the USA. His fellow passengers, performer Gene Vincent, Cochran's fiancée, Sharon Sheeley, deputy tour manager Patrick Tomkins and the driver, George Martin, all survived the crash. The plaque features an illustration of Cochran's Gretsch guitar which was in the taxi on the fateful night and later impounded at the local police station, where young police cadet David Harman (himself a pop star by 1965, named Dave Dee) was entrusted with taking care of the instrument. The guitar must have been sprinkled with stardust: just days before the accident the Gretsch had been carried to Cochran's waiting car in London by helpful 13-year-old fan Mark Feld, who later became Marc Bolan.

LOCATION 052: on the A4 in Chippenham, heading east after passing under the railway viaduct in the town, on the grass verge to the left of the road before heading up Rowden Hill.

Front page news: 29 others died on bank holiday roads
Right: Cochran's roadside plaque

SALISBURY
BUDDY HOLLY SPOTTED IN WOOLWORTHS!

What is now Salisbury's Odeon cinema was formerly the Gaumont where Buddy Holly and The Crickets performed three shows on March 22nd 1958. The Tudor revival, grade II listed building is situated close by what was the Old George Hotel on the High Street, where Holly's entourage stayed. The singer, who visited Woolworths to buy a new pen to write a letter home to his folks and visited the store's new American Soda-Bar, described the hotel as "a real old, quaint place". Holly would have been dismayed to know that both Woolworths and the hotel are no more, although the Old George Hotel's 13th-century frontage can still be admired on the High Street as it stands as the entrance to Salisbury's new shopping centre.

LOCATION 053: The Odeon, 15 New Canal, postcode SP1 2AA

SWINDON
XTC'S MAGIC ROUNDABOUT

Swindon-born XTC band member Colin Moulding wrote 'English Roundabout' a track on the band's most successful album English Settlement. The song is about Swindon's famously large and convoluted motorists' nightmare the so-called Magic Roundabout. Cue this four-minute insistent, choppy track to press and play as you travel through the roundabout for maximum effect.

LOCATION 044: too complicated to pinpoint! Best found by heading for the nearby Swindon Town football ground, postcode SN1 2ED

South West of England

OLD WARDOUR CASTLE STING'S WHITE RUIN AND FIELDS OF GOLD

This 14th-century castle was the album cover location shoot for Sting's Ten Summoner's Tales. Inside the distinctive white ruin, Sting is pictured together with his Icelandic horse Hrímnir. The Police man's fifth solo album was an all-Wiltshire affair, recorded at his Elizabethan manor, Lake House, at Wilsford cum Lake. The 1993 release included one of Sting's best-loved songs, 'Fields Of Gold'.

LOCATION 045: open to the public, Wardour Castle lies two miles south-west of Tisbury, postcode SP3 6RR. Lake House is a private, heavily protected house

Sting and Hrímnir in the courtyard at OldWardour Castle

LONGLEAT LORD BATH'S STATELY HOME GOES POP

Always full of innovative ideas, Lord Bath (the 7th Marquess of Bath) came up with an ingenious plan in the early Sixties to raise some much needed cash to help run the vast estate at Longleat. The novel introduction of lions to roam his parkland would wait until 1966. Two years earlier, he came up with a potentially more dangerous idea: outdoor pop concerts. A 1961 appearance by local clarinet chart-topper Acker Bilk proved successful enough before Billy J. Kramer and The Dakotas topped the first Longleat pop bill in May 1964, attracting 12,153 fans and causing traffic chaos stretching six miles from the historical house. Ill-equipped for his first pop invasion, the Marquess promised "stronger barriers and barbed wire" for any future event, and a month later a rain-swept concert by The Bachelors (arriving at Longleat with film actress Diana Dors) passed off more quietly. Confident that he was getting the hang of organising by now, the Marquess pulled off his biggest coup in August 1964 when 16,000 turned out to see The Rolling Stones performing "in person and on the

steps" of his stately home, as the adverts proclaimed. More than 200 mostly female fans were treated for fainting by a team of nurses, incidents never repeated as future Longleat concerts became rather sedate affairs. One more gig that year by Heinz and The Wild Boys (filling in for last-minute cancellations The Hollies) and 1965 appearances by Freddie and The Dreamers, The Seekers and Adam Faith failed to recapture the drama of the summer of '64. But the gamble of organising large-scale outdoor pop concerts had been prototyped at Longleat, and soon the idea would take root in neighbouring Somerset before mushrooming nationwide.

LOCATION 046: off the A36 between Bath and Salisbury (A362 Warminster to Frome road). Postcode: BA12 7NW

Fans held back by a chicken wire fence watch pop funsters Freddie and The Dreamers at Longleat

TROWBRIDGE
RADIOHEAD DEBUT AT THE PSYCHIC PIG

Mark Johnston and George Hodgson's Psychic Pig club has enjoyed some great nights in three different venues around Trowbridge since its first event in 1984. Hardly the best attended but certainly the most famous gig came when, for a fee of £50, a group advertised as On A Friday turned up, only to announce that they would be christening a new band name. Thus in 1991, Radiohead were born at the Psychic Pig, impressing the organisers as much for their domestic neatness as the music played that night. Before leaving, Thom Yorke and co. tidied up the club and even washed up their own cups and dishes!

❝They were the politest bunch of young men I have ever met.❞
Radiohead booker George Hodgson

LOCATIONS 047 and 048: The Psychic Pig venues in Trowbridge: Civic Hall, St Stephen's Place, BA14 8AH; Trax nightclub, 46-47 Church Street; The Hub, 2 Wicker Hill, BA14 8JS

STONEHENGE A ROCK MECCA FOR STONES, BYRDS AND SPINAL TAP

A place of lunar and solar worship since 3100 BC, Stonehenge was a mecca for freaks and hippies in the Sixties, drawn to the most breathtakingly spiritual location in Britain. In 1968, Rolling Stones Mick Jagger and Keith Richards acted the perfect hosts for a tourist visit by American group The Byrds. Gram Parsons was clearly in awe of Mick and Keith and the trip to the famous stones precipitated Parsons leaving The Byrds when the remaining band members left for a controversial tour of South Africa. Leaving a South Kensington club in the early hours, the party headed west out of London in Richards' Bentley, walked the last stretch to the ancient standing stones and later breakfasted

on kippers in a nearby Salisbury pub. By 1972, Stonehenge began to stage annual free pop festivals. Space rockers Hawkwind made frequent appearances and attendance figures reached a peak in 1984 when 30,000 descended on the historic site. A year later, clashes between police and new-age travellers made the news headlines in the so-called 'Battle of the Beanfield'. This battle field, a short distance from the standing stones, prevented the festival and summer solstice celebrations from taking place again following government intervention. There is no record of the band Spinal Tap having actually visited the ancient site, but their track 'Stonehenge' and its appearance in the movie This Is Spinal Tap included the

hilarious, shambolic Stonehenge stage set, which prompted an angry Nigel Tufnel to describe the none too epic creation as "a Stonehenge monument on the stage that was in danger of being crushed by a dwarf."

❛The famous Stonehenge trip we went on at three in the morning with Mick Jagger and Keith Richards and their current girlfriends along with myself, my wife, Roger McGuinn and his wife... and Gram Parsons, desperately trying to win favour with our old friends Mick and Keith.❜

Chris Hillman

LOCATION 048: north of the A303, close by its junction with the A344

Wiltshire's finest at the height of their pop powers: Dave Dee, Dozy, Beaky, Mick and Tich pictured in early 1968

SALISBURY CIVIC SOCIETY

Dave Dee, Dozy, Beaky, Mick and Tich

In recognition of their outstanding contribution to popular music and celebrating the 40th anniversary of their chart topping hit single 'The Legend of Xanadu' 1968-2008

SALISBURY DAVE DEE, DOZY, BEAKY, MICK AND TICH REMEMBERED

The Wiltshire group that topped the chart in 1968 with 'The Legend Of Xanadu' are remembered with a Salisbury Civic Society blue plaque (above right) outside the City Hall. The plaque was unveiled on the 40th anniversary of their most successful single release. The venue, which has hosted The

Beatles, The Stones, Cream, David Bowie, Led Zeppelin and Pink Floyd, is still a great place to catch the best of British live music.

LOCATION 049: Salisbury City Hall, Malthouse Lane, postcode SP2 7TU. Website: www.cityhallsalisbury.co.uk

Born in Wiltshire

James Blunt (b. 22 Feb 1974, Tidworth)
Rick Davies, vocals/ keyboards, Supertramp (b. 22 Jul 1944, Swindon)
Dave Dee (b. 17 Dec, Salisbury, d. 9 Jan 2009)
Dave Gregory, guitar, XTC (b. 21 Sep 1952, Swindon)
Justin Hayward, vocals, The Moody Blues (b. 14 Oct 1946, Swindon)
Mark Lamarr, presenter (b. 7 Jan 1967, Swindon)
Colin Moulding, bass XTC (b. 17 Aug 1955, Swindon)
Colin Newman, vocals/ guitar, Wire (b. 16 Sep 1954, Salisbury)
Billie Piper, vocalist / actress (b. 22 Sep 1982, Swindon)

South West of England

CHESIL BEACH
ECHOES OF A BEACH IN CANADA

Martha and The Muffins' 1980 Top 10 hit 'Echo Beach' was a fictitious location dreamed up by the band's Mark Gane. Though inspired by his local Sunnyside Beach on Lake Ontario, Canada, Gane's song was released as a single in a picture sleeve showing a map of the extraordinary 18-mile-long Chesil Beach.

LOCATION 050: at the eastern end of the beach, accessed by taking the B3157 and south to the Abbotsbury Swannery, situated at postcode DT3 4JG

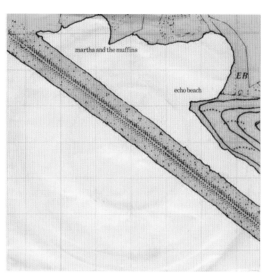

Martha and The Muffins' Chesil Beach picture sleeve

DURDLE DOOR
AN OCEAN ALBUM COVER SCENE

Ocean Colour Scene's album North Atlantic Drift carries images of the natural coastal archway Durdle Door on its cover. The May 2003 photo shoot was the work of renowned snapper Lawrence Watson.

LOCATION 051: approximately 5 miles south of the A352 at West Lulworth, postcode BH20 5RS

ISLE OF PURBECK **IN A BIG COUNTRY**

The Big Country video for the band's 1983 hit 'In A Big Country' was shot at various locations on the Isle of Purbeck. Not a real island, the Dorset peninsula's tourist hotspots Corfe Castle, the seaside resort of Swanage and the white cliffs of Old Harry Rocks are all locations for what proves to be an almost Enid Blyton-esque Famous Five-like storyline involving the band members and a mysterious dark-haired girl. All that's missing are the lashings of ginger beer.

LOCATIONS 052 and 053: the A351 to the coast at Swanage (postcode BH19 1) takes in Corfe Castle (postcode BH20 5ED) on route

BRIDPORT **A PROPER MUSIC SHOP**

Quite unusual this, a shop that sells just about everything the music-lover requires. Records, musical instruments, radios and music related T-shirts and books. Bridport Music has intelligently diversified from its record shop roots and survived the fate of so many small town independents.

LOCATION 054: 33A South Street, Bridport, postcode DT6 3NY. Website www.bridportmusic.com

HENGISTBURY HEAD
PHISH'S GIANT BALL

The Slip Stitch and Pass album cover from US rock band Phish features a giant ball of wool pursuing a running figure on the shoreline at Hengistbury Head. A 1997 live offering, the cover was yet another classic image created by Storm Thorgerson.

LOCATION 055: turn left on to The Broadway from the B3059 in Southbourne, postcode BH6 4NA

Cat Stevens

EYPE PJ HARVEY'S CLIFFTOP RECORDING BASE FOR LET ENGLAND SHAKE

Having first contemplated London or Berlin as a recording base for her eighth album, PJ Harvey eventually settled on a magical place closer to home. The clifftop church of St Peter's, a few miles from where she grew up in the Dorset village of Corscombe, was rehearsal space and studio for her second Top 10 album Let England Shake. For a five-week period in 2010, the remote 19th century church, now the coastal village of Eype's Centre for the Arts, became the project's creative hub. On a snowy night in December that year, St Peter's was fittingly also the album's launch venue when PJ Harvey previewed Let England Shake ahead of its critically acclaimed release and Mercury prize in 2011.

❛It's very remote, on top of a cliff, and has a graveyard which has trees bent by the wind. It's a classic, misty surrounding but actually a beautiful place and a place I was very familiar with and often walk through, so it felt a part of me.❜ PJ Harvey describes the church where she recorded Let England Shake

LOCATION 056: St Peters Church, Mounts Lane is in the village of Eype, a mile west of Bridport, just south of the A35, postcode DT6 6AL

Photographer Cat Stevens captures the Let England Shake sessions. "I was struck by what a lovely atmosphere had been created in St Peters. A group of old friends recording the songs live, in one take. I had a wonderful time documenting it."

Born in Dorset

**Robert Fripp (b.16 May 1946, Wimborne)
Alex James, bass, Blur (b. 21 Nov 1968, Boscombe)
Rick Kemp, bass, Steeleye Span (b. 15 Nov 1941, Little Hanford)
Greg Lake (b. 10 Nov 1948, Bournemouth)
Steve Lamacq, radio presenter, (b. 16 Oct 1965, Bournemouth)
Darrell Sweet, drums, Nazareth (b. 16 May 1947, Bournemouth)**

‘In June 1966 my boss, Reg Calvert, had been shot dead by a business rival. Radio City, the pirate radio station based on a WWII sea fort that he owned and I worked for, was silent, occupied by more than a dozen heavies armed with guns and knives.’

Tom Edwards, retelling events on Shivering Sands (in the Thames estuary) to the Daily Mail

ROCK ATLAS
South East England
UK and Ireland Edition

South East England

ISLE OF WIGHT

Home to poet Alfred Lord Tennyson, the IOW attracted the new order of pop poetry when the likes of Bob Dylan, Leonard Cohen, Joni Mitchell and Joan Baez arrived to make the IOW Festivals some of the most significant events in British pop history. With a larger gathering than Woodstock, the island's 1970 festival was also Britain's biggest. It showcased Jimi Hendrix's final UK performance, a fact commemorated by a statue to the guitarist at Freshwater. Retro rock 'n' roll movie That'll Be The Day was filmed on the island at Shanklin and Ryde, where actor pop stars David Essex, Ringo Starr, Billy Fury, Keith Moon and Viv Stanshall expressed their love for the place. In the spirit of Tennyson, who surrounded himself with island visitors Edward Lear, Gilbert and Sullivan and Jenny Lind, the singer-songwriter Robyn Hitchcock is perhaps the modern-day equivalent, finding the place an inspiration that draws him back regularly for performances to charm his loyal followers. The island features poetically in his song 'Airscape'.

❛Cliffs suspended in the heat" and "the sun reflected from the waves. Inshore it spangles.❜
Robyn Hitchcock's 'Airscape'

EAST AFTON HENDRIX HEADLINES UK'S BIGGEST FESTIVAL

LOCATION 057: east out of Freshwater on the B3399 Newport Road

Originally scheduled for Churchill's Farm, Calbourne, the county council found the site unsuitably "high, windy and damp" for the third Isle of Wight Festival and agreed that East Afton Farm near Freshwater should host a gathering later reported as being larger than that at Woodstock. A good case could be put forward for this event being better organised and boasting an even better line-up than the most famous festival in rock history a summer earlier. Jimi Hendrix, John Sebastian, Ten Years After, The Who, Sly & The Family Stone, Richie Havens and Joan Baez all reprised their Woodstock performances on a bill that also included Joni Mitchell (whose performance drew four encores), Leonard Cohen, Miles Davis, The Doors, Free, Jethro Tull, Taste, Emerson, Lake and Palmer, Chicago and Donovan. What Woodstock had that the East Afton festival did not was a blockbuster movie watched by millions. Had the 600,000 who made it to the Isle of Wight in 1970 been immortalised on the big screen in the same way, then Hendrix's version of 'God Save The Queen' might have lived in the memory just as long as his wonderfully distorted reworking of 'The Star Spangled Banner' did at Woodstock.

❛No I'm not getting £30,000, or whatever, for this one and I'm not living on some luxury yacht. Leonard Cohen and I are living in a nice little hotel around here, with breakfast at a quarter-to-nine.❜
Joan Baez

FRESHWATER THE JIMI HENDRIX STATUE

As a lasting memorial to Jimi Hendrix and the historic 1970 music festival, Dimbola Lodge museum is the location for a statue of the world's most famous guitarist, who died just three weeks after his performance at the third Isle of Wight Festival close by at East Afton Farm. Decisions regarding the placing of the statue, commissioned by music promoter John Giddings, have been controversial. The National Trust denied permission to site it at the original festival location and Dimbola Lodge curator Brian Hinton checked-out the planning permission regulations before the life-size Hendrix bronze was positioned outside in the museum grounds. A local faction, vehemently opposed to the honouring of the American rock star, campaigned to stop what some considered an outrageous monument to a "junkie". Happily, the statue still survives in its spot at the former residence of Julia Margaret Cameron, the home of the celebrated Victorian photographer. The building is now a museum to her work and also provides visitors with an exhibition of the colourful history behind the Isle of Wight's music festivals.

Alan Simpkins: Isle of Wight Images

❝Janie Hendrix **wrote to me from Seattle thanking me for helping to save the statue and saying how Jimi would have been proud to be associated with the great Victorian poets and artists whose work he so loved.**❞
Museum curator Brian Hinton

LOCATION 058: the Jimi Hendrix statue is in the garden at Dimbola Lodge Museum, Terrace Lane, Freshwater Bay. Postcode: PO40 9QE. Website: www.dimbola.co.uk

GODSHILL THE 1968 'ISLE OF WIGHT POP FESTIVITY' SITE

The story of pop festivals on the Isle of Wight began when used as a means to raise funds for the island's swimming pool association. The one-hundred-acre Hells Field at Ford Farm, in the south of the island near Godshill, was the setting for what was advertised as "The Great South Coast Bank Holiday Pop Festivity". The August 1968 one-nighter was compered by John Peel, and those present saw headliners Jefferson Airplane make their British debut. The 10,000 fans also enjoyed performances by the Crazy World of Arthur Brown, Tyrannosaurus Rex, The Move, The Pretty Things, and Fairport Convention, whose vocalist Iain Matthews (who sang with his eyes tight shut) recalled "I started Leonard Cohen's 'Suzanne' in darkness, when I opened my eyes at the end of the song it was dawn."

LOCATION 059: north of Niton on the A3055

ROBIN HILL BESTIVAL'S 'EDEN'

This annual September event, organised primarily by DJ Rob da Bank and wife Josie, began in 2004, attracting 10,000 fans, expanding to more than 40,000 festival-goers by 2009. Perceived as something of an antidote to the more corporate commercial events, Bestival has tended to find its niche as the friendly family festival situated in what the da Banks promote as a "veritable garden of eden".

LOCATION 060: Downend Road, postcode PO30 2NU

South East England

WOOTTON DYLAN HEADLINES THE 1969 ISLE OF WIGHT FESTIVAL OF MUSIC

The second Isle of Wight Festival attracted 150,000 music fans from around the world. A greatly increased gathering compared to the first festival assembled in the fields a short distance from Woodside Bay, to the north of the island. Bob Dylan was the big draw for a crowd that included Beatles John Lennon, George Harrison and Ringo Starr and assorted celebrities including Francoise Hardy, Jane Fonda, Roger Vadim, Keith Richards, Mick Jagger, Peter Wyngarde, Terence Stamp and Cilla Black. The Who (whose helicopter was involved in an accident on landing), Pentangle, Richie Havens, Tom Paxton, The Moody Blues, Joe Cocker, Family, The Nice and The Pretty Things provided the supporting bill. Most entertaining performance of the weekend came from the Bonzo Dog Doo-Dah Band's explosions, bubble-blowing machine and Viv Stanshall's public information announcements, which kept the crowd informed about the comings and goings at the festival site.

❝Bert Weedon is tunnelling from Middlesbrough and is believed to be under the Irish Sea.❞
Viv Stanshall

❝We had wanted to land on the stage but they wouldn't let us.❞
Pete Townshend

LOCATION 061: north of the A3054 at Wootton Bridge

BEMBRIDGE BOB DYLAN'S BED & BREAKFAST

When Bob Dylan was invited to appear at the second Isle of Wight Festival in 1969, the organisers sold him on the idea by sending both their own movie and booklet of the island's best features. Dylan and family were invited to spend a two-week, all expenses paid holiday with a $50,000 festival appearance fee for dad. As it turned out, an accident on board the ocean liner Queen Elizabeth II prevented son Jesse, and as a consequence daughter Maria, joining Dylan and wife Sara when the couple agreed to come and settle into their holiday hideaway at Forelands Farm, Bembridge. Visited by George Harrison, Ringo Starr and John Lennon while enjoying all the home comforts of the idyllic farm bed and breakfast, Dylan spent the fortnight consuming healthy quantities of pies, porridge, tea and honey, playing tennis (badly according to housekeeper Judy Gascoyne), sailing and making excursions to Queen Victoria's Osborne House and Quarr Abbey to experience the monks chanting. Meanwhile, Dylan's backing group, The Band, made good use of the farm's barn and set up their equipment for rehearsals for what would be Dylan's first major live performance since his serious motorcycle accident in 1966.

❝After supper some evenings [Bob] would ask if I would like him to sing something. I would demote George Harrison to go fetch things from the kitchen and help me do the washing up so I would not miss anything.❞
Judy Gascoyne

LOCATION 062: Forelands Farm Lane, postcode PO35 5TJ. Status: private residence

QUARR ABBEY SCOTT WALKER'S WALK ON THE QUIET SIDE

At the height of his fame, The Walker Brothers' Scott Walker discovered he hadn't the temperament to deal with the fame of being a swinging 60s pop star and spent some time at Quarr Abbey. This beautiful medieval monastery provided both peace and seclusion and the opportunity for the singer to study the Gregorian chanting of the Abbey's monks, something Bob Dylan witnessed on a day trip when staying locally while performing at the island's 1969 pop festival. Sadly for Scott Walker, his adoring fans soon discovered his whereabouts and would hammer on the Abbey doors or enter the grounds to catch a glimpse of their pop idol.

LOCATION 063: north of the A3054 between Fishbourne and Binstead, postcode PO33 4ES. The Abbey invites organised group tours. www.quarrabbey.co.uk

RYDE THE 'TICKET TO RIDE'

'Ticket To Ryde' anyone? The seaside town to the island's north is said to have been the inspiration for The Beatles' 1965 chart-topper 'Ticket To Ride'. In 1960, before they found worldwide fame, Paul McCartney and John Lennon hitch-hiked down to the Isle of Wight to visit Paul's cousin Elizabeth and her husband Mike Robbins, who ran the Bow Bars pub in Ryde. McCartney revealed that the line had come about as a memory of a British Railways ticket issued for a trip to the town of Ryde. The island also gets a mention in McCartney's Sgt Pepper's Lonely Hearts Club album track 'When I'm Sixty-Four', where, "Every summer we can rent a cottage in the Isle of Wight".

LOCATION 064: 74 Union Street, postcode PO33 2LN

Born on the Isle of Wight

Boon Gould, guitar, Level 42 (b. 4 Mar 1955, Shanklin)
Phill Jupitus, presenter (b. 25 Jun 1962, Newport)
Mark King, vocals, Level 42 (b. 20 Oct 1958, Cowes)
Nathan King, vocals, Level 42 (b. 29 Aug 1970, Cowes)
David Steele, bass/keyboards, Fine Young Cannibals (b. 8 Sep 1960, Cowes)

HAMPSHIRE

The affluent county of Hampshire has more than its fair share of inspirational homes and houses where popular music's classic chords were struck. Farley House, Headley Grange and Stargroves played host to increasingly affluent Seventies rock stars who hit upon a new way of recording their music away from the claustrophobia of London's studios. Hampshire also boasts one of England's finest cathedrals, Winchester, which inspired two very different stories - three if you count the fact that Led Zeppelin's John Paul Jones came within a whisker of leaving the band to become the cathedral's organist in 1971. Then there's what amounts to The Beatles' least successful gig (Aldershot), a rare 90s protest song ('Twyford Down') and the UK's only Top 10 hornpipe ('Portsmouth'). And finally, quite why the county has given birth to a preponderance of drummers is anyone's guess but, at various times, Coldplay, King Crimson, Manfred Mann, Razorlight, The Troggs, Uriah Heep and The Zombies have all been driven on rhythmically by a Hampshire man.

ALDERSHOT THE BEATLES PLAY TO 18 FANS AT THE PALAIS

The good people of Hampshire's military town weren't to know, but they could have witnessed history in the making on December 9th 1961. Just 18 fans turned out to see what was supposed to be The Beatles' first gig outside Hamburg and their native north-west. The booking by northern promoter Sam Leach went horribly wrong. John, Paul, George and Pete Best were scheduled to do a show at Aldershot's Palais Ballroom, but a pre-arranged sizeable advertisement heralding the band's appearance in local newspaper The Aldershot News failed to appear and The Beatles were left to perform to a scattering of non-paying punters, some of whom had been persuaded to attend following a quick dash round the local pubs to press-gang a crowd of fans.

❝Halfway through one number George and Paul put on their overcoats and took to the floor to dance the foxtrot together, while the rest of us struggled along, making enough music for them and the handful of spectators.❞
Beatles drummer Pete Best

LOCATION 065: The Palais Ballroom, corner of Queen's Road and Perowne Street, postcode GU11

South East England

FARLEY CHAMBERLAYNE THE BIRTH OF BRITISH FOLK-ROCK

According to Q magazine, "folk-rock's defining moment" came with the release of Fairport Convention's album Liege & Lief. The beginning of something special in British folk can be traced back to the group's eight-week stay at Farley House in the remote village of Farley Chamberlayne during the summer of 1969. The group's bass guitarist Ashley Hutchings recalled what he remembered as "a sense of adventure" and the "uplifting" atmosphere of the large Queen Anne house where they wrote, rehearsed and lived the Liege & Lief experience. In between the periods spent inventing British folk-rock, the group lived the rural lifestyle to the full with kite-flying, football on the lawn, trips to the local pub and even a spot of busking in nearby Winchester.

❝Being in that house certainly helped form the music.❞
Ashley Hutchings

LOCATION 066: near the village of Braishfield, on the A3090, Farley House, Farley Lane, Farley Chamberlayne, postcode SO51. Status: private residence

WINCHESTER A GRAMMY - WINNING CATHEDRAL SONG

Foundations for Winchester's vast cathedral were laid in 1079. The best part of a thousand years later it became the inspiration for an astonishingly successful transatlantic hit single. The New Vaudeville Band's 'Winchester Cathedral' was a UK No.4 hit and topped the US Billboard Hot 100 for three weeks in 1966, selling more than a million copies in the process. The British sextet were the creation of Geoff Stephens, who, hired as a staff songwriter in London's Denmark Street, was gazing one day at a calendar on the office wall. Stephens was intrigued by the architecture on a picture of Winchester Cathedral below the dates and set about writing a song to capture his enthusiasm for the subject.

LOCATION 067: postcode SO23 9LS

SOUTHAMPTON SEAL OF APPROVAL FOR THE JOINERS

The Joiners Arms first promoted live music as far back as the late Sixties when Jimi Hendrix is rumoured to have dropped in en route to or from the Isle of Wight Festival. By 1988, every other Tuesday was set aside for the legendary 'Next Big Thing' nights. The organiser's clever knack of booking bands already popular but about to hit huge saw 600 queue down the street for The Charlatans in 1990 and a similar level of excitement greeted the visit of the Manic Street Preachers in 1991. Brett Anderson of Suede and The Verve's Richard Ashcroft each rate their gigs at the Joiners in 1992 as among their best ever. The Joiners has a reputation for superb hospitality, which may have encouraged Oasis, Coldplay, The Libertines and Radiohead to also play what NME announced as "undoubtedly the most relevant venue in the south".

LOCATION 068: St Mary's Street, postcode SO14 1NS. Website: www.joinerslive.co.uk

EAST END STICKY FINGERS AT STARGROVES

Stargroves ticks all the boxes in any competition for the most rock 'n' roll mansion in Britain. Oliver Cromwell famously stayed there, and more recent visitors have recorded some of rock's most popular albums. The Rolling Stones (Sticky Fingers and Exile On Main St) and Led Zeppelin (Physical Graffiti and Houses Of The Holy) were among a number to be created inside the old walls. At various times owned by Mick Jagger and Rod Stewart, the estate also attracted The Who, utilising the grand surroundings and The Rolling Stones' mobile recording unit to good effect when recording their tour de force, 'Won't Get Fooled Again'.

LOCATION 069: three miles west of the A34 at the village of East End (part of the larger village of East Woodhay), postcode RG20 0AE. Stargroves is a private house. There are public footpaths around the estate

TWYFORD DOWN M3 MADNESS

'Twyford Down' was a hit single for acid jazz exponents Galliano, taken from their 1994 Top 10 album The Plot Thickens. The track was created as their protest at the excavation of a large chunk of an 'Area of Outstanding Natural Beauty' near Winchester to lay a new two-mile stretch of the M3.

LOCATION 070: the distinctive M3 motorway cutting near Winchester

HEADLEY RADICAL RECORDINGS BY LED ZEPPELIN AT THE GRANGE

Some of Led Zeppelin's best work was created at Headley Grange. Built in 1795, the rambling retreat certainly had an atmosphere when the band moved in for the duration of their stay 176 years later. "It was very Charles Dickens" according to guitarist Jimmy Page, whose room was at the very top of the former poorhouse. "Dank and spooky" is how he remembered it. "It became lighter as a result of our stay there," he told Guitar magazine. Using The Rolling Stones' mobile recording unit, the band harnessed the house's acoustics to maximum effect with John Bonham's drumming captured in the hall on tracks such as 'When The Levee

Breaks'. Although most famous as the place where Robert Plant was reported to have written 'Stairway To Heaven' in one day, the rural retreat was already a favourite of Fleetwood Mac, who recommended it to Led Zeppelin. Genesis created much of The Lamb Lies Down On Broadway here and Ian Dury and Elvis Costello also recorded or rehearsed there.

❛We did ['Going To California'] with all of us sitting outside on the grass playing mandolins and whatever else was around.❜
Led Zeppelin's John Paul Jones, recalls a winter recording

Headley Grange: once a poor house, now one of rock's stateliest of homes - it's even got a stairway to heaven!

❛There's this kind of Zeppelin heritage and it's fine for us to be glib about that, but the family there had had their gates nicked in the run-up to the O2 [gig] because they had Headley Grange written on them! I felt bad about that.❜
Jimmy Page, speaking to Mojo magazine about his return to Headley Grange in 2009 while filming the movie It Might Get Loud

LOCATION 071: just south of the B3002, Liphook Road, Headley, postcode GU35 8N. Status: private house. Don't make Jimmy Page feel 'bad' - stay away from those gates!

WINCHESTER
GRAHAM NASH'S BIRTHDAY 'TRIP' TO THE CATHEDRAL

"Standing on the grave of a soldier who died in 1799 and the day he died was a birthday and I noticed it was mine" was the poignant line written by Graham Nash in 'Cathedral', the epic five-minute track on Crosby, Stills and Nash's 1977 album CSN. Nash had visited the cathedral on his 32nd birthday while under the influence of LSD in 1974. The subject of the song is a grave inscription to British Army officer Hugh Foulkes, prominently marked on Winchester Cathedral's central aisle floor. "There were graves on the floor and one of them attracted my attention and my legs started to waver, not shake, but just waver, you know, like a divining rod - it was real strange" was how Nash later described his moving experience while "flying in Winchester Cathedral", as the song says.

❛The incident was: getting up in the morning at six, getting into this old Rolls-Royce that we'd hired for the day, going over to this dealer's in London and picking up some acid, dropping the acid and then going through Richmond Park with the ultimate goal of ending up in Stonehenge – and we went through Winchester on the way.❜
Graham Nash

LOCATION 072: postcode SO23 9LS. Website: www.winchester-cathedral.org.uk

PORTSMOUTH MIKE OLDFIELD'S HIT HORNPIPE

Mike Oldfield's update of a traditional folk melody from 1701 gave him his highest-placed single when 'Portsmouth' peaked at No.3 in the chart in 1976.

LOCATION 073: the well-known maritime and Royal Navy-based city nicknamed "Pompey" lies an hour's drive south of London

Born in Hampshire

Rob da Bank, DJ (b. 24 Jun 1974, Warsash)
Carl Barât, guitar/vocals, The Libertines (b. 6 Jun 1978, Basingstoke)
Amelle Berrabah, Sugababes (b. 22 Apr 1984, Aldershot)
Ronnie Bond, drums, The Troggs (b. 4 May 1940, Andover, d. 13 Nov 1992)
Andy Burrows, drums, Razorlight (b. 30 Jun 1979, Winchester)
Will Champion, drums, Coldplay (b. 31 Jul 1978, Southampton)
Craig David (b. 5 May 1981, Southampton)
Michael Giles, drums, King Crimson (b. 1 Mar 1942, Waterlooville)
Hugh Grundy, drums, The Zombies (b. 6 Mar 1945, Winchester)
Steve Hillier, keyboards, Dubstar (b. 14 May 1969, Southampton)
Roger Hodgson, vocals, Supertramp (b. 21 Mar 1950, Portsmouth)
Mike Hugg, drums, Manfred Mann (b. 11 Aug 1942, Gosport)
Howard Jones (b. 23 Feb 1955, Southampton)
Paul Jones, vocals/harmonica, Manfred Mann (b. 24 Feb 1942, Portsmouth)
Lee Kerslake, drums, Uriah Heep (b. 16 Apr 1947, Bournemouth)
Steve Lamacq, presenter (b. 16 Oct 1965, Basingstoke)
Laura Marling (b. 1 Feb 1990, Eversley)
Scott Mills, presenter (b. 28 Mar 1973, Eastleigh)

Mickie Most, producer/music mogul (b. 20 Jun 1938, Aldershot, d. 30 May 2003)
Paul Newton, bass, Uriah Heep (b. 21 Feb 1948, Andover)
Roland Orzabal, vocals/guitar, Tears For Fears (b. 22 Aug 1961, Portsmouth)
Reg Presley, vocals, The Troggs (b. 12 Jun 1941, Andover)
Peter Staples, bass, The Troggs (b. 3 May 1944, Andover)
Jef Streatfield, guitar, The Wildhearts (b. 8 Jun 1971, Southampton)
Mike Vickers, guitar/saxophone, Manfred Mann (b. 18 Apr 1940, Southampton)
Dave Wright, guitar, The Troggs (b. 21 Jan 1944, Winchester, d. 10 Oct 2008)

Andover born and bred cave-dwelling troglodytes The Troggs

BERKSHIRE

Less rock evocative perhaps than the Mississippi, but the River Thames running through this royal county has drawn a host of well-heeled and indeed high-heeled rock glitterati to its towns and villages. Aside from gathering together the individuals who would be Led Zeppelin and the Spice Girls, Berkshire played a huge part in the mod movement's enjoyment of some terrific live music at the various Ricky Tick clubs around the county. Berkshire can also proudly claim to have Elton John as a resident, one of the world's best established annual festivals at Reading, the grandeur of Lennon's Tittenhurst home and the less grand but charming Reading pub where he and Paul McCartney played a gig as holidaying teenagers in 1960.

OLD WINDSOR ELTON'S WOODSIDE MANSION

Two miles south of the royal residence of Windsor Castle lies the only slightly more modest home of Elton John. World statesmen and women are regular visitors to either establishment, particularly since Elton began hosting his annual White Tie & Tiara Balls to benefit the Elton John AIDS Foundation at his Woodside home. Sir Elton's eight-bedroom, Queen Anne-style property is accessed through electric gates and a gravelled drive flanked by immaculately tended white rose bushes. Inside, floral opulence is everywhere in a house full of vases of flowers. Outside, the obsessive nature of the owner is reflected in the formerly laid-out gardens on the 37-acre property which feature a lake, Orangery, the White Scented Gardens, an Italian garden, a Roman terrace, a secret garden and enough garaging for a fleet of cars that once made most motor museums green with envy but now houses his burgeoning collection of modern art.

LOCATION 074: going south out of Old Windsor and turn right on to Crimp Hill, where the private residence of Woodside is approximately one mile on your left. Postcode: SL4 2HL

ETON THE JAM'S POSH SCHOOL PROTEST

"Sup up your beer and collect your fags there's a row going on down near Slough" wrote The Jam's Paul Weller. Eton public school is the destination in the class war song by Britain's angry young mod trio. Paul Weller wrote and recorded 'The Eton Rifles' in 1979, prompted by reports a year earlier of a march by Right to Work and Rock Against Racism protestors who congregated outside the school, a symbol of posh privilege and wealth to the burgeoning socialist movement during the years of Margaret Thatcher's Conservative government.

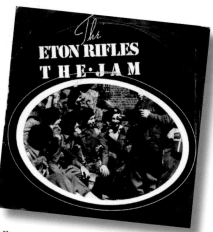

LOCATION 075: there is no direct access for vehicles over the Thames from Windsor to Eton. Pedestrians can walk across Windsor Bridge and up Eton High Street to Eton College, a distance of about half a mile. Postcode: SL4 6DW

HOOK END THE STUDIOS WHERE PIGS MIGHT FLY

Now a superbly appointed residential studio complex, Hook End Manor has variously been owned by Ten Years After's Alvin Lee, Pink Floyd's Dave Gilmour and producer and all-round pop person Trevor Horn. However well appointed the recording facilities might be, it is the 16th-century Elizabethan house and surrounding countryside that has drawn the likes of Radiohead, Morrissey, Iron Maiden, Kaiser Chiefs, Robbie Williams and Megadeth to book in and work. In addition to Dave Gilmour's floating recording studio aboard the Astoria houseboat, nearby on the Thames, Hook End Manor was used to record parts of Pink Floyd's 1987 album A Momentary Lapse Of Reason. During Gilmour's ownership of Hook End, one of the group's famous giant inflatable pig stage props was stored in an outbuilding of the property.

LOCATION 076: the village of Hook End is slightly north east of the A4074 that joins Reading and Wallingford, postcode RG8 0UE. The house and studio are a private residence. Website: www. hookendstudio.com

South East England

PANGBOURNE THE BOATHOUSE BIRTHPLACE OF LED ZEPPELIN

Jimmy Page's beautiful riverside home at Pangbourne was the location where the component parts of Led Zeppelin were assembled. In 1968, Yardbirds guitarist Page decided to start a new group and enlisted the services of organist and bass player John Paul Jones, vocalist Robert Plant and drummer John Bonham. Page owned the Boathouse between 1967 and 1975 and the property was the band's early HQ, where they first met and later rehearsed by climbing a ladder to the first floor. The property has attracted many visiting Led Zeppelin pilgrims down the years. According to a report in the Sunday Times, one inquisitive visitor in 2003, apologising for any intrusion, asked the then owner Graham Gore, "Did you know that a group used to be here?" Gore broke off from mending his son's car in the Boathouse garage to reply, "You mean Led Zeppelin? Why, are you a fan?" "No," replied a no doubt amused Robert Plant, "I was the singer."

LOCATION 077: the Boathouse, 4 Shooters Hill, Pangbourne,

The former Boathouse, Pangbourne, home of Jimmy Page

postcode RG8 7DU. Best viewed from the opposite bank of the River Thames, this private residence is a short walk from the centre of the village of Pangbourne

MAIDENHEAD THE SPICE GIRLS' HOMELY HQ

When Heart Management placed an advertisement in British entertainment newspaper The Stage, they recruited a group of girls who matched all the requirements spelled out in the ad. "R.U.18-23 with the ability to sing/dance? R.U. streetwise, outgoing, ambitious and dedicated?" Mel B, Geri, Mel C, Victoria and Emma answered emphatically "yes!"

and bonded together in a home base in 1993 provided for them in Boyn Hill Road, Maidenhead, by Heart's financier Chic Murphy.

LOCATION 078: a quiet Maidenhead address and a private residence, the Spice Girls' house was at 58 Boyn Hill Road, postcode SL6 4HJ

SUNNINGDALE RINGO, JOHN AND YOKO'S TITTENHURST PARK HOME

This Georgian house was home to John Lennon and Yoko Ono from 1969-1971 before the house, estate and recording studio were purchased by Ringo Starr, who owned it between 1973 and 1988. The place is familiar to so many music fans due to its frequent appearance in Beatles film footage and photos. Two days after The Beatles' final recording session, John, Paul, George and Ringo wandered the 72-acre estate for the group's last photocall on August 22nd 1969. The Daily Mail's Monte Fresco, the group's assistant Mal Evans and American Ethan Russell all snapped away and Russell's Tittenhurst pictures were included on the front and back of The Beatles' US album release Hey Jude. Most memorable of all are the images from the 'Imagine' video (taken from the album/movie Imagine) of John and Yoko outside and inside Tittenhurst's white walls. At the beginning of the 'Imagine' video, as John and Yoko entered the house, the couple's equivalent of a welcome mat was weirdly and typically a simple message etched into the glass above Tittenhurst's front door: 'THIS IS NOT HERE'.

Revered singer-songwriter Nick Drake was an excited house guest at Tittenhurst in 1971. John and Yoko had relocated to New York, leaving domestic staff in charge of the upkeep of the house in readiness for their return. Caretaker Paul Wheeler had been a friend of Drake at Cambridge University, and following the completion of his Pink Moon album Drake spent at least one visit soaking up the atmosphere of the rock star lifestyle at the house that had been home and creative hub for Lennon's Imagine recordings earlier that year.

❛The worst band I ever played with in my life. I had Eric Clapton, Elton John, Keith Richards, Ronnie Wood and I all playing in my studio in Tittenhurst in 1985. Too many leaders.❜
Ringo Starr, talking to Q in 1991

LOCATION 079: north of the village of Sunningdale on the A329, postcode SL5 0PN. Status: private estate

The Tittenhurst Park house and grounds

The cover for US album Hey Jude depicts John, George, Paul and Ringo at Tittenhurst

Pete Nash www.britishbeatlesfanclub.co.uk

WINDSOR AND NEWBURY THE RICKY-TICK CLUBS

Perhaps Berkshire's biggest contribution to rock history came with the establishing of the wonderfully titled Ricky-Tick club. The name was coined in the 1920s and 30s as a description for syncopated music, but it was the organ-based jazz-influenced rhythm and blues sounds that encouraged fans to flock to the Ricky-Tick's various locations across Berkshire. Promoter John Mansfield tapped into the rapidly growing enthusiasm for new bands like The Rolling Stones who broke big at the first Ricky-Tick location at the Star & Garter hotel in Windsor back in January 1963. They literally brought the house down, with walls and ceilings shedding crumbling masonry, forcing a move down to the riverside Thames Hotel. By May 1964, the Ricky-Tick had a very different home at Clewer Mead. This derelict mansion was a mecca to mods who travelled from as far as north London to groove to the music provided by the likes of Zoot Money, Graham Bond and Georgie Fame. Like most music clubs at the time there was no alcohol to be had, but the old house had a room converted into a coffee bar, a games room and a room set aside for the new early-60s recreation of TV watching. You can see a perfect reconstruction of the club in the 1966 movie Blow-Up. The director, Michelangelo Antonioni, was keen to use the real Windsor venue but the local council was in the process of trying to oust the Ricky-Tick from Clewer Mead. At great expense and effort, the club's fixtures and fittings were transported to the film's studio in Borehamwood, Hertfordshire, where the Ricky-Tick was recreated

for a sequence in the movie where The Yardbirds (featuring both Jeff Beck and Jimmy Page) performed in front of a bussed-in crowd of the club's mods.

‘Mods used to drive down from north London, come down the North Circular, past the Ace Cafe and the June rockers and the A4 where there would be little pockets of mods on their scooters waiting for the convoy to come by. They would join it and then when they got to Slough, turn left into Eton, over the

bridge and there was a cafe with hundreds of motorbikes outside and the rockers would be jeering at them and they'd all go to the club.’
John Mansfield

On May 20th 1966, the Ricky-Tick in Newbury was the setting for a massive falling-out by members of The Who. Famously fiesty on stage, this particular gig took their trademark aggression a stage further when John Entwistle and Keith Moon arrived late and Pete Townshend and Roger Daltrey took to the stage backed by support band The Jimmy Brown Sound. Entwistle and Moon finally arrived midway through the performance of 'My Generation', prompting Townshend to strike Moon over the head with his guitar in front of 800 Ricky-Tick club witnesses. Worse was to come. When refused payment for the gig, The Who's van ran out of petrol a short distance down the A4 on the journey back to London. With his injuries from the gig requiring stitches, Moon recuperated in a nursing home before going on to announce to the media that he and Entwistle would be leaving The Who. He later backtracked and both rejoined within a week.

‘I don't know who hit who first but it ended up as an almighty punch-up on stage as punches are thrown on stage and cymbals are being thrown around and guitars smashed on heads and Roger Daltrey was going wild shouting for the crowd to riot.’
John Mansfield

LOCATIONS 080, 081, 082, 083 and 084: at Windsor (all gone), Newbury (Corn Exchange), Maidenhead and farther afield at The Stoke Hotel Guildford, and Hounslow

READING THE THAMES-SIDE FESTIVAL THAT SAW NIRVANA'S LAST STAND

It's testament to the success of this annual festival by the River Thames that so many legendary performances have ended up on CD and DVD. Nirvana, Hawkwind, Level 42, Samson, Ten Years After and Marillion have all been captured and given the 'Live at Reading' treatment. But it was Nirvana's greatest (and final) UK performance at the 1992 Reading Festival that fans remember with most enthusiasm. This festival hasn't always been located in its current Richfield Avenue site. Perpetually close to the River Thames, the festival began in 1961 as a jazz and blues-based event at Richmond Athletic Ground and moved further west to Windsor, then Sunbury, before settling at Reading.

LOCATION 085: Richfield Avenue, postcode RG1 8EQ. www.readingfestival.com

SULHAMSTEAD KATE BUSH'S ISLAND HOME

Iron gates, high walls and security cameras protect Kate Bush's privacy at her island home by the Kennet and Avon Canal at Tyle Mill, just east of the A4 on the road to the village of Sulhamstead.

LOCATION 086: Status: private house and grounds

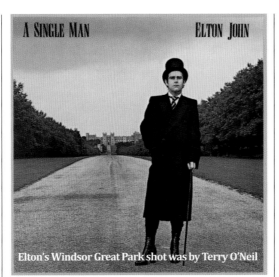

Elton's Windsor Great Park shot was by Terry O'Neil

WINDSOR GREAT PARK ELTON'S PHOTOSHOOT ON THE LONG WALK

Windsor Castle and Windsor Great Park are where the front cover for his 1978 album A Single Man was shot. The photo features an uncharacteristically soberly dressed Elton in undertaker black. Appropriate perhaps as darker tracks on the LP recorded nearby at The Mill, Cookham, included 'Madness', 'Reverie' and 'Song For Guy.'

LOCATION 087: south of the castle (postcode SL4 1NJ) on the Long Walk, which is a public right of way

Born in Berkshire

Cliff Bennett (b. 4 June 1940, Slough)
Mark Brzezicki, drums, Big Country (b. 21 Jun 1957, Slough)
Tim Dorney, keyboards, Republica (b. 30 Mar 1965, Ascot)
Danny Goffey, drums, Supergrass (b. 7 Feb 1974, Slough)
Sarah Harding, Girls Aloud (b. 17 Nov 1981, Ascot)
Chesney Hawkes (b. 22 Sep 1971, Windsor)
Jonny Male, guitar, Republica (b. 10 Oct 1963, Windsor)
Mike Oldfield (b. 15 May, 1953, Reading)
Irwin Sparkes, vocals/guitar The Hoosiers (b. 5 Mar 1981, Reading)
Will Young (b. 20 Jan 1979, Wokingham)

READING THE NERK TWINS PAY (AND PLAY) THEIR DUES AT THE FOX & HOUNDS

During the 1960 Easter weekend, John Lennon and Paul McCartney played a couple of acoustic sessions to drinkers at the Fox & Hounds in Reading. The two friends had hitch-hiked down to stay at Paul's cousin Betty's pub in the Reading suburb of Caversham. Both lads served behind the bar and absorbed some good show-business advice from Betty's husband, a former Butlins entertainments manager. He advised them on what to play to his Saturday night punters and suggested the duo kick off with a lively instrumental number instead of launching straight into Paul's favoured 'Be-Bop-A-Lula'. So, this unique rock 'n' roll meets country and western gig saw Lennon and McCartney perched on stools with their guitars beginning with their version of Les Paul and Mary Ford's 'The World Is Waiting For The Sunrise'.

❝It was a lovely experience that came from John and I just hitching off down there. At the end of the week we played in the pub as The Nerk Twins. We even made our own posters.❞
Paul McCartney, from the Anthology interviews

LOCATION 088: north of the centre of Reading over the River Thames at 51 Gosbrook Road, Caversham, postcode RG4 8BS

South East England

OXFORDSHIRE

The epicentre of the vibe created by folk-rock pioneers and mainstays Fairport Convention is the village of Cropredy, where their annual festival has been going for ever. The same rural summer sunshine their festival appears to guarantee has drawn Traffic, XTC, Paul Weller and Mike Oldfield to seek out Oxfordshire rural retreats for the creation of some of these artists' finest work. In keeping with its history as a place where cerebral activity has thrived, the city of Oxford has produced a calibre of band famed for their thoughtful, intricate lyrics. Foals, Stornoway, Supergrass and Radiohead, top the list of a wave of music, much of which has been nurtured in the small area of the city called Jericho. The county's greatest claim to rock immortality and worldwide musical acclaim came when schoolboys Thom Yorke, Colin Greenwood, Ed O'Brien, Phil Selway and Jonny Greenwood formed a group at Abingdon public school that would later become a music obsession for some and a terrific earner worldwide for the British music industry. East of Oxfordshire is the palatial estate where the county's most famous rock resident, George Harrison, lived, gardened, filmed and recorded for the greater part of his life before his death in 2001.

HENLEY-ON-THAMES DUSTY SPRINGFIELD'S MEMORIAL STONE

Henley is the town where Dusty Springfield lived out the final years of her life and the parish church of St Mary the Virgin is a much visited spot for her loyal fans. Here a funeral congregation, including Lulu, Elvis Costello and the Pet Shop Boys, came to pay their last respects to the iconic singer after her death in 1999. There is a memorial stone in the churchyard where some of her ashes are buried, the remainder having been scattered by her brother Tom Springfield in Ireland. Go to the Rock Atlas Republic of Ireland, Lislarkin entry and the Greater London W8 section for additional information on these Dusty memorials.

LOCATION 089: St Mary the Virgin churchyard is on the A4130 (Hart Street) in the centre of Henley-on-Thames. Postcode: RG9 2AU

CHIPPING NORTON
ELTON JOHN: THE PIED PIPER OF CHIPPING NORTON

An NME report in 1975 by Steve Turner nominated the launch party for Elton John's new label Rocket Records as one of the most notable media events of the decade. In keeping with the train-themed label logo, Elton laid on a football special with disco and ferried the press and guests from London's Paddington to Oxfordshire. Alighting at the Oxfordshire station of Kingham, the media scrum then followed Elton - acting, as Turner put it, "as a 20th-century Pied Piper" - through the streets complete with marching band, to the local hall for much merrymaking before the return trip to Paddington. At this time the residents of Chipping Norton were hardly unfamiliar with the sight of rock and pop legends visiting the town. Edwin Starr, Status Quo, Duran Duran, Gerry Rafferty, Jeff Beck, Fairground Attraction and Alison Moyet are just some of the musicians that recorded or rehearsed

The new Rocket label is launched at Chipping Norton in 1972

at Chipping Norton Recording Studios from 1972 to 1999.

LOCATION 090: Chipping Norton is about 20 miles north-east of Oxford on the A44. The grade II listed building that once housed the recording studios is at 28 New Street, postcode OX7 5LJ

ASTON TIRROLD TRAFFIC GO BACK TO THE COUNTRY

Here lies the secluded white cottage surrounded by farmland where the group Traffic escaped to gain some rural inspiration and rehearse new material in 1967. The idyllic spot, complete with beehives, was tucked away down a dirt track with stunning views from the makeshift cement platform rehearsal stage where the group would play on warm summer evenings. The stone-floored cottage had no running water and no electricity at the start of their three-year rented residence, but the band members set about creating their own unique lifestyle, with many visitors dropping by despite the geographical isolation of the place. Eric Clapton, Pete Townshend, John Bonham, Ginger Baker and Joe Cocker were all house guests. Leon Russell even premiered a new song he'd just completed on the cottage piano called 'Superstar.' By 1969, rock fans everywhere had become aware of Traffic's music haven, following the release of the Mr. Fantasy and Traffic albums and numerous press reports about the band's "back to the country" commune. Rolling Stone magazine reported the experience in depth with Traffic's Steve Winwood pictured outside the cottage on the front cover.

❛I think the sound of the room is very interesting, like every room has its own character, and the room in the cottage where we do rough takes of the songs has its own special quality, because it is an old house and you can tell what kind of room the sound was recorded in when you listen to the tape.❜ Steve Winwood, talking to Rolling Stone in 1968

❛Stevie Winwood was always my favourite singer, that blue-eyed soul sound. It had been our ambition from the start to convince him to join Crosby, Stills and Nash – I wanted an organ player who could sing the blues. He was exceptionally kind to me, but every time I trudged across the moors to see him, he was always occupied.❜ Stephen Stills

LOCATION 091: south of the village of Aston Tirrold where Spring Lane meets the A417 is a lane on the opposite side of

Rolling Stone wrote about Traffic at Aston Tirrold and the cottage features on the sleeves below this main road which in turn branches off right into a dirt track leading to Sheepcot Farm. Status: private. Postcode: OX11 9DS

CROPREDY FAIRPORT'S CONVENTIONS IN THE SUN

Music festivals featuring Fairport Convention in the village of Cropredy can be dated back to 1976. The band's bass-playing founder member Dave Pegg and his family settled in the village and Fairport's Cropredy Convention started life as a private back garden event with a few hundred guests. What began as the end of the band (they played what they believed to be their final outdoor gig at Cropredy in 1979) was actually a rebirth with a burgeoning fanbase seeded and grown through decades of tours and recordings. Their festival has now expanded to stretch over

Blessed with sunshine: the Cropredy Convention site

three days and attracts up to 20,000 at the annual August get-together. Joining Fairport Convention on the bill in recent years have been folk favourites Seth Lakeman, John Martyn and Ralph McTell, plus Steve Winwood, Supergrass and Jools Holland's Rhythm 'n' Blues Orchestra.

LOCATION 092: the current festival site is east of the village of Cropredy, immediately over the Cropredy Bridge, postcode OX17 1PQ, which spans the River Cherwell and Oxford Canal. Check out the extremely helpful Cropredy section of the website www. fairportconvention.com

OXFORD RADIOHEAD'S SOUTH PARK HOMECOMING

With their album Amnesiac top of the chart a month earlier Radiohead made a triumphant homecoming appearance at Oxford's South Park in July 2001. Torrential rain failed to dampen the spirits of 42,000 adoring fans, who also witnessed performances by fellow local lads Supergrass plus Beck, Sigur Ros and Humphrey Lyttelton.

❛It's what you dream of really. Having a show like that in what was my local park at the time was quite something. Looking out into the audience and seeing the pandemonium is an image that will stay with me.❜
Phil Selway, Radiohead

LOCATION 093: south of the A420 Headington Road at Cheney Lane, postcode OX3 7QJ

OXFORD 'CREEP' VIDEO AT THE ZODIAC

Formerly called the Co-op Dining Hall, The Venue and then The Zodiac, this 1,000-plus-capacity music theatre was where Radiohead's 'Creep' video was shot on the old main stage. The band's management company were responsible for funding the venue's re-opening in 1995. Oxford's premier music spot now continues to do business, re-named as the O2 Academy.

LOCATION 094: the O2 Academy, 190 Cowley Road, postcode OX4 1UE

HENLEY-ON-THAMES GEORGE HARRISON'S FRIAR PARK MANSION

The quiet Beatle's estate at Friar Park is strongly associated with his hugely successful debut solo album All Things Must Pass. One track in particular, 'Ballad Of Sir Frankie Crisp (Let It Roll)', acts as a guided tour of the Friar Park 120-room Neo-Gothic mansion's caves, maze, woods and "Ye long walks of Coole and Shades", as Harrison puts it. Frank Crisp was an earlier owner of Friar Park who designed the gardens and began a collection of whimsical statues and gnomes, a trend embraced by Harrison (a keen gardener), who included some of his garden gnomes on the All Things Must Pass album cover shot at Friar Park. Harrison purchased the estate in 1970 and lived there until his death in 2001. His debut album wasn't the only chart-topper recorded at the estate's studio. Shakespear's Sister's No.1 single

'Stay' and their album, Hormonally Yours, was recorded there.

LOCATION 095: heading west from the centre of Henley-on-Thames, follow Market Place into Gravel Hill. The private Friar Park estate begins on the right after the right-hand turn to Hop Gardens. Postcode: RG9 2EH

Friar Park, George and gnomes on the 2001 re-issue cover of All Things Must Pass

OXFORD SUPERGRASS AND RADIOHEAD TAKE OFF IN JERICHO

Jericho is a historic suburb of Oxford, just a short walk north-east of the city centre, and is a place where A&R people would flock to see new bands. In 1986, The Jericho Tavern witnessed the very first gig by local boys On A Friday, who would soon become Radiohead, and a performance by Supergrass in 1994 was so good it instantly bagged them a recording contract. Built in 1818, The Jericho continues to promote great live music in this quiet corner of Oxford. It was local record shop the Manic Hedgehog that gave On A Friday the name for

their final demo tape. It included tracks that would resurface on the band's Pablo Honey debut album, released under new name Radiohead.

❝It's such a weird place and it's very important to my writing.❞
Thom Yorke describes Oxford in an early interview

LOCATION 096: a short walk north-east of the city centre, The Jericho Tavern is at 56 Walton Street, postcode OX2 6AZ. Website: www.thejerichooxford.co.uk

South East England

SHIPTON-ON-CHERWELL WELLER AT THE MANOR

Now the private property of the Marquess of Headfort, The Manor at Shipton-on-Cherwell was once a rural residential recording studio owned by Richard Branson, ostensibly to service his Virgin Records stable of artists. The place gave the right amount of freedom and inspiration that enabled Mike Oldfield to create his 17-million-copy-shifting album Tubular Bells. It also famously fitted the bill perfectly when a mellowing Paul Weller, seeking a new base to record some folkier material in 1993, hit upon The Manor for his new album Wild Wood. Weller so enjoyed the experience that his next album Stanley Road was another product of the The Manor's rural vibe, this time with a guest appearance by Steve Winwood, who had himself returned to some traditional British roots music during Traffic's immersion in the Oxfordshire countryside three decades earlier. Apparently, Traffic's Jim Capaldi had tipped-off Winwood about Weller's Wild Wood and he was approached to play at The Manor on Stanley Road's 'Woodcutter's Son' and 'Pink On White Walls'. The Strawbs, Gong and XTC made tracks there more than once before Radiohead and Cast became The Manor's last bookings in 1995.

❛The Manor was just really magical. In fact, everyone who came down sensed it.❜
Paul Weller

LOCATION 097: two miles north of Kidlington, postcode OX5 1JL

Mapledurham Mill and a cloaked friend are all you need to recreate this famous Black Sabbath photo shoot

MAPLEDURHAM MILL THE FIRST BLACK SABBATH ALBUM COVER

The ghostly cloaked figure on the front cover of Black Sabbath's debut album is standing in a winter landscape in front of Mapledurham Mill, on the River Thames. The building, which dates back to the 15th century, was photographed from the lawns of Mapledurham House.

LOCATION 098: a short distance west of the A4074, north-west of Reading. Postcode: RG4 7TR. Status: public paid admission. Website: www.mapledurham.co.uk

OXFORD SUPERGRASS ON 'SHOTOVER HILL'

A track on the band's 1999 album, the hill is a 557ft-high beauty spot.

❛It's actually a hill in Wheatley and we used to go up there and the travellers used to be there and we used to get a bit of smoking done and see all these mad travellers with their dogs. It's just a little story about that, remembering walking up the hill and coming back down three hours later after a few smokes and it's raining. It was a really beautiful place as well, and it's a very visual song. It talks about how you can see the glow of the caravans and they're smoking stuff and you can smell it all. It's looking back to our youth. We all remember it really well, so it was good to get together and write about it.❜
Gaz Coombes

LOCATION 099: east of Oxford, Old Road, postcode OX3 8TB

BUCKINGHAMSHIRE

The former home of Three Men in a Boat author Jerome K Jerome invaded by The Small Faces, an eye-popping High Wycombe hostelry enjoyed by the Kings of Leon and a Victorian railway station timewarp for Welsh band Man are three key stories in the annals of Buckinghamshire rock. Noel Gallagher is a Little Chalfont resident and Paul Weller writes a less than loving lyric about Milton Keynes, but it's the cast of characters passing through the county town of Aylesbury (on a par with San Francisco according to Ian Hunter) with its significant court, club and market square that perhaps gives the county its greatest rock 'n' roll claim to fame.

HIGH WYCOMBE STRIP PUB DEBUT FOR KINGS OF LEON

The hugely successful band formed in Nashville, Tennessee, made their UK debut in High Wycombe's extraordinary White Horse pub in February 2003. The young band's first impression of the British live circuit was not what they were expecting but not altogether unfavourable. In addition to beer and big screen football, the White Horse offered entertainment of a more exotic nature. This warm-up gig and an encounter with the pub's naked dancers was followed the next day by a rather more traditional introduction to Britain's music venues up the A40 at The Zodiac in Oxford.

❛It was a strip joint by day then at night they'd have bands playing, so when we got there, there was a bunch of naked women in our dressing room, changing clothes. We thought this is definitely the life!❜
Matthew Followill, Kings of Leon, talking to Mojo magazine

Kings of Leon: from Nashville to High Wycombe's White Horse

LOCATION 100: 95 West Wycombe Road, postcode HP11 2LR

AYLESBURY 'KEEF' IN COURT

In January, at the start of what would become a particularly difficult 1977 for Keith Richards, Aylesbury Crown Court was the setting for a high-profile court case for The Rolling Stones' guitarist. Found guilty on some but not all of a catalogue of drug possession charges, he was also fined £25 for failing to produce a current MOT certificate or tax disc while driving. His misdemeanours escalated to an altogether more international level in February when he was infamously arrested by the Canadian Mounties in Toronto.

❛The next day, The Final Day, can only be likened to Cup Final Fever. Oop fer der bust, and so on. By this time the big, forbidding-looking front gates of Aylesbury Crown Court were locked up to keep the maddening crowd at bay.❜
The trial, as reported by Tony Parsons for NME

LOCATION 101: Market Square, postcode HP20 1XD

AYLESBURY 'MARKET SQUARE HEROES' AND THE BRITISH SAN FRANCISCO

Aylesbury was the spiritual setting for 'Market Square Heroes' the song that gave the Buckinghamshire-formed band Marillion their first hit in 1982. Inspired by the inner city riots across England the previous spring and summer, Marillion's vocalist Fish remembers writing the song's lyrics in nearby St Mary's churchyard. Mott The Hoople's Ian Hunter is another to have gained inspiration from the town.

❛Aylesbury is like a little San Francisco. It's one of those places where everything seems to start... The people there seem to sense what's going to happen. In fact, the atmosphere of Aylesbury got to me to such an extent that I was seriously considering moving there... but I moved to America instead.❜ Ian Hunter, talking to Mojo in 2009

LOCATION 102: the town centre, postcode HP20 1UF

South East England

AYLESBURY FROM MANDRAKE PADDLE STEAMER TO ZIGGY AT FRIARS

Even if you never attended a gig there - the club had 87,000 members by the time it closed in 1984, so many did - no-one who bought a music paper in the Seventies could have failed to notice the weekly gig ads topped by the distinctive gothic Friars logo. Opening with Mike Cooper and Mandrake Paddle Steamer on June 2nd 1969 at New Friarage Hall, Friars relocated to the Borough Assembly Hall from 1971 until 1975, when it moved to its current Civic Centre home. Promoter David Stopps oversaw the conveyorbelt of prog rock's finest that put Aylesbury on the music map and managed the 2009 40th anniversary gig that saw Friars return to the town once more. No band has been as crucial to the ongoing success story as The Groundhogs, who returned to play the anniversary gig along with early Friars favourites Edgar Broughton and The Pretty Things. Back in the day, Captain Beefheart, Genesis, Mott The Hoople and Fleetwood Mac all appeared before new-wavers, and punks became the Friars' new customers when The Flamin' Groovies and The Vibrators took the place by storm in 1976. Before the end came, The Clash, U2, The Jam, The Ramones and The Police all put in memorable appearances. Friars played an important part in David Bowie's development from thoughtful singer-songwriter to full-blown rock 'n' roll superstar. September 25th 1971 was the date of his memorable first performance at the club in front of the Friars' faithful, who each paid ten shillings to watch a captivating performance

that left him promising, "When I come back I'm going to be completely different." How focused, driven and true to his word was he? January 29th, 1972 saw his return in the guise of Ziggy Stardust. It was a life-changing introduction to a whole new direction in music for him. It was equally life-changing for many in the audience that night who witnessed a set list including the new Ziggy album plus revved-up classics 'I Feel Free' by Cream and 'Around And Around' by Chuck Berry.

❛Some audiences could be a bit hairy for a better word, you were never sure of the reaction. But at Friars, it was run like a family club almost. Everybody... not just backstage, but the audience too seemed to know each other. There was a wonderful camaraderie about it.❜
Jake Burns, Stiff Little Fingers

Andy Fairweather Low plays to a packed Borough Assembly Hall Below: the queue outside Friars before the gig

LOCATION 103: Civic Centre, Market Square, postcode HP20 1UF. For the continuing Friars drama visit the website: www.aylesburyfriars.co.uk

TAPLOW STATION COVER FOR MAN'S FIRST CHART ALBUM

The fine Victorian architecture of Taplow station is pictured on Man's 1973 album cover Back Into The Future, photographed by Ruan O'Laughran. The Victorian characters pictured on the platform (from left to right on the gatefold sleeve) were Man people Angie Davies, Will Youatt, Plug's daughter, Howard 'Plug' Davies (tour manager/roadie), Ella Ryan, Phil Ryan, Linda Williams, Micky Jones, Terry Williams, Jenny Jones, Noel Ryan and Jeff Hooper (sound engineer). Jones came up with the idea for the title of the album and Youatt the concept for the sleeve design. The double LP was the Welsh band's first to chart and it gave them a No.23 hit, which remains their highest-placed entry.

❛The photo session was a good laugh. We turned up at Taplow station, which was all derelict. We used the old waiting rooms to change in - the boys in one room, the girls in the other. The station is on the Wales to Paddington main line, so every 15 minutes an express would come thundering through. I think passengers thought they were going through some sort of time warp!❜ Micky Jones, Man

LOCATION 104: the station is south of Taplow, east of Maidenhead, postcode SL6 0NU

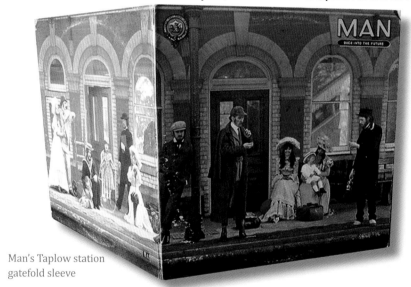

Man's Taplow station gatefold sleeve

MARLOW SMALL FACES AT MONKS CORNER

The former home of writer Jerome K Jerome was the spot for a final burst of creativity for The Small Faces in the period after No.1 album Ogdens' Nut Gone Flake. According to keyboards man Ian McLagan, Monks Corner was where 1968 hit single 'The Universal' was partly recorded. The birdsong, barking dog and Steve Marriott's acoustic guitar were all taped in the garden on their old mono cassette machine. Marlow was also the starting point for Small Faces and Faces bass player Ronnie Lane's new venture in 1974, The Passing Show, a rock and folk tour travelling the country in a circus-style big top.

LOCATION 105: west of Marlow, Monks Corner, Marlow Common, postcode SL7 2QR.Status: private residence

MILTON KEYNES THE STYLE COUNCIL WERE "NOT SO KEYNE"

Hardly affectionate, Paul Weller was "not so keyne" as the lyric says, but not every town has a song written about it, even if the sentiments involved are less than flattering. 'Come To Milton Keynes' didn't quite manage to put Buckinghamshire's new town on a rock 'n' rolling par with 'Galveston', 'Memphis' or 'Tulsa', but it did give The Style Council their 9th Top 30 hit back in the summer of 1985.

LOCATION 106: for a taste of what Paul Weller was describing, leave the M1 at junction 14

Born in Buckinghamshire

Nicholas Bracegirdle, aka Chicane (b. 28 Feb 1971, Chalfont St Giles)
Terry Cox, drums, Pentangle (b. 13 Mar 1937, High Wycombe)
Paul Ferguson, drums, Killing Joke (b. 31 Mar 1958, High Wycombe)
Adam Ficek, drums, Babyshambles (b. 1974, Bletchley, Milton Keynes)
Kris Ife, singer-songwriter (b. 16 Jun 1946, Aylesbury)
John Otway (b. 2 Oct 1952, Aylesbury)
Tim Rice, lyricist (b. 10 Nov 1944, Amersham)
Justin Sullivan, vocals, New Model Army (b. 8 Apr 1956, Jordans)

South East England

SURREY

A handy distance for wealthy rock star commuters into London, Keith Moon, John Lennon, Ringo Starr, Eric Clapton and Stephen Stills have all lived the rock royalty lifestyle in some of Surrey's most attractive properties. The affluent county can also boast what's generally accepted as the largest audience to watch Bob Dylan when his Bobness played Blackbushe Aerodrome. Birth county of such luminaries as Roger Waters, Paul Weller, Petula Clark and Peter Gabriel, it even has a Bow Wow Wow beauty spot and a cracking family-orientated annual festival, GuilFest. And, let's hear it for the town of Woking, which seems to have given birth to more pop people than any place that size has any right to.

CAMBERLEY DYLAN'S AERODROME PICNIC AT BLACKBUSHE

A crowd of 175,000 rock fans turned up at this Surrey airfield in 1978 to see Bob Dylan top the bill in what promoter Harvey Goldsmith advertised as 'The Picnic at Blackbushe Aerodrome'. Present day pilgrims might find it tough to work out exactly where the stage would have been where the great man (bedecked in top hat) performed on that July weekend. The exact position where Dylan, supported by local boy made god Eric Clapton, Joan Armatrading, Graham Parker and The Rumour and Lake performed is a short stroll due north of the aerodrome control tower. On the day of the concert, a sea of humanity stretched from the fence near the A30 to a stage with no giant screens. Even a privileged ligger like Ringo Starr complained he couldn't see anything from his VIP vantage point. Still, at least Dylan gave good audio value for money for £6-a-head ticket-holders crammed together on the runway: watching from what seemed like miles away, Dylan disciples witnessed a three-hour-long performance.

LOCATION 107: on the A30, three miles west of Camberley, postcode GU17 9LQ

❝He rang my agent. Not his manager. Dylan himself personally. That was great. The idea of it.❞
Joan Armatrading recalls her invitation to play Blackbushe!

CHERTSEY KEITH MOON'S ECCENTRIC HOME: REBUILT BY VINCE CLARKE

Possessor of the largest kit in rock, The Who's larger than life drummer Keith Moon lived at 'Tara', a home built of pyramids and named by the original owner after the southern mansion in Gone with the Wind. The eccentric structure was party central during Moon's ownership between 1971 and 1975, when he sold the place to Kevin Godley. The 10cc man then sold in turn to Erasure's Vince Clarke, who demolished the place but, to his credit, created an equally eccentric rock star fantasy home featuring a futuristic snail shell-like house and recording studio. Still standing as it did in the 70s at the bottom of the winding drive to the house is a building that was a familiar and much-loved part of Keith Moon's life in the Seventies, his handily placed local hostelry, the Golden Grove pub.

LOCATION 108: St Ann's Hill Road, Chertsey, postcode KT16 9EN. Status: private residence

GUILDFORD FUN FOR ALL THE FAMILY AT GUILFEST

Guilfest was started in 1992 by local businessman and festival fan Tony Scott. This annual mid-July festival doesn't make any cutting-edge or cult claims. It's possibly Britain's most family-orientated music festival, attracting 20,000 fans to line-ups featuring pop and rock's more enduring bands. In 2011, the wide-ranging bill included Public Image Ltd and James Blunt.

LOCATION 109: a short walk north of the centre of Guildford at Stoke Park, London Road (A3100), postcode GU1 1SW. Website: www.guilfest.co.uk

REIGATE BOW WOW WOW 'GO WILD IN THE COUNTRY'

In a 1981 reconstruction of Manet's famous painting Le déjeuner sur l'herbe, Bow Wow Bow posed for the cover of their See Jungle! See Jungle! Go Join Your Gang, Yeah. City All Over! Go Ape Crazy album (and the following year's 'Last of The Mohicans' EP) at a location discovered by photographer Andy Earl. The Surrey beauty spot, overlooked by the North Downs, is a 200-acre woodland area but not the most private place for a photoshoot involving a degree of nudity. Although the

Andy Earl's Priory Park photoshoot

cover failed to get used in the UK and US, it presents a much seen image due to the controversial nudity of singer Annabella Luwin, who was only 15 at the time.

❛He came up with the idea of copying Déjeuner on Saturday and we shot it on Monday. I drove round Surrey looking for locations in my old Land Rover and found this spot at Priory Park, near Reigate.❜
Photographer Andy Earl recalls Malcolm McLaren's concept

LOCATION 110: south of Reigate town centre. Accessed via Park Lane at the park's western side, postcode RH2 7RL

EWHURST 'LAYLA' AT CLAPTON'S HURTWOOD HOME

Eric Clapton moved into this 1910 Italian-styled villa in 1969 and it was here he wrote 'Layla' for Pattie Boyd, who later became his wife at Hurtwood. The house became love nest, band rehearsal HQ for Delaney and Bonnie and Friends and Derek and The Dominos and home to the reclusive guitarist during his darkest days when addicted to drugs. Memphis-born Domino, Bobby Whitlock, recalled writing songs with Clapton by the fireside at Hurtwood, although 'Layla', Clapton's signature song and the standout track on Derek and The Dominos' album Layla And Other Assorted Love Songs, was one song Clapton worked on alone in his bedroom. When Eric finally did marry Pattie, in 1979, a party to celebrate the occasion at Hurtwood saw Mick Jagger, George Harrison, Paul McCartney, Denny Laine, Ginger Baker and Lonnie Donegan join Eric on stage for a jam in the garden.

❛We wrote ['I Looked Away'] then we went down the village pub. Sausages and beer❜
Dominos keyboard player Bobby Whitlock

LOCATION 111: the private grade II listed residence Hurtwood Edge, postcode GU6 7NW and the Windmill pub at Pitch Hill, which adjoins the estate's gardens at postcode GU6 7NN on Ride Way

RIPLEY ERIC CLAPTON'S BIRTHPLACE

Britain's most famous exponent of the electric guitar was born and raised in the comparative comfort of the Surrey stockbroker belt. This historic village had a great pull on Eric Clapton's affections in a non-musical sense. Aside from being born here and raised by his grandparents, Ripley was a significant place in the formation of the game of cricket, which Clapton enthusiastically plays and watches. In fact, the 250-year-old local cricket club is situated on the village green, reputed to be England's largest.

LOCATION 112 1 The Green (postcode GU23 6AJ) is in the centre of the village, off the B2215. Status: private residence

WOKING WELLER'S 'TOWN CALLED MALICE'

The Jam's single 'A Town Called Malice' is reported to have been based on Woking, a town much changed since the young Paul Weller kicked a ball about in his local streets. The title of his best known solo album, Stanley Road, is the Woking back street where he grew up. His former two-up two-down Victorian family home is a distant memory as the road has been redeveloped as a one-way street with offices and flats. Joining Stanley Road is Walton Road, where the teenage Weller played some of his first gigs at the then Working Men's Club, now the Woking Liberal Club.

LOCATIONS 113 and 114: the Woking Liberal Club, 23 Walton Road, GU21 5DL, is just a short walk away from one-time Weller family home in Stanley Road

> ❛ Brookfield House was a magical place. There were ghosts. And I had wonderful bursts of creativity there. ❜
>
> Stephen Stills

> ❛ I did manage to get out and about in the surrounding countryside. Loved going to the Guildford Train Station to escape to London when Stephen gave us a weekend pass. ❜
>
> Chris Hillman, Manassas band member

> ❛ Johnny's workroom/office was virtually untouched. It still has faded album covers and photos on the wall. The recreation room, where Manassas rehearsed, was much the same. It even seemed the same family of swans still inhabited the waterways there. ❜
>
> Al Perkins, Manassas pedal steel guitarist, describes a return visit in 2008

ELSTEAD SELLERS, STARR AND STILLS AT BROOKFIELD

A beautiful estate made remarkable by the property-buying chain that saw Peter Sellers sell to Ringo Starr, who sold to Stephen Stills. The 15th-century oak-beamed house, complete with Japanese deer pond, waterfowl and stables was owned by Peter Sellers when he married Britt Ekland. The actor added a cinema above the garage and, at vast expense, imported a beautiful front door all the way from Italy. Rumour has it that Ringo later 'adapted' the door by cutting a cat flap in it for the family's Siamese cats. During Ringo's time, the place was the location for a meeting convened in January 1969 to attempt to get The Beatles back together to finish the Let It Be album. George Harrison was the defector summoned to Brookfield and the attempt to 'get back' was successful, the four switching recording from the "cold and not very nice atmosphere" at Twickenham, as George put it, to their studio at Savile Row. When Stephen Stills first rented, then bought the house from Ringo, his period in Surrey coincided with a rich vein of form in 1970. Escaping the infighting surrounding super-group Crosby, Stills, Nash & Young back in the States, Stills set about writing and recording his first solo

Manassas, pictured in the Brookfield garage

Atlantic Records

Peter Sellers returns to Brookfield to visit Stephen Stills and the subject of Stills' song 'Johnny's Garden', John the gardener

Henry Diltz

album, commuting from Brookfield up to London's Island Studios, where both Eric Clapton and Jimi Hendrix contributed to the LP. A second burst of activity two years later saw Stills fly in his new band Manassas for rehearsals before they hit the road to tour. Manassas band member Chris Hillman recalled how much the three months of foggy, cold British weather affected a bunch of musicians more used to the sun of California. He also remembers being visited by Bernie Leadon of the Eagles, who played him cuts from the band's debut album, which they were recording in London with producer Glyn Johns at the time. Through all the rock 'n' roll changes at Brookfield, one thing was constant: the presence of the estate's gardener John. A calming influence over all he met, Stills even wrote a song about him. 'Johnny's Garden' appeared on the first Manassas album, but it wasn't the only legacy left by the pipe-smoking herbalist that had a profound effect on all Brookfield's tenants: Peter Sellers based his performance of Chance the Gardener on John in the 1979 movie Being There.

LOCATION 115: Fulbrook Lane, Elsted, postcode GU8 6LG. Status: private residence

South East England

RIPLEY BLACK BARN STUDIO HAS THE "VIBE"

"More vibe than you can shake a stick at" and "bucketloads of vibe" is how this rural recording studio advertises itself. Anyone needing to see how that vibe translates visually can see clearly what has attracted the likes of Joss Stone, Bo Diddley and Gary Numan to the Surrey countryside. The album cover for 22 Dreams, by local boy Paul Weller, is the perfect calling card. The 2008 release's sleeve depicts the idyllic setting where he spent a year recording the 21 tracks.

Street, beyond the White Horse pub, postcode GU23 6AL

Paul Weller's 2008 album cover depicts the idyllic setting in which the music was recorded

LOCATION 116: the private studios are near Dunsborough Park, just north of Ripley High

WEYBRIDGE LENNON'S KENWOOD AND RINGO'S SUNNY HEIGHTS HOMES

The house where John Lennon lived at the height of Beatlemania between 1964 and 1968, Kenwood was so much associated with this period in 60s music culture that the house sign is reported to have been sold at auction in 2003 for a staggering $20,400. The house dates back to 1913, when it was appropriately built by Love & Sons. Some of Lennon's home movie, footage shot at Kenwood later turned up on the Imagine: John Lennon movie and the cover of The Beatles' sixth chart-topping album, Rubber Soul, was photographed in the garden. Inside the house an old circus poster Lennon had bought in Sevenoaks, Kent, decorated the living room wall. On one particular Kenwood get-together, he and Paul McCartney turned the characters named in the poster into the Sgt Pepper track 'Being For The Benefit Of Mr Kite'. The Saint George's Hill estate on which Kenwood stands also

provided homes to newly minted 60s pop stars Tom Jones and Cliff Richard. A year after John Lennon's move to the estate, the newly married Ringo Starr followed suit, buying nearby Sunny Heights on South Road. When Lennon and first wife Cynthia divorced, Kenwood was sold to chart-topping hits songwriter Bill Martin, who wrote 'Puppet On A String', 'Congratulations' and 'Back Home'.

LOCATION 117: from Weybridge station take the B374 south, turning left into South Road, straight on to Cavendish Road, which curves to the left, before turning in to Wood Lane and Kenwood, postcode KT13 0JU. Sadly, for both residents and visitors, a spate of burglaries led to the construction of security gates at the entrance to the entire Saint George's Hill estate, preventing anything but distant viewing of these Beatle bases

Born in Surrey

Mick Avory, drums, The Kinks (b. 15 Feb 1944, East Molesey)

Rick Buckler, drums, The Jam (b. 6 Dec 1955, Woking)

Eric Clapton (b. 30 Mar 1945, Ripley)

Petula Clark (b. 15 Nov 1932, Epsom)

Gus Dudgeon, producer (b. 30 Sep 1942, Woking, d. 21 Jul 2002)

Bruce Foxton, bass/vocals, The Jam (b. 1 Sep 1955, Woking)

Peter Gabriel (b. 13 Feb 1950, Chobham)

Simon Gallup, bass, The Cure (b. 1 Jun 1960, Duxhurst)

Dana Gillespie, folk/pop singer (b. 30 Mar 1949, Woking)

Dave Greenslade, keyboardist (b. 18 Jan 1943, Woking)

Dan Hawkins, guitar, The Darkness (b. 12 Dec 1976, Chertsey)

Justin Hawkins, vocals/guitar, The Darkness (b. 17 Mar 1975, Chertsey)

Glyn Johns, producer (b. 15 Feb 1942, Epsom)

Steve Lillywhite, producer (b. 1955, Egham)

Nick Lowe (b. 24 Mar 1949, Walton-on-Thames)

Rick Parfitt, vocals/guitar, Status Quo (b. 12 Oct 1948, Woking)

Jimmy Pursey, vocals, Sham 69 (b. 9 Feb 1955, Hersham)

Andrew Ridgeley, guitar/vocals, Wham! (b. 26 Jan 1963, Windlesham)

Mike Rutherford, guitar, Genesis (b. 2 Oct 1950, Guildford)

Lol Tolhurst, drums/keyboards, The Cure (b. 3 Feb 1959, Horley)

Roger Waters, bass/vocals, Pink Floyd (b. 6 Sep 1943, Great Bookham)

Paul Weller (b. 25 May 1958, Woking)

Pete Wiggs, keyboards, Saint Etienne (b. 15 May 1966, Reigate)

WEST SUSSEX

The South Downs sweep down to the sea to a spot rock pirate Keith Richards calls both home and 'God's Little Acre'. The West Sussex countryside was an inspiration to Cat Stevens and also provided the right environment for the young Paul Weller to nail a life-changing spot of song writing and Paul McCartney to shoot a 1979 Christmas video down the pub. The county's Bluebell Railway presented Elton John with a location that gave a passable impression of an American railroad station for the cover of his second hit album, and West Sussex gave birth to Britain's most brilliantly monikered punk poet Attila the Stockbroker, born in the genteel town of Southwick.

HORSTED KEYNES ELTON'S TUMBLEWEED CONNECTION

Situated on the delightful Bluebell Railway, Horsted Keynes station is the spot where Elton John's cover photo for Tumbleweed Connection was shot. The station buildings and platforms have changed little since Elton, lyricist Bernie Taupin and photographer David Larkham made the trip in 1970. The station is a throwback to Britain's pre-war steam era but could pass for a railroad halt in the American West and was a good fit for Elton's country-themed album.

LOCATION 118: public station, east of the B2028, less than two miles outside the village of Horsted Keynes, postcode RH17 7

Elton's Horsted Keynes connection

SELSEY BILL PAUL WELLER'S HOLIDAY SCRIBBLINGS

"Save up their money for a holiday, to Selsey Bill or Bracklesham Bay", as The Jam's 'Saturday's Kids' goes. Paul Weller wrote 'The Eton Rifles' while holidaying in his parents' caravan at the seaside headland of Selsey Bill. Both songs surfaced on Setting Sons, the band's 1979 album. The southern-most spot on the West Sussex coast also gets an honourable mention in 'Driving In My Car', where, according to Madness, "I drive up to Muswell Hill, I've even been to Selsey Bill."

LOCATION 119: Selsey Bill seafront, postcode PO20 9DB

MIDHURST CAT STEVENS' SUSSEX MEDITATION

When Cat Stevens suffered an almost fatal bout of tuberculosis in 1968, he was hospitalised for a lengthy period at Midhurst's King Edward VII Hospital. However uncomfortable his slow period of recuperation, Stevens would look back on the period and admit to a significant side effect. It gave the singer-songwriter, who had already charted with 'Matthew And Son' and 'I'm Gonna Get Me A Gun', a period to reflect on his intensive life as a young pop star and begin a new direction in his career. The three months spent in bed and outside in the hospital's beautiful grounds were followed by a further nine months spent recovering at home. The enforced absence from the music business produced a move away from commercial pop songs to a reflective, acoustic phase. During this period of recovery, he wrote more than 30 new songs. These new folk-based offerings didn't go down well with his then producer Mike Hurst, which in turn led to a departure from Deram Records. Island Records were more appreciative, signing the new Cat Stevens and releasing Mona Bone Jakon, which began a sequence of Island album releases that peaked with Catch Bull At Four, a US chart-topper.

❛I got into meditation, deep in the Sussex countryside, and that began my earnest search for the road, and ultimately, to find out what's at the end of it.❜ Cat Stevens

LOCATION 120: Kings Drive, postcode GU29 0BL, due west of the A286 north of Midhurst. Status: the hospital and grounds are in the process of being redeveloped as a residential site

South East England

David Cole / Rex Features

Keith Richards' home base in Britain since 1966 is Redlands, the Elizabethan farmhouse in the West Sussex coastal countryside discovered by a house hunting Richards when he and his Bentley took a wrong turning, winding up at Redlands, which was miraculously for sale. From spotting the place to buying it took from midday to evening that same day, a whirlwind of activity that involved a return trip to London to grab the necessary £20,000 cash for a transfer of the deeds in front of the picturesque house's fireplace that night. Redlands was the setting for the most publicised drugs bust in rock history involving Keith, Mick Jagger and friends. On that winter's evening on February 12th 1967, one friend, Marianne Faithfull, was to suffer the indignity forever associated with that Mars bar story, a rock myth according to the gallant Richards. More productively, the house was where Rolling Stones classic 'Jumping Jack Flash' was born, a song inspired by Redlands' gardener Jack Dyer's early morning activities. In an interview with the Independent in 2000, he referred to his thatched and moated property and the nearby village as "God's Little Acre". The genuine article when it comes to proper rock star status, Richards is a popular figure in these parts. He generously forked out £30,000 to help renovate the community's West Wittering Memorial Hall in the village centre at the junction of Rookwood Road and Elms Lane.

Fire and raids: Mick Jagger and Keith Richards smile for the camera on Keith's beautifully manicured lawn at Redlands

❛I love that village. They've always been smooth with me.❜ Keith Richards

LOCATION 121: north out of West Wittering on the B2179, left into Redlands Lane, PO20 8QE. Status: private residence

ASHURST **THE FOUNTAIN'S 'WONDERFUL CHRISTMASTIME'**

The Fountain Inn was the location for the video shot to promote Paul McCartney's 1979 single 'Wonderful Christmastime'. A packed pub sees McCartney hamming it up festive style at the piano in the Fountain's dining room, and outside the then whitewashed frontage displays a large sign advertising the now defunct Portsmouth-based Brickwoods Brewery. Despite making quite an impact, it is doubtful whether McCartney visited the pub more than once, unlike Ashurst resident the actor Sir Laurence Olivier, who from 1973 until his death in 1989 was something of a regular customer.

LOCATION 122: the Fountain Inn is just off the B2135 in the village of Ashurst, four miles north of Steyning. Postcode: BN44 3AP

Born in West Sussex

Attila the Stockbroker, poet/musician (b. 21 Oct 1957, Southwick)

Brett Anderson, vocals, Suede (b. 29 Sep 1967, Haywards Heath)

Jeremy Cunningham, bass, the Levellers (b. 2 Jun 1965, Cuckfield)

Robin Goodridge, drums, Bush (b. 10 Sep 1966, Crawley)

Antony Hegarty, vocals, Antony and The Johnsons (b. 1971 Chichester)

Luke Pritchard, vocals, The Kooks (b. 2 Mar 1985, Worthing)

Leo Sayer (b. 21 May 1948, Shoreham-by-Sea)

Bob Stanley, keyboards, Saint Etienne (b. 25 Dec 1964, Horsham)

Nick Van Eede, vocals, Cutting Crew (b. 14 Jun 1958, Cuckfield)

Bruce Welch, guitar, The Shadows (b. 2 Nov 1941, Bognor Regis)

West Sussex-born Brett Anderson

EAST SUSSEX

Brighton proves to be a prominent centre of music culture through its once infamous (now just famous) connection to the Mods and Rockers pitched battles of the sixties, later popularly documented in The Who's Quadrophenia album and movie. A city stuffed full of lively music venues, it has two of the more extraordinary places to take in the live music experience. The architectural splendour of the Dome was where Abba enjoyed their career-defining Eurovision Song Contest win and Brighton's pebble beach has rattled to a series of huge gigs witnessing the DJ decks dexterity of local resident Norman Cook. The city even has a large enough pool of talent to boast its very own pavement-starred Walk of Fame. Farther afield, East Sussex's grandest homes and gardens provided newsworthy residences for Brian Jones, Jimmy Page and farmer Roger Daltrey, who likes nothing better than walking the Sussex Weald. The county also throws up the quirkiest of locations. Seek out the secluded church and its pump organ featured on a British Sea Power track written about the East Sussex coastline and its dramatic Seven Sisters.

❛We'd go down to Brighton and sit on the beach looking windswept and interesting. I first met Rod Stewart that way, hitching on the Purley Way with a guy called Italian Tony. ❜ Ralph McTell

BRIGHTON JOHN PEEL AT THE PRINCE ALBERT

A memorial to the much-loved DJ John Peel in the form of a vast mural dominates the side wall of The Prince Albert pub in Frederick Place. Never one to big himself up, Peel might well have shied away from such a giant-sized tribute and would no doubt have disapproved of the subject of the Banksy artwork that shares the wall with him. An additional painting depicts his beloved Liverpool's archrivals Manchester United, represented by an image of George Best.

LOCATION 123: the Prince Albert pub is on the corner of Trafalgar Street and Frederick Place, postcode BN1 4ED

A giant-sized tribute to John Peel at The Prince Albert

Janet Bateman

South East England

BRIGHTON QUADROPHENIA MOD HOTSPOTS

The spiritual home of Mod culture, Brighton is still a place you can shop for all the right gear while soaking up the atmosphere of the Sixties scene so grittily portrayed in The Who's 1973 rock opera and 1979 movie Quadrophenia. The Lanes and North Laine are shoppers' paradises and the seaside city appears to positively encourage scooter runs and Mod weekenders these days: a far cry from almost half a century ago when teenagers on Lambrettas and Vespas would gather by word of mouth all points south of Crawley and Croydon on the A23 to weekend in Brighton. Fashion, dancing and scooters were the Mods' main obsessions but their violent clashes with gangs of rockers (or greasers) were what made front-page news. The Brighton Sea-Life Centre, formerly the seafront aquarium, was the setting for one of the bloodiest battles in 1964, restaged as a scene in Quadrophenia. The movie's famous sex scene when Mod Jimmy (played by Phil Daniels) and girlfriend Steph (Leslie Ash) get it together in a narrow alley is still down

Little East Street (off East Street) and the hotel where bellboy Ace (Sting) worked is the magnificent Grand Hotel, which dominates the seafront.

❛Outside the aquarium at about 6am on Bank holiday Monday morning we emerged into the morning light after dancing all night. The place was surrounded with rockers and up on the roof of the hotel opposite were camera men: funny that! That was a fair old punch up. The rockers obviously didn't take account of the French blues that most of the guys were blocked up (not me - never taken drugs myself). Anyway, we won that one. Later on that day it all kicked off again under the pier. I remember being in a bit of a tricky spot, with only 20 of us to 30 or 40. All of a sudden there were mods everywhere. We got out and the rockers got stoned.❜ Retired fire officer Pete Hopcraft recalls his trip to Brighton as a 16-year-old Mod in 1964

LOCATION 124: all the above can be explored within a short distance of Brighton's seafront, postcode BN2 1TB

Daily Mirror

In two dramatic pictures — all the fury and the hate of the scrap-happy Whitsun Wild Ones

LIVING FOR KICKS

Portrait of a Mod in action at Brighton yesterday

Daily Sketch

Beach crowds take cover from battling Mods and Rockers

WILDEST ONES YET

BRIGHTON THE WALK OF FAME

Based on the popular American concept of awarding pavement stars to celebrities, songwriter and producer David Courtney brought the idea to Brighton's Marina in 2002. A trail of plaques honour current

and former residents Norman Cook, Annie Nightingale, Zoe Ball, Gaz Coombes, Steve Ellis, The Levellers, Kevin Rowland, Leo Sayer, Dusty Springfield, Brighton Eurovision winners Abba and Brighton's

mod figureheads The Who.

LOCATION 125: Brighton Marina, 18 Waterfront, postcode BN25 5WA. Website: www.walkoffame.co.uk

BURWASH COMMON FARMER DALTREY'S COUNTRY MANOR

Always a keen angler, The Who's lead singer Roger Daltrey achieved a life-long ambition when he got to manage his very own trout fishery on the 400-acre farm he calls home. Daltrey originally purchased the 20-room, 400-year-old Holmshurst Manor property in 1972 for the excellent views it afforded some of East Sussex's most beautiful countryside. But, having taken on the place, he thrived in the day-to-day running of the estate, instantly catching the farming bug. Accepted by the locals after decades living and working in the area, he has now become something of an authority on the fishery business and cattle management.

❝I always loved space. I must have been four years old, playing on the bomb sites in London, but I called it 'running away to the country'. Now I love walking on the Sussex Weald. ❞
Roger Daltrey, interviewed by The Times (2008)

LOCATIONS 126 and127: Lakedown Trout Fishery is just north of the A265 at Swife Lane, postcode TN21 8UX. Website: www. lakedowntroutfishery.co.uk. Holmshurst Manor is at postcode TN19 7JP

BRIGHTON FATBOY SLIM'S BIG BEACH PARTIES

Local resident and DJ Norman Cook provided Brighton with its best attended musical event when a larger than anticipated 250,000 attended his Fatboy Slim concert on the beach in the summer of 2002. Subsequent events, branded the Big Beach Boutique, have attracted more modest but manageable crowds to the beachfront. The former member of The Housemartins took a new alias in 2008 when calling his new act BPA – the Brighton Port Authority.

LOCATION 128: Brighton beach, postcode BN2 1TB

HARTFIELD BRIAN JONES' HOUSE AT POOH CORNER

News reports still circulate more than forty years after the death of Rolling Stone Brian Jones about the mysterious circumstances surrounding his death at his Cotchford Farm estate. In 1969, the guitarist and founder member of the band was discovered dead, aged 27, in the swimming pool of the house once owned by author A.A. Milne. The 16th-century building is the House at Pooh Corner that Milne wrote about in his Winnie the Pooh stories. The innocent world of children's literature is at odds with Jones' rock 'n' roll lifestyle, which, at varying levels, included loud music annoying the neighbours and sending his Vespa scooter through the front window of local Hartfield pub The Haywaggon Inn. Recent wear and tear on the infamous swimming pool at Cotchford Farm prompted a dubious sale of underwater rock memorabilia when recent owners elected to sell the pool's tiles to Jones fans priced at £100 each. A second tenuous music connection to Cotchford Farm comes courtesy of Kenny Loggins' whimsical song 'House At Pooh Corner', also recorded by The Nitty Gritty Dirt Band.

LOCATION 129: south on the B2026 out of the village of Hartfield, turning right on to Cotchford Lane, postcode TN7 4DN. Status: private residence

Cotchford Farm: little changed since Brian Jones owned the place

South East England

HASTINGS STONES AND HENDRIX ON THE PIER: RIOTS ON THE BEACH

Burnt to a cinder in 2010 and requiring multi-million-pound investment to return it to its former glory, Hastings pier was a thriving business when Britain's top pop and rock groups played the pier ballroom. Gene Vincent, Jimi Hendrix, Pink Floyd, The Hollies, The Who, Tom Jones and Genesis all performed there in the 60s and 70s with The Rolling Stones making four appearances at an entertainment centre that offered the usual pier activities. The Stones were booked for the Saturday of the infamous 1964 Bank Holiday weekend when mods and rockers ran riot at the seaside resort the Monday following. Just as controversial, by reputation at least, an early Sex Pistols appearance at the pier made such an impression on one young music fan that she set about forming a band (X-Ray Spex) and changing her name to Poly Styrene. The July 1976 gig saw the Pistols bizarrely supporting Budgie, and two years later X-Ray Spex were a star attraction at the pier themselves.

LOCATION 130: Hastings pier is situated close by White Rock (A259). Postcode: TN34 1EU

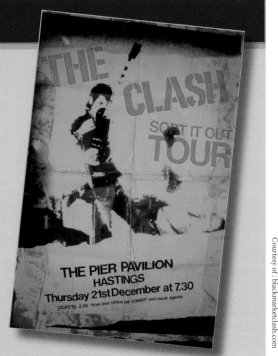

LULLINGTON BRITISH SEA POWER'S CHURCH SONG

The smallest church in Sussex (some say smallest in England) is featured in the 2003 British Sea Power song about this part of East Sussex. The 20-seat flint building, which dates from the 13th century, sits atop a wooded hill above the Cuckmere Valley. Band member Hamilton added the melancholy organ part to 'The Smallest Church In Sussex' by sneaking inside the tiny Church of the Good Shepherd to play the pump organ.

LOCATION 131: Lullington is a tiny hamlet, a short stroll east of the village of Alfriston. Postcode: BN26 5QY

PEASMARSH PAUL McCARTNEY'S COUNTRY ESTATE

The modest buildings at Blossom Wood Farm were acquired by Paul McCartney back in 1975, and he and wife Linda began creating their perfect country home. As unshowbusiness-like and grounded as he could make it for his growing family, Paul set about designing a new farmhouse himself ("like a glorified council house", according to one acquaintance) and eventually extended the grounds to the vast 933-acre estate it is today. The place is newsworthy as the location for the country's largest population of wild boar. The tusked creatures that met with extinction in Britain hundreds of years ago share the vast wooded estate with sheep, crops, a specially excavated conservation pond, the six-bedroom house and a studio converted from the farm's old windmill.

❛Walking into the recording studio felt like walking on to the set of Star Trek. He kept his original Hofner guitar from his Beatles days in a secret panel underneath the floor. There was a small circular hook that he pulled on and a bit of the floor came up, seamlessly.❜
A quote by one invited guest to the windmill studio, from the London Evening Standard

LOCATION 132: north-west of the A259 and the coastal town of Rye. Postcode: TN31 6UU.Status: private residence

PETT LEVEL DAVID BOWIE ON THE BEACH

With added solarisation effects, the beach and cliffs at Pett Level were the backdrop for Bowie's 1980 Ashes To Ashes video.

LOCATION 133: the shoreline between Rye and Hastings, a few miles off the A259. Postcode: TN35 4EH

PLUMPTON JIMMY PAGE'S MOATED MANSION

Plumpton Place is the former home of Jimmy Page. You have to say the Led Zeppelin guitarist had great taste when buying his various properties. The Elizabethan house's moat was home to the first carp introduced to Britain, and the estate is entwined in the history and development of that most British of apples, the Cox's Pippin. Page's tenure lasted from 1971 to 1980, during which time a sequence from the Led Zeppelin movie The Song Remains The Same with him playing a hurdy gurdy was filmed next to his property. Local pub the Half Moon benefited from Page's patronage, the guitarist even performing one charity gig there with Ronnie Wood under the pseudonym Arms & Legs, back in 1977.

LOCATION 134: east of the church and Plumpton College. Postcode: BN7 3AF. Status: a private residence but surrounded by public footpaths

Born in East Sussex

Tony Banks, keyboards, Genesis (b. 27 Mar 1950, East Hoathly)
Tom Chaplin, vocals/guitar, Keane (b. 8 Mar 1979, Battle)
Dave Clarke, DJ/producer (b. 19 Sep 1968, Brighton)
Shirley Collins, folk singer (b. 5 Jul 1935, Hastings)
Simon Fuller, manager/TV producer (b. 17 May 1960, Hastings)
Dave Greenfield, keyboards, The Stranglers (b. 29 Mar 1949, Brighton)
Ed Harcourt, singer-songwriter (b. 14 Aug 1977, Wootton)
Dan Hipgrave, guitar,
Toploader (b. 5 Aug 1975, Brighton)
Annie Holland, bass, Elastica (b. 26 Aug 1965, Brighton)
Peter 'Spider' Stacy, The Pogues (b. 14 Dec 1958, Eastbourne)
Suggs (Graham McPherson), vocals, Madness (b. 13 Jan 1961, Hastings)
David Van Day, vocals, Dollar/Guys 'n' Dolls (b. 28 Nov 1956, Brighton)
Johnny Wakelin, singer-songwriter (b. 1939, Brighton)
Samantha Womack (née Janus), UK entry, 1991 Eurovision Song Contest (b. 2 Nov 1972, Brighton)

KENT

Stations, caves, a castle and even a sea fort provide Kent's 'Garden of England' with a vigorous crop of music locations. Responsible for the birth of Mick Jagger and Keith Richards, Dartford was the starting point for the formation of Britain's most enduring rock 'n' roll band, The Rolling Stones. Their arch-but-friendly rivals The Beatles favoured the county, with significant visits in 1967. Though 250 miles from the real Strawberry Fields, Kent's Knole Park was the setting for rock's first music video by The Fab Four who also finished off filming their Magical Mystery Tour ten miles east at West Malling. The remarkable tunnelled music venue that was Chislehurst Caves, the inspirational big 'listening ears' at Dungeness and Chas Hodges' 'Margate' all fall within the county that also gave birth to Keane, Shane MacGowan, Kevin Ayers and Joss Stone.

CANTERBURY CARAVAN'S ST DUNSTAN'S ALBUM COVER

Local prog-rockers Caravan featured an illustration of a Canterbury street on the cover of their 1976 hit album Blind Dog At St Dunstan's. The band members were frequent visitors to the pubs in the St Dunstan's area of the city. The cover illustration depicts the busy St Dunstan's Street with the medieval Westgate gatehouse in the background, said to be the oldest in England. Caravan were one of a number of groups in the Sixties that begat what became known as the Canterbury scene. Emanating from the group The Wilde Flowers, those associated with the movement, Robert Wyatt, Hugh Hopper, Steve Hillage, Kevin Ayers and Daevid Allen, were not all locals but formed various bands when meeting in the city as students.

St Dunstan's Street pictured with Canterbury's imposing Westgate gatehouse in the background

LOCATION 135: to find the spot where the blind dog stood, head for Westgate, located where the main A290 crosses the Great Stour River in Canterbury city centre. Postcode: CT1 2BQ

South East England

BECKENHAM EVERYTHING'S HUNKY DORY AT HADDON HALL

Beckenham was the place where Bowie's alter-ego Ziggy Stardust was born and where the ideas flowed on some of his most enduring songs such as 'Life On Mars', conceived and composed late one afternoon after "a beautiful day, sitting on the steps of the bandstand" at Beckenham Park. The park was just a short walk from home at Haddon Hall, a fake gothic mansion where young David's early Seventies transformation from misfit and misfiring songwriter to man on a mission to create an extraordinary career and persona took place. First in the basement, then elevated to a room overlooking the gardens, Bowie slaved away on an endless diet of cigarettes, coffee and tea supplied by doting wife Angie. This period of creative energy and determination paid off and songs written and composed at this time formed the classic albums Hunky Dory and Ziggy Stardust And The Spiders from Mars, which would confirm his place in the rock star firmament. With nothing left of Haddon Hall these days, the only recognition of Bowie's presence in Beckenham is at the spot where, as plain David Jones, he played some of his earliest gigs at the Three Tuns

Bowie on the lawns of Haddon Hall: Ziggy Stardust and a surge of early Seventies classic songs were created in the room with the veranda to Bowie's right

pub in the High Street, now a restaurant. Backroom folk recitals gradually evolved into more experimental performances, an initiative Bowie dubbed The Arts Lab. A red plaque marks this key location in Bowie's development as an international superstar, a vital and solitary point of pilgrimage for those seeking out Bowie's Beckenham.

LOCATION 136: the plaque is on the wall of Zizzi, 157 High Street, Beckenham, postcode BR3 1AE. The demolished Haddon Hall was at 42 Southend Road, now Shannon Way, postcode BR3 1WG

CHISLEHURST KENT CAVES ECHO TO THE SOUND OF ROCK'S FINEST

These man-made subterranean tunnels echoed to the sounds of rock's finest when used as Britain's weirdest music venue in the Sixties and Seventies. Far out and deep down, Chislehurst Caves attracted The Rolling Stones, David Bowie and Jimi Hendrix. DJ Johnny Stewart wasn't impressed by the innovative sounds of The Pink Floyd in 1966. He responded to a radio commercial for a "Radio Caroline night out at Chislehurst Caves - this week Pink Floyd" by jumping on his Lambretta GT 200 and riding in a small mod convoy from Bromley to the caves. "What a load of rubbish, I thought at the time. Five tunes and five shillings to get in. What a waste of money! Status Quo were on the following week but I never returned."
In 1974, the caves proved the perfect extravagant underground location for a media bash to celebrate the release of Silk Torpedo by the Pretty Things, the first record on Led Zeppelin's new Swan Song label. An NME report by Steve Turner listed scantily-clad nymphets, nuns in stockings and suspenders, escapologists and fire-eaters all laid on courtesy of Swan Song's (then) generous £5,000 party budget.

LOCATION 137: sandwiched between the B264 to the north and the A222 to the south at Caveside Close, postcode BR7 5NL. Status: now a visitor attraction. Website: www.chislehurstcaves.co.uk

DARTFORD MICK AND 'KEEF''S RAILWAY EPIPHANY

Although they had met years before when both attended Wentworth Primary School, the significant meeting place for two young students who would form the world's most enduring rock band happened in October 1961 at Dartford railway station. Rock legend has it that Mick Jagger and Keith Richards got into conversation when sharing a railway carriage on a Sidcup-bound train from Dartford station. Richards had noticed, with admiration, the records Jagger had with him that day, hard-to-buy releases that Jagger had purchased by mail order. Other reports suggest the two simply exchanged words on the platform, but what is certain is that they immediately bonded through their enthusiasm for American blues music. At the time of writing, a 9 or 10-foot-high bronze statue to mark the meeting is at the planning stage. A short walk west of the station is local music and arts venue The Mick Jagger Centre, and the local council have honoured the two Stones by naming streets in a new estate near to Keith's Spielman Road boyhood home Stones Avenue, Babylon Close, Ruby Tuesday Drive, Dandelion Row, Little Red Walk, Lady Jane Walk, Angie Mews, Rainbow

Dartford station in the early Sixties

Close, Cloud Close, Satisfaction Street and Sympathy Street.

LOCATIONS 138, 139 and 140: for Mick and Keith's meeting of minds, go to Station Approach, postcode DA1 1BP. Less than a mile west of the station is The Mick Jagger Centre, Shepherd's Lane, postcode DA1 2JZ. Website: www.themickjaggercentre.com. The Stones streets are currently under construction at new housing development The Bridge, less than two miles from the town centre just south of the Queen Elizabeth II Thames crossing, postcode DA1 5PA

CHISLEHURST SIOUXSIE'S 'HONG KONG GARDEN'

The inspiration behind Siouxsie and The Banshees' 1978 single 'Hong Kong Garden' was a small Chinese restaurant on the busy Chislehurst High Street. The local band's debut hit (Siouxsie grew up in the town) made No.7 and the lyrics were written as a result of Siouxsie's experiences of the racial abuse suffered by the staff at the hands of local thugs.

❛I'll never forget, there was a Chinese restaurant in Chislehurst called 'The Hong Kong Garden'. Me and my friend were really upset that we used to go there and like, occasionally when the skinheads would turn up it would really turn really ugly. These gits would just go in en masse and just terrorise these Chinese people who were working there. We'd try and say 'leave them alone', you know. It was a kind of tribute.❜Siouxsie Sioux

LOCATION 141: Noble House, 101 High Street, Chislehurst, postcode BR7 5AG

HERNE BAY PIRATE RADIO AND SLADE AT SHIVERING SANDS

Photo: P.A Woodhead (www.flickr.com/photos/pawoodhead)

Shivering Sands is the somewhat dispiriting-sounding location where Screaming Lord Sutch launched his Radio Sutch pirate radio station in the Thames Estuary in 1964. Situated on an abandoned World War II sea fort, the station then became Radio City and was dogged by controversy before its government shut down in 1967. The 1975 movie Slade in Flame used this location for some dramatic scenes of the fictitious band Flame (played by Slade) visiting Radio City.

LOCATION142: off the coast from the town of Herne Bay, postcode CT6 5NE

SEVENOAKS FIRST POP PROMO MOVIE SHOT BY THE BEATLES

Knole Park, with its stately home surrounded by a deer park, provided the location for the mini movie The Beatles made to accompany their psychedelic masterpiece 'Strawberry Fields Forever'. Over two cold, crisp winter days in early 1967, the four Beatles arrived on set driving their black Mini Coopers and rode around the park on large white horses. At one point an observer witnessed John Lennon larking about singing "Hey, Hey, We're The Monkees", the theme song from the brand new US TV show, as the group filmed a scene jumping from a tree. While staying in the town, Lennon also happened upon the subject matter for a new song that would end up on the group's next album, Sgt Pepper's Lonely Hearts Club Band. He wandered into a local antique shop and purchased an old Victorian circus poster. The names of the performers on the bill that so fascinated him would become the characters included in the lyrics of 'Being For The Benefit Of Mr Kite'.

LOCATION 143: Knole Park is within a short walk east of Sevenoaks town centre. Postcode: TN15 0RP. Status: open to the public. Website: www. nationaltrust.org.uk/main/w-knole. The site of the antique shop is unknown

ROCHESTER SCHOOLBOY JAGGER INSPIRED BY RAMBLIN' JACK

Bob Dylan famously counts Ramblin' Jack Elliott as a huge influence on his music, but the New York-born folk legend also had a very immediate effect on the young Mick Jagger. Ramblin' Jack found himself at Rochester railway station after a visit to a ship moored in the dock back in the Fifties and put on an impromptu performance for Jagger and his school mates.

❛We were waiting for a train back to London and there was a group of schoolchildren on the other platform across the tracks from us and I thought, 'Well, look at those kids just standing around bored. I think I'll play them a little music. What the heck.' And I just got the guitar out of my case and started yodelling and playing cowboy songs to these kids across the way. They appreciated it and I think they even clapped. But I didn't know one of those kids was young Mick Jagger. He told me about it when I met him about 20 years later in a hotel in Canada. He said that was the first time he'd seen me and that he ran right out the next day and bought a guitar. He must have been about 12, 14 years old or something like that.❜ Ramblin' Jack Elliott

LOCATION 144: the station is situated off the High Street. Postcode: ME1 1HQ

TONBRIDGE FIRST MEETING FOR KEANE SCHOOLBOYS

All three members of Keane first met when students at Tonbridge School. Tim Rice-Oxley, Tom Chaplin and Richard Hughes were all boarding schoolboys.

LOCATION 145: High Street, Tonbridge, postcode TN9 1JP

MARGATE CHAS & DAVE'S SEASIDE HIT

A big fan of the whole cockle, whelk, jellied eel eating, bucket and spade business of British seaside holidays, Chas Hodges chose Margate as a subject for song-writing for purely commercial reasons. "We were doing an advert for Courage Best Bitter about going down to Margate, so we used that to give it an extra plug on the telly." 'Margate' hit the chart in 1982 and was memorably included in The Jolly Boys, a feature length episode of the BBC comedy show Only Fools and Horses.

❛Margate is pronounced "Margit" where I'm from.❜ Chas Hodges

LOCATION 146: at the end of the A28 on the north-eastern tip of the Kent coast. Postcode: CT9 1HG

DENGE ROCK ART AT THE 'LISTENING EARS'

The Dungeness coastal landscape is shaped by the strange architectural splendour of the sound mirrors that are featured as cover artwork on Turin Brakes' Ether Song album and hit single 'Long Distance'. Constructed as a Royal Air Force early warning system for incoming aircraft, the Denge mirrors are often referred to as 'Listening Ears' and have also featured in The Prodigy video for 'Invaders Must Die' and Blank & Jones' Monument album cover and video for 'A Forest'.

LOCATION 147: between Lydd-on-Sea and Greatstone-on-Sea. Postcode: TN29 9NL. Access with guided walks. www.andrewgrantham.co.uk/soundmirrors

ROLVENDEN IAN DURY'S TOAD HALL

When Ian Dury and The Blockheads' success began to realise a degree of financial security, Dury rented his very own rock star mansion. Toad Hall in the village of Rolvenden had a swimming pool and a spiral staircase leading to a tower with views over the Kent countryside which, despite his disability, Dury would ascend with the aid of his minder, Fred "Spider" Rowe. Author Will Birch's Ian Dury: The Definitive Biography points to Toad Hall as the place where both

Dury and writing partner Chaz Jankel completed work on what would become the new wave No.1 single 'Hit Me With Your Rhythm Stick'. Jankel worked diligently in the garage to create the keyboard melody while Dury finalised the lyrics, which he'd kept on a scrap of paper since the song's conception three years earlier.

LOCATION 148: Toad Hall is west of Rolvenden, south of the B2086, in Sandhurst Lane, TN17 4QP. Status: private residence

Above: Ian Dury's view from Toad Hall, which he rented for the peace and quiet that might benefit his songwriting

Right: scenes from this Ian Dury biopic were based on his Rolvenden home

WEST MALLING **THE MAGICAL MYSTERY TOUR FINALE**

The Beatles' Magical Mystery Tour of the south-west of England in 1967 should have seen the band end their journey at Shepperton film studios for filming interior scenes for the movie. Instead, they were forced to switch location to West Malling when it transpired that nobody had booked Shepperton for shooting the outstanding scenes. The movie's ballroom sequence for 'Your ... ... filmed in the disused ... g and 'I Am The ... A ticket- ... eet

LOC... remain at the former RAF West Malling, south of the town just off the A228. Postcode: ME19

ROCHESTER **CLANNAD CASTLE COVER**

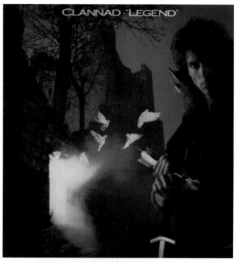

The group were Irish, the location ought to have been Nottingham, but Clannad's cover artwork for their 1984 Legend album, sound-tracking the TV series Robin of Sherwood, was photographed at Rochester Castle.

LOCATION 150: the centre of Rochester, close by the bridge over the River Medway. Postcode: ME1 1SW The castle is open to the public.

Rochester doubles for Nottingham Castle

Born in Kent

Kevin Ayers (b. 16 Aug 1944, Herne Bay)
Gary Barden, vocals, Michael Schenker Group (b. 27 Aug 1955, Tunbridge Wells)
Peter Blake, pop artist (b. 25 Jun 1932, Dartford)
Bill Bruford, drums, King Crimson (b. 17 May 1949, Sevenoaks)
Billy Childish, singer/guitarist (b. 1 Dec 1959, Chatham)
Richard Coughlan, drums, Caravan (b. 2 Sep 1947, Herne Bay)
Roger Dean, album cover artist (b. 31 Aug 1944, Ashford)
Anne Dudley, keyboards, Art of Noise (b. 7 May 1956, Chatham)
Guy Fletcher, keyboards/guitar, Dire Straits (b. 24 May 1960, Maidstone)
Gordon Giltrap, guitarist (b. 6 Apr 1948, Brenchley)
Paul Hartnoll, keyboards, Orbital (b. 19 May 1968, Dartford)
Phil Hartnoll, keyboards, Orbital

(b. 9 Jan 1964, Dartford)
Richard Hughes, drums, Keane (b. 8 Sep 1975, Gravesend)
Rick Huxley, guitar, The Dave Clark Five (b. 5 Aug 1942, Dartford)
Mick Jagger, vocals, The Rolling Stones (b. 26 Jul 1943, Dartford)

Joss Stone: born in Kent, raised in Devon

Matt Letley, drums, Status Quo (b. 29 Mar 1961, Dartford)
Shane MacGowan (b. 25 Dec 1957, Tunbridge Wells)
Phil May, vocals, The Pretty Things (b. 9 Nov 1944, Dartford)
Mike Ratledge, keyboards, Soft Machine (b. Apr 1943, Maidstone)
Noel Redding, bass, The Jimi Hendrix Experience (b. 25 Dec 1945, Folkestone, d. 11 May 2003)
Keith Richards, guitar, The Rolling Stones (b. 18 Dec 1943, Dartford)
Crispian St Peters, singer-songwriter (b. 5 Apr 1939, Swanley, d. 8 Jun 2010)
Dave Sinclair, keyboards, Caravan (b. 24 Nov 1947, Herne Bay)
Richard Sinclair, guitar, Caravan (b. 6 Jun 1948, Canterbury)
Joss Stone (b. 11 Apr 1987, Dover)
Dick Taylor, guitar, The Pretty Things (b. 28 Jan 1943, Dartford)
Pete Tong DJ (b. 30 Jul 1960, Hartley)

ROCK ATLAS

Greater London

UK and Ireland Edition

'Famously dubbed a white elephant as the Millennium Dome, it is now the world's most popular music arena overtaking New York's Madison Square Gardens' most-tickets-sold-in-a-year record.'

GREATER LONDON

With the exception of Liverpool and Manchester for short spells, London has been the undisputed heartbeat of the British music scene and the nation's capital of rock. London's domination is split up into a number of geographical centres of excellence with very distinctive contributions to British popular music. In the middle of it all, Soho gave us the clubs and coffee bars that propagated pop and rock from jazz, blues, skiffle and R&B roots. North London had its Kinks and Dave Clark Five, from the East came geezers Small Faces, Ian Dury, Dizzee Rascal and Billy Bragg, south of the river gave us the kitchen sink drama of homebodies Squeeze and a black urban DIY and pirate radio scene and out west was where those well-heeled enclaves of Richmond, Twickenham and Harrow had the venues that propelled Stones, Who and Cream to worldwide fame from exotic but ramshackle places like Crawdaddy, Eel Pie and Klooks Kleek.

Never the easiest of places to organise for listings books like this one, the London entries in Rock Atlas have been arranged by postcode, beginning with East London (E) and moving clockwise through the South-East (SE), South-West (SW), West (W), North-West (NW) and finally the North (N).

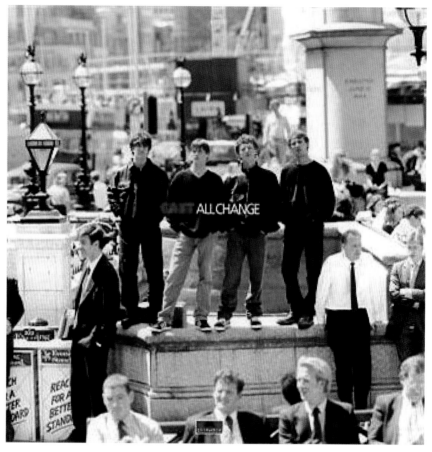

EC3 CITY OF LONDON CAST COVER FOR ALL CHANGE

Liverpool band Cast chose a spot outside The Royal Exchange between Cornhill and Threadneedle Street to pose in typical four-lads-down-from-Liverpool style for the cover of their 1995 album All Change.

LOCATION 151: the Royal Exchange, postcode EC3V 3LL

Four lads down from Liverpool make a stand in the City of London

EC1
A FILTHY McNASTY HOME FROM HOME FOR SHANE MACGOWAN

This Islington pub is home from home for the Pogues/Popes man Shane MacGowan. Filthy McNasty's has been his rendezvous point of choice with reporters and mates including Johnny Depp. The Tunbridge Wells-born Irishman has also been known to shoot the odd video here, surrounded by walls decorated with his gold records. Fellow rock 'n' roll scallywag Pete Doherty once worked behind the bar, returning to gig with his band The Libertines in a venue that has created a knack for nurturing poets and pop stars.

LOCATION 152: a short walk from Angel tube station at 68 Amwell Street, Islington, postcode EC1R 1UU

EC1 KESTREL HOUSE TOWER BLOCK COVER FOR THE STREETS' DEBUT

The beautifully photographed Islington tower block appears on the cover of the debut album by Mike Skinner (aka The Streets). Birmingham-born Skinner admitted loving London (Hampstead Heath in particular), without ever living in a tower block, when quizzed by Time Out.

LOCATION 153: Kestrel House, City Road, Islington, postcode EC1

German photographer Rut Blees Luxemburg's photo for the 2002 album

E1 A MADNESS INTRODUCTION TO THE HISTORY OF NORTON FOLGATE

The Liberty Of Norton Folgate, the ninth studio album from Madness, helped draw attention to one of the oddest districts of London. The lengthy title track tells the story of an area of East London that was, until 1900, a real independent state in the manner of the 1949 fictitious subject of the Ealing comedy film Passport To Pimlico.

LOCATION 156: follow the cobbled Folgate Street, east of the A10 and Broadgate Tower, postcode EC1 6DB

A short walk from Liverpool Street Station takes you to the strange world of Norton Folgate

E2 THE 'UP THE BRACKET ALLEY'

The promotional video for the title song from The Libertines' 2002 album Up The Bracket was filmed in an alley in Bethnal Green and namechecks nearby Vallance Road (once home to the notorious Kray twins at No.178) in the opening line. Fans of the band have turned the Up The Bracket Alley into a Libertines-based message wall with lyrics and graffiti comments. This spot, just south of Regent's Canal (also seen briefly in the video), is a short walk from the flat in Teesdale Street once shared by the band's Carl Barât and Pete Doherty. Most of the debut album's tracks were written and conceived here. Adding further interest to these locations was the 2011 movie There Are No Innocent Bystanders, in which Barât revisits the area for a spot of Libertines nostalgia.

LOCATIONS 154 **and** 155: 'Up The Bracket Alley' (real name Hare Row) is off Cambridge Heath Road, postcode E2 9BT. A short stroll takes you to Barât and Doherty's former flat, nicknamed the Albion Rooms, at 112a Teesdale Street, postcode E2 6PU

DAGENHAM IS TERRY VENABLES 'DAGENHAM DAVE'?

The 1995 Morrissey single 'Dagenham Dave' carried a photo of Dagenham-born footballing celebrity Terry Venables on the cover.

LOCATION 157: London suburb north of the A13, postcode RM10 8

Greater London

E17 EAST 17 AND PARKLIFE IN WALTHAMSTOW

Pop group East 17 (also named E-17 and East Seventeen) named themselves after the postcode of the area they came from and titled their 1993 chart-topping debut album Walthamstow. The North-East London district, famous for its greyhound stadium, was also the location for photoshoots for the cover of a second Walthamstow-based No.1 album when Blur's Parklife pictures were shot there in 1994.

LOCATION 158: the greyhound stadium, still standing but closed for racing, is off the A112 in Walthamstow, postcode E4 8SJ

THE JAM SNAPPED AT ST KATHARINE DOCKS

The Jam's compilation album of all their hits, Snap!, carries a snap of the three band members out for a stroll at St Katharine Docks.

LOCATION 160: St Katharine Docks, off the River Thames, postcode E1W 1LA

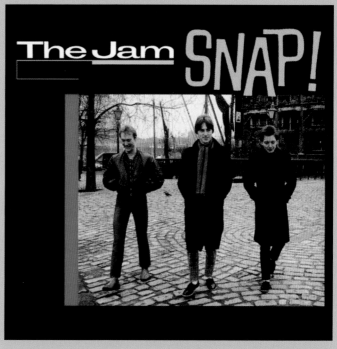

The Jam photographed well before the break-up of the band and release of the 1983 album this picture appeared on

E12 LITTLE ILFORD'S 'ITCHYCOO PARK'

Close to Steve Marriott's childhood home in East Ham and bordered by the North Circular Road is this small park immortalised in the Small Faces song. Twice a Top 10 hit, in 1967 and 1975, Itchycoo Park was a favourite place well known to the band members from their childhood. It was full of stinging nettles that, according to Ronnie Lane, caused the itching and scratching that led to the song's title.

LOCATION 159: Little Ilford Park is bordered on the eastern side by the A406 North Circular Road. Accessed by Church Road and Dore Avenue, postcode E12 6JT

DAGENHAM VILLAGE BLUES AT THE ROUNDHOUSE

Still a music venue to this day, the Roundhouse pub has been described as East London's premier location for rock during the period between 1969 and 1975, when promoting bands as the Village Blues Club. Everyone from Led Zeppelin in the early days to Dr Feelgood during the height of pub rock have played the distinctive white building. And how about this for an East End honour? In 1999, Barking-born Billy Bragg, said to be lined-up to narrate a locally made documentary movie about the place, had a road named after him on the site of the old Roundhouse car park.

LOCATION 161: Lodge Avenue and Bragg Close, Dagenham, postcode RM8 2HY

Born in East London

Damon Albarn (b. 23 Mar 1968, Whitechapel)

John Ashton, guitar, The Psychedelic Furs (b. 30 Nov 1957, Forest Gate)

Kenny Ball, jazz trumpeter (b. 22 May 1930, Ilford)

Jet Black, drums, The Stranglers (b. 26 Aug 1938, Ilford)

Marc Bolan (b. 30 Sep 1947, Hackney, d. 16 Sep 1977)

Graham Bond, British R&B musician (b. 28 Oct 1937, Romford, d. 8 May 1974)

Andy Bown, keyboards, Status Quo (b. 27 Mar 1946, City of London)

Mick Box, guitar, Uriah Heep (b. 8 Jun 1947, Walthamstow)

Billy Bragg (b. 20 Dec 1957, Barking)

Vince Clarke, keyboards/guitar, Erasure (b. 3 Jul 1960, South Woodford)

Phil Collen, guitar, Def Leppard (b. 8 Dec 1957, Hackney)

Jamie Cullum (b. 20 Aug 1979, Rochford)

Jules De Martino, multi-instrumentalist, The Ting Tings (b. 16 Jul 1969, East London)

Rob Dean, guitar, Japan (b. 23 Apr 1953, Clapton)

Dizzee Rascal (b. 1 Oct 1985, Bow)

Ian Dury (b. 12 May 1942, Harrow, d. 27 Mar 2000)

Darren Emerson, DJ, Underworld (b. 30 Apr 1971, Hornchurch)

Dave Evans (The Edge), guitar, U2 (b. 8 Aug 1961, Barking)

Paloma Faith (b. 21 Jul 1985, Hackney)

Gabrielle (b. 16 April 1970, Hackney)

Tim Gane, guitar/keyboards, Stereolab (b. 12 Jul 1964, Barking)

Martin Gore, keyboards/guitar, Depeche Mode (b. 23 Jul 1961, Dagenham)

Steve Harris, bass, Iron Maiden (b. 12 Mar 1956, Leytonstone)

Brian Harvey, East 17 (b. 8 Aug 1974, Walthamstow)

Imogen Heap, singer/songwriter (b. 9 Dec 1977, Havering)

John Hendy, East 17 (b. 26 Mar 1971, Barking)

Steve Hillage (b. 2 Aug 1951, Chingford)

Alan Howard, bass, Brian Poole & The Tremeloes (b. 17 Oct 1941, Dagenham)

Kenney Jones, drums, The Small Faces/Faces/The Who (b. 16 Sep 1948, Stepney)

Kano, rapper (b. 21 May 1985, East Ham)

Gary Kemp, guitar, Spandau Ballet (b. 16 Oct 1959, Smithfield)

Ronnie Lane (b. 1 Apr 1946, Plaistow, d. 4 Jun 1997)

Nicko McBrain, drums, Iron Maiden (b. 5 Jun 1952, Hackney)

Steve Marriott, vocals/guitar, (b. 30 Jan 1947, East Ham, d. 20 Apr 1991)

Tony Mortimer, East 17 (b. 21 Oct 1970, Stepney)

Dave Munden, drums, Brian Poole & The Tremeloes (b. 2 Dec 1943, Dagenham)

Plan B (Ben Drew), rapper (b. 22 Oct 1983, Forest Gate)

Brian Poole, vocals, Brian Poole & The Tremeloes (b. 2 Nov 1941, Barking)

Andy Powell, guitar, Wishbone Ash (b. 19 Feb 1950, Stepney)

Jeff Rich, drums, Status Quo (b. 8 Jun 1953, Hackney)

Helen Shapiro (b. 28 Sep 1946, Bethnal Green)

Sandie Shaw (b. 26 Feb 1947, Dagenham)

Phil Smith, guitar, Haircut 100 (b. 1 May 1959, Redbridge)

Leeroy Thornhill, The Prodigy (b. 8 Oct 1969, Barking)

Louise Wener, vocals, Sleeper (b. 30 Jul 1966, Gants Hill)

Keith West (b. 6 Dec 1943, Dagenham)

Ricky West, guitar, Brian Poole & The Tremeloes (b. 7 May 1943, Dagenham)

Wiley, rapper (b. 19 Jan 1979, Bow)

Cliff Williams, bass, AC/DC (b. 14 Dec 1949, Romford)

Jah Wobble (b. 11 Aug 1958, Stepney)

Brentwood-born Curved Air vocalist Sonja Kristina made her stage debut as a 13-year-old at Romford's Swan Folk Club

Curved Air

BTM records

Greater London

SE7 THE WHO PUT THE BOOT IN AT CHARLTON

Charlton Athletic football ground has changed much since the damp day in 1976 when The Who made a record-breaking appearance there. The Harvey Goldsmith promoted concert was one of three visits to English (Charlton), Welsh (Swansea City) and Scottish (Celtic) football stadia. At Charlton's Valley football ground on May 31st, The Who set the unenviable record as the world's loudest group when their 120-decibel output bagged them a place in The Guinness Book of Records. Responsibly, Pete Townshend would later write to the book's editor, Norris McWhirter, to politely make a case for the removal of the record-breaking category that had begun to seriously affect his hearing. Other acts playing on a day when 76,000 official ticket-holders were joined by many with forgeries, included Little Feat and The Sensational Alex Harvey Band. The Who had played the football ground two years earlier in the summer of 1974 when Lou Reed, Humble Pie and Bad Company also rocked the Valley on a sunny day marred by outbreaks of crowd violence.

LOCATION 162: the much-changed football ground is at Floyd Road, Charlton, postcode SE7 8BL

SE1 WAPPING WINGS OVER LONDON TOWN

More famous for 'that Scottish song' than the title track featuring barkers and rozzers, the cover picture for London Town was shot from Wapping Ironically for an album so strongly linked to the capital city, it was a single release from London Town about a remote Scottish outpost that was most significant. 'Mull Of Kintyre' provided Paul McCartney and Wings with a single release that eclipsed anything sold by The Beatles, or anybody else for that matter.

LOCATION 163: Tower Bridge, River Thames, SE1 2UP

SE4 SECRET BROCKLEY VENUE HOSTS KINGS OF LEON

The intimate surroundings of Brockley's Rivoli Ballroom played host to a secret gig by just about the biggest band in the world on October 27th 2010. Here amid the chandeliers and retro glamour, Kings of Leon showcased tracks from their new album Come Around Sundown. The 260 lucky free ticket-holders assembled for a BBC Radio 1 broadcast were also treated to some of the band's previous hits before heading back out the doors of this small but perfectly formed dance hall, said to be the capital's only remaining intact 1950s ballroom.

LOCATION 164: 350 Brockley Road, postcode SE4 2BY

SE1 THE KINKS' 'WATERLOO SUNSET'

The Kinks' 'Terry and Julie' love song written by Ray Davies is often referred to as the benchmark of great songwriting by the generation of London songsmiths that followed. Revered by the likes of Paul Weller and Suggs and written about a couple who meet every Friday at Waterloo Station, the song surprisingly stalled at No.2 in 1967, prevented from topping the singles chart by The Tremeloes' 'Silence Is Golden'.

❝It would make me proud to hear Frank Sinatra singing 'Waterloo Sunset'. That song came to me in a dream. I woke up singing it in my sleep. ❞
Ray Davies talking to Ira Robbins

LOCATION 165: Waterloo Bridge, SE1

SE1 THE SAVAGE GARDEN MARKET

South-East London's famous food market was given the guided tour treatment by Darren Hayes in the video for the Australian duo's penultimate hit single 'Hold Me'.

LOCATION 166: 8 Southwark Street, SE1 1TL

SE14 GOLDSMITHS NURTURES ROCK AND POP CREATIVES

Specialising in the arts and culture, this magnate for creative types was where student Damon Albarn, Graham Coxon and Alex James formed the nucleus of Blur. Others benefiting from what this constituent college of the University of London had to offer were John Cale, Neil Innes, Malcolm McLaren, Brian Molko and Rob da Bank.

LOCATION 167: 8 Lewisham Way, postcode SE14 6YZ

SE15 A PULP B-SIDE

A B-side to single 'Razzmatazz', final track on Pulp's 1993 Intro album, recalling an utterly awful party that Jarvis Cocker attended, '59 Lyndhurst Grove' was written as a well-intentioned warning to the wife of an architect he met there. His concern that she was headed for a life of misery "married to this prick", as he put it, led him to write to her enclosing a copy of the CD. No reply was forthcoming.

LOCATION 168: 59 Lyndhurst Grove, Camberwell, SE15 5AW. Status: private residence

PRS

SE9 ELTHAM DEBUT FOR STATUS QUO

Before you can begin rockin' all over the world, you have to pay your dues. The Welcome Inn (now the Edens residential development) where Status Quo first performed in 1967 may have burned down in 2006 but that fact didn't stop PRS for Music marking the event with a plaque on the site in 2010.

Francis Rossi and Rick Parfitt attend the unveiling of the plaque commemorating their first gig supporting Episode Six, who later evolved into Deep Purple

LOCATION 169: in Well Hall Road, postcode SE9 6UB

❝I remember the gig very well. It was the first we played after Rick [Parfitt] joined us. He wore the green and yellow striped blazer I got married in.❞
Francis Rossi

SE10 EARLY GREENWICH GIGGING FOR SQUEEZE

Some of pop's most thoughtful songwriting came out of South London in the 1970s courtesy of Greenwich-based band Squeeze. Their lyrical kitchen sink dramas incorporated a number of key local locations. One of the best examples was 'King George Street', a single from the 1985 album Cosi Fan Tutti Frutti. The band were propelled to fame on the back of gigs in the Greenwich area at the Bricklayers' Arms, the now demolished Northover (Catford), Hardy's Free House, the Deptford Arms and The Bell. A plaque to commemorate one of their earliest gigs was unveiled at the Greenwich Dance Agency, Borough Hall, Greenwich, in 2010.

❝I've always stayed in this area and I love this area – I don't think I'll ever leave. But I've seen it change, and it's now harder for bands to get started.❞
Glenn Tilbrook, 2010

LOCATIONS 170 and 171: King George Street, postcode SE10 8QB. The Borough Hall plaque is on Royal Hill, postcode SE10 8RE

SE10 THE O2: A GREAT BRITISH MUSIC EXPERIENCE

Once famously dubbed a hugely expensive white elephant, London's Millennium Dome was regenerated by AEG Europe as the world's most popular music arena, overtaking New York's Madison Square Garden's record for most-tickets-sold in a year record. Imagine turning the O2 structure upside down as a giant dish: O2 boffins have calculated that it would take Niagara Falls 15 minutes to fill it with water or, if you prefer, 3.8 billion pints of beer. In addition to the 20,000-capacity arena, the O2 boasts, nightclubs, cinema screens and a curving mall of eateries. But, most significant for this book is the interactive museum of popular music the British Music Experience, opened in 2009. At this unique

visitor attraction, budding musicians can play a wide range of guitars, keyboards and drums and view legendary handwritten lyrics, memorabilia and famous outfits from 60 years of British music history.

LOCATION 172: Peninsula Square, SE10 0DX. Website: www. britishmusicexperience.com

The giant messageboard outside the O2 following the King of Pop's death in 2009

WELLING KATE BUSH'S CHILDHOOD HOME

East Wickham Farm was the family home where Kate Bush lived with her doctor father, mother and two older brothers, John and Paddy. Her inbuilt wonder and love of music and outpouring of songs, written when a schoolgirl, all began here surrounded by her musical family. Famously 'discovered' and encouraged by David Gilmour and signed to EMI as a songwriting prodigy, the teenage Kate Bush also formed the KT Bush Band with brother Paddy and three friends, playing South London pubs. The secluded 350-year-old farmhouse home offered a base for an idyllic

childhood and subsequently a secure and private environment for her work. The conversion of one of the farm's barns into a 24-track studio in 1983 was significant. It gave Kate, who now had four Top 10 albums to her credit, a financial and creative independence to take as long as she wanted over future projects.

LOCATION 173: the large farmhouse is almost impossible to see through impenetrable undergrowth and is situated in a surprisingly built-up area on Wickham Street, Welling, postcode DA16 3DA. Status: private residence

Gered Mankowitz for EMI

Kate Bush, who shares a birthday with Wuthering Heights author Emily Bronte, wrote her 'version' at East Wickham Farm

SE18 THE HOUSE THAT MADE BOY GEORGE

In 1974, the 14-year-old George O'Dowd moved house to 171 Shooter's Hill, where his metamorphosis into chart-topping Culture Club singer, DJ and solo star Boy George began. George, together with mum, dad, his sister and four brothers, moved to this Edwardian semi from their cramped 1930s council house at 29 Joan Crescent, two miles away on Eltham's Middle Park estate.

'I would never dare go knock on the door and say 'I used to live here, can I come in?'
Boy George, when filming the Channel 4 documentary about his childhood homes

Both homes were featured in the 2010 Channel 4 TV documentary The House That Made Me, enabling George, somewhat reluctantly it has to be said at first, to return to his childhood surroundings, where the programme makers had faithfully reproduced the 70s interiors in both houses.

LOCATIONS 174 and 175: both private residences are at 29 Joan Crescent, Eltham, postcode SE9 5KR, and 171 Shooter's Hill, postcode SE18 3HP

Born in South East London

Ginger Baker, drums, Cream (b. 19 Aug 1939, Lewisham)
Easther Bennett, Eternal (b. 11 Dec 1972, Croydon)
Vernie Bennett, Eternal (b. 17 May 1971, Croydon)
John Bentley, bass, Squeeze (b. 16 Apr 1951, Deptford)
Alan Blakely, guitar, Brian Poole & The Tremeloes (b. 1 Apr 1942, Bromley)
Boy George, vocals, Culture Club (b. George O'Dowd, 14 Jun 1961, Bexley)
Kéllé Bryan, Eternal (b. 12 Mar 1975, Lewisham)
Kate Bush (b. 30 Jul 1958, Bexleyheath)
Captain Sensible (Ray Burns), bass, The Damned/solo (b. 23 Apr 1955, Balham)
Norman Cook (Fatboy Slim), DJ/producer/keyboards (b. 31 Jul 1963, Bromley)
Jay Darlington, keyboards, Kula Shaker (b. 3 May 1968, Sidcup)
Chris Difford, guitar, Squeeze (b. 4 Nov 1954, Greenwich)
Mickey Finn, drums, T. Rex (b. 3 Jun 1947, Thornton Heath, d. 11 Jan 2003)
Matthew Fisher, guitar, Procol Harum (b. 7 Mar 1946, Croydon)

Jerome Flynn, Robson & Jerome (b. 16 Mar 1963, Bromley)
Simon Friend, guitar, Levellers (b. 17 May 1967, Upper Norwood)
Peter Grant, music manager (b. 5 Apr 1935, South Norwood, d. 21 Nov 1995)
Steve Harley (b. 27 Feb 1951, Deptford)
Charlie Heather, drums, Levellers (b. 2 Feb 1964, Bromley)
Ken Hensley, keyboards, Uriah Heep (b. 24 Aug 1945, Plumstead)
Nick Heyward (b. 20 May 1961, Beckenham)
Jools Holland (b. 24 Jan 1958, Blackheath)
Steve Jansen, drums, Japan (b. 1 Dec 1959, Beckenham)
John Paul Jones, bass, Led Zeppelin (b. 3 Jan 1946, Sidcup)
Louise (Redknapp, née Nurding) (b. 4 Nov 1974, Lewisham)
Jacqui McShee, vocals, Pentangle (b. 25 Dec 1943, Catford)
Les Nemes, bass, Haircut 100 (b. 5 Dec 1960, Croydon)
Horace Panter (Sir Horace Gentleman), bass, The Specials (b. 30 Aug 1953, Croydon)
Mica Paris (b. 27 Apr 1969, Lewisham)
Maxi Priest (b. 10 Jun 1961, Lewisham)
Danny Rampling, DJ (b. 15 Jul 1961, Streatham)
Francis Rossi, vocals/guitar, Status Quo (b. 29 May 1949, Forest Hill)
Siouxsie Sioux (b. 27 May 1957, Southwark)
Tommy Steele (b. 17 Dec 1936, Bermondsey)
Poly Styrene, vocals, X-Ray Spex (b. 3 Jul 1957, d. 25 Apr 2011, Bromley)
David Sylvian, vocals, Japan (b. 23 Feb 1958, Beckenham)
Glenn Tilbrook, vocals/guitar, Squeeze (b. 31 Aug 1957, Woolwich)
Tinie Tempah, rapper (b. 7 Nov 1988, Plumstead)
Steve Peregrin Took, drums, T. Rex (b. 28 Jul 1949, Eltham, d. 27 Oct 1980)
Paul Tucker, keyboards, Lighthouse Family (b. 12 Aug 1968, Crystal Palace)
Alan White, drums, Oasis (b. 26 May 1972, Eltham)
Steve White, drums, The Style Council (b. 31 May 1965, Bermondsey)
Marty Wilde (b. 15 Apr 1939, Blackheath)
Bill Wyman (b. 24 Oct 1936, Lewisham)

Greater London

SW1 'PARTY CENTRAL' FOR THE SMALL FACES AT WESTMORELAND TERRACE

Described as 'Party Central' by keyboards man Ian McLagan, 22 Westmoreland Terrace was The Small Faces' home for 12 glorious months, during which time the band racked-up four Top 10 singles. Under the watchful eye of an Austrian housekeeper, McLagan, Steve Marriott and Ronnie Lane arrived in the Pimlico property rented for them by manager Don Arden at the tail end of 1965. Drummer Kenney Jones stayed with his mum and dad in Stepney, and as a result probably missed much of the mayhem that took place at Westmoreland Terrace. One memorable visit by Brian Epstein to No.22 saw The Beatles manager experience his first LSD trip. Following the most creative and productive period in their career, they left Pimlico for good on Christmas Eve 1966.

LOCATION 176:
22 Westmoreland Terrace, Pimlico, postcode SW1V 4. Status: private residence

The Small Faces hit a chart purple patch while living at Westmoreland Terrace: their year-long residency included four Top 10 singles and this No.3 album

SW1 BRIAN EPSTEIN'S CHAPEL STREET HOME

This is the exclusive Belgravia property where Brian Epstein lived and then tragically died in 1967. His home, from December 1964 (and from 1966 his work base) was like the man himself, fashionably smart and immaculately turned out. Often parked outside would be his choice of transport for the day, the red Rolls-Royce or the Silver Bentley. A launch party for the press for the Sgt Pepper's Lonely Hearts Club Band album was held here on May 19th 1967, at which Paul McCartney met photographer Linda Eastman for only the second time.

LOCATION 177: 24 Chapel Street, postcode SW1X7. Status: private residence

SW1 'BORIS THE SPIDER' AT THE SCOTCH OF ST JAMES

A favourite haunt for musicians in London's swinging Sixties, The Beatles (and in particular Paul McCartney) found The Scotch of St James a haven of relative privacy and a convenient short distance from their Savile Row daytime base. It was at this late-night bolt-hole that the Fab Four could escape from public pressure and keep up to date with the fast-changing music scene. The tartan-decorated club was where Jimi Hendrix first caused a stir on his arrival in the UK. An impromptu performance on September 24th 1966 accompanied by the club's house band was his first astonishing appearance, followed quickly by a Jimi Hendrix Experience private showcase on October 19th. Although the media would ramp up the competitiveness between the Sixties acts, it was at The Scotch of St James where The Who, The Stones and The Beatles could relax together with a drink and a smoke. One typical night out enjoyed by The Who's John Entwistle and Rolling Stone Bill Wyman saw the two bass guitarists playing a naming game listing imaginary pets. This particular creative conversation led to Entwistle recording Who track 'Boris The Spider', a creature born at The Scotch of St James.

LOCATION 178: now the Directors Lodge Club, 13 Mason's Yard, Duke Street, postcode SW1Y 6BU

SW1 THE NEW BOOTS AND PANTIES!! SHOP

Axford's was the clothing shop on Vauxhall Bridge Road where Ian Dury posed with his six-year-old son Baxter for the photograph that adorns the cover of the singer-songwriter's 1977 album New Boots And Panties!! Suggested by Dury to photographer Chris Gabrin, the location was chosen after an abortive attempt to get a cover picture outside Dury's nearby flat at The Oval. The three then made the short journey to Vauxhall Bridge Road. Gabrin's hastily parked Mini van can be seen across the road outside Woolworths in the window reflection. Axford's had originally been pointed out to Drury by his good friend, the artist Peter Blake. Hardly worth recommending for a pilgrimage, just about all that's left of this Seventies location is the pavement. But, here is one site and visual stop on pop's timeline that should be marked with a plaque. The photoshoot was lovingly recreated in 2010 Ian Dury biopic Sex & Drugs & Rock & Roll.

LOCATION 179: 306 Vauxhall Bridge Road, postcode SW1V 1

Ian and Baxter Dury outside Axford's

SW3 CHELSEA SONGS, KINGS ROAD HIPPIES AND PUNKS AT THE WORLD'S END

Immediately north of the River Thames, hip, trendy and wealthy Chelsea has been regularly referenced in pop and rock, but not always positively. Elvis Costello's critical hit '(I Don't Want To Go To) Chelsea' in 1978 was an attempt to articulate what he thought the place stood for. Less critical was Jon Bon Jovi's biggest UK solo hit 'Midnight In Chelsea', written with the assistance of Dave Stewart and Bruce Willis. Chief inspiration for the 1997 No.4 hit was the New Jersey frontman's stay in a Chelsea basement observing and writing about London's red buses, homeless drunks, Goths and Sloane Rangers. Disappointingly, the single's video was shot in Manhattan.

The open all hours three-storey Chelsea Drugstore where Mick Jagger sang about standing in line "with Mr Jimmy" from The Stones' 'You Can't Always Get What You Want' has long since ceased trading. This architectural icon of the Sixties was an early attempt to introduce a US-style drug store to London. Drugs, records, coffee and alcohol bars and magazines are no longer on offer as the building has adopted a more recent US import. The junction of Royal Avenue and No.49 The King's Road is currently a McDonald's restaurant.

Around the same time in the late Sixties the western, World's End district of The King's Road began to attract a steady stream of rock stars raiding a new wave of clothes emporiums. The uniquely styled shop Granny Takes A Trip led the way and fed a craving for more exotic stage gear championed by regular customers Marc Bolan and Rod Stewart.

In 1971, Malcolm McLaren and Vivienne Westwood began a cultural revolution at

It was here in 1975 at the boutique called SEX, now Vivienne Westwood's World's End, that a green-haired John Lydon auditioned for the Sex Pistols, singing along to Alice Cooper's 'I'm Eighteen' on the shop's jukebox

the then shabby end of The King's Road. They kick-started the Fifties' rock 'n' roll revival look that so dominated early to mid-Seventies pop with their Let It Rock shop. With the best jukebox for miles and shelves stocked with brothel creepers, luminous ties and socks, the shop at No.430 evolved into SEX, the famous punk boutique, a magnet for the fast-developing punk movement sported that new fashion by using The Kings Road as a vast al fresco catwalk. Tom Petty gives a more up-to-date guided tour of this rag bag of clothing stores in 'Kings Road', from his 1981 hit album Hard Promises.

LOCATION 180: The King's Road, postcode SW3

SW5 DYLAN HEADS FOR THE TROUBADOUR IN 1962

A bohemian-style coffee house since 1954, the Troubadour has played host to a wide variety of performers including Sammy Davis Jr, Jimi Hendrix, Paul Simon and Joni Mitchell. Still a wonderfully atmospheric place to eat, drink and take in live music, the Troubadour's best claim to fame came from Bob Dylan's first UK gig on a cold November night in 1962. The emerging folk singer was in Britain to record a part acting in BBC TV play, The Madhouse On Castle Street. Before heading for London, established US folk singer Pete Seeger had singled out the Troubadour as a place the 21-year-old Dylan must visit. The coffee bar's Tuesday night folk organiser, Anthea Joseph, only recognised him on his arrival from the front cover of US folk magazine Sing Out!, which fans could buy from Collets record shop in Tottenham Court Road. During this same winter, Dylan also made impromptu appearances at other key folk spots, The King & Queen in Foley Street and the Pindar of Wakefield in Gray's Inn Road.

Left: Dylan in the Troubadour basement in November 1962

Bottom left: Davey Graham performing at the Troubadour

Below: Little-changed and still hosting some lively music: the Troubadour

❝**Dylan didn't seem as interested in performing as he was in listening. I felt quite like a native in the presence of an anthropologist.**❞
Troubadour folk night organiser Anthea Joseph

LOCATION 181: 263 Old Brompton Road, Earls Court, postcode SWA 9JA. Website: www.troubadour.co.uk

Alison Chapman McLean

SW17 STATUS QUO'S TOOTING TURNING POINT

Around the time Status Quo were enjoying the success of their fourth hit single 'Down The Dustpipe', they played a significant gig in Tooting. The year was 1970 and, booked to play the Castle pub, they realised their audience was evolving. That night Status Quo evolved too. For the first time the band played to a crowd sitting cross-legged in their trench coats on the floor. Clutching their pints and nodding their heads, Quo adapted their performance accordingly. As the Castle stage was no more than a few inches high, Quo guitarists Rick Parfitt and Francis Rossi "had to get down to the audience" as Parfitt put it. So, heads bowed and legs apart, the famous Quo stance came into being. Musically this also marked their development into mega-selling album rock property. Currently live music takes a back seat at the Castle, which these days advertises quiz nights and Salsa classes.

LOCATION 183: 38 Tooting High Street, postcode SW17 0RG

SW6 MICHAEL JACKSON'S STATUE AT FULHAM FOOTBALL CLUB

When Michael Jackson died in 2009, Mohamed Al Fayed commissioned this extraordinary statue in memory of his friend. Originally, the memorial to "The King of Pop" was to have been sited at the multi-millionaire's Harrods store in Knightsbridge, but when Fayed sold the property he then had the statue erected at the home of Fulham Football Club, where he is Chairman. The 7ft-6in-tall plaster and resin Jacko sits on a 2.5-ton granite base inscribed with the words and music from the singer's 1988 single 'Man In The Mirror'. Not all Fulham football fans thought the location of the statue was appropriate, and even Jackson may have wondered how this memorial ended up inside a football ground overlooking the River Thames, where he did once attend a game at Craven Cottage, sat in the director's box with Chairman Al Fayed.

❛It may seem an unusual thing to do, but those of us who know and love the chairman are not surprised at all. The tribute fits perfectly for him.❜
Fulham footballer Dickson Etuhu

LOCATION 184: Fulham Football Club, Craven Cottage, Stevenage Road, postcode SW6 HH. Note that the statue is situated inside the stadium at the corner of the Hammersmith and Riverside stands but can be viewed from the Thames river path. For access to the stadium, check out the Fulham FC website at www.fulhamfc.com

Michael Jackson's riverside statue was unveiled before the Premier League football match between Fulham and Blackpool on April 3rd 2011

SW7 'A HOST OF STARS' AT THE ALBERT HALL

Opened in 1871 and one of very few music venues to offer a performer the experience of being virtually surrounded by their audience, the grand Royal Albert Hall continues to operate as a special place for rock watching. Said to be Paul Weller's favourite place to play, the building was almost one-hundred years old before pop and rock made a debut in the mid-Sixties. Billed back then as 'A Host of Stars', the old place echoed to the music of The Spencer Davis Group, The Yardbirds, The Small Faces, The Mindbenders, Them, The Moody Blues, Unit 4 Plus 2, The Nashville Teens and The Zombies in 1966 for a Dick Clark US TV show. Both Cream and Led Zeppelin have particularly memorable associations with the place that also hosted late Eighties Brit Awards shows. And, when Eric Clapton (probably the Royal Albert Hall's most regular performer) and friends wanted the perfect venue for an opportunity to say a musical goodbye to George Harrison, here is where the great and good paid tribute to the former Beatle a year after his death, at the Concert For George in 2002.

LOCATION 185: Kensington Gore, postcode SW7 2AP

Greater London

SW6 MUMFORD & SONS AT PIMPERNEL & PARTNERS

UK folk-rock outfit Mumford & Sons were pictured in the window of an address on south-west London's grooviest thoroughfare when snapped for their Sigh No More album cover in 2009. Photographer Max Knight spent nine hours getting the finished result at the location on The Kings Road. The cover shows all four band members plus their friend (and Laura Marling's multi-instrumentalist) Pete Roe looking out of a floor window in the building next door.

Mumford & Sons at No.596 Kings Road

❝One of the toughest shoots I've ever done. We had to battle the heat, the traffic (shooting across the main road) and the reflection off the glass window. The shoot also took place on Wimbledon Finals day...it was super distracting as it was a boiling hot day and the pub across the road was full of people with ice-cold beers, cheering on the tennis.❞
Photographer Max Knight

LOCATION 186: at vintage and replica French furniture shop Pimpernel & Partners, 596 King's Road, postcode SW6 2DX

SW8 PINK FLOYD'S PIG

The inclusion of a pig on the sleeve of the Pink Floyd's Animals album cover in 1977 began a close association with the animal throughout the band's stop-start career. The LP cover's inflatable pig, conceived by the band's Roger Waters, was launched and tethered floating above the defunct Battersea Power Station for the photoshoot. After three days of airborne activity, the forty-foot-long helium-filled balloon broke free and famously caused mayhem with flights at nearby Heathrow Airport. The pig eventually crash-landed in a Kent farm but was hastily puncture-repaired and returned for one last attempt at a perfect photo which failed. The final cover was a composite of at least two different photographs to get the desired effect.

LOCATION 189: 188 Kirtling Street, Nine Elms, postcode SW8 5BP

SW11 'THE GIRL FROM CLAPHAM' AND THE 'WINDY COMMON'

Clapham Common and railway station junction is the setting and euphemism for one of Britain's greatest song stories. Referencing 'the girl from Clapham' and 'the windy common', 'Up The Junction' by Squeeze was a No.2 hit in 1979 for the South London band, who nabbed the title from the 1963 novel, TV drama and subsequent movie of the same name. Manfred Mann failed to chart with their 'Up The Junction' theme song

The 'Up The Junction' theme tune to the movie starring Dennis Waterman and Suzy Kendall

(see picture sleeve left) to the 1968 movie but the track and the storyline of teenage abortion and social depravation was picked up and turned into a late-Seventies pop classic by Squeeze songwriters Chris Difford and Glenn Tilbrook.

LOCATIONS 187 and 188: Clapham Junction, postcode SW11 2QP, and Clapham Common, postcode SW4 7

The final result of the protracted photoshoots for Animals

SW10 HOME TO THE EMBRYONIC STONES

"Truly disgusting" was how Keith Richards described the living conditions at the address where The Rolling Stones spent the cold winter of 1962-63. Most importantly it was a base for obsessionally honing the skills to enable them to emulate Mick Jagger, Keith Richards and Brian Jones' American blues heroes. Here they studied and copied the Muddy Waters and Bo Diddley records they would listen to on the flat's one luxury item, Brian Jones' huge radiogram. When the cold and squalor got too much they would cash-in empty bottles and head for the nearby Wetherby Arms pub at 500 King's Road, for a drink and a warm, to ponder their future.

LOCATION 190: 102 Edith Grove, Chelsea, sandwiched between the River Thames and The King's Road, postcode SW10 0NH. Status: private residence

The then "truly disgusting" but now rather delightful Edith Grove home of Jagger, Richards and Jones

SW13 RECORDING HEAVEN AT OLYMPIC STUDIOS

This former theatre then film studio in Barnes began its new life as a recording studio in the mid-Sixties. For any young rock fan hell-bent on filling their autograph book, the doorway of Olympic Studios must have made the most profitable hovering point. Attracted by the smart Barnes location and superior acoustics, the likes of Led Zeppelin, The Rolling Stones, The Who and Dusty Springfield were all regular visitors. Even The Beatles strayed from Abbey Road to commence recordings for 'All You Need Is Love'. Olympic was where supergroup Blind Faith assembled to record their transatlantic chart topping debut album, Procol Harum delivered 'A Whiter Shade Of Pale', The Small Faces created 'Lazy Sunday' and the Eagles began their recording career with 'Take It Easy' and the remaining bunch of songs on their first two albums. Later beneficiaries of the Olympic acoustics were Queen, who selected the place for A Night At The Opera, and The Verve, who recorded the classic Urban Hymns here. Despite recent album recordings by Babyshambes (Shotter's Nation in 2007) and U2 completing work on No Line On The Horizon in 2008, the famous old studio is now closed, with the building's future as a recording facility uncertain after EMI sold it in 2009.

LOCATION 191: 117 Church Road, Barnes, postcode SW13 9HL. Status: private offices

The entrance to Olympic Studios where classic single 'Itchycoo Park' by The Small Faces and tracks for Traffic's Mr Fantasy album were recorded on the same day in 1967

Martin Downham

Greater London

SW15 MARC BOLAN'S ROADSIDE SHRINE

When Marc Bolan died in a car crash on September 16th 1977, his devoted fans decided to mark the location of the tragedy with a shrine to the T. Rex glam rock icon. This is the spot in Barnes where the purple Mini he and girlfriend Gloria were travelling in struck a tree at speed near the railway bridge on Queens Ride. It is the focal point for fans to pay their respects and leave a memento, message or flowers. The message board, sculptured bust and memorial stone of Bolan are all situated on the steep heavily wooded embankment that drops away from the stretch of road where Bolan met his death.

The Bolan bust attracts a variety of mementos

LOCATION 192: a shady embankment at the junction of Queens Ride and Gipsy Lane, Barnes, postcode SW15

SW15 PUTNEY'S HALF MOON PUB ROLLS WITH THE TIMES

This Putney pub's first regularly organised music nights began under the Folksville banner in 1963. American folk and blues legends Sonny Terry and Brownie McGhee, Champion Jack Dupree and Arthur Crudup all played The Half Moon, augmented by the best of new British folk, Roy Harper, Ralph McTell, Bert Jansch and John Martyn. The venue has rolled with the times, and British R&B and pub rock movements saw top exponents John Mayall's Bluesbreakers to Dr Feelgood play the Half Moon. U2 and Kate Bush have a particular soft spot for the place: U2 played their first sold-out gig on their debut UK tour here and Kate made her public performance debut billed as the KT Bush Band. In May 2000, The Half Moon played host to a private Rolling Stones get-together in memory of Keith Richards' personal assistant Joe Seabrook, who had died just a month or so earlier. The band, who had

played the venue four decades previously, all assembled to party, with Ronnie Wood and Richards jamming with the night's hired band. Pictures of the acts that have played the place decorate the walls of this traditional pub, which was thankfully saved from gastro-pub anonymity in 2009 to continue a menu of wall-to-wall live music.

The Half Moon has reverberated to the sounds of every milestone music genre since 1963

LOCATION 193 93 Lower Richmond Road, Putney, postcode SW15 1EU. Website: www.halfmoon.co.uk

SW9 'ELECTRIC AVENUE', 'THE GUNS OF BRIXTON' AND BOB MARLEY WAY

Built in the 19th century, Brixton's Electric Avenue was named to mark one of the earliest shopping streets to enjoy electric lighting. This lively thoroughfare was the title of Eddy Grant's biggest hit, which made No.2 on both sides of the Atlantic. A frequent topic for songwriters, Brixton and its recent volatile history has featured in graphic tracks by The Clash ('The Guns Of Brixton') and Carter-The Unstoppable Sex Machine ('And God Created Brixton'). Recent local exports Alabama 3 were formed in Brixton in the Nineties, becoming world famous for 'Woke Up This Morning', the theme to American TV's The Sopranos. This track features on the band's 1997 album Exile On Coldharbour Lane, which is a mile-long stretch of road connecting both Brixton with Camberwell.

LOCATIONS 194 and 195: Electric Avenue and Brixton Market is bordered by the A23, the B223 and the A2217 (Coldharbour Lane), postcode SW9 8JX. A short walk south from the market on the B223 Railton Road brings you to Bob Marley Way, postcode SE24 0LP

SW15 SANDY DENNY'S PUTNEY VALE GRAVESTONE

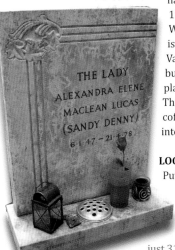

The honey-voiced folk singer who suffered a brain haemorrhage in 1978 and died in a Wimbledon hospital is buried at Putney Vale Cemetery. At her burial, a lone piper played 'Flowers Of The Forest, as her coffin was lowered into the ground.

LOCATION 196: Putney Vale Cemetery, Stag Lane, postcode SW15 3DZ

Sandy Denny was just 31 when she died

KT3 WIMBLEDON'S UNHALFBRICKING COVER

The cover photograph for Fairport Convention's first hit album Unhalfbricking was shot at Arthur Road in Wimbledon. The composition of this 1969 cover, sans band name or album title, depicts Fairport Convention singer Sandy Denny's parents Edna and Neil outside their home. Sandy and the rest of the band are assembled on the lawn, and the precise location is pinpointed by the appearance of St Mary's Church (Broadway Court) in the photo's misty background.

LOCATION 197: Arthur Road, Wimbledon, postcode KT3 6LX

Eric Hayes' photo of Edna and Neil (and Fairport Convention) at Arthur Road, Wimbledon, was shot in the early spring of 1969

Born in South West London

Emma Anderson, vocals, Lush (b. 10 Jun 1967, Wimbledon)
Iain Baker, keyboards, Jesus Jones (b. 29 Sep 1965, Carshalton)
Jeff Beck (b. 24 Jun 1944, Wallington)
David Bowie (b. 8 Jan 1947, Brixton)
Dave Brock, vocals/guitar, Hawkwind (b. 20 Aug 1941, Isleworth)
Richard Butler, vocals, The Psychedelic Furs (b. 5 Jun 1956, Kingston upon Thames)
Tim Butler, bass, The Psychedelic Furs (b. 7 Dec 1958, Teddington)
Sandy Denny, vocals, Fairport Convention (b. 6 Jan 1947, Merton Park, d. 21 Apr 1978)
Chris Dreja, guitar, The Yardbirds (b. 11 Nov 1945, Surbiton)
Mel Gaynor, drums, Simple Minds (b. 29 May 1960, Balham)
Ed Harcourt, singer/songwriter (b. 14 Aug 1977, Wimbledon)
Mick Jones, guitar, The Clash (b. 26 Jun 1955, Brixton)
Simon Kirke, drums, Bad Company/Free (b. 28 Jul 1949, Lambeth)

Dee C. Lee, vocals, The Style Council/solo (b. 6 Jun 1961, Balham)
Tom McGuinness, bass, Manfred Mann (b. 2 Dec 1941, Wimbledon)
John Martyn (b. 11 Sep 1948, New Malden, d. 29 Jan 2009)
Alex Patterson, The Orb (b. 15 Oct 1959, Battersea)
Tom Rowlands, keyboards, The Chemical Brothers (b. 11 Jan 1971, Kingston upon Thames)
Rat Scabies (Christopher Millar), drums, The Damned (b. 30 Jul 1957, Kingston upon Thames)
Paul Simonon, bass, The Clash (b. 15 Dec 1955, Brixton)
Skin (Deborah Dyer), vocals, Skunk Anansie (b. 3 Aug 1967, Brixton)
Dave Swarbrick, violin, Fairport Convention (b. 5 Apr 1941, New Malden)
Mick Talbot, keyboards, The Style Council (b. 11 Sep 1958, Wimbledon)
Porl Thompson, guitar, The Cure (b. 8 Nov 1957, Wimbledon)
Ben Watt, guitar/keyboards, Everything But The Girl (b. 6 Dec 1962, Barnes)
Florence Welch, vocals, Florence + The Machine (b. 28 Aug 1986, Camberwell)

Greater London

WC1 BOB MARLEY REMEMBERED AT RIDGMOUNT GARDENS

When Bob Marley first came to the UK in 1972, he lived at this quiet, rather stately mansion block at Ridgmount Gardens, a short stroll from the busy Tottenham Court Road. In 2006, Mayor of London Ken Livingstone, who organised a commemorative plaque in partnership with the Nubian Jak Community Trust, described the internationally famous reggae artist as 'quite simply a musical genius.' The plaque unveiling was attended by children from Paddington Green Primary School, who read aloud a potted history of Marley's life's work and Students from St Martin-in-the-Field who sang 'Redemption Song' from the 1980 Bob Marley and The Wailers album Uprising.

LOCATION 198: 34 Ridgmount Gardens, postcode WC1E7

Bob Marley's first London home and the plaque unveiled in 2006

W1 'YESTERDAY' WRITTEN AT THE ASHER FAMILY HOME

Doctor and Mrs Asher lived in Wimpole Street along with their talented actress daughter Jane and fledgling pop singer son Peter. They obligingly provided a London base for Jane's boyfriend Paul McCartney, who was their attic room lodger for three years until 1966. To avoid the press and fans, Paul would often gain access to and from the property via back doors, side doors and adjacent roof tops. Paul thrived at No.57 in this naturally artistic and creative environment, rattling off a few tunes along the way, including 'Yesterday', pop's most-covered song.

LOCATION 199: 57 Wimpole Street, postcode W1G 8YW. The private residence is on your right just before the intersection with New Cavendish Street

W1 SEVEN DECADES OF NEW MUSIC AT THE 100 CLUB

The 100 Club has promoted live music in the same premises since 1942, when jazz was the draw. The subterranean venue at No.100 on London's busy Oxford Street has witnessed a number of significant music events, not least Britain's first punk festival over two chaotic nights in September 1976. Newly assembled acts sporting provocative names such as The Damned, The Clash, Siouxsie and The Banshees, The Buzzcocks and a headlining Sex Pistols took to the stage in an atmosphere of mutual aggression between the audience and the performers. This was a catch-all opportunity for the British music press to witness several bands desperate to prove themselves at the vanguard of the new punk movement. The 100 Club event provided the many assembled journalists with all the copy they needed to spread the news about this new, largely London based phenomena nationwide. An equally important introduction to a new era occurred in 1992 when the 100 Club hosted new outfit Suede, a gig that revitalised interest in the club and led to the venue enjoying jam-packed houses for visits by a conveyor belt of indie rock bands such as Oasis, Travis, Catatonia and Kula Shaker.

LOCATION 200: 100 Oxford Street, postcode W1D 1LL. Website: the100club.co.uk

W1 EMI MANCHESTER SQUARE AND THE ICONIC BALCONY

The original location of this iconic stairway was on a first-floor landing at EMI's London HQ in Manchester Square, where if you lent over the balcony you looked down into the EMI reception area. This is the spot where photographer Angus McBean looked up to snap The Beatles for their Please Please Me debut album cover. The balcony featured again on covers for The Beatles red (62-66) and blue (67-70) greatest hits albums. The Blue album's updated shot of the Fab Four was a picture originally shot by McBean for the cover of the shelved Get Back album. Neither EMI nor the balcony remain at Manchester Square. Moving offices to Hammersmith in 1995, EMI also moved the increasingly iconic staircase, which they described as "a very important part of Beatles history and EMI history". Re-erected in the Hammersmith offices' staff café, together with a commemorative plaque, there it stayed until the structure moved once more to EMI Group HQ in Wrights Lane, Kensington. Describing the EMI fixtures and fittings as "like fragments of the true cross" in his biography McCartney, author Christopher Sandford revealed that the current owner of the banisters and staircase is none other than Paul McCartney himself. Former EMI PR director Brian Southall witnessed much trespassing at Manchester Square: "Loads of fans used to come by to try and re-create the photo but were usually chased off by security because to get the shot they actually had to stand on EMI private property and the corporation weren't having any of that!"

LOCATION 201: No.20 Manchester Square, postcode W1U 3PZ. Status: private offices. If you're visiting, stop for a drink in the Devonshire Arms at 7 Duke Street, off the southern end of the Square where The Beatles did the same thing

The most famous balcony in pop!

EMI's former London HQ at No.20 Manchester Square

W1 ZAPPA, HENDRIX AND THE BEATLES AT THE SPEAKEASY

Four consecutive nights at the Speakeasy Club by Bob Marley and The Wailers helped the band create a name for themselves during their first British tour as a newly signed act with the Island label. That short, sold-out residency in May 1973 was witnessed by audience members including Eric Clapton, Jeff Beck and members of Deep Purple and The Who. Other Speakeasy acts you didn't get to see every night of the week in Britain included the extraordinary Mothers Of Invention featuring Frank Zappa in 1967 and King Crimson's debut there in May 1969. Back in the day when the nearby Marquee club didn't have a bar, and the local pub The Ship chucked out after last orders the Speakeasy would come into its own as an after-midnight wind-down place where musicians, journalists and photographers would mingle the night away. One night, on the eve of the release of Sgt Pepper's Lonely Hearts Club Band, American group The Turtles arrived in London and headed straight for the Speakeasy to find The Beatles in a booth enjoying a quiet night out. Additionally, as The Turtles' Howard Kaylan later boasted, in one night he met Graham Nash, Donovan, Brian Jones and Jimi Hendrix, who, in turn, legend has it, once jammed with Paul McCartney's girlfriend Jane Asher's mum and failed in an attempt to lure Marianne Faithfull away from boyfriend Mick Jagger.

❛The Speakeasy in Margaret Street, that's where bands could go after their gigs - it was a late club and I often used to see John Lennon or Keith Moon, whoever, or Phil May. ❜
Yardbirds drummer Jim McCarty

LOCATION 202: north of the junction of Oxford Street and Regents Street, 48 Margaret Street, postcode W1W 8SE

W1 HMV PLAQUE MARKS KEY BEATLES EVENT

Between the Boots and Foot Locker stores on Oxford Street is the location of the original HMV store. Here, Beatles manager Brian Epstein was directed to get The Beatles' demo tapes transferred to disc for convenience when touting them round the record labels. The engineer, liking what he heard during the transfer, suggested Epstein approach EMI Publishing on the top floor, which eventually resulted in their first hit 'Love Me Do' being released in 1962. Look out for the large wall plaque which reminds passers-by that this was once a prestigious record store with an important connection to The Beatles' eventual success story.

LOCATION 203: 363-367 Oxford Street, postcode W1C 2LA

Where The Beatles set up shop

W1 THE APPLE BOUTIQUE ON BAKER STREET

The Beatles' well-intended but ultimately unsuccessful adventure into retail marketing opened in December 1967. The exterior of their clothes and fashion shop represented the optimism of the time, with a building-wide psychedelic landscape painted by Dutch artists The Fool. Months later, at the bureaucratic insistence of local councillors, the building was whitewashed over, heralding the end of this altruistic folly. Having lost money virtually since it opened, The Beatles decided to close the store in July 1968 and give away the remaining stock, although they craftily spent a night or two beforehand helping themselves to some of the finer items. Once the shop had finally closed, ever the opportunist, Paul McCartney wrote the title of their forthcoming single 'Hey Jude' in the whitewashed shop windows. Look out for the building's blue plaque which, strangely, namechecks only John Lennon.

LOCATION 204: 94 Baker Street, at the junction with Paddington Street, postcode W1U 6FZ. The building is currently occupied by an employment agency

West London

WC1 SEX PISTOLS DEBUT AT ST MARTINS COLLEGE OF ART

If St Martins wasn't exactly the place where UK punk was born, it was certainly where the Sex Pistols launched their bid to get noticed. Here, after lugging their equipment on foot from their nearby base in Denmark Street, they played their first gig, which lasted no longer than 20 minutes. The raucous debut on November 6th 1975 ended in chaos when, legend has it, they literally had the plug pulled on them by St Martins student Stuart Goddard, who, years later, would transform himself into Adam Ant. Other former St Martins students who made a name for themselves in music include Jarvis Cocker, Polly Jean Harvey, Sade, Shane MacGowan, Clash members Joe Strummer, Paul Simonon and Mick Jones, Bonzo Dog Doo-Dah men Vivian Stanshall and Neil Innes and Sex Pistol Glen Matlock.

❝I would like to say that punk started when we did our first show at St Martins School of Art. I don't know if that's quite true or not, but we certainly put the cat among the pigeons. Remember, this was a good year before any other bands were really playing around. ❞
Glen Matlock

LOCATION 205: the 7th floor of the Central Saint Martins College of Art & Design, 107 Charing Cross Road, postcode WC1B 4AP

Glen Matlock with a copy of the plaque that sits above the security desk at St Martins

W1 HENDRIX BLOWS THE AUDIENCE AWAY AT THE BAG O' NAILS

The dramatic rise in popularity of Jimi Hendrix can be traced back to a significant performance in Kingly Street

Having made his UK public debut in October at the nearby Scotch of St James, Jimi Hendrix (now billed as The Jimi Hendrix Experience) literally blew some of his audience away on November 25th 1966 at a special reception for inquisitive musicians and journalists. At the showcase gig for the new group, some of the audience fled the tiny Bag O' Nails club battered by the trio's high-volume performance. Among those present who stayed to witness a hugely significant gig were The Beatles, The Who and Donovan. That night, The Jimi Hendrix Experience enjoyed a promotion push generated by thrilled musicians' word-of-mouth recommendations and an interview with Record Mirror. By the end of the following month, The Jimi Hendrix Experience were a national TV curiosity, as seen on Ready Steady Go! and Top Of The Pops, interviewed by Radio Caroline and courting contract offers from the likes of Who management duo Chris Stamp and Kit Lambert. The Bag O' Nails was also a favourite after-hours Beatles haunt and the place where Paul McCartney met his future wife Linda at a Georgie Fame gig in May 1967. The young photographer Linda Eastman was in the UK from the US checking out the London rock scene. Elsewhere in Kingly Street, look out for the former studio and darkroom at Picture Story Publications Ltd at No.21, where The Beatles posed for a photo session with Fiona Adams behind the camera. No.62 was once La Valbonne, another nightclub frequented by the Fab Four.

LOCATION 206: 9 Kingly Street, Soho, postcode W1B 5PH

Greater London

W1 CARNABY STREET: SMALL FACES FASHION AND FANCLUB

The epicentre of the swinging Sixties, Carnaby Street was more specifically the hub of the Mod movement's universe, a fact still evident today judging by the target iconography, scooters and parkers on display. The street became a new base for London's rag trade out of necessity when World War II bombs destroyed much of the East End's tailoring businesses. Those most fashionable of Mods, The Small Faces, were managed from an office in Carnaby Street by the highly efficient and some would say down right frightening larger-than-life character Don Arden. From this base, Arden would pay the band in clothes tokens for the local boutiques and shops rather than actual cash. The office was also the home of

The Small Faces' fanclub, where sacks of mail would arrive containing requests for signed photos, offers of marriage, a variety of gifts and, on one occasion, a dog. In 2007, the band's drummer, Kenney Jones, unveiled a plaque at the building where Don Arden and The Small Faces worked.

❝Our office was above a shop called John Stephens. There was John Stephens, Lord John, a shoe shop called Toppers. We had accounts in the shops down there and so we spent a lot of money on shirts. In other words, that's how we got our money, because we couldn't get it any other way, so we became fashion gurus walking about in the latest togs.❞ Kenney Jones

LOCATION 207: currently a Puma store at the southern end of Carnaby Street (Nos.52-54), postcode W1F 9QD

The plaque reads:

CITY OF WESTMINSTER
IMPRESARIO
DON ARDEN
AND MOD BAND
"SMALL FACES"
(STEVE MARRIOTT, RONNIE LANE, KENNEY JONES, IAN MCLAGAN AND JIMMY WINSTON)
WORKED HERE
1965-1967

W1 THE BEATLES LAST STAND ON THE SAVILE ROW ROOFTOP

The Beatles, as a public unified band, ended on the January 30th 1969 with an extraordinary lunchtime concert on the rooftop of their Apple HQ at Savile Row. Paul McCartney had worked at trying to reinvigorate the band by getting them to play to a live audience. The filmed rehearsals in the cold, cavernous Twickenham film studios had stretched them to bad-tempered breaking point. Lennon remained exasperatingly uncommunicative, Harrison was frustrated at the lack of attention given to his songs and the usually affable Starr was impatient to get the project out of the way so that he could start on his movie, The Magic Christian. Decamping to the new Apple Studios in the basement of their Savile Row HQ, they had at least managed some semblance of rehearsing, but a location for the live show could not be agreed. The Roundhouse, the Royal Albert Hall, The Cavern and even makeshift stages in India or Africa were all discussed and dismissed until, with overall interest in

the project waning, they all agreed to play up on the roof of the central London building. On that bitterly cold winter's lunchtime, The Beatles, plus Billy Preston, assembled on the roof and ran through their repertoire of new songs, including 'Don't Let Me Down' and 'I've Got A Feeling', plus an oldie from 1962, 'One After 909'. A local bank manager objected to the noise and disruption and called in the police to stop the gig. Fears that they might be dragged from the stage and arrested came to nothing. The police merely asked them to turn their amps down. It was left to Lennon, at the end of their last run-through of 'Get Back', at the end of their last ever public live performance, to turn to the onlookers, assembled on adjacent rooftops and swarming below in Savile Row, and announce, "I'd like to say thank you on behalf of the group and ourselves and I hope we passed the audition."

LOCATION208: 3 Savile Row, postcode W1S 3

The famous Savile Row offices and rooftop today

W1 (WHAT'S THE STORY) BERWICK STREET?

The Oasis best-selling album (What's The Story) Morning Glory? features a cover shot of radio DJ Sean Rowley and the album's producer Owen Morris passing each other in an otherwise deserted Berwick Street. So, the cover doesn't picture either of the Gallagher brothers, as some people originally thought. However, the Soho street, which was once a mecca for fans of independent record shop browsing, coincidentally joins the aptly-named Noel Street.

LOCATION 209: Berwick Street, Soho, postcode W1F

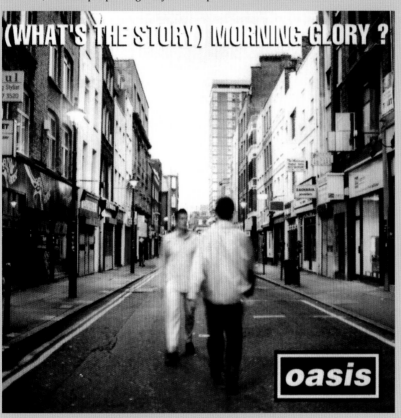

No Gallaghers: Berwick Street, as pictured on the UK's third best-selling album

W1 GERRY RAFFERTY'S 'BAKER STREET'

Gerry Rafferty's biggest hit was a biographical song recalling his days spent busking in the capital. Rafferty would stay in a friend's flat off Baker Street when visiting London from his home in Scotland and the homesick song was written as a joyous end to a period of isolation from releasing music following legal problems when a member of Stealers Wheel.

LOCATION 210: Baker Street tube station, postcode W1U 6SF

W1 THE BEATLES AT THE PALLADIUM AND BRIAN EPSTEIN'S LONDON OFFICE

Argyll Street's Palladium theatre hosted three concerts by The Beatles between 1963 and 1964. Most memorable was their appearance on the hugely popular weekly TV show, Val Parnell's Sunday Night at the London Palladium. Broadcast nationwide on October 13th 1963 at a time when, in the UK, there were only two television channels, this performance was a pivotal point in their career. This enabled their by now well-honed act to be broadcast into millions of homes for maximum impact. Reporting on the Palladium performance the following day, newspapers printed "Beatlemania!" headlines and pictured the crowds of screaming girls who caused chaos on the pavements outside. Across Argyll Street from the Palladium at No.s 5-6 is the office block where Beatles manager Brian Epstein held court. His North End Music Stores (NEMS) HQ office was set up here in 1964 after a brief spell in Covent Garden. Argyll Street provided a more convenient central venue for The Beatles and other artists belonging to the Epstein management stable. Once the business base had shifted from Liverpool to London, press interviews and management of The Beatles, Cilla Black, Gerry and The Pacemakers and Billy J. Kramer and The Dakotas were taken care of here in Argyll Street.

LOCATIONS 211 and 212: Argyll Street, Oxford Circus, postcode W1F 7TF

Greater London

W1 SKIFFLE IS BORN AND CLIFF FINDS TWO SHADOWS AT THE 2i's

The 2i's Coffee Bar in Old Compton Street billed itself as the 'home of the stars'. Musicians Hank Marvin, Joe Brown, Tommy Steele, Bruce Welch, Cliff Richard and Adam Faith were all fans and performers at the centre of a new youth movement. Professional wrestler Paul Lincoln ran the 2i's, which encouraged the new breed of Fifties teenagers to enjoy whooshing frothy coffee at Formica tables and skiffle music in the cramped basement. Skiffle found a home at the 2i's thanks to Wally Whyton's request to the owners for a place to 'busk' for his group The Vipers. Business at the coffee bar had been poor but The Vipers regular performances began to create the packed atmosphere where regular fans, musicians and agents made it the place to be seen, perform and do business. Back in early 1958, Harry Webb, Norman Mitcham and Terry Smart were three school friends looking for bookings. Billed as The Drifters, acting manager John Foster sensed the potential evident in singer Webb (Cliff Richard) and managed a booking for the Hertfordshire trio at the 2i's. Mitcham and Smart were enthusiastic amateurs but lacked the charisma of singer Webb, who was soon grabbing rave notices on Jack Good's Oh Boy! TV show. By 1959, and with a national tour looming, the search for more accomplished musicians by Foster bore fruit on another visit to the 2i's. Cliff recalled, "He came back from the 2i's club and said, 'I've found a guitarist. He plays like James Burton who played for Ricky Nelson and ultimately ended up playing for Elvis and he looks like Buddy Holly. And, he's got a friend.' So, Bruce Welch and Hank Marvin came home and we sang and played together. It was obvious we were going to click so I asked them to join me." Welch and Marvin, who in addition to performing at the club also worked behind the bar serving the customers orange juice, were soon joined by Jet Harris and Tony Meehan and the newly-named Shadows line-up was complete.

Where it all began: commemorated by this plaque, the 2i's' downstairs performance area is now a storage area for the bar and restaurant that currently occupies No.59 on this still vibrant Soho street

SITE OF THE 2i's COFFEE BAR (1956-1970) BIRTHPLACE OF BRITISH ROCK 'N ROLL AND THE POPULAR MUSIC INDUSTRY — CITY OF WESTMINSTER — ROBERT MANDRY

❛In 1958 the 2i's was the fuse for the explosion that was to come in the world of UK rock 'n' roll. It was just a little cafe with an old battered piano in the basement in Old Compton Street. But it had a soul and a buzz. ❜
Guitarist Joe Moretti

LOCATION 213: the 2i's is currently the Boulevard Bar & Dining Room, 59 Old Compton Street, Soho, postcode W1D 6HR

W1 WHEN HARRY BECAME CLIFF AT THE SWISS TAVERN

A short walk from the site of the 2i's Coffee Bar was the Swiss Tavern (now Comptons), the pub where in 1958 a young singer entered named Harry Webb and left as Cliff Richard. Harry Greatorex, who ran a ballroom in Ripley, Derbyshire, was on a scouting mission in London at the 2i's Coffee Bar and wanted to book Harry Webb and The Drifters, but the young Harry was adamant that the posters must advertise just "The Drifters". Greatorex insisted that he had to have an Elvis or Jerry Lee Lewis type of name up front to promote the act, so the band set about thinking one up.

❛We went to a little pub round the corner, ordered a shandy, sat down and thought of names. The last combination of names was Russ Clifford [then] Cliff Russard. I thought, wait a minute, forget Russard – Cliff, (rock face!), then we got to Cliff Richards with an 's' on the end and then Ian Samwell, who wrote 'Move It!' for me said, 'Take the 's' off. That means you've got two Christian names - Cliff Richard – and it could be a tribute to Little Richard.' And that's how it came about. I thought, that sounds good - "Cliff Richard and The Drifters". Then of course we changed Drifters to Shadows. The 'd' I think was important. The 'd' of Richard, the 'D' of Drifters and the 'd' of Shadows. There was a link and it was rhythmical. ❜
Cliff Richard

LOCATION 214: Comptons, 51-53 Old Compton Street, Soho, postcode W1D 6HN

The pub where Harry became Cliff

W1 THE MEMORIAL TO KIRSTY MACCOLL

Soho Square is the fitting location of a memorial to singer-songwriter Kirsty MacColl, who died tragically in Mexico in 2000. A ceremony when a bench was unveiled in her memory was witnessed by 150 family, friends and fans, accompanied by a broadcast of her song 'Soho Square', from the 1993 album Titanic Days, in which MacColl sang about shivering pigeons, naked trees and 'an empty bench in Soho Square'.

LOCATION 215: the bench and plaque can be found at the southern end of Soho Square, postcode W1D

Kirsty MacColl
1959 – 2000
"One day I'll be Waiting There.
No Empty Bench in Soho Square"

Kirsty's 'empty bench' in Soho Square

Martin Downham

W1 KEITH MOON REMEMBERED AT THE MARQUEE

Owned by Harold Pendleton and based at 165 Oxford Street, The Marquee was said to have been the first venue where a London audience saw an electric guitar. This seminal moment occurred in 1958 when Pendleton and Chris Barber tracked down US bluesman Muddy Waters and brought him to the former Marquee ballroom, in a cinema basement. In the Sixties it was Pendleton who introduced the predominantly jazz-based audiences to the music of the new British R&B movement, featuring the genre's innovators Alexis Korner and Cyril Davies (Blues Incorporated). Young R&B band The Rolling Stones made their Marquee debut supporting Davies, and by 1964 the venue had moved to Wardour Street where the likes of The Who and The Yardbirds became fixtures. Progressive and punk sounds found a home at the

club before yet another move to 105-107 Charing Cross Road until 1995, when the name vanished. Years later The Marquee reappeared, launched at the Islington Academy (16 Parkfield Street) in 2002, and between 2004 and 2005 Leicester Square was its home. What appears to be the absolute end came following a short period at 14 Upper St Martin's Lane on February 12th 2008. A plaque remembering Keith Moon at the best known Marquee location in Wardour Street is all that remains of one of Britain's best-loved music brands. The Who drummer, who

CITY OF WESTMINSTER

KEITH MOON
1946 - 1978

LEGENDARY ROCK DRUMMER
WITH 'THE WHO'

PERFORMED HERE AT
THE SITE OF THE
MARQUEE CLUB
IN THE 1960s

THE HERITAGE FOUNDATION

Keith Moon's plaque marks the position of the world famous Marquee

died in 1978, was honoured at the plaques' unveiling in 2009, an event attended by his 88-year-old mother and Roger Daltrey.

❝I used to go to the Marquee three or four times a week. I was always at the front of the queue because I went straight from school. I went so often that the management got to know me. They invited me in and I used to sweep the floor and put the chairs out before the audience arrived.❞

Phil Collins, interviewed by Johnny Black for Music Week

LOCATION 216: the Marquee commemorative plaque is at 90 Wardour Street, Soho, postcode W1F 0. Website: www. themarqueeclub.com

Greater London

W1 ZIGGY IN HEDDON STREET

The subject of a recent renovation as an area of pavement eateries, Heddon Street is famously the spot where David Bowie was photographed for his Ziggy Stardust And The Spiders From Mars album cover. Although the prominent illuminated 'K. West' sign and the back cover original red telephone box are long gone, the street has changed little and a replacement phone box has been installed for those Bowie pilgrims wishing to emulate his back cover pose. Bowie's 'motivation' for photographer Brian Ward's cover shoot that wet night in January 1971 was to carry off a look inspired by characters from A Clockwork Orange and William S. Burroughs' The Wild Boys. The colour-tinted front cover picture was nearer to an alien landing in London and remains one of the most powerful ever rock 'n' roll images, selected for the series of British album cover designs reproduced on Royal Mail postage stamps in 2010.

Although the K. West sign was removed and auctioned as a valuable item of memorabilia, Heddon Street at night still retains that Ziggy Stardust vibe

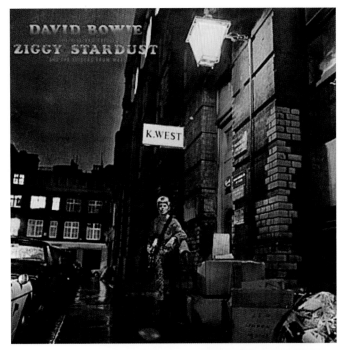

Heddon Street in 2011, and the Bowie phone box still attract Bowie fans keen to recreate the Ziggy Stardust album back cover pose

Martin Downham

LOCATIONS 217 and **218:** Ziggy Stardust front cover: 23 Heddon Street; back cover: the Heddon Street alleyway, postcode W1B 4BQ

W1 TOMMY ROCKING AT RONNIE SCOTT'S

East London-born Ronald Schatt later changed his name to Ronnie Scott, and with the help of fellow sax-playing friend Pete King opened his first jazz club at 39 Gerrard Street in 1959. The former tea bar was the perfect refuge for like-minded fans of American jazz. But by the 60s the club moved to larger premises at 47

Frith Street, where rock acts appeared in addition to the jazz legends who had helped make it the coolest place to play in London. Special Ronnie Scott's nights included the premiere of rock opera Tommy by The Who, an appearance by Jimi Hendrix days before his death and a debut showcase by the much vaunted

Humble Pie. The smaller venue within a venue, Upstairs at Ronnie's, also played host to a stream of hopefuls including Soft Machine, The Jam and XTC.

LOCATION 219: in 1965, Ronnie Scott's moved to 47 Frith Street, Soho, postcode W1D 4HT

W1 PILL POPPING TO THE LATEST R&B SOUNDS AT THE FLAMINGO

Early Sixties London clubs, previously set up for jazz fans, grudgingly allowed the new R&B acts a session or two. The Flamingo Club in Wardour Street was a good example, with its famous all-nighters. Georgie Fame and The Blue Flames were at the forefront of acts who were now incorporating soul, bluebeat and pop style sounds into the jazz they had been playing since the mid-Fifties. Fame's own British take on R&B had been accelerated by his switch from piano to Hammond organ, backed up by The Blue Flames' powerful rhythm base of saxophone, guitar and congas. Now dancing to this music through to dawn, Flamingo Club-goers kept their energy levels up by amphetamine pill-popping and the relatively new British craze for drinking Coca-Cola and scoffing American-style hot-dogs.

❛I would come out of the Flamingo at 4 o'clock in the morning after a night of watching bands when I couldn't take the heat anymore and I had to get some air. As I was leaving John Mayall would be coming in carrying his keyboard on his shoulders down into the depths to set up. ❜ Eric Burdon

LOCATION 220 33-37 Wardour Street, Soho, postcode W1F 0

Georgie Fame was a regular at Nos.33-37 Wardour Street

W1 MAYFAIR AUDITION SEEKING SPICE GIRLS

Danceworks Studios in Mayfair was the setting for the auditions to recruit four talented singers/dancers that would become the Spice Girls. From 11am to 5.30pm on March 4th 1993, a conveyorbelt of 400 hopefuls strutted their stuff. Among their number on that first day were eventual Spice Girls Victoria Adams, Melanie Brown and Melanie Chisholm.

❛WANTED: R. U. 18-23 with the ability to sing/dance? R U streetwise, outgoing, ambitious and dedicated? ❜ Heart Management advertisement in The Stage newspaper

LOCATION 221: 16 Balderton Street, Mayfair, postcode W1K 6TN

W1 LES COUSINS IN GREEK STREET

Martin Downham

The former home of Les Cousins

The oddly named Les Cousins Club was formerly a skiffle hang-out before opening as a folk and blues venue in 1965. The owner wasn't called Les Cousins: indeed, Les Cousins wasn't a person at all, the club being appropriately named after the naive country boy in the 1959 French movie Les Cousins who moved to the city under the influence of his decadent cousin. Resident performers were British R&B guru Alexis Korner and folk singer-songwriter Roy Harper, who recorded his 1969 live album here. The club was briefly re-opened in 2004 for a special tribute concert to Nick Drake.

LOCATION 222: 49 Greek Street, Soho, postcode W1D 4EG

Greater London

W1 JOHN, PAUL, JIMI AND RINGO AT MONTAGU SQUARE

The English Heritage blue plaque on the wall of 34 Montagu Square indicates only a small proportion of the rock history associated with this ground-floor and basement flat. The plaque unveiled by Yoko Ono in 2010 informs that John Lennon lived there in 1968 but understates this regency house's important role in the lives of three other rock legends. The first home that John and Yoko shared together, it was here that the two were photographed naked for the couple's Two Virgins album cover and Lennon worked on material for The Beatles' White Album. The capital's most celebrated rock and pop residence began its colourful history in 1965 when Flat No.1 at No.34 was purchased and lived in by Ringo Starr and wife Maureen. Needing more space with the arrival of son Zak, the Starrs soon vacated Montagu Square and Paul McCartney moved in during 1966, utilising the basement as a recording studio and worked on, among other things, 'Eleanor Rigby'. The next tenant, later that same year, was Jimi Hendrix, who set up home in the basement with girlfriend Kathy Etchingham and his manager Chas Chandler, who, along with his girlfriend Lotta, took the first floor. Here Hendrix formed The Experience and wrote at least one classic hit, 'The Wind Cries Mary', and in a less productive mood reportedly threw paint at the walls during an acid trip. This led owner/landlord Ringo to re-decorate the place with white interiors throughout, a look that prevails to this day. After Hendrix moved to nearby Brook Street, in came John and Yoko before Ringo eventually sold up in 1969. The most desirable rock 'n' roll pad in London has attracted many tourist visitors down the years and at least one would-be rock star purchaser in Noel Gallagher, who was thwarted in his plans to buy in 2001.

❝People from all corners of the world will come to London and see this plaque with love for John and the memory of what he was.❞
Yoko Ono at the plaque unveiling in 2010

LOCATION 223: 34 Montagu Square is a private residence, postcode W1H 2LJ

London's most celebrated rock 'n' roll residence and the plaque at No.34

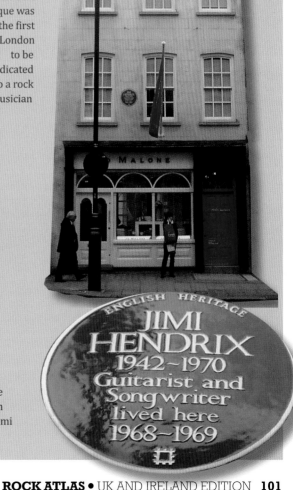

W1 HENDRIX AND HANDEL: 'NEIGHBOURS' IN BROOK STREET

A blue plaque on the wall at 23 Brook Street marks the former home of Jimi Hendrix, where the guitarist lived on and off between 1968 and 1969. Unveiled by Pete Townshend in 1997, the plaque sits next door to another at No.25, where, two-hundred years earlier, the composer Handel once lived. Handily placed, it was little more than a ten-minute walk across Regent Street and into Soho for Hendrix to relax or jam at The Bag O Nails or head north of Oxford Street to the Speakeasy.

The first-floor flat where Jimi Hendrix lived with girlfriend Kathy Etchingham. The blue plaque was the first in London to be dedicated to a rock musician

LOCATION 224: 23 Brook Street, postcode W1K 4HA

Kathy Etchingham's biography describes the time spent sharing the Brook Street flat with the variously shy, wild, free spirit that was Jimi Hendrix

Greater London

THE BEE GEES
BARRY, ROBIN & MAURICE GIBB
COMPOSED AND STAYED HERE
1968-1980
CITY OF WESTMINSTER
THE HERITAGE FOUNDATION

W1 THE BEE GEES' LONDON BASE

Bee Gees manager and producer Robert Stigwood's Brook Street home was the base for all the band's significant activities from 1968 to 1980. During this 12-year period at Brook Street the trio composed songs, took care of Bee Gees business and first met John Travolta, the star of Saturday Night Fever, the movie that re-ignited the Gibb brothers' astonishing career as disco superstars. The house carries a green plaque, which was unveiled by Robin Gibb in 2008.

Bee Gees base: Robert Stigwood's former organisation HQ

LOCATION 225: 67 Brook Street, postcode W1K 4NJ

W1 WORLD'S FIRST HARD ROCK

An ideal stop on any tour of London's rock locations, this Hard Rock Café was the original and first of 150 (and counting) Hard Rock's to open back in 1971. Famous for food and rock memorabilia, the original restaurant has created its own niche in music history and still houses Eric Clapton's Lead II Fender guitar, the first ever item of memorabilia donated to the chain. Also on display: Pete Townshend's Gibson Les Paul guitar, Mitch Mitchell's Jimi Hendrix Experience black Gretsch drum kit and Adam Clayton's Fender Telecaster bass.

LOCATION 226: 150 Old Park Lane, postcode W1K 1QZ

W1 THE STONES, BLUR, LIVE8 AND JAMES TAYLOR AT HYDE PARK

At 2.30pm precisely on Friday June 13th 1969 the bandstand at the south-east corner of Hyde Park was the venue for an unconventional photocall. "Mick, Keith, Bill and Charlie invite you to meet their new guitarist" read the invitation to the press. Joining The Rolling Stones that day was Welwyn Garden City-born Mick Taylor. The former John Mayall's Bluesbreakers guitarist's arrival in the Stones was a PR masterstroke, on a par with the signing of a star footballer. The event preceded the famous Stones in the park free concert, when the band remembered the recently deceased founding member Brian Jones, found dead in his Cotchford Farm swimming pool 22 days earlier. However, it was The Pink Floyd, Jethro Tull, Roy Harper and Tyrannosaurus Rex who first started the tradition of playing free in Hyde Park when their June 29th 1968 event kicked-off proceedings. Major concert events, sadly no longer 'free', have been frequent

down the decades. Recent highlights include Live8 (2006) and the reformation of Blur (2009). On a somewhat smaller scale, Hyde Park has always had its fair share of buskers, none more celebrated than the newly signed Apple label artist James Taylor back in 1968. In between Beatles recording breaks on The White Album, the young American singer-songwriter used the downtime to record his debut album. And, with no time for gigging and rent to pay, Taylor would make the journey from his temporary home in Earls Court to busk in the Hyde Park subway.

❛ There was this underground passage by Hyde Park where people liked to play, because the echo was good. You couldn't walk across the street there, so people had no choice but to come past you.❜
James Taylor

LOCATION 227: west of Park Lane, postcode W1

W2 STIFF AND BLACKHILL AT ALEXANDER STREET

This Bayswater address was the HQ for Stiff Records, where the business side of things was overseen by Jake Riviera and Dave Robinson. Through this door passed Elvis Costello, Nick Lowe, Ian Dury, Madness and The Pogues en route to their meteoric rise to critical acclaim in the late-Seventies new wave era. With the punk and new wave scenes unsettling the old order of progressive rock, it was perhaps symbolic that the Stiff premises had once been the home of Pink Floyd's Roger Waters. Blackhill Enterprises, who looked after Floyd's interests, had also been based at No.32, which makes this tiny portal with managed artists Marc Bolan, Kevin Ayers, The Clash and Roy Harper a veritable music business hotbed. It was from these offices that Blackhill Enterprises organised the early free Hyde Park music festivals starring the likes of Blind Faith.

Stiff one: the first Stiff single - 'So It Goes' by Nick Lowe

LOCATION 228: Stiff Records was at 32 Alexander Street, which is now Gallery 32, postcode W2 5NU

W2 CROSBY, STILLS & NASH'S BAYSWATER HIDEAWAY

In November 1968, Californian David Crosby, Texan Stephen Stills and Lancashire's Graham Nash departed the US West Coast vibe of Laurel Canyon for the cold winter of London's Bayswater. Mixing Everly Brothers-style harmonies with lyrics as insightful as anything Dylan was producing at the time, the three decamped to a top-floor flat on Moscow Road to rehearse material for their first album. Amid the joint-smoking fog of creativity, the place soon became open house for journalists and inquisitive record company types. Visitors who heard CSN play live, acoustic and as yet unrecorded versions of 'Marrakesh Express' and 'Suite: Judy Blue Eyes' included George Harrison, who surprisingly declined to sign them for Apple. Ironically, once signed to Atlantic and back in the US, some in the music press soon began describing CSN as "America's answer to The Beatles".

❛All Joints Must Be Re-Weighed At Time Of Purchase.❜ The sign in the window of the flat on Moscow Road, stolen from a local Bayswater butcher's shop by David Crosby

LOCATION 229: 16 Moscow Road is the unconfirmed address, near the junction with Salem Road, postcode W2 4BT

W1 HOWLIN' WOLF AND HIS ALL-STAR BAND AT PICCADILLY CIRCUS

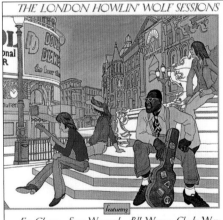

Howlin' Wolf and his band of famous fans at the statue of Eros

In Spring 1970, revered American bluesman Howlin' Wolf visited London to record a super session album with a bunch of his UK fans. Those fans included Eric Clapton, Steve Winwood, Bill Wyman and Charlie Watts. The cover for the resulting album of recordings at Olympic Studios was released in 1971, carrying artwork depicting the all-star band on the steps of the statue of Eros in Piccadilly Circus.

LOCATION 230: statue of Eros, Piccadilly Circus, postcode W1J 9EY

WC2 TIN PAN ALLEY ON DENMARK STREET

London's equivalent of the original New York City-based Tin Pan Alley is stuffed with music history. Musicians and fans still get a buzz and a tingle of nostalgia wandering down the street where instrument shops and offices look much as they did back in the post-war period when songwriters and publishers set up shop. At various times, Denmark Street has seen the recording of the first Rolling Stones album at No.4 (Regent Sounds Studio), the launch of the New Musical Express at No.5, the address where both the Sex Pistols and The Clash made their base at No.6, the launch of Melody Maker at No.19, Mills Music where Elton John once worked as a £5-a-week office boy at No.20, and the street's only remaining recording facility, Tin Pan Alley Studio, at No.22.

LOCATION231: Denmark Street, postcode WC2H

The studio (walls insulated by egg cartons as Keith Richards recalls) where The Stones recorded their debut album over five days in January 1964

Every musician visiting London can't resist a spot of window shopping in Denmark Street

WC2 THE MONMOUTH STREET HOME OF THE BEATLES' FAN CLUB

When Beatles manager Brian Epstein moved his business HQ down from Liverpool, he relocated the centre of his NEMS organisation to this trendy street near Seven Dials, Covent Garden. His arrival here in 1963 created a massive increase in work for the local postal service, as this became the address of the group's fan club at the start of Beatlemania. In 2010, a plaque marking this spot was unveiled by Cilla Black, another of Epstein's management stable of stars.

LOCATION232: at 13 Monmouth Street, postcode WC2H 8

WC2 THE BLITZ CLUB

Originally centred around a few dozen extraordinarily flamboyant art students, mostly from St Martins, a new movement developed its identity at the Blitz Club near Holborn tube station. Three key characters were the pioneers-in-chief of the New Romantic fashion and music explosion based at this former World War II wine bar. Taking care of the Blitz cloakroom was a young Boy George, DJ duties were handled by Rusty Egan and Steve Strange played the host with, at his discretion, only those weird or wonderful enough permitted entry.

LOCATION 233: 4 Great Queen Street, Holborn, postcode WC2B 5DG

Martin Downham

W4 THE BEATLES FILM SET AT STRAND-ON-THE-GREEN

A running theme of The Beatles' second movie Help! was the pursuit of Ringo Starr, who at one point is chased down Post Office Alley and into the City Barge pub on one of the most picturesque stretches of the Thames' London embankment. The scene involving all four Beatles in and around this location at Strand-on-the-Green climaxes with Ringo's encounter with a fully-grown tiger in the pub's basement. Scenes inside the pub were shot in the studio.

Strand-on-the-Green: a Beatles Help! location

LOCATIONS 234 and 235: The City Barge, 27 Strand-on-the-Green, and Post Office Alley, postcode W4 3PH

W8 & W14 QUEEN'S KENSINGTON MILE

A trio of Queen locations can be visited within a one-mile stretch of Kensington. For the key place of pilgrimage, head for the green door at Logan Place, which is covered in messages from around the world remembering that this is the place where Freddie Mercury lived, then tragically died, in 1991. A convenient short walk will take you to an important pub in Queen band history. The Kensington was the Queen local where Freddie Mercury met Brian May and Roger Taylor and would often hold meetings to talk Queen business over a drink or two. Dr Feelgood enjoyed a lengthy residency here at the height of pub rock mania. Nearby is the first-floor building where Freddie and Roger both sold the latest fashions in the early Seventies at Kensington Market. The market building has been demolished but the flat once shared by all the group in Sinclair Road, Kensington, still stands.

LOCATIONS 236, 237 and 238: Freddie's former home is at Garden Lodge, 1 Logan Place, Kensington, postcode W8 6QN. The Queen flat is at 36 Sinclair Road, postcode W14 0NH. Both these addresses are private residences. The Kensington pub is at 54 Russell Gardens, postcode W14 8EZ

WC2 DYLAN'S SUBTERRANEAN HOMESICK BLUES AT THE SAVOY HOTEL

Immortalised in D. A. Pennebaker's movie Don't Look Back a sequence filmed in an alley close to the Savoy hotel has become one of the all-time great music videos. When Bob Dylan visited London in the spring of 1965 he stayed at the Savoy. On May 8 he left his hotel suite with Pennebaker and friends, American singer-songwriter Bob Neuwirth and US beat poet Allen Ginsberg, and headed for the back streets behind the Savoy, taking a set of handwritten cue cards to accompany the lyrics to 'Subterranean Homesick Blues'. At the entrance to Savoy Steps instead of miming to the song he captioned key words and phrases from the lyrics as the camera rolled with the cue cards earlier painted by Dylan, girlfriend Joan Baez and his new British friends Alan Price and Donovan. At his Savoy suite, a day after the 'Subterranean Homesick Blues' shoot, Dylan met Donovan again and all four Beatles (in London filming Help!), who brought along Alma Cogan.

LOCATION 239: little has changed since the shooting of the memorable promotional film in 1965. The exact spot, where Dylan performed his much-copied inventive cue-card routine, is at the entrance to Savoy Steps (position yourself with your back to Savoy Hill), postcode WC2R 0

Greater London

W8 BILL WYMAN'S STICKY FINGERS

The American-style restaurant opened by owner Bill Wyman in 1989 was named after the Rolling Stones album released 18 years earlier. The walls of Sticky Fingers are crammed full with rock memorabilia from the bass guitarist's collection.

LOCATION 240: 1A Phillimore Gardens, Kensington, postcode W8 7QG. Website: www. stickyfingers.co.uk

Former Stone Bill Wyman at his Kensington rock restaurant

W8 DUSTY SPRINGFIELD'S KENSINGTON HOME

The house in Aubrey Walk was where Dusty Springfield lived from 1968 until she relocated to the USA in 1972. Two years after the singer's death in 1999, a plaque was unveiled on the front wall in memory of what many music fans would regard as Britain's most talented and charismatic female singer. Following rebuilding work, a second plaque was unveiled in 2011.

LOCATION 241: 38 Aubrey Walk, postcode W8 7JG. Status: private residence

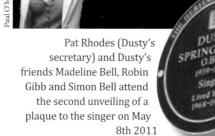

Paul O'Mara

Pat Rhodes (Dusty's secretary) and Dusty's friends Madeline Bell, Robin Gibb and Simon Bell attend the second unveiling of a plaque to the singer on May 8th 2011

W12 TOWNSHEND'S WHITE CITY

In 1985, The Who's Pete Townshend released White City: A Novel, which was actually an album about this area in West London where the White City Stadium (venue for London's 1908 Olympic Games) once stood. The demolition of the stadium was the subject of a song ('White City') written by Shane MacGowan for The Pogues' 1989 album Peace And Love.

LOCATION 242: White City, postcode W12 7TS

W2 KULA SHAKER'S PETER PAN PILGRIMAGE

Kula Shaker's 2010 album Pilgrims Progress features Kensington Gardens' famous Peter Pan statue on the cover. The band's video for the album's first single, 'Peter Pan (R.I.P)' was also shot in the royal park.

LOCATION 243: enter Kensington Gardens from the north side Bayswater Road entrance, near Lancaster Gate tube station. Postcode: W2 2UE

Kula Shaker's fourth album release, covered by Peter Pan

W10 WESTWAY FLYOVER: A KISS, CLASH AND JAM

The Westway flyover is hardly as evocative an inspiration to song-writers as Route 66 or the New Jersey Turnpike, but this stark, functional, elevated carriageway has not been lost on Britain's grittier bands. The Clash were, it would seem, most lyrically and photographically attached to it. The Westway gets a starring role in 'London's Burning', features in the title of the band's documentary movie Westway To The World and is pictured on the cover of their 1999 live album From Here To Eternity. Others to share their fascination for the massive escape route out of the capital include The Jam, whose 1977 album cover This Is The Modern World pictures the trio looking all smart casual in the structure's shadows, Bloc Party, who use an aerial view on their 2007 album A Weekend In The City, and Blur, The Pretty Things and Pete Doherty, who each weave the Westway into their song lyrics. A photograph shot here by Jimmy Page's daughter Scarlet was dominated by the apparently 'wasted' model Lucy Joplin, on the receiving end of a full-on kiss by a male model at a football pitch under the Westway which provided the cover image for the Stereophonics' No.1 album Performance And Cocktails.

LOCATION 244: Westway flyover, postcode W10

TW2 ALAN FREEMAN'S HERITAGE FOUNDATION PLAQUE

A blue plaque unveiled in the presence of Robin Gibb and Rick Wakeman marks Australian-born DJ Alan Freeman's final residence at The Brinsworth House retirement home. The much-loved broadcaster, who uniquely combined a knowledgeable enthusiasm for music with a talent for legendary catchphrases, died in 2006.

LOCATION 245: at the private care home, 72 Staines Road, Twickenham, postcode TW2 5AL

W9 BBC MAIDA VALE STUDIOS

When the BBC broadcast live sessions by quest musicians, here is where they have frequently taken place down the years. Most famous of these were the Peel Sessions recorded for John Peel's radio shows from 1967 to 2004. Many of the broadcasts ended up as record releases, a trend kick-started by the Fab Four whose 1994 release The Beatles: Live At The BBC gathered together 69 songs recorded for Light Programme broadcasts from shows such as Top Gear and Saturday Club from 1963 to 1965. There's a small plaque on the wall in Studio 3 which marks Bing Crosby's last recording here on October 11th 1977, and electronic music buffs and sci-fi fans will know that it was at Maida Vale where the BBC Radiophonic Workshop conjured up the theme tune to Dr Who.

LOCATION 246: Delaware Road, postcode W9 2LG

TW1 RINGO STARS AT THE TURK'S HEAD

Twickenham pub The Turks Head was the location used during a scene involving Ringo Starr in The Beatles' first movie A Hard Day's Night in 1964. A popular local with film studio staff at nearby Twickenham Film Studios, the pub was also the venue for the traditional wrap party with cast and crew attending.

LOCATION 247: 28 Winchester Road, Twickenham, postcode TW1 1LF

W9 DUFFY'S 'WARWICK AVENUE'

When Duffy met up with co-writers Eg White and Jimmy Hogarth to finish work on 'Warwick Avenue', she had already completed most of the lyrics. At the time, the subject of the Rockferry album track was a place she had never visited, a name she plucked with no specific reason from a London Underground tube map. The resulting saturation radio play of the spring 2008 smash hit single means few can journey in or out of this station on the Bakerloo Line without recalling the waves Never having visited Warwick Avenue before writing the song, Duffy was quickly snapped for this press shot of defiant emotion from Duffy's tearful back-of-a-taxi-cab video performance, now forever linked to this posh pop location.

LOCATION248: near Little Venice, Paddington, postcode W9 2PT

TW1 STRAWBS LAUNCHED FROM TWICKENHAM

In 1963, a banjo, guitar and mandolin trio, Dave Cousins, Tony Hooper and Arthur Phillips, made their debut in a back room folk club in Clapham. Without a name to call themselves, Dave Cousins quickly rectified the problem by deciding on The Strawberry Hill Boys as band rehearsals were frequently based at Strawberry Hill in Twickenham. A couple of years passed before the band's name morphed with familiarity into The Strawbs, whose frequent line-up and genre changes would establish them as chart stars with massive hits 'Lay Down' and 'Part Of The Union'.

LOCATION 249: Waldegrave Road, Twickenham, postcode TW1 4SX

TW1 HIPPIE HAVEN AND MECCA FOR MUSIC FANS AT EEL PIE ISLAND

Connected to the real world by a slender footbridge, Eel Pie Island is a fantasy island in the River Thames which drew musicians and fans in the Fifties and Sixties to the hotel, which sadly burned to the ground in 1971 and was demolished. The hotel began promoting jazz in the Fifties at a time when the island was bridgeless and gig-goers would ferry across or even swim in some cases. Never the easiest of places to play, even in the Sixties, groups would have to manhandle their amps and instruments over the new tiny pedestrian bridge. Acker Bilk, The Who, The Rolling Stones, The Yardbirds and Rod Stewart all played this unique location during their early careers. The isolated community still has a wind chime resonance that on a sunny summer's day gives off a Laurel Canyon, hippie-style vibe. Although the

The pedestrian-only access to the 550-metre-long island, where first the Eel Pie Island Hotel and later Colonel Barefoot's Rock Garden hosted and entertained musicians and fans in the swinging Sixties

island is liberally sprinkled with arts and crafts studios, The Eel Pie Recording Studios isn't one of them. The currently redundant Pete Townshend-owned recording facility is situated on the mainland on the Thames' south-west bank, downriver of Richmond Lock at The Boathouse, Ranelagh Drive.

LOCATION 250: cross the bridge to Eel Pie Island in the River Thames at Twickenham, postcode TW13DY

TW9 RICHMOND'S CRAWDADDY CLUBS

In 1963, the Crawdaddy club was made famous due to its increasingly popular resident band, The Rolling Stones. This crucial venue in the development of The Stones was perfectly situated for drawing large groups of R&B fans from all over London due to its location opposite Richmond station. This was where The Beatles ventured out to West London for their first opportunity to see The Stones play. The club was named after the Bo Diddley song 'Hey Crawdaddy' or 'Craw Dad', with which The Stones would close their performances. Once they had charted with 'Come On', their fan base began spilling out onto the streets of Richmond and they moved to larger venues, to be replaced at the Crawdaddy by The Yardbirds. The importance of this

key club is underlined by the first major rock magazine in America naming itself Crawdaddy! in 1966. The popularity of the brand name saw a larger live venue take off at Richmond Athletic Ground, where the Richmond Athletic Association's clubhouse and grandstand area presented Crawdaddy performances as R&B groups made way for future rock gods Led Zeppelin and Pink Floyd.

❛My favourite place, looking back, was the Station Hotel, Richmond, just because everything really kicked off from there.❜ Keith Richards reflects in his autobiography, Life

LOCATION 251: formerly the Station Hotel, now The Bull, 1 Kew Road, Richmond, postcode TW9 2NQ

The site of the former Crawdaddy, at what used to be known as the Station Hotel, where large numbers of Stones fans would overflow onto Kew Road

Martin Downham

Greater London

TW10 IAN DURY'S SOLAR-POWERED MUSICAL BENCH

Donated by his family, Ian Dury's extraordinary memorial is tucked away in a quiet garden in Richmond Park. On the face of it, an inscribed park bench in peaceful Poet's Corner would seem an inappropriate way to remember one of pop music's larger than life characters. Closer inspection reveals a large 'Reasons to be Cheerful' carved inscription, but it's the solar-powered arm rests that make the bench special. By plugging in any standard set of headphones, visitors can enjoy a set of Dury's tracks and hear the great man's Desert Island Discs BBC radio interview,

broadcast four years before his death in 2000. The bench's location in Richmond Park marks a favourite place that Dury often visited during his life.

❛My luxury would be a working item... an 8-track home recording studio with a solar panel... that would keep me happy forever.❜ Ian Dury, who would have approved of his solar-powered memorial, chooses his luxury item on Desert Island Discs

LOCATION 252: Poet's Corner, near Pembroke Lodge, Richmond Park, postcode TW10

An Ian Dury fan tunes-in to the great man in Richmond Park

TW10 TWO RONNIES AT THE WICK

When advertised for sale in 1971, The Wick came complete with its own separate cottage, gypsy caravan and gardens sloping down to the River Thames. Currently owned by Pete Townshend, The Wick has 'previous' in rock star home ownership terms. Originally the property of Ronnie Wood,

the guitarist shared the bank-busting purchase, persuading fellow Faces mate Ronnie Lane to buy the cottage at the bottom of the garden. The Wick is where Wood lived and rehearsed his 1974 solo album I've Got My Own Album To Do in the house's purpose-built basement studio. Mick Jagger, Keith Richards, Mick Taylor, George Harrison, Ian McLagan and Rod Stewart all made musical contributions at The Wick studio and no doubt enjoyed a frame or two on Ronnie's snooker table, once owned by the sport's legendary champion Joe Davis.

LOCATION253: Richmond Hill, Richmond, postcode TW10 6RN. Status: private residence

Ronnie, doing his own thing at The Wick

Martin Downham

TW1 BEATLES' HELP! HOUSES IN TWICKENHAM

Although indoor shots of the linked Beatles homes in Help! the movie were filmed at nearby Twickenham Film Studios, the external scenes showing the Fab Four entering each of their individual terraced houses were shot in Ailsa Avenue. For the record, Ringo Starr lived at No.5, John Lennon next door at No.7, Paul McCartney at No.9 and George Harrison at No.11.

LOCATION 254: 5, 7, 9 and 11 Ailsa Avenue, Twickenham, postcode TW1 1NF. Status: private residences

TW13 FREDDIE MERCURY'S STAR

Born in Zanzibar, but less exotic Feltham was where the boy who became Freddie Mercury first made his home in the UK, a fact honoured by the unveiling of a large decorative plaque in November 2009. Freddie's fellow Queen band member and friend Brian May, who also grew up in Feltham, joined Freddie's mother Jer Bulsara to pay tribute to the rock legend, who died in 1991, at the unveiling of the Hollywood-style star imbedded in the pavement of the Centre shopping piazza. More than 2,000 of the singer's fans, together with the local Mayor and Queen tribute band Mercury attended the ceremony. The four years at his family home in Feltham from 1964 to 1968 coincided with his discovery and passion for music, shared with Brian May, who recalled often visiting Freddie at his Gladstone Road home.

❛I grew up in Walsham Avenue about 200 yards from where [Freddie] lived but we never met until later. Freddie invited me around to his house and we sat listening to Jimi Hendrix. ❜ Brian May's teenage memories in Feltham

LOCATION 255: The Centre, Feltham, postcode TW13 4GU

Born in West London

Lily Allen (b. 2 May 1985, Hammersmith)

Adam Ant (b. 3 Nov 1954, Marylebone)

Simon Bartholomew, guitar, The Brand New Heavies (b. 16 Oct 1965, Ealing)

Betty Boo (b. 6 Mar 1970, Kensington)

Keisha Buchanan, Sugababes (30 Sep 1984, Westminster)

Jean-Jacques Burnel, bass, The Stranglers (b. 21 Feb 1952, Notting Hill)

Tony Butler, bass, Big Country (b. 13 Feb 1957, Shepherd's Bush)

Phil Collins (b. 30 Jan 1951, Chiswick)

Paul Cook, drums, Sex Pistols (b. 20 Jul 1956, Hammersmith)

Elvis Costello (b. 25 Aug 1954, Paddington)

Mikey Craig, bass, Culture Club (b. 15 Feb 1960, Hammersmith)

Roger Daltrey (b. 1 Mar 1944, Hammersmith)

Eliza Doolittle (b. 15 Apr 1988, Westminster)

John 'Rhino' Edwards, bass, Status Quo (b. 9 May 1953, Chiswick)

John Entwistle, bass/vocals, The Who (b. 9 Oct 1944, Chiswick, d. 27 Jun 2000)

Adam Faith (b. 23 Jun 1940, Acton, d. 8 Mar 2003)

Andy Fraser, bass, Free (b. 3 Jul 1952, Paddington)

Justine Frischmann, vocals/guitar, Elastica (b. 16 Sep 1969, Twickenham)

Charlotte Hatherley, guitar, Ash/solo (b. 20 Jun 1979, Chiswick)

Steve Jones, guitar, Sex Pistols (b. 3 Sep 1955, Shepherd's Bush)

John "Speedy" Keene, Thunderclap Newman (b. 29 Mar 1945, Ealing, d. 21 Mar 2002)

Bob Kerr, Bonzo Dog Doo-Dah Band (b. 14 Feb 1940, Kensington)

Jan Kincaid, drums/keyboards, The Brand New Heavies (b. 17 May 1966, Ealing)

Andrew Levy, bass, The Brand New Heavies (b. 20 Jul 1966, Ealing)

John McVie, bass, Fleetwood Mac (b. 26 Nov 1945, Ealing)

Glen Matlock, bass, Sex Pistols (b. 27 Aug 1956, Paddington)

Brian May (b. 19 Jul 1947, Hampton)

Crispian Mills, vocals, Kula Shaker (b. 18 Jan 1973, Hammersmith)

Ian Mosley, drums, Marillion (b. 16 Jun 1953, Paddington)

Annie Nightingale, broadcaster (b. 1 Apr 1942, Osterley)

Gary Numan (b. 8 Mar 1958, Hammersmith)

Andrew Loog Oldham, manager (b. 29 Jan 1944, Paddington)

David O'List, guitar, The Attack/The Nice (b. 13 Dec 1948, Chiswick)

Andrew Ranken, drums, The Pogues (b. 13 Nov 1953, Ladbroke Grove)

Keith Relf, vocals/harmonica, The Yardbirds (b. 22 Mar 1943, Richmond, d. 14 May 1976)

John Renbourn, guitar, Pentangle (b. 8 Aug 1944, Marylebone)

Paul Samwell-Smith, bass, The Yardbirds (b. 8 May 1943, Richmond)

Seal (Seal Henry Samuel) (b. 19 Feb 1963, Paddington)

Labi Siffre (b. 25 Jun 1945, Hammersmith)

Heather Small, vocals, M People (b. 20 Jan 1965, Ladbroke Grove)

Roger Ruskin Spear, multi-instrumentalist, Bonzo Dog Doo-Dah Band (b. 29 Jun 1943, Hammersmith)

Richard Thompson, vocals, Fairport Convention (b. 3 Apr 1949, Notting Hill)

Daniel Woodgate, drums, Madness (b. 19 Oct 1960, Maida Vale)

Greater London

NW1 ROCK CELEBRITY SANCTUARY AT THE HAWLEY ARMS

Famous as the pub that Razorlight, Pete Doherty frequent and a favourite location of the late Amy Winehouse, the place was very nearly demolished as a result of the 2008 Camden Market fire that came close to destroying this gem of a building. An eclectic schedule of music takes place in the first-floor bar, but it's the music-themed wall decorations, jukebox and positive feel of a place that has survived some tough times that make this pub so special.

Surviving and prospering after the Camden Market fire: The Hawley Arms re-opened just eight months after the blaze

LOCATION 256: 2 Castlehaven Road, postcode NW1 8QU

NW1 BOB DYLAN'S CAMDEN VIDEO WALKABOUT

Reportedly tempted to buy a house in North London to be near his friend, musician and producer Dave Stewart, Bob Dylan has a soft spot for the environs of Camden, a fact underlined by Stewart's video to accompany Dylan's World Gone Wrong album. The 1993 film for the album's stand-out track 'Blood In My Eyes' followed the top-hatted Dylan as he mingled with the locals on the streets and sat at a table in, what was at the time, the Fluke's Cradle café. The cover of the album pictures Dylan at Fluke's Cradle, sitting below a painting by Irish artist Peter Gallagher, which received an enormous boost in value as a result of its inclusion.

LOCATION 257: the Fluke's Cradle café is now the Max Orient restaurant at 275 Camden High Street, postcode NW1 8QS

Dylan sits below Peter Gallagher's L'Etranger, the subject of a legal wrangle when the painting was featured in this album cover shot at Fluke's Cradle

NW1 KEY MOMENTS IN ROCK HISTORY AT THE ROUNDHOUSE

Once a gin barrel storehouse and 19th-century railway engine shed and turntable, this circular structure first became a music venue when hosting an all-night rave featuring Pink Floyd and Soft Machine to celebrate the launch of underground newspaper The International Times on October 14th 1966. When, in the following spring, the UFO club moved out of its Tottenham Court Road basement, the Roundhouse seemed like a sensible new venue, until a few months there saw the club continually make a loss and fold. But by this point the Roundhouse had built a name as a music venue and in the autumn of 1968 The Doors and Jefferson Airplane played a double-billed gig under the Middle Earth Club banner. Making an even bigger mark on British music history was the July 4th 1976 performances by American prototype punks The Ramones and The Flamin' Groovies. The insolent stage presence, a high-speed thirty-minute set and Dee Dee Ramone spurting blood from a cut finger all over his white Fender Precision bass left an instant

impression that something shocking was happening. The Ramones' appearance accidentally prompted the beginnings of a rethink in rock values that would trigger a backlash against established rock superstars and lay the foundations of the UK punk movement. Although closed as a music venue in 1983, the Roundhouse returned to the live music scene again in 2006. Revamped but still retaining the best of what Sixties UFO club organiser Joe Boyd described as a "magnificently decaying brick hulk", the Roundhouse has recently rocked its 3,000-capacity foundations to memorable gigs by Paul McCartney, Morrissey and Robbie Williams. Talking Heads founder David Byrne literally played the building when his innovative 2009 project invited fans to make music from a pump organ wired up to the Roundhouse's pillars, pipes and beams.

LOCATION 258: Chalk Farm Road, postcode NW1 8EH. Website: www.roundhouse.org.uk

NW5 TALLY HO! IT'S PUB ROCK

The precise point at which a new music genre takes off is naturally impossible to pin down. But in the case of pub rock it was very much a location-associated accidental birth. On May 3rd 1971, the Tally Ho pub Sunday lunchtime jazz combo were about to disappoint the regulars with a no-show when the landlord enlisted the help of local band Eggs Over Easy to fill the slot. Formed by New Yorkers Austin de Lone and Jack O'Hara, the band were conveniently billeted a short stroll way at 10 Alma Street. A pub residency flourished and once they eschewed the jazz covers and began trotting out their own three-or four-hour sets of country rock, pub rock was up and running with the Tally Ho geographically at the centre of the movement. If you fancy a pub rock pub crawl, The Bull & Gate, also a key player in the genre's early days, is close by on Kentish Town Road.

LOCATIONS 259,260, 261: though this area of London is well served musically by the Forum (9-17 Highgate Road, postcode NW5 1JY) and The Bull and Gate pub(389 Kentish Town Road, postcode NW5 2TJ), the Tally Ho at 9 Fortress Road was reduced to a pile of rubble for redevelopment in 2006. No.10 Alma Street, postcode NW5 3DJ

Greater London

NW1 THE NUTTY BOYS' BIG BREAK AT THE DUBLIN CASTLE

Claims to fame for this busy pub include the setting for Coldplay's first gig, the location for Madness video 'My Girl' and career kick-starts for Travis and a number of others who made their first tentative steps here courtesy of the much-missed, late landlord Alo Conlon, who turned the pub into a music venue in 1979. The spiritual home of local 'Nutty Boys' Madness in their early days, the hundreds of acts who have graced the 150-capacity Dublin Castle include The Specials, Arctic Monkeys and Babyshambles. Suggs reveals how he blagged a crucial early break for Madness with Alo Conlon opposite.

❛He asked us what we played and we said country and western, and jazz - we thought that would be the thing to say when going in to ask for a gig at an Irish pub.❜
Suggs

Where Madness began a career not singing country and western

LOCATION 262: 94 Parkway, Camden, postcode NW1 7AN

NW1 THE BEATLES ARE WAXED, WEDDED AND SENTENCED

The imposing Marylebone Register Office is where Paul McCartney married Linda Eastman in March 1969, breaking the hearts of numerous Beatlemaniacs who still thought, after nearly ten years, they might just be 'in with a chance' with the last remaining Beatle bachelor. Ringo Starr married Bond girl Barbara Bach at the same venue in 1981, with his two surviving band-mates as guests of honour. Meanwhile, a short distance away at the Marylebone Magistrates' Court in November 1968, John Lennon pleaded guilty to unauthorised drugs possession. A short walk east along Marylebone Road will take you to Madame Tussauds where the four wax figures of The Beatles are displayed, depicting them in happier days.

LOCATION 263: Marylebone Road, postcode NW1 5PT

Where Paul married Linda and Ringo married Barbara

NW3 SUPERNOVA HEIGHTS

When your second album threatens to become the biggest-selling since The Beatles' Sgt Pepper's Lonely Hearts Club Band, you are entitled to name your new gaff to reflect your elevation to rock superstardom. The track 'Champagne Supernova' from (What's The Story) Morning Glory? was Noel Gallagher's inspiration for decoratively naming his home Supernova Heights. The Oasis guitarist and songwriter left Primrose Hill and moved to the country in 1999.

LOCATION 264: 9 Steele's Road, Belsize Park, postcode NW3 4SE. Status: private residence

NW1 CAMDEN HIGH STREET'S ELECTRIC BALLROOM

The former Carousel Ballroom got a new name and a new purpose in 1978 when live music took centre stage at the Electric Ballroom on Camden High Street. Dizzee Rascall, Stereophonics, Paolo Nutini and Public Image have been recent additions to a gig list that has included, U2, Oasis, The Clash and Red Hot Chilli Peppers down the years. As popular as ever, the venue has added themed club nights Sin City, Shake and Inferno to the 1,100 capacity venue on two levels.

LOCATION 265: 184 Camden High Street, postcode NW1 8QP. www. electricballroom.co.uk

NW6 'ROCK ISLAND LINE' AT BROADHURST GARDENS

The Decca recording studios in West Hampstead created some of Britain's most historically vital music moments. Not so vital for The Beatles, but nevertheless worthy of note, is the fact that these studios were the first port of call in London on the Fab Four's rise to becoming the greatest band in popular music history, a rise that would cause Decca no little embarrassment after they decided to pass on the opportunity to sign The Beatles following the band's demo session audition at Broadhurst Gardens on New Year's Day 1962. Acts who did end up passing the audition for Decca in the early Sixties included The Rolling Stones, Fleetwood Mac and John Mayall's Bluesbreakers, but the studios' seminal moment came with a recording by Lonnie Donegan several years earlier on July 13th 1954. Recorded in the still standing Studio 2, his revved-up version of an old American country blues song by Lead Belly would prove to be a skiffle classic and just what the new breed of British teenagers had been waiting for. Evidence suggests that Decca's release of 'Rock Island Line' was a major jolt forward in British popular music's development into a new independent youth movement.

The Broadhurst Gardens building still contains the walls if not the fixtures and fittings to Studio 2

The Decca studio single release that changed everything

LOCATION 266: now a rehearsal space for the English National Opera at 165 Broadhurst Gardens, West Hampstead, postcode NW6 3AX

NW5 JEFFERSON AIRPLANE AT PARLIAMENT HILL FIELDS

Vaguely advertised, heavily rained upon and with an anti-hippie, hostile element amongst the crowd, a nevertheless "happy to be here" Jefferson Airplane played the first of a series of free festivals at Parliament Hill Fields. This Camden Council initiative on September 4th 1968 saw Fairport Convention also perform on the tiny bandstand in front of a crowd estimated in the low hundreds. The following May brought three more Camden Free Fringe festivals at the bandstand, headlined by Pink Floyd, Procol Harum and Fleetwood Mac.

LOCATION 267: Highgate Road, Hampstead, postcode NW5 1QR

NW1 RHYTHM 'N' BOOZE AT DINGWALLS

Situated in the heart of the vibrant atmosphere at Camden Lock Market, Dingwalls has been a music venue since 1973. Named after the Victorian building's original owner, you can still see timber yard owner T.E. Dingwall's name painted on the outside wall. The large shed-like building began its new life as a live music venue during the advent of glamrock and flourished as a punk hotspot when The Ramones played there in 1976, watched, significantly, by impressionable members of the recently formed but still little-known bands The Clash, Sex Pistols and The Damned. Advertised as purveyors of Rhythm 'n' Booze in the Eighties, various artists including Blondie, The Doors, Dr Feelgood and the Foo Fighters have performed at this canal-side music mecca.

LOCATION 268: Middle Yard, Camden Lock, postcode NW1 8AB. Website: www. dingwalls.com

Greater London

NW8 BILLY FURY AND PAUL McCARTNEY'S ST JOHN'S WOOD HOMES

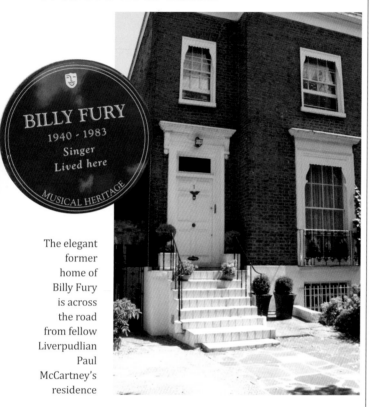

The elegant former home of Billy Fury is across the road from fellow Liverpudlian Paul McCartney's residence

No.7 Cavendish Avenue has been owned by Paul McCartney since 1966. A convenient short stroll from Abbey Road, this provided relatively easy access for fans to get close to the only London-based Beatle during the mid-Sixties, whereas John, George and Ringo had retreated to secluded private outer-London estates in Esher and Weybridge. Patient fans were treated to regular glimpses of their idol, with some exceptionally lucky ones witnessing Paul perched on a windowsill late one evening premiering his new song, 'Blackbird'. The garden featured a unique, domed sun-house where The Beatles, as part of a day-long photo session that took them from London's Docklands to St John's Wood, assembled for a few final shots, along with Paul's sheepdog, Martha. Across the road, marked by a blue plaque, is the one-time home of Paul's neighbour and fellow Liverpudlian Billy Fury.

LOCATIONS 269 and **270:** 7 Cavendish Avenue (McCartney) and 1 Cavendish Avenue (Billy Fury), St John's Wood, postcode NW8 9JE. Status: private residences

NW10 GINGER'S FRONT ROOM SUPERGROUP REHEARSAL

In 1966, bass player Jack Bruce and guitarist Eric Clapton arrived at Ginger Baker's north London house to rehearse together for the first time. The blues jam that day in Baker's small front room was so successful that the trio decided they were on to something and Cream was born. The Braemar Avenue property became a hive of band activity and a silk-screen press set-up in Ginger's garden shed was used to run off the band's first posters.

❝It was very obvious we had something unique.❞
Jack Bruce on that first rehearsal at Ginger Baker's house

LOCATION 271: Braemar Avenue, off the A4088, south-west of Brent Reservoir, postcode NW10 0DJ

NW1 CHALK FARM MADNESS

The attractive Edwardian frontage of Chalk Farm tube station was actually a late replacement location for the cover shoot of the Madness album Absolutely in 1980. The band were to have assembled outside Camden station, but with too many pedestrians and cars about Madness and their photographer headed half a mile north-west to the quieter Chalk Farm station.

LOCATION 272: Adelaide Road, postcode NW3 2BP

Madness, sporting the appropriate baggy trousers

NW8 THE ABBEY ROAD STUDIOS AND ZEBRA CROSSING

Martin Downham

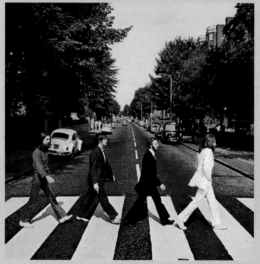

The most famous zebra crossing in the world is featured on The Beatles' Abbey Road album cover and the image is one of only six photographs taken on August 8th 1969 by photographer Iain Macmillan. It's almost impossible to replicate the photograph yourself without teetering atop a stepladder placed in the middle of the road. Given the sheer volume of traffic in the area, this is not recommended. A few metres from the zebra crossing is the recording home of The Beatles, where most – but not all – of their 200-plus songs were recorded under the guidance of producer and so-called fifth Beatle George Martin. Favouring Studio 2, The Beatles went from straight rock 'n' rollers, recording their first album in a day, through to the epic Sgt Pepper's Lonely Hearts Club Band album. During the final splintered days The Beatles could be found solo in other studios, or even corridors, within Abbey Road, recording their separate parts for later releases such as The White Album. But The Beatles' reliance on the studios is just one chapter of the Abbey Road story's impact on British popular music. Glenn Miller made his final recording here in 1944 and Cliff Richard and The Drifters' sensational 'Move It!' (1958), Pink Floyd's psychedelic masterpiece The Piper At The Gates Of Dawn (1967), Kate Bush's first No.1 album Never For Ever (1980) and Radiohead's transatlantic chart-topper Kid A (2000) were all created in this white, rather plain Georgian townhouse.

LOCATION 273: 3 Abbey Road, St John's Wood, postcode NW8 9AY. Status: private studios

Top left: the Abbey Road Studios entrance

Top right and above: the most photographed zebra crossing in the world was given Grade II listed status by the government in 2010. Care needs to be taken when reproducing the cover - a number of people have been injured by cars when standing in the middle of Abbey Road

The West End Lane location for what was once Klooks Kleek

NW6 KLOOKS KLEEK AND MOONLIGHT AT THE RAILWAY

Aside from being around the corner from the Decca recording studios and a handy place to relax after a hard day's recording, the Railway Hotel was the home of R&B club Klooks Kleek. The club catered for an R&B audience entertained by John Mayall, Graham Bond, Georgie Fame and their various combos. Encouraged by a growing demand for British blues, the club's upstairs room (with no stage) helped develop lengthy careers for Eric Clapton, The Rolling Stones, Peter Green, Jethro Tull, Ten Years After and Cream. The club closed in 1970, only to re-open again soon after to support a new wave of young live performers including The Jam, The Cure and Uriah Heep at what was then called the Moonlight Club.

LOCATION 274: the Railway Hotel, or more recently, Railway Tavern, 100 West End Lane, postcode NW6 2LU

NW3 MADNESS ON PRIMROSE HILL

Madness LP The Rise & Fall (1982) features an almost Penny Lane-like tour on the track 'Primrose Hill'. The cover photograph for this, the band's fifth hit album, is a panoramic view of London from Primrose Hill, with the band typically engaged in a variety of whacky activities.

LOCATION 275: postcode NW3

NW1 BEATLES IN STORE AT BAKER STREET

Shop here for all your Fab Four requirements. An ideal place to purchase Beatles memorabilia: with a superb range of merchandise ranging from badges and posters for a few pounds to collectable figurines and gold discs for hundreds.

LOCATION 276: 231 Baker Street, postcode NW1 6XE. Website: www. beatlesstorelondon.co.uk

WEMBLEY ARENA

Built in just six months as a swimming pool for the 1934 Empire Games, hence the name Empire Pool, this building in the shadow of Wembley Stadium became London's 12,000-capacity indoor concert venue in 1978. The renamed Wembley Arena, attracted mega draws the Eagles, Madonna and Bruce Springsteen and was the subject of a major revamp by LiveNation in 2006.

LOCATION 277: Arena Square, Engineers Way, postcode HA9 0AA

HARROW THE WHO'S BIG LEGACY

The Who's 1971 album Meaty Beaty Big And Bouncy nicely rounded up their hits to that point, with the cover artwork reflecting a pictorial history from the band's beginnings. Photos appearing on the inside of the gatefold package depict a key venue in their rise to fame, the Railway Hotel. Sadly no longer standing, this is where The Who became a regular draw for their loyal Mod fan-base from 1964 and where Pete Townshend began his famously destructive on-stage guitar-smashing activities.

The relatively new development of flats on the old Railway Hotel site have been fittingly named after the band's drummer and vocalist. Keith Moon House and Roger Daltrey House serve as a constant reminder of the incredibly exciting music and mayhem created in this otherwise quiet suburban corner of North West London.

LOCATION 278: Keith Moon House and Roger Daltrey House, next to the station, High Street, Harrow, postcode HA3 5BP

NORTHWOOD HILLS ELTON'S DEBUT

The Northwood Hills Hotel was the place where local boy Reginald Dwight made his performance debut as a 15-year-old in 1962. Paid £25 a week, his repertoire back then extended little further than Jim Reeves and Ray Charles covers. Still hosting live music but now operating as modern Indian sports club the Namaste Lounge, the building proudly displays a PRS plaque to mark Reggie's Thursday through to Sunday evening performances that began a career spanning six decades.

LOCATION 279: Northwood Hills, 66 Joel Street, postcode HA6 1LL

NW8 RAK STUDIOS AND MICKIE MOST'S BLUE PLAQUE

In 1969, after a highly successful career as a pop star in South Africa, Hampshire-born producer and music entrepreneur Mickie Most created his own RAK record label and recorded a conveyorbelt of hit records from the RAK recording studios in St John's Wood. Most, who died aged 64 in 2003, is remembered for RAK pop classics by Mud, Racey, Suzi Quatro, Kim Wilde, Hot Chocolate, Steve Harley and CCS and, pre-RAK, the production credit on the astonishing recording of 'The House Of The Rising Sun' by The Animals. The studio carries a blue plaque next to the front entrance.

LOCATION 280: private studios, 42-48 Charlbert Street, St John's Wood, postcode NW8 7BU

WEMBLEY ROCK AT THE HOME OF FOOTBALL

A common location for the world's largest bands to strut their stuff these days, but it wasn't always so. Stadium rock at the home of English football kicked off in the early Seventies when a half-filled stadium hosted a rock 'n' roll revival concert. By 1974, the old ground was packed to capacity when 72,000 attended the final date for Crosby, Stills, Nash & Young after what had been a gruelling stadium tour of the USA. This one-off British appearance saw the supergroup top a bill also featuring The Band and Joni Mitchell. So successful was the day that summer concerts became something of a fixture with Elton John, the Eagles and The Beach Boys entertaining fans on the hallowed turf next. By 1985, there was no other British venue capable of hosting the most publicised outdoor music event since Woodstock and the combination of Wembley and a perfect sun-drenched summer's day did Live Aid proud. The newly-built stadium, complete with spectacular arch, replaced the old Wembley with its twin towers in 2007 and continues to host some of the world's biggest music events.

LOCATION 281: Empire Way, postcode HA9 0WS

Large scale stadium rock concerts first came to Wembley in 1974 (above) and are now a common event, hosting the likes of Take That (top) on their record-breaking 2011 Progress tour

Greater London

NW3 SUEDE AND PJ HARVEY CREATE A STIR DOWN THE WHITE HORSE

1984 author George Orwell was once a customer at Hampstead's White Horse pub, and it was obviously the place to get noticed in 1991. Here was the setting for Suede's first gig and an early PJ Harvey performance that led to them being hurriedly signed up by the Too Pure label.

LOCATION 282: the White Horse Pub, 154 Fleet Road, Hampstead Heath, postcode NW3 2QX

Born in North West London

Hugh Cornwell, vocals, The Stranglers (b. 28 Aug 1949, Tufnell Park)

Fearne Cotton, presenter (b. 3 Sep 1981, Northwood)

Jerry De Borg, guitar, Jesus Jones (b. 30 Oct 1960, Kentish Town)

Adam Devlin, guitar, The Bluetones (b. 17 Sep 1969, Hounslow)

Steve Ellis, vocals, Love Affair (b. 7 Apr 1950, Edgware)

Marianne Faithfull (b. 29 Dec 1946, Hampstead)

Ian Gillan, vocals, Deep Purple (b. 19 Aug 1945, Hounslow)

Harvey Goldsmith, promoter (b. 4 May 1946, Edgware)

Jack Good, producer (b. 7 Aug 1931, Greenford)

Jet Harris, bass, The Searchers (b. 6 Jul 1939, Kingsbury, d. 18 Mar 2011)

Billy Idol (b. 30 Nov 1955, Stanmore)

Elton John (b. 25 Mar 1947, Pinner)

Tony Kanal, bass, No Doubt (b. 27 Aug 1970, Kingsbury)

Johnny Kidd, vocals, Johnny Kidd & The Pirates (b. 23 Dec 1935, Willesden, d. 7 Oct 1966)

Paul Kossoff, guitar, Free (b. 14 Sep 1950, Hampstead, d. 19 Mar 1976)

Hugh McDowell, cello, Electric Light Orchestra (b. 31 Jul 1953, Hampstead)

Ian McLagan, keyboards, The Small Faces/The Faces (b. 12 May 1945, Hounslow)

Dave Mattacks, drums, Fairport Convention (b. 13 Mar 1948, Edgware)

Tony Meehan, drums, The Shadows (b. 2 Mar 1943, Hampstead, d. 28 Nov 2005)

Keith Moon, drums, The Who (b. 23 Aug 1946, Wembley, d. 7 Sep 1978)

Mark Morriss, vocals, The Bluetones (b. 18 Oct 1971, Hounslow)

Scott Morriss, bass, The Bluetones (b. 10 Oct 1973, Hounslow)

Richard Oakes, guitar, Suede (b. 1 Oct 1976, Perivale)

Jimmy Page (b. 9 Jan 1944, Heston)

Larry Parnes, manager (b. 1930, Willesden, d. 4 Aug 1989)

Dave Parsons, bass, Bush (b. 2 Jul 1965, Hillingdon)

Steve Priest, bass, The Sweet (b. 23 Feb 1948, Hayes)

Gavin Rossdale, vocals, Bush (b. 30 Oct 1965, Kilburn)

Slash (Saul Hudson) guitarist, Guns N' Roses (b. 23 Jul 1965, Hampstead)

Dusty Springfield (b. 16 Apr 1939, West Hampstead, d. 2 Mar 1999)

Chris Squire, bass, Yes (b. 4 Mar 1948, Kingsbury)

Screaming Lord Sutch (b. 10 Nov 1940, Hampstead, d. 16 Jun 1999)

Chris Thomas, producer (b. 13 Jan 1947, Perivale)

Mick Tucker, drums, The Sweet (b. 17 Jul 1947, Harlesden, d. 14 Feb 2002)

Rick Wakeman (b. 18 May 1949, Perivale)

Ronnie Wood (b. 1 Jun 1947, Hillingdon)

Richard Wright, keyboards, Pink Floyd (b. 28 Jul 1943, Hatch End, d. 15 Sep 2008)

Marianne Faithfull, was born in Hampstead and grew up in Reading and on her father's commune, Braziers Park in Oxfordshire

Ellen Von Unwerth/TT Records

N1 PUB ROCK, PINTS AND PUNK AT THE HOPE & ANCHOR

The early to mid-Seventies revival of basic no frills country, rock and blues, dubbed pub rock, was chiefly associated with this Islington boozer. Hardly a genre, it was rock and it was played in pubs during an economically depressed decade. Pub landlords began to realise that to chase the younger punters' pound they needed the added attraction of live music, something that pre-Seventies would have been a deterrent to increased takings. Nowhere epitomised the new London-based scene better than the Hope & Anchor, where Ducks Deluxe, Brinsley Schwarz, Chilli Willi and The Red Hot Peppers, Bees Make Honey, Kilburn and The High Roads and Dr Feelgood strutted their stuff on the small stage here and at a growing number of pubs - the Tally Ho (where it all began), The Greyhound and The Bull and Gate - in pub rock's London heartland. When pub rock morphed into punk, the Hope & Anchor took this proper new genre in its stride, which is more than can be said for Jonathan Ross. Attending his first ever gig at the Hope & Anchor in 1977, he cracked his head on the low ceiling pogo-ing along to X-Ray Spex.

LOCATION 283: 207 Upper Street, Islington, postcode N1 1RL

Islington's Hope & Anchor where, along with 30 other punters, you would have witnessed Joy Division's London debut on December 27th 1978

N1 RICHARD ASHCROFT AND FAT LES: DOING THE HOXTON WALK

Fans of mega hit single 'Bitter Sweet Symphony' by The Verve can, if they care to, walk in Richard Ashcroft's footsteps to recreate the video filmed in Hoxton. The famous video walk begins where Falkirk Street joins Hoxton Street then heads north on the eastern side of the street. This short journey promoting The Verve's 1997 No.2 hit was reproduced to promote World Cup record 'Vindaloo' a year later, when Fat Les (Keith Allen and a growing gang of walkers including young daughter Lily Allen) parodied Ashcroft's deadpan walk to camera.

LOCATION 284: Hoxton Street, postcode N1 6SH

N3 A NORTHERN LINE LOVE SONG AT 'FINCHLEY CENTRAL'

The subject of The New Vaudeville Band's third hit single was a jaunty story of love lost on London Underground's Northern Line. 'Finchley Central' was a 1967 No.11 hit for the septet, led by 1920s dance band fan Geoff Stephens, born in nearby New Southgate. Mega hits about British locations don't end there. See their million-selling entry in Hampshire.

LOCATION 285: Station Road, Finchley, postcode N3 2RY

N2 THE FORTIS GREEN KINKS KONNECTIONS

The front room in Denmark Terrace where Ray and Dave Davies constructed the 'You Really Got Me' riff on the family piano

Linking Muswell Hill to East Finchley is the area and road called Fortis Green, the place where Kinks Ray and Dave Davies spent their childhood growing up in Denmark Terrace. Across the road from the Davies household is local pub The Clissold Arms, which once remembered the brothers with pictures and memorabilia including a plaque marking this spot as the site in 1960 of Ray and Dave's Kinks debut. The Clissold Arms even got a namecheck in Dave's 2002 Bug album track 'Fortis Green' but currently the Kinks association only stretches to a few framed photos.

LOCATIONS 286 and 287: the Davies' childhood home is at 6 Denmark Terrace and The Clissold Arms is opposite at 115 Fortis Green, postcode N2 9HR

N15 DAVE CLARK'S BOYHOOD HOME

Dave Clark, drummer and leader of the stomping Dave Clark Five, who patented the Tottenham Sound, grew up at 208 Philip Lane, Tottenham. Situated above the Williams Brothers grocery store and opposite what was the Greyhound (now the Botany Bay) pub, this was the rented family home of a teenager whose group briefly gave The Beatles a run for their money in the transatlantic superstar stakes in the mid-Sixties. It was here that The Dave Clark Five rehearsed for what would be a stratospheric rise from the band's home base at the Tottenham Royal to the top of the American singles chart and 18 appearances on the Ed Sullivan Show.

LOCATION 288: on the corner with Kitchener Road at 208 Philip Lane, Tottenham, postcode N15 4HH. Status: private residence

N16 AMY'S 'BACK TO BLACK' ABNEY PARK CEMETERY

The sombre video to singer songwriter Amy Winehouse's signature hit song 'Back To Black' was filmed in the grounds of Abney Park Cemetery. The magnificently gothic Abney Park Chapel is the backdrop to the end of the funeral procession as Amy symbolically buries her broken heart. Abney Park additionally gave its name to the American band of that name, who also titled their first album after the cemetery. The band's Washington-born frontman Robert Brown once lived close to the cemetery when studying in London.

LOCATION 289: entrance to the cemetery is from Stoke Newington High Street, postcode N16 0LH. Nearby Gibson Gardens (opposite the cemetery entrance a fork left) and Chesholm Road (a little way south) feature during earlier scenes in the video

Vocalist Robert Brown named his band after the Stoke Newington cemetery near to where he lived when an American student in London

N4 FINSBURY PARK'S ROCKING RAINBOW

Originally a cinema, this prominently situated Finsbury Park structure was well known to rock fans in the Seventies as the Rainbow Theatre. The Moorish-styled interior had been lavishly designed to reproduce the look of a Spanish village. Formerly the Astoria, the 3,000-seat venue played host to Cliff Richard, The Beatles and The Beach Boys in the Sixties before its transformation as North London's stylish home of rock music on November 4th 1971 when The Who performed the Rainbow's opening gig. In its heyday, the Rainbow saw memorable performances by David Bowie (1972), Stephen Stills' Manassas (1972), Van Morrison (1973), Stevie Wonder (1974) and Little Feat (1975) before finally closing its doors to rock music in January 1982. The venue's last post, so to speak, was sounded by the heavy metal band UFO, who were reported to have been using the venue as a rehearsing space the week the building's lease was offered for sale. The building is once again in constant public use as the UK HQ for the Universal Church of the Kingdom of God, whose owners have beautifully maintained the grade II listed interior. Rock fans who remember cramming into the grand foyer, pint in hand, will be pleased to know that the famous star-shaped fish pond they avoided falling into remains in all its glory.

LOCATION 290: in the fork between Isledon Road and Seven Sisters Road, 232-238 Seven Sisters Road, postcode N4 3NX

Beautifully restored and maintained by the present owners, the Rainbow's grand entrance hall and fish pond

Greater London

N7 MUSIC, MAYHEM AND MURDER AT JOE MEEK'S HOLLOWAY ROAD BASE

High up on a wall on Holloway Road is a small plaque dedicated to one of British pop's larger-than-life characters. The plaque tells anyone who chances to glance up that it marks the spot where record producer Joe Meek lived and worked. Carrying an image of the Telstar satellite and dubbing him "The Telstar Man", the small black disc can only hint at the innovation and mayhem that went on in the three-storey flat where the Gloucestershire-born Meek created his unearthly recordings. Europe's first independent producer led a volatile existence, which ended when he shot dead his landlady Violet Shenton (who owned the ground-floor leather handbag and suitcase shop). He then turned the gun, owned by his protégé and lover Heinz, on himself that fateful day back in February 1967. The chaotic surroundings inside 304 Holloway Road were brilliantly reconstructed for the Joe Meek biopic Telstar in 2008.

LOCATION 291: currently grocery store Holloway Express at 304 Holloway Road, N7 6NJ. The plaque is above the two 'L's in 'Holloway'

Top left: the building where Joe Meek practised his recording wizardry on Holloway Road

Top right: the Joe Meek-produced 'Telstar' was the first single by a British group to top the US chart and gave its name to this 2008 movie

N4 SLADE POSE IN ROCK STREET

Never a hit album, Whatever Happened To Slade (1977) nevertheless makes a thoroughly essential entry in Rock Atlas. The band were photographed up against the wall for the album cover and CD booklet in the appropriately named Rock Street. Pictured standing next to billboard images of their earlier skinhead selves, the band were also photographed farther down Rock Street outside house numbers 6 and 8.

LOCATION 292: Rock Street, Finsbury Park, postcode N4 2DN

With glamrock's glitter fading, Slade recorded this out-and-out rock offering in 1977

N8 SWEET DREAMS AT DAVE STEWART'S CHURCH

In the Nineties, Bob Dylan came calling on his friend Dave Stewart at The Church. Unaware that he'd arrived at the wrong address on nearby Crouch End Hill, he asked the woman who answered the door if Dave was at home. As she happened to be the wife of a plumber called Dave, she invited her visitor in to wait for his return. Minutes later the plumber returned home to find Dylan waiting for him in the living room drinking a cup of tea.

Once an Agapemone church, then utilised by animators Bob Bura and John Hardwick for the creation of their Trumpton, Camberwick Green and Captain Pugwash children's TV shows, this beautiful church (and the house next door) was eventually bought as a recording studio by musician David A. Stewart in the Seventies. A five-minute walk north from The Church to The Broadway is where Dave and Annie Lennox formed The Tourists when living above the Spanish Moon record shop. Back at The Church, they later went on to complete work on Sweet Dreams (Are Made Of This) album as the Eurythmics. In 2003, the building changed hands again when singer-songwriter David Gray bought the place.

LOCATIONS 293 and 294: just south of the centre of Hornsey on the A1201 at 145H Crouch Hill, postcode N8 9QH. Dave and Annie's flat was at 28 The Broadway, a five-minute walk away, postcode N8 9SU

N10 A FAIRPORT CONVENTION

Can there have been a more naturally chosen band name than Fairport Convention? The group that has sported a myriad of line-up changes began life in the childhood home of guitarist Simon Nicol. The name of his family's house was the large North London property called 'Fairport', and as Nicol's friends, first Ashley Hutchings then Richard Thompson, 'convened' there to rehearse, Fairport Convention presented itself as their perfectly logical new group name.

LOCATION 295: 'Fairport' stands at the corner of Fortismere Avenue and Fortis Green Road, postcode N10 3BQ. Status: private residence

The Muswell Hill house where Fairport Convention began in 1967

Greater London

N22 'ALLY PALLY' PLAYS HOST TO THE DEAD AND MTV

Always a music venue able to offer that little bit more, Alexandra Palace has staged the annual Brit Awards with its attendant indoor funfair and many a large scale rock event, beginning with the epic 14 Hour Technicolor Dream, staged to benefit underground newspaper The International Times in 1967. On the bill that April night, and the next morning until sunrise when Pink Floyd brought proceedings to a dramatic end, were a succession of the counter-culture's most far-out acts including Yoko Ono, Soft Machine and The Crazy World Of Arthur Brown. Most of the 6,000 present inside were 'stoned', some taking advantage of the banana skin joints freely available while watching more than 30 musicians and poets, some playing simultaneously on two stages. In between this and recent enormous events such as the MTV Europe Music awards, The Grateful Dead, The Stone Roses, Blur, Travis and The Strokes have all played noteworthy gigs here.

❝ The whole thing was rather like the last struggle of a doomed tribe to save itself from extinction.❞
The Sunday Mirror's 1967 review of the 14 Hour Technicolor Dream at 'Ally Pally'

LOCATION 296: Alexandra Palace Way, Wood Green, postcode N22 7AY

N8 THE KINKS' KONK STUDIOS AND RAY'S CAFE

When the brothers Ray and Dave Davies decided to invest some of the proceeds from new songs like 'Lola' and 'Apeman' in a recording studio, they settled on a base close to home for their new venture. Created by The Kinks for their own recordings in the early Seventies, Konk would come to play host to Blur, Depeche Mode, The Stone Roses, Massive Attack and the Arctic Monkeys. A short walk turning right out of Konk to the parade of shops curving round into Church Lane is the location of the doorway where the photoshoot for the 2007 Ray Davies solo album Working Man's Café took place. The café pictured on the remainder of the CD packaging (The Lane Cafe) is a further minute's walk away, heading south on Tottenham Lane.

LOCATION 297: Konk is at 84-86 Tottenham Lane near the corner with Church Lane, Crouch End, postcode N8 7EE. Website: www.konkstudios.com
The Lane Cafe is at 55 Tottenham Lane, postcode N8 9BD

Ray Davies in the doorway on Tottenham Lane, photographed for the cover of his Working Man's Café album

N19 MUSWELL HILLBILLIES AT THE ARCHWAY TAVERN

The pub scene depicted on the front cover of The Kinks' 1971 album Muswell Hillbillies was, confusingly, photographed two miles from the band's spiritual home in Muswell Hill. To find the right kind of pub and stage a back cover picture of the band posing under a sign to Muswell Hill, they decamped to the Archway Tavern and, for the signpost, to a small traffic island where Castle Yard meets Southwood Lane.

LOCATION 298: the Archway Tavern, Archway Close, postcode N19 3TD

Born in North London

Adele (b. 5 May 1988, Tottenham)

Jazzie B (Trevor Beresford Romeo), DJ/producer, Soul II Soul (b. 26 Jan 1963, Hornsey)

Mark Bedford, bass, Madness (b. 24 Aug 1961, Islington)

Brian Bennett, drums, The Shadows (b. 9 Feb 1940, Palmers Green)

Melanie Blatt, All Saints (b. 25 Mar 1975, Camden)

Johnny Borrell, vocals/guitar, Razorlight (b. 4 Apr 1980, Muswell Hill)

Wallis Buchanan, didgeridoo, Jamiroquai (b. 29 Nov 1965, Crouch End)

Jonny Buckland, guitar, Coldplay (b. 11 Sep 1977, Islington)

Emma Bunton, Spice Girls (b. 21 Jan 1976, Finchley)

Clem Cattini, drums, The Tornados/ Johnny Kidd & The Pirates (b. 28 Aug 1937, Stoke Newington)

Dave Clark, drums, The Dave Clark Five (b. 15 Dec 1942, Tottenham)

Terry Coldwell, East 17 (b. 21 Jul 1974, Islington)

B.J. Cole, pedal steel guitar (b. 17 Jun 1946, Enfield)

Chris Cross, bass, Ultravox (b. 14 Jul 1952, Tottenham)

Dana (b. 30 Aug 1951, Islington)

Lenny Davidson, guitar, The Dave Clark Five (b. 30 May 1944, Enfield)

Dave Davies, guitar/vocals, The Kinks (b. 3 Feb 1947, Fortis Green)

Ray Davies, vocals, The Kinks (b. 21 Jun 1944, Fortis Green)

Alison Goldfrapp (b. 13 May 1966, Enfield)

Tony Hadley (b. 2 Jun 1960, Islington)

Brian Harvey, East 17 (b. 8 Aug 1974, Walthamstow)

Chas Hodges, Chas & Dave (b. 28 Dec 1943, Edmonton)

Mark Hollis, vocals/guitar, Talk Talk (b. 4 Jan 1955, Tottenham)

Steve Howe, guitar, Asia/Yes (b. 8 Apr 1947, Holloway)

Ashley Hutchings, guitar, Fairport Convention (b. 26 Jan 1945, Southgate)

Bob Johnson, guitar/vocals, Steeleye Span (b. 18 Mar 1944, Enfield)

John Keeble, drums, Spandau Ballet (b. 6 Jul 1959, Islington)

Martin Kemp, bass, Spandau Ballet (b. 10 Oct 1961, Islington)

Dave Knights, bass, Procol Harum (b. 28 Jun 1945, Islington)

Joe Leeway, vocals/percussion, Thompson Twins (b. 15 Nov 1955, Islington)

Leona Lewis (b. 3 Apr 1985, Islington)

Shaznay Lewis, All Saints (b. 14 Oct 1975, Islington)

John Lydon (aka Johnny Rotten) (b. 31 Jan 1956, Finsbury Park)

Derrick McKenzie, drums, Jamiroquai (b. 27 Mar 1962, Islington)

Malcolm McLaren (b. 22 Jan 1946, Stoke Newington, d. 8 Apr 2010)

Sir George Martin, producer (b. 3 Jan 1926, Highbury)

George Michael (b. 25 Jun 1963, East Finchley)

Alan Murphy, guitar, Level 42 (b. 28 Nov 1953, Islington, d. 19 Oct 1989)

Dave Murray, guitar, Iron Maiden (b. 23 Dec 1956, Edmonton)

Simon Nicol, guitar, Fairport Convention (b. 13 Oct 1950, Muswell Hill)

Dave Peacock, Chas & Dave (b. 24 May 1945, Enfield)

Marco Pirroni, guitar/vocals, Adam & The Ants (b. 27 Apr 1959, Camden Town)

Simon Raymonde, Cocteau Twins (b. 3 Apr 1962, Tottenham)

Martin Rushent, producer (b. 11 Jul 1948, Enfield, d. 4 Jun 2011)

Mike Smith, vocals/keyboards, The Dave Clark Five (b. 6 Dec 1943, Edmonton, d. 28 Feb 2008)

Alvin Stardust (b. 27 Sep 1942, Muswell Hill)

Geoff Stephens, The New Vaudeville Band/songwriter (b. 1 Oct 1934, New Southgate)

Rod Stewart (b. 10 Jan 1945, Highgate)

Charlie Watts, drums, The Rolling Stones (b. 2 Jun 1941, Islington)

Sean Welch, bass, The Beautiful South (b. 12 Apr 1965, Enfield)

Chris White, bass, The Zombies (b. 7 Mar 1943, Barnet)

Amy Winehouse (b. 14 Sep 1983, Southgate, d. 23 Jul 2011)

ROCK ATLAS

Eastern England

UK and Ireland Edition

STAR HIRE

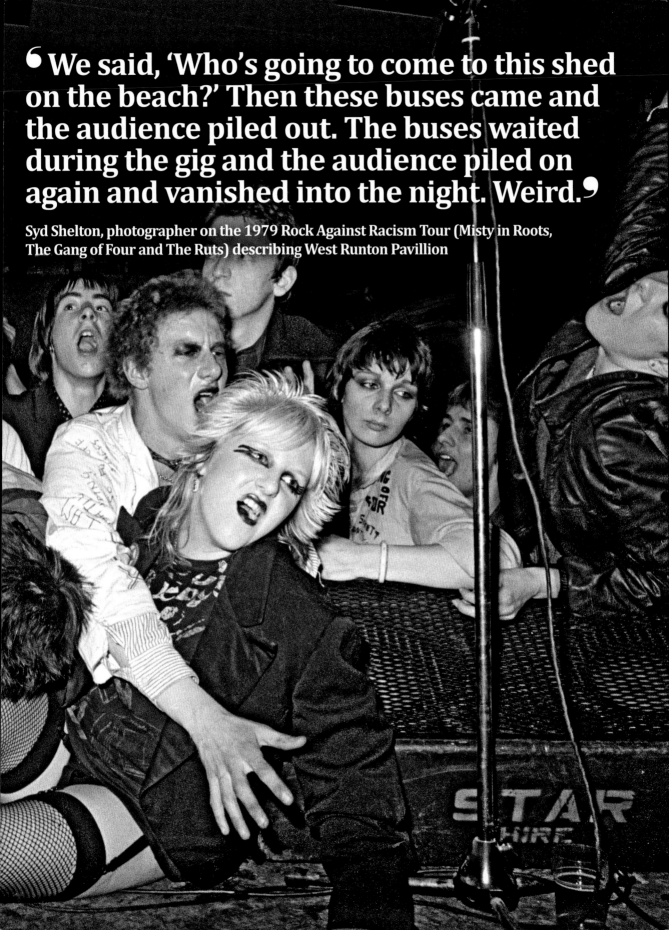

'We said, 'Who's going to come to this shed on the beach?' Then these buses came and the audience piled out. The buses waited during the gig and the audience piled on again and vanished into the night. Weird.'

Syd Shelton, photographer on the 1979 Rock Against Racism Tour (Misty in Roots, The Gang of Four and The Ruts) describing West Runton Pavillion

Eastern England

HERTFORDSHIRE

Within the Hertfordshire county boundary you can explore Knebworth's 'Stately Home of Rock', the spot where British rock 'n' roll ignited for Cliff Richard when he first heard a new song called 'Heartbreak Hotel', a Welwyn Garden City pub where Led Zeppelin played a seminal gig and the 350-year-old country house where Ritchie Blackmore named a new group Black Sabbath. This is the county for Zombies, video shoots, location beginning and ending eras in the Queen timeline, the birthplace of jazz man and (crucially) skiffle enthusiast Chris Barber and a village pub with no beer where Fairport Convention made their home. There's Elton John's obsession with his local football club, the talented Tewin family Wilde, plus Little Richard's rock 'n' roll rescue act in Watford. And, if you travel a short distance up the A1, there remains a reminder, every time you head out of London, of the Canterbury prog rock outfit Hatfield And The North, who took their name from a road sign now irritatingly reworded to read "The North And Hatfield".

CHESHUNT NOISY REBEL CLIFF UPSETS THE NEIGHBOURS

Born in India and raised in Hertfordshire, Cliff Richard (Harry Webb as he was then) moved into a new family home on the Bury Green Estate in Cheshunt in 1951. The new, modern, three-bedroom council house at 12 Hargreaves Close was a massive improvement for a family forced to share temporary accommodation with relatives since moving to England two years previously. This is the house where Cliff practised with his mates Terry Smart and Norman Mitcham when forming the original Drifters. Steve Turner's biography of Cliff Richard shows just what a rebel the young Cliff could be. In it he researched the local council files and discovered a complaint about the noise emanating from No.12 by a neighbour at No.11, requesting that the late-night skiffle sessions cease. The resulting hand-written council record read "son not willing to cooperate". There's a plaque to mark Cliff's association with the house and a development of flats nearby in Cheshunt has been named after the singer at Cliff Richard Court.

LOCATIONS 299 and **300:** the house at Hargreaves Close (postcode EN7 5BB) is west of the A10 Great Cambridge Road. Cliff Richard Court is at High Street, Cheshunt, postcode EN8 0BE. Status: both are private residences

ALDBURY
OASIS WERE THERE THEN

An Oasis folly? Not the complete disaster of a release many have panned, the band's Be Here Now set a record for the fastest-selling album in 1997, shifting an incredible 663,389 copies in just three days. The setting for the cover shoot was certainly no architectural folly. Photographed at the suitably opulent former home of Playboy Club chief Victor Lownes, Stocks House was the perfect location for sinking a Rolls-Royce in the swimming pool and arranging a selection of thought-provoking items chosen by Noel Gallagher from the BBC props department. When a hotel, Stocks House was a favourite watering hole for Who drummer Keith Moon, and the house and grounds became a video director's favourite when selected for filming Madness ('It Must Be Love'), Fun Boy Three ('Summertime') and Kajagoogoo ('Hang On Now'). The house is currently the private residence of jockey and trainer Walter Swinburn.

LOCATION 301: north of the picturesque village of Aldbury, Stocks Road, Aldbury, postcode HP23 5RX

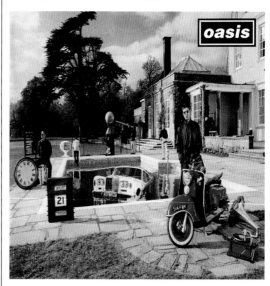

Stocks House provides the setting for the cover of Oasis' record-breaking follow-up to (What's The Story) Morning Glory?

HODDESDON CLIFF 'DISCOVERED' AT THE FIVE HORSESHOES

In March 1958, The Drifters featuring Harry Webb made their debut at Forty Hill Badminton Club, a short distance down the A10 from Harry Webb's Cheshunt home. But their most significant gig came farther north up the A10 a little later, one mid-week evening, at the Five Horseshoes pub in Burford Street, Hoddesdon. There they met 'Teddy Boy' John Foster, who would become their manager. Foster, crucially, had both a telephone (rare at the time) and enough experience of Soho's

Demolished in 1967, the Five Horseshoes pub where John Foster discovered what he saw as Britain's own Elvis

legendary 2i's Coffee Bar venue to blag them a booking there that would prove crucial.

❝I looked at the singer in his white shirt and black trousers and I saw Elvis. Something told me, yes, he's going to be big.❞
John Foster talent scouts in Hoddesdon. (From Steve Turner's Cliff Richard: The Biography)

LOCATION 302: the pub, now demolished, stood in Burford Street, postcode EN11 8JW

CHESHUNT THE WOLSEY HALL WHO GIGS

A seemingly unremarkable venue, Cheshunt's Wolsey Hall was a regular stepping stone for The Who on their career curve upwards. The band made four appearances here, the first of which was as The High Numbers on October 11th 1964. The venue's "Sunday Scene" promised "raving R&B" at a ticket price of five shillings to see the band, who had recently changed their name from what had been The Who.

The Windmill Lane venue promised "raving R&B" for just five shillings

They returned a month later to Cheshunt, this time billed as The Who. Their act at this time, which was peppered with Motown covers – Martha Reeves' 'Heatwave' was a particular favourite – was about to get a boost with a 23-date residency at London's Marquee Club. Back to Wolsey Hall they came "by popular request" on November 18th 1965 before their final Cheshunt appearance on December 1st of that year. Four weeks before this gig, the band's 'My Generation' had stormed the singles chart and by 1966 Wolsey Hall was just not big enough to accommodate the increasing number of fans who wanted to witness their popular brand of power pop.

LOCATION 303: close to the town centre in Windmill Lane, postcode EN8 9AA

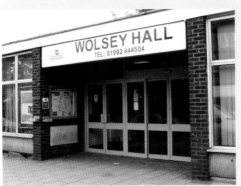

HERTFORD BALLS PARK INCIDENT AS SMILE BECOME QUEEN

November 14th 1970 was the day Queen first played a gig under that name. Balls Park College was the venue for the crowning of Queen. Booked originally for the college's winter ball as Smile, organisers thought they might be imposters when Roger Taylor's drum kit was set up bearing the bass drum logo "Queen". When quizzed about this, the band explained that they had recently decided on a name change after their previous gig at The Cavern Club, made famous by The Beatles on Liverpool's Mathew Street.

LOCATION 304: no longer a college, the buildings are in private ownership. Postcode: SG13 8AR

Eastern England

KNEBWORTH THE STATELY HOME OF ROCK

The gothic mansion and grounds that doubled as Wayne Manor in the first Tim Burton-directed Batman movie, Knebworth House has the distinction of being the largest single-stage rock venue in the country, hosting some of Britain's largest outdoor music events. The estate began temporarily shipping out the herds of deer and opening its gates to live rock shows as early as 1974's Bucolic Frolic, which attracted 60,000 fans to watch The Allman Brothers headline a bill also boasting Van Morrison, The Doobie Brothers, The Sensational Alex Harvey Band, Mahavishnu Orchestra and Tim Buckley. In 1975, with the sound travelling as far as the county town of Hertford, 80,000 attended Knebworth Park, excited by the prospect of witnessing performances from Pink Floyd, Steve Miller Band, Captain Beefheart, Roy Harper and Linda Lewis. Then 1976 saw Mick Jagger drop in for tea and leave his Y-fronts at the foot of his four-poster guest room bed when The Rolling Stones drew 100,000 to Knebworth Fair, joined by 10cc, Hot Tuna, Lynyrd Skynyrd, Todd Rundgren's Utopia and The Don Harrison Band. The Stones were massively late on stage due to someone pouring a bottle of beer into the mixing desk.

Knebworth House

❛Aw right, Knob-worth?!❜
Mick Jagger on stage in 1976

A Midsummer Night's Dream in 1978 saw a more modest 60,000 turn out for Genesis, Jefferson Starship, Tom Petty, Devo, Brand X and The Atlanta Rhythm Section and a second 45,000 attended the advertised Oh God, Not Another Boring Old Knebworth with Frank

Zappa headlining a cutting-edge bill featuring The Tubes, Peter Gabriel, The Boomtown Rats, Rockpile and Wilko Johnson's Solid Senders.

❛I was 14 [when The Stones played] and we have little mementos of that. We have a pair of very smart red underpants left at the bottom of

Mick Jagger's bed which are now in the safe.❜
Henry Lytton-Cobbold, current owner of Knebworth House

The more stately titled 1979 Knebworth Festival saw Led Zeppelin play over two Saturdays to a crowd of 200,000, supported by The New

Barbarians, Todd Rundgren, Southside Johnny and The Asbury Dukes, The New Commander Cody Band, Chas & Dave and Fairport Convention.

Knebworth 80, with The Beach Boys, Mike Oldfield, Elkie Brooks, Santana, Lindisfarne and The Blues Band attracted a crowd of 45,000 but signalled the end of rock at Knebworth for a time while Jazz and Cliff Richard took over. However, The Return of Knebworth Fair in 1985 laid on a heavy-duty line-up featuring Deep Purple, Scorpions, Meat Loaf, UFO, Mountain, Mama's Boys and Alaska, boosting the attendance to 80,000.

❛The Beach Boys joined my brother's 12th birthday party - Dennis Wilson ate the entire cake.❜
Henry Lytton-Cobbold

It's a Kind of Magic had Queen (their last gig with Freddie Mercury), Status Quo, Big Country and Belouis Some, drawing 120,000 punters in 1986 before a four year gap, after which the same number attended Pink Floyd, Paul McCartney, Mark Knopfler, Eric Clapton, Elton John, Phil Collins, Genesis, Robert Plant and Jimmy Page, Cliff Richard and The Shadows, Status Quo and Tears For Fears.

❛This is an enormous place even by our standards. I tell you it looks BEAUTIFUL from up here!❜
Freddie Mercury surveys the 120,000 crowd in 1986

Genesis came back in 1992, supported this time by The Saw Doctors and Lisa Stansfield and watched by 90,000.

The Knebworth attendance record was smashed when Oasis drew 250,000 fans over two nights in 1996. The Prodigy, Manic Street Preachers, Ocean Colour Scene, The Charlatans, Cast, Chemical Brothers, Kula Shaker and The Bootleg Beatles were in support for the most oversubscribed tickets in British rock history.

2001 saw a return to live music with 35,000 grooving to a Ministry of Sound event in nine marquees, before the massive 2003 Robbie Williams concerts drew 375,000 over three nights, the Robster ably assisted by Moby, Ash, Kelly Osbourne and The Darkness. Hedgestock with The Who in 2006 and then the Sonisphere Festival in 2009 featuring Metallica, Linkin Park, Lamb of God and Mastodon returned Knebworth to its rock roots once more, a tradition set to continue.

Top left: fans get ready to enjoy what Robbie Williams later rated "the pinnacle of my career".

Above left: Beach Boy Al Jardine chats to Henry Lytton-Cobbold and friends on the roof of the house

Right: the UK's largest single-stage rock venue

❛I think after this... it's all downhill. This is the pinnacle of my career right now, so come and see me in a holiday camp like Butlins in around five years with Oasis.❜
Robbie Williams (2003)

LOCATION 305: a short distance off the A1(M) at Stevenage. Website: www.knebworthhouse.com

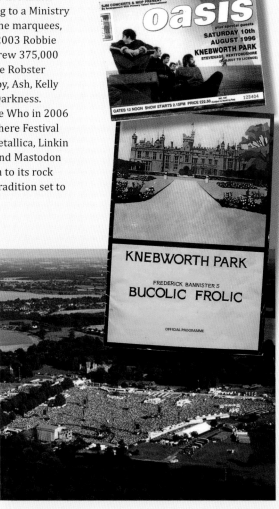

Eastern England

LITTLE HADHAM **FAIRPORT CONVENTION AT THE ANGEL**

Following the band's living, working and sharing a house ethos that worked so successfully in Hampshire a year earlier, Fairport Convention moved to the Hertfordshire village of Little Hadham in 1969. They made their home for more than a year in what had been village pub, The Angel. More than a dozen band members, wives, children and roadies shared one bathroom and one kettle in the basic accommodation. Despite the spartan conditions, the band enjoyed visits from many musicians keen to share their hippie-style hospitality. Drummers Cozy Powell and John Bonham and Nick Drake (rehearsing material for his Bryter Layter album) would all make the trek out to Hertfordshire. After a hard day's writing and rehearsing, local pub The Nags Head was the destination most nights for a spot of unwinding. The band were made welcome by the local community and even staged local fundraising gigs for St Cecilia's church organ fund and the Hertfordshire Police benevolent fund, with a crowd of around 3,000 turning up in a meadow in nearby Much Hadham. Their stay at The Angel came to an enforced end shortly after the release of their 1971 Top 10 album Angel Delight, named after their stay in the former pub. Positioned precariously on a sharp corner of the main A120, the building was struck by a lorry, which careered into what was band member Dave Swarbrick's living quarters. The Dutch lorry driver died instantly but Fairport's fiddle player miraculously survived the accident. Fairport's Simon Nicol recalls, "Swarb's was the [room] with the chevrons on the wall, Richard's [Thompson] is the one above. The entire front wall and the chimney in the corner collapsed on the truck, leaving the floor of RT's room hanging loose in space. A bottle of

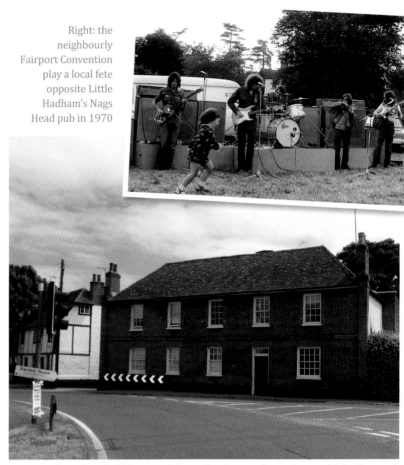

Right: the neighbourly Fairport Convention play a local fete opposite Little Hadham's Nags Head pub in 1970

Dave Swarbrick's room (above the chevrons) was the one hit by the truck

Poteen was rescued from the rubble and was shared with the fire service once the body of the driver and his rather bashed-up co-pilot were removed... As a palliative for extreme shock, it's right up there with hot, sweet tea!"

❛The layout was still that of a pub. Downstairs, there were two bars that we used as bedrooms, and a huge pub kitchen, which became our communal living space. There was also a function room, about 30ft x 15ft, which we used for rehearsals, and next to it was a kind of hovel, where our roadies lived.❜
Fairport Convention band member Richard Thompson, in a 2006 interview with The Sunday Times

LOCATIONS 306 and 307: the former Angel Inn is on the A120 at the crossroads in Little Hadham, postcode SG11 2DQ. Status: private residence. The Nags Head pub Fairport Convention visited as their local is a short walk south of The Angel at Hadham Ford, postcode SG11 2AX

MARKYATE THE ZOMBIES' 'BEECHWOOD PARK'

Once a nunnery, now a prep school, Beechwood Park gave its name to the Zombies song that appeared on their 1967 album Odessey And Oracle. The atmospheric track was written by the group's bass guitarist Chris White, whose father owned a local general store from where he and Chris would deliver goods to the girl's school.

LOCATION 308: Beechwood Park School (now co-ed) is south-west of the A5 at Markyate. Postcode: AL3 8AW

The Zombies, with Barnet-born and Markyate-raised Chris White (centre)

TEWIN THE WILDE FAMILY HOME

The Thatched Rest is the aptly-named home of one of British rock 'n' roll's earliest stars. Marty Wilde's family base is where high profile music careers began for daughter Kim Wilde and son Ricki Wilde. Marty's wife and mother to Kim and Ricki had her own noteworthy pop moment as a member of The Vernons Girls. Joyce Baker, as she was back in the Fifties, married Marty in the first heavily publicised pop star wedding before the couple moved to Hertfordshire. In 1996, Kim Wilde managed a slightly quieter ceremony of her own in nearby Codicote, where she would live with her future husband, the actor Hal Fowler. The wedding did nevertheless have its rock 'n' roll photo opportunity when Kim arrived at Codicote's St Giles' Church accompanied by father Marty.

LOCATION 309: The Thatched Rest is on Queen Hoo Lane, postcode AL6 0LT. Status: private residence

Hertfordshire's rock 'n' roll wedding: Kim arrives at St Giles' Church accompanied by father Marty

The Wilde family Hertfordshire home and Marty Wilde's music room

Eastern England

WATFORD ELTON SUPPORTS HIS LOCAL FOOTBALL CLUB

With his Seventies pop career skyrocketing and his local football team languishing in the old Third Division, Elton John put on what the Watford Observer claimed was the first outdoor rock concert to be staged at a football stadium. The 1974 gig, which raised almost £30,000 for his beloved Watford F.C., drew a crowd of 30,200 to the Vicarage Road football ground to see a bill that included Nazareth and Rod Stewart. According to the local paper, many fans deliberately fainted in order to be helped backstage by the St John Ambulance crew in a bid to get near the show's stars. Elton, who later became Watford Chairman during some of the club's most successful years, returned to play al fresco football fund-raisers at the stadium in 2005 and 2010.

LOCATION 310: the Vicarage Road stadium is a short walk from the town centre. Postcode: WD18 0ER

The Watford Football Club Hornets shirt badge, adapted for the 1974 concert programme

How the Watford Observer reported on "the first ever [concert] to be staged in a British football stadium"

A rare old treat from Hornet Herc

"HERC" The Hornet has injected some new qualities into Vicarage Road, Watford — dynamism, money and worldwide attention. At yesterday's glorious bash, Mr Elton Hercules John gave 30,200 fans a rare old treat and the disconsolate Newcastle side a chance to forget their Wembley blues.

Rod Stewart in spectacular action with Elton John

Peaceful show 'like a family outing'
by TERRY BURKE

Elton blasts out a number to captivate the huge audience

RIDGE THE NAMING OF DEEP PURPLE

Deeves Hall in the village of Ridge was the setting for auditions that led to the formation of Deep Purple. An advertisement in the pages of Melody Maker in 1967 assembled the remaining musicians that would create the group Roundabout, who name-changed to Deep Purple in April 1968.

❛We had a list [of band names] on the wall at Deeves Hall. One morning Deep Purple was on it. After intense interrogation it turned out that Ritchie [Blackmore] had put it up. The reason was that it was his grandmother's favourite song.❜
Jon Lord (Deep Purple)

LOCATION 311: Deeves Hall, Deeves Hall Lane, Ridge, postcode EN6 3LS. Located close to junction 23 of the M25 at its intersection with the A1. Status: private residence

WATFORD LITTLE RICHARD TO THE RESCUE AT THE GAUMONT

Carrying on the British musical hall tradition of great variety bills, promoter Don Arden was attempting the teenage equivalent for pop music in the early Sixties. By the time his 1963 package tour arrived at the Watford Gaumont, the advertised Everly Brothers, Bo Diddley, Rolling Stones and Mickie Most line-up was failing to attract sufficient interest at the box office. The Watford leg of the tour on October 5th hit a significant turning point when Little Richard was added to the mix. Arden took typically forceful action, and after reportedly phoning the American star 20 times, Richard relented and joined the tour in Hertfordshire. The excitable rock 'n' roller didn't disappoint his audience, pounding out his hits, at one point clambering on top of his piano, stripping off everything but his trousers and giving an incendiary performance that garnered four encores.

LOCATION 312: tragically all that remains of the old cinema is the road name Gaumont Approach, a stone's throw from the building's original site at 65 High Street, Watford. Postcode: WD17 1LJ

WALTHAM CROSS CLIFF HEARS ELVIS FOR THE FIRST TIME

A massively important few minutes in the future career of the teenage Cliff Richard took place on the streets of Waltham Cross one Saturday in May 1956, when he unknowingly discovered Elvis Presley on a car radio. Picture the scene and let Cliff describe what happened that spring day that changed his life:

❝I can remember the moment I first heard Elvis because I was with some buddies of mine and we were walking round a town called Waltham Cross which was a few miles away from where I lived. And I remember this car pulling up. It was a little tiny store, a hole-in-the-wall type place, a newsagents, Asplans it was called. Anyway, the car pulled up and he must have been in a rush. The engine was still running, the windows were down. He ran in to buy, perhaps, cigarettes and a newspaper. We're all going 'Ahhh, I'm going to have one of these when I grow up.' You know – that sort of thing. And then we heard Elvis singing – well we didn't know who it was – we heard 'Heartbreak Hotel', didn't know what the title was. And before it had finished the car had gone. And we thought – we were – deflated thinking "We've got to find out who this person is.❞

LOCATION 313: the shop formerly known as Asplan's was in the Four Swannes area of Waltham Cross, postcode EN8 7HH

WELWYN GARDEN CITY LED ZEP TAKE OFF AT THE CHERRY TREE

A Waitrose supermarket now dominates the building where the Cherry Tree pub once entertained music fans. In the same week their debut album first stormed the chart, Led Zeppelin played here at the pub's Bluesville '69 Club in April 1969. The Cherry Tree also catered for Tamla and soul fans on various nights of the week, but it was the staggering performance by a group who were on the cusp of rock superstardom that most will recall best.

❝I remember [Jimmy] Page's strange antics with his weird box of sounds. An incredible, powerful noise vibrating the wooden floorboards.❞
Baldock schoolboy Andy Clare at the Cherry Tree

LOCATION 314: Welwyn Garden City town centre, Bridge Road, postcode AL8 6AB

Born in Hertfordshire

Rod Argent, vocals/keyboards, The Zombies/Argent (b. 14 Jun 1945, St Albans)
Paul Atkinson, guitar, The Zombies (b. 19 Mar 1946, Cuffley, d. 1 Apr 2004)
Russ Ballard, guitar/vocals, Argent (b. 31 Oct 1945, Waltham Cross)
Chris Barber (b. 17 Apr 1930, Welwyn Garden City)
Colin Blunstone, vocals, The Zombies (b. 24 Jun 1945, Hatfield)
Chris Britton, guitar, The Troggs (b. 21 Jan 1944, Watford)
Martin Carthy (b. 21 May 1941, Hatfield)
Ray Cooper, percussionist (b. 19 Sep 1945, Watford)

Alesha Dixon (b. 7 Oct 1978, Welwyn Garden City)
Robert 'Lu' Edmonds, guitar, Public Image Ltd (b. 9 Sep 1957, Welwyn Garden City)
Bruce Gilbert, guitar, Wire (b. 18 May 1946, Watford)
Geri Halliwell, Spice Girls (b. 6 Aug 1972, Watford)
Bob Henrit, drums, Argent (b. 2 May 1944, Broxbourne)
Simon Le Bon, vocals, Duran Duran (b. 27 Oct 1958, Bushey)
David 'Buster' Meikle, vocals/guitar, Unit 4 + 2 (b. 1 Mar 1942, Goffs Oak)
Peter Moules, bass, Unit 4 + 2 (b. 14 Oct 1944, Barnet)

Mat Osman, bass, Suede (b. 9 Oct 1967, Welwyn Garden City)
Brian Parker, vocals/guitar, Unit 4 + 2 (b. 1940, Cheshunt, d. 2000)
Jim Rodford, bass, Argent (b. 7 Jul 1941, St Albans)
Jerry Shirley, drums, Humble Pie (b. 4 Feb 1952, Waltham Cross)
Mick Taylor, guitar, John Mayall's Bluesbreakers/The Rolling Stones (b. 17 Jan 1949, Welwyn Garden City)
Storm Thorgerson, album cover designer (b. 1944, Potters Bar)
Tracey Thorn, vocals, Everything But The Girl (b. 26 Sep 1962, Brookmans Park)
Dave Vanian, vocals, The Damned (b. 12 Oct 1956, Hemel Hempstead)

BEDFORDSHIRE

There's an air of transience about Bedfordshire's rock claims to fame, which may have something to do with the two main roads (the A1M and the M1) that link north and south through the county. Luton's Ritz cinema hosted visits by The Beatles and P.J. Proby, who famously split his trousers, causing nationally reported outrage at the now demolished Gordon Street location. And it was late one night after Christmas 1978 that Joy Division's Ian Curtis was rushed to Luton & Dunstable Hospital when travelling home north from a gig, suffering from what was later diagnosed as the singer's first epileptic seizure. On a brighter note, the Duke and Duchess of Bedford were among the first land owners to welcome hippies and rock music into their home at Woburn Abbey and Dunstable's California Ballroom was a magnet for Britain's Motown and soul music aficionados in the Sixties and Seventies.

CARDINGTON
TAKE THAT MAKE PROGRESS IN THE OLD AIRSHIP HANGARS

The giant airship hangars at RAF Cardington form the dramatic backdrop to the cover of the Propellerheads' 1998 hit album Decksandrumsandrockandroll. Since the demise of airship travel, the sheds have been used for movie-making and rock rehearsals. Big enough to house two Wembley Stadiums inside, one shed has been booked for tour practice by Paul McCartney, AC/DC, Rod Stewart and U2. In 2011, the Take That production team built the group's entire outdoor show stage for secret rehearsals for the forthcoming Progress Live Tour (Britain and Europe's biggest ever) inside one of the giant Cardington hangars.

LOCATION 315: three miles south-east of Bedford at Shortstown, near Cardington, postcode MK42 0TF

DUNSTABLE SOUL CENTRAL AT THE CALIFORNIA BALLROOM

Gone but not forgotten by thousands of soul fans, the building that was the California Ballroom was demolished to make way for a Dunstable housing estate. A familiar gig for beat groups in the early Sixties, the second half of the decade saw a succession of soul greats from Ike and Tina Turner to James Brown double ticket prices and crank up the excitement. Running from 1960 to 1979, this extraordinary venue became the southern epicentre of Britain's obsession with soul and Motown music, although the likes of Cream, The Who, Traffic and Jimi Hendrix kept up a fine tradition of outstanding rock performances, with a healthy number of glam rock acts booked as the Seventies wore on. But if you grooved to the records of Percy Sledge, Jimmy James & The Vagabonds, Johnny Johnson & The Bandwagon, Arthur Conley and Edwin Starr, the 'Cali' was the first place to check out your favourites live. All that remains today to mark the location is a reference on a standard street sign for Royce Close, which reads, 'Site of the California Ballroom 1960-1979 and pool 1935-1970.'

LOCATION 316: Royce Close, postcode LU 2NT. For the extended history of the 'Cali', visit: www.california-ballroom.info

WOBURN THE FESTIVAL OF FLOWER CHILDREN

One of Britain's earliest pop festivals, a three-day "happening" at Woburn Abbey in 1967's, Summer of Love, saw a bill topped by The Small Faces, The Move, Eric Burdon and Jeff Beck. Taking place "by kind permission of his Grace The Duke of Bedford", an advertisement at the time went on to describe the August Bank Holiday event as a "Festival of the Flower Children". This new iniative by the Duke provided some spectacular moments for the national press to report. At one point during the proceedings a hot-air balloon floated over dropping flowers on the 12,000-strong crowd below. Although not exactly rife, capitalism did rear its ugly head according to reports in one Sunday newspaper. An interview revealed that a disgruntled hippie had paid 30 shillings (£1.50) for a three-day ticket and then been disgusted to discover that a hot dog would set him back a further one shilling and nine pence (8p). The following summer saw a second event simply promoted as the Woburn Music Festival at which Jimi Hendrix, Pentangle, Geno Washington, Family, Roy Harper and Donovan all featured.

❝My fondest memories of [Woburn]were that I was on stage and I saw people starting to tear trees down to make fires because they were camping out for the night and The Duke of Bedford and his wife came along. I said 'I'm very sorry sir about the trees, it's really disgusting.' He says 'Oh never mind – we can always grow some more. In fact you're probably saving my old man some work because we have to trim them for the coming year.' Wow man, how loose can you get?❞
Eric Burdon

LOCATION 317: Woburn Abbey (postcode MK17 9WA) is close by junction 12 or 13 of the M1

Born in Bedfordshire

Mick Abrahams, guitar, Jethro Tull (b. 7 Apr 1943, Luton)
David Arnold, composer (b. 23 Jan 1962, Luton)
Clive Bunker, drums, Jethro Tull (b. 30 Dec 1946, Luton)
Neil Conti, drums, Prefab Sprout (b. 12 Feb 1959, Luton)
Duke D'Mond, vocals,

Barron Knights (b. 25 Feb 1943, Dunstable, d. 9 Apr 2009)
Gilson Lavis, drums, Squeeze (b. 27 Jun 1951, Bedford)
Martin McCarrick, guitar/cello, Therapy? (b. 29 Jul 1962, Luton)
Paul Young (b. 17 Jan 1956, Luton)

CAMBRIDGESHIRE

Spiritual home to Pink Floyd, Cambridge oozes rock sophistication and can also claim to be Britain's annual central pilgrimage point for folk fans with the famous festival, located since 1964 at Cherry Hinton Hall. The Beatles, Stones and Hendrix have all played the wider county, although few of the original venues they played (none in the case of Peterborough) are still intact. Wisbech is a town that saw more than its fair share of Sixties beat groups leave an impression at the town's opulent Corn Exchange, which turned out to be a particularly significant destination on The Rolling Stones' 1963 schedule of appearances. But, it's the Cambridge Corn Exchange we head for first for, Syd Barrett's last gig and a 1974 Drifters' riot.

CAMBRIDGE
RIOTING DRIFTERS FANS AND SYD'S LAST STAND

It wasn't until 1965 that the good folk of Cambridge ceased exchanging corn and hired out this magnificent asset as a place of entertainment. The best of British has performed here including The Beatles, Iron Maiden and Dizzee Rascal. In 1972, in the same year it was converted into a properly designated concert venue, the place witnessed the final public appearance of local legend Syd Barrett when his band Stars supported The MC5. Two years later and the management were faced with a near riot when 1,000 Drifters fans showed their displeasure when informed that the band would not be appearing.

LOCATION 318: Wheeler Street in Cambridge city centre, postcode CB2 3QB

Cambridge Corn Exchange: setting for a near riot by Drifters fans and the final public performance by Syd Barrett

Eastern England

CAMBRIDGE SYD BARRETT'S SEMI-DETACHED

The Pink Floyd madcap genius Syd Barrett retreated from the fame and success he once enjoyed in Pink Floyd, penning classic hits 'Arnold Layne' and 'See Emily Play', by living as something of a recluse until his death aged just 60. In a semi-detached house in the cul-de-sac at 6 St Margaret's Square, he spent his days painting pictures and making his own furniture but leaving the 1930s three-bedroom house largely lacking any modernisation from the time his mother owned the property in the 1950s. A shrine to a hugely creative but ultimately troubled soul who settled for the simple life, the house has attracted much interest from Syd's fans: one or two were even reported to have camped in the long, narrow garden during his tenancy. Like most of his followers, they were no doubt feeling the need to in some way protect the fragile but precious character that helped spark the British psychedelic music movement.

LOCATION 319: private residence to the south-east of the city centre, postcode CB1 8AQ

The former home of Syd Barrett

GRANTCHESTER PINK FLOYD'S POETIC RIVERBANK MEADOWS

Pick the right day in early summer and you can see and feel why Grantchester Meadows was such an inspirational location for Pink Floyd's song of the same name. The pastoral track, all birdsong and acoustic guitar strumming with Roger Waters' lyrics and vocals, appeared on the band's 1969 album Ummagumma. The recommended method of discovering this idyllic spot is to wander lazily out of Cambridge on the River Cam's

Grantchester Meadows: creative inspiration in abundance

footpath to Grantchester with the seven-minute-plus track on repeat on your mp3 player.

LOCATION 320: from the M11 at junction 12, head towards Grantchester village High Street. Turn left at the green and enter the meadows at the end of the road, past the Red Lion pub, postcode CB3 9NF

'Grantchester Meadows' appears on Ummagumma, whose front cover artwork by Hipgnosis was created at Storm Thorgerson's girlfriend's home in Long Shelford, a village two miles south of Grantchester

CHATTERIS
HALF MAN HALF BISCUIT'S 'ENVY OF THE FENS'

The track 'For What Is Chatteris...' appears on Half Man Half Biscuit's 2005 album Achtung Bono. The song appears to sound like a Tourist Information leaflet, promoting an apparently perfect Fenland town with three good butchers, two fine chandlers and a first-class cake shop, not to mention its famed brass band. But as the Half Man Half Biscuit song goes, "...if you're not there, I may as well be in Ely or St Ives."

LOCATION 321: 20 miles north of Cambridge where the A141 meets the A142, postcode PE16

STRETHAM **THE DIVISION BELL ALBUM COVER**

A field near Stretham was the temporary site for the three-metre-high sculptures photographed for the cover of Pink Floyd's album The Division Bell. Created by Storm Thorgerson, these vast metallic busts were sculpted by Aden Hynes and John Robertson from artist Keith Breeden's illustrations and photographed with Ely Cathedral clearly visible in the background. The two sculptures are currently on display as museum exhibits in the US at Cleveland's Rock & Roll Hall of Fame.

LOCATION 322: east out of Stretham on the A1123, the field is on your left just before the bridge over the River Cam, with views of Ely Cathedral in the distance. Postcode: CB6 3LJ

Ely Cathedral and the flat fields outside Stretham form the setting for Pink Floyd's The Division Bell album cover

WISBECH
A ROLLING STONES MILESTONE AT THE CORN EXCHANGE

Wisbech was no music outpost, hosting a growing number of rock and pop shows in the Sixties. It played a significant part in the development of the increasing popularity of The Rolling Stones in the summer of 1963. That July proved to be a career-defining milestone. A week or two before their first hit 'Come On' entered the chart, the band made their TV debut on Thank Your Lucky Stars and made the jump from the club circuit to ballrooms around the country. Wisbech was the place where the band made their debut in this larger type of venue, when they appeared at the Corn Exchange on July 20th. Despite the significance of the gig, there seems little empathy between the Corn Exchange crowd attending and Keith Richards in particular, who referred to the male Wisbech fans as hostile 'yokels' in his biography Life.

LOCATION 323: still standing near the town centre at 1 North Brink, postcode PE13 1JR

Born in Cambridgeshire

Syd Barrett, vocals/guitar, Pink Floyd (b. 6 Jan 1946, Cambridge)
Andy Bell, vocals, Erasure (b. 25 Apr 1964, Peterborough)
Matthew Bellamy, vocals/guitar, Muse (b. 9 Jun 1978, Cambridge)
Andrew Eldritch, vocals, The Sisters of Mercy (b. 15 May 1959, Ely)
David Gilmour, vocals/guitar, Pink Floyd (b. 6 Mar 1946, Cambridge)
Maxim, vocals, The Prodigy (b. 21 Mar 1967, Peterborough)
Aston Merrygold, JLS (b. 13 Feb 1988, Peterborough)
Olivia Newton-John (b. 26 Sep, 1948, Cambridge)
Owen Powell, guitar, Catatonia (b. 9 Jul 1967, Cambridge)
Tom Robinson (b. 1 Jun 1950, Cambridge)
Phil Selway, drums, Radiohead (b. 23 May 1967, Hemingford Grey)

Eastern England

ESSEX

The county is home to the swanky, all mod cons, mega V Festival at Chelmsford's Hylands Park, but there's also a gritty determination about Essex's musical activity dating back over more than half a century. After all, this is the coastline that was washed away in the tragic floods of 1953 and witnessed the brave resistance movement that was pirate radio off the port of Harwich (Radio Caroline South). It has its fair share of posh rock star homes and gardens: Rod Stewart's is particularly magnificent and there's the "all too beautiful" cottage homes of Steve Marriott. But, it's the glorious seaside locations of Southend and Canvey Island that helped create a small but significant music revolution. This was a raw, no-frills, but appealingly flash sound that pushed the likes of pub rock innovators Dr Feelgood into the national limelight.

ARKESDEN STEVE MARRIOTT'S COTTAGE FIRE AND TRAGIC DEATH

This is the village where mod icon Steve Marriott lived and tragically died in 1991. The former Small Faces and Humble Pie band member was found dead at the scene of a fire at the 16th-century cottage he rented in the village High Street. At 6.30 on the morning of April 20th, a passing motorist saw the property ablaze and called the fire brigade. One officer attending the emergency call-out was Keith Dunatis, a fan of Marriott's, who identified the rock star's body immediately and successfully rescued the collection of guitars and recording equipment. Compounding the tragedy was the fact that Marriott, after a period of relative inactivity, had returned the day before from a productive trip to the US, working once more on an album with former Humble Pie band mate Peter Frampton.

LOCATION 324: approximately eight miles north of Bishop's Stortford, just west of the M11. The cottage is opposite the Axe & Compasses pub (Marriott's local) in Arkesden village High Street, postcode CB11 4EX. Status: private residence

BILLERICAY
IAN DURY'S 'BILLERICAY DICKIE'

When Ian Dury incorporated a British music hall sensibility to his songs, 'Billericay Dickie' from his most popular album New Boots And Panties!! created his sauciest seaside postcard character yet. The 40,000 townspeople of Billericay have been trying to live it down ever since. Essex girls from Shoeburyness and Burnham-on-Crouch also get a namecheck but it's the randy bricklayer that constantly brings a smirk whenever the name of the town gets an airing.

LOCATION 325: east of the A12 between the M25 and Chelmsford, postcode CM12

CANVEY ISLAND A WARNING FROM BRITISH SEA POWER

'Canvey Island', a track on British Sea Power's 2008 Top 10 album Do You Like Rock Music? is a song written by the band's Yan (Peter Wilkinson) as an obvious warning of the problems of climate change, remembered through the dreadful floods in 1953 that so devastated Canvey, claiming the lives of 58 of the island's inhabitants. The band was memorably filmed for the BBC's Culture Show playing the track at waterfront pub The Monico.

LOCATION 326: The Monico is at 1-3 Eastern Esplanade, postcode SS8 7DN

CHAPPEL AND WAKES COLNE BLUR'S RAILWAY SHED REUNION

Honoured by a PRS for Music plaque, the East Anglian Railway Museum was the unusual location for Blur's first gig. Damon Albarn, Graham Coxon, Alex James and Dave Rowntree returned to the Colchester museum's Goods Shed twenty years on from their first public performance in 1989 to kick-off their much-publicised 2009 reunion tour.

LOCATION 327: north of the A1124, eight miles west of Colchester at Station Road, postcode CO6 2DS. Website: www.earm.co.uk

The first PRS for Music plaque awarded to commemorate Blur's first gig

CANVEY ISLAND DR FEELGOOD'S HOME DOWN BY THE JETTY

Spiritual home to Dr Feelgood, Canvey Island has a salty character and special atmosphere preserved in something of a decades-old timewarp. The band probably rejected any thoughts that the landscape was anything other than a petrochemical wasteland when their brand of pub rock helped spearhead the new genre that turned them from local heroes into R&B media favourites. Mid-Seventies albums Down By The Jetty and Malpractice sounded as belligerent and gloriously seedy as their surroundings, but a certain affection for the place was obvious on album covers picturing the band at home in Canvey Island locations. The jetty in question can be found a stone's throw from the waterfront Lobster Smack pub.

Dr Feelgood: spelling out their background on the beach in front of the Labworth restaurant

The band's last album featuring frontman Lee Brilleaux was titled Down At The Doctors simply because it was recorded down at Canvey's Dr Feelgood Music Bar in January 1994, 10 weeks before the singer's death. The venue is, like Lee, no longer standing and sadly missed, but the cover of this live album carries an image of the band in front of the place at 21 Knightswick Road, where now stands the Oysterfleet Hotel and a plaque honouring Brilleaux. The 2009 Julien Temple-directed movie Oil City Confidential provides the perfect introduction to the band and this oddly romantic Essex outpost.

LOCATION 328, 329, 330 and 331: there's only one way into Canvey Island - via the A130.

Favoured spot for more than one photoshoot was the Art Deco building currently called The Labworth restaurant, situated on the beach front, postcode SS8 7DW. The Oysterfleet Hotel is at 21 Knightswick Road, postcode SS8 9PA, and the Lobster Smack pub down by the jetty is on Haven Road, postcode SS8 0NR. The Admiral Jellicoe pub, pictured on the cover of the band's fifth album Be Seeing You, is at 283 High Street, postcode SS8 7RS

❛**The murky water. The flaming towers on the horizon at the oil refineries. I think it's beautiful. In the evening the mists surge around, like dry ice at a concert.**❜
Dr Feelgood's Wilko Johnson, in an interview given to Mojo

Down their local: Dr Feelgood worked, rested and played at the Admiral Jellicoe

Eastern England

COLCHESTER BEER HOUSE SHOOT FOR MARILLION'S BEST

The bar room setting for the cover shoot for Marillion's 1987 No.2 album Clutching At Straws was photographed at Colchester's Beer House pub. In the cut and paste days before computer graphics, images of Robert Burns, Dylan Thomas, Truman Capote and Lenny Bruce were added to the front cover bar scene at what was then called The Baker's Arms. Hurriedly put together by a designer working against an impossible deadline, the sleeve unsurprisingly didn't meet with lead singer Fish's approval. "The worst Marillion sleeve which also housed our best album to date," he later reflected.

LOCATION 332: a short walk south-east of the centre of Colchester at 126 Magdalen Street, postcode CO1 2LF

Famous faces prop up the bar at The Beer House pub

EPPING ROD STEWART'S COUNTRY LIFE

Living for long periods of the year in the US, Rod Stewart finds it impossible to distance himself from the traditional British lifestyle and has, like so many of the professional footballers he admires, bought himself a country pile in Essex. Wood House near Epping famously boasts a full-sized football pitch complete with dug-outs, where Rod the former mod's Vagabonds F.C. have staged many a match down the years. The estate only became Rod's place when he successfully outbid King Constantine of Greece for the property in 1986. Completing the archetypal British setting for the man who no doubt yearns for California when in Essex and Essex when on the West Coast is Rod's good old English local, the Theydon Oak, where he has been frequently spotted downing the odd red wine or two. Putting a whole new meaning on the description "free house", so good for trade and so pally with the landlord is Rod that apparently he hasn't bought a drink there in more than

20 years. Sadly, one unfulfilled footnote to this location's entry remains just that: Shortly before his death, Michael Jackson was reported to have plumped for Wood House as his base for the relatively easy trip down the nearby M11 into London for his projected marathon of O2 gigs in 2009 and 2010.

❝Rod's not a bad player. He's got a pitch in his back garden. Unbelievable pitch. Wembley would die for it❞
Football legend, Denis Law, gives his verdict after watching Rod's team take on Iron Maiden

LOCATIONS 333 and 334: Wood House is south of Epping High Street and almost within earshot of the M25. Postcode: CM16 5HT. Status: private residence. The Theydon Oak pub can be found at 9 Coopersale Street, Epping, postcode CM16 7QJ

Rod's home and the Theydon Oak pub

RCA Music Mark Seliger

HARLOW **FREE ROCK FOR ALL IN HARLOW TOWN PARK**

Harlow Town Council upset some residents but hugely impressed others with their free rock concerts staged in Harlow Town Park during the Seventies. A broad selection of rock, pop and folk acts helped make Harlow hip, attracting decent crowds – 20,000 in the case of a riotous visit by the Bay City Rollers in 1974 – to play at the new town's futuristic park Bandstand. Five dates were set during the spring and summer of 1973 with Atomic Rooster, Chicken Shack, Arthur Brown, Mungo Jerry and Hawkwind all headlining. Space rockers Hawkwind made a memorable return in 1974, supported by Magic Michael and Michael Moorcock, a year in which Fairport Convention, Clancy and Sassafras also made appearances. Thin Lizzy and Man topped the bill in 1975. Others putting in an appearance, before the council's initiative was scaled down, included Judas Priest and 10cc.

LOCATION 335: The Showground Bandstand still hosts concerts (although not currently of the scale of the seventies events) in the town park framed by Edinburgh Way to the north and Mandela Avenue to the south. Postcode: CM20

HARLOW
CATHOLIC CHURCH IS DJ MIX COVER

The Chemical Brothers' album cover image for Brothers Gonna Work It Out is an extraordinary architectural gem that would not look out of keeping in the US Mid-West. But it's the Our Lady of Fatima Catholic Church in Harlow new town that adorns the duo's DJ mix album from their 1998 compilation release.

LOCATION 336: a short distance east of the town centre at Howard Way, postcode CM20 2NS

The Chemical Brothers' various artists' Catholic church album cover

MORETON HUMBLE PIE'S HIDEAWAY AT BEEHIVE COTTAGE

Spotted driving around the winding lanes of this part of Essex in a white Aston Martin fitted with a record player, Steve Marriott lived the rock 'n' roll lifestyle in this remote setting just west of the small village of Moreton. Here the guitarist and singer-songwriter resided along with dogs, cats, geese and a horse that he would famously ride to the local pub. Purchased in 1968 shortly before his career took an international upturn with the formation of Humble Pie, the property boasted a detached building for guests and recording which became Clearsound Studio, a place where Peter Frampton was a frequent visitor during the secret formation and rehearsing of the supergroup's new material. Larger scale band rehearsals would take place at nearby Magdalen Laver Village Hall. Watch out for the High Laver Bridge if you are driving around these parts. Rock legend has it Marriott once bounced over it a little too quickly in the Aston Martin and landed in the river below.

❛We went down to Steve's little town in Essex at Magdalen Laver Village Hall, and we got it together in the country as Traffic had just done before us. That was our first time in the studio, with Andy Johns, you know, as the engineer. It doesn't get much better.❜
Peter Frampton, talking to Modern Guitars Magazine

LOCATION 337: three miles north of the A414 Harlow Road, in the village of Moreton. Postcode: CM5 0DR. Status: private residence

Top: Marriott's Moreton: the Beehive Cottage studio.
Above: "Bridge of sighs" (remember 'Itchycoo Park'?) where Marriott ended up in the river.
Right: made in Essex: Steve Marriott's Humble Pie

WEELEY THE PEOPLE'S FESTIVAL

August Bank Holiday weekend 1971 saw over 100,000 rock fans descend on this 200-acre site five miles from the coast at Clacton-on-Sea for an event headlined by The Faces. Promoted as "The People's Festival", tickets were £1.50 for the entire weekend at an event that had everything: A great British bill including Barclay James Harvest and a 45-piece orchestra, fires, gang fights, Hells Angels and some decent weather. Weeley Festival ended with Stray (complete with firework display) playing until dawn on the Tuesday.

LOCATION 338: the festival site is bordered by a railway line to the north, the B1441 to the west and bisected by public footpaths. Postcode: CO16 DH

❛This festival is not a "bread trip", every penny it makes will go to aid Bangladesh, Shelter and other important community charities.❜
Statement by the local Round Table festival organisers in 1971

SOUTHEND-ON-SEA THE KURSAALS' FLYERS AND FEELGOODS

Although the last live music gig was as far back as 1977, the Kursaal Ballroom's opulent foyer, exterior walls and famous dome still stand today as a reminder of some memorable occasions since its opening in 1901 at the heart of what was claimed to be the world's first theme park. Now converted as a venue for ten-pin bowling, this remarkable structure saw Thin Lizzy turn out for the dubious honour of performing at the place for the final time. Among the many acts gracing this fine venue during its pre-punk heyday were the Kursaal Flyers, who took their name from a mocked-up wild-west train that featured in the annual Southend Carnival. Around half the tracks on Dr Feelgood's 1976 chart-topping live album Stupidity were recorded here.

LOCATION 339: Eastern Esplanade, postcode SS1 27G

Feelgood factor: live at Southend's Kursaal

Born in Essex

Najma Akhtar, singer (b. 1964, Chelmsford)

Victoria Beckham, Spice Girls (b. 17 Apr 1974, Harlow)

Jet Black, drums, The Stranglers (b. 26 Aug 1938, Ilford)

Pauline Black, vocals, The Selecter (b. 23 Oct 1953, Coggeshall)

Graham Bond, British R&B musician (b. 28 Oct 1937, Romford, d. 8 May 1974)

David Byron, vocals, Uriah Heep (b. 29 Jan 1947, Epping, d. 28 Feb 1985)

Keith Christmas, singer-songwriter (b. 13 Oct 1946, Wivenhoe)

Vic Collins, guitar, Kursaal Flyers (b. 10 Sep 1950, Rochford)

Tony Connor, drums, Hot Chocolate (b. 6 Apr 1947, Romford)

Tina Cousins (b. 20 Apr 1974, Leigh-on-Sea)

Sarah Cracknell, vocals, Saint Etienne (b. 12 Apr 1967, Chelmsford)

Jamie Cullum, jazz musician, presenter (b. 20 Aug 1979, Rochford)

Graeme Douglas, guitar, Kursaal Flyers (b. 22 Jan 1950, Rochford)

Dave Gahan, vocals, Depeche Mode (b. 9 May 1962, North Weald)

Paul Gray, bass, Eddie & The Hot Rods (b. 1 Aug 1958, Rochford)

Roy Hay, guitar/keyboards, Culture Club (b. 12 Aug 1961, Southend-on-Sea)

John Hendy, East 17 (b. 26 Mar 1971, Barking)

Steve Hillage (b. 2 Aug 1951, Chingford)

Liam Howlett, keyboards, The Prodigy (b. 21 Aug 1971, Braintree)

Neil Innes, Bonzo Dog Doo-Dah Band/The Rutles (b. 9 Dec 1944, Danbury)

Wilko Johnson, guitar, Dr Feelgood (b. 12 Jul 1947, Canvey Island)

Nick Kamen (b. 15 Apr 1962, Harlow)

Sonja Kristina, vocals, violin, Curved Air (b. 14 Apr 1949, Brentwood)

John Leyton (b. 17 Feb 1939, Frinton-on-Sea)

Alison Moyet (b. 18 Jun 1961, Billericay)

Peter Nelson, bass, New Model Army (b. 22 Sep 1958, Colchester)

Scott Robinson, Five (b. 22 Nov 1979, Basildon)

Dave Rowntree, drums, Blur (b. 8 May 1964, Colchester)

Jon Sevink, violin, Levellers (b. 15 May 1965, Harlow)

Twink (John Alder), drums/vocals, The Pink Fairies/The Pretty Things (b. 29 Nov 1944, Colchester)

Ricky West, guitar/vocals, Brian Poole & The Tremeloes (b. 7 May 1943, Dagenham)

Cliff Williams, bass, AC/DC (b. 14 Dec 1949, Romford)

Eastern England

SUFFOLK

The relative lack of large towns in Suffolk meant that Ipswich managed to monopolise booking just about every act worthy of a place in the A-Z of rock legends. In fact, such was the standing of the town's famous Gaumont that it even has its own rock-related biography written about it. The county can also brag about attracting the likes of John Peel to its bosom for 33 happy years of residency and giving birth to that 21st-century hit-making machine The Darkness, and it has the closest piece of mainland to another Peel-related location, pirate station BIG L. Felixstowe pier was start point for Britain's largest chain of independent record stores, Andy's Records, whose HQ became based in Bury St Edmunds, and five miles out of Southwold lies the setting for Suffolk's very own miniature impression of Woodstock, Latitude Festival which stages its three days of music, poetry and comedy every July.

FELIXSTOWE RADIO LONDON'S FINAL BROADCAST

On August 14th 1967, off-shore pirate station Radio London played its final record. "Big L time is three o'clock - Radio London is closing down" came the announcement that millions of pop fans had dreaded as 'A Day In The Life' by The Beatles brought to an end three years of broadcasts from converted mine-sweeper the Galaxy. When the British government introduced legislation outlawing the off-shore broadcasts, it led to all nine DJs and three engineers leaving the ship for good. Among the Big L contingent picked up and dropped off at Felixstowe quayside was DJ John Peel. From Felixstowe, the party made their way to Ipswich to catch a train to London's Liverpool Street Station, where 1,000 angry demonstrating fans had assembled.

LOCATION 340: The Dock, postcode IP11 3SY

GREAT FINBOROUGH JOHN PEEL COUNTRY

West of Stowmarket lies the village of Great Finborough where John Peel lived, worked and received numerous guests from the world of music. The thatched cottage where he often broadcast BBC programmes from his home studio also contained the much-loved DJ's world-famous record collection. Peel Acres is just a short stroll from St Andrew's Church, where John is buried. His York stone gravestone bears an epitaph few would be surprised at: "Teenage dreams so hard to beat", a line from Peel's all-time favourite record, 'Teenage Kicks' by The Undertones, footnotes a gravestone also adorned by a representation of the badge of his beloved Liverpool F.C.

LOCATION 341: Peel Acres is a private residence. St Andrew's churchyard can be located just north of the centre of the village by heading up Church Road. Postcode: IP14 3AD

The St Andrew's Church headstone

Peter Tarleton

GILLINGHAM **THE DARKNESS FORMED AT AUNTIE'S PUB**

The Swan pub and motel was the spot where Justin and Dan Hawkins formed retro glam rockers The Darkness. The brothers had already been in a band, Empire, which hadn't exactly set the world alight, but on Millennium Eve they dramatically began the new century with a new resolution and confidence that would lead to No.1 album Permission To Land in 2003. Surrounded by family and friends at their aunt's pub that night, the two Hawkins brothers recall someone selecting Queen's 'Bohemian Rhapsody' on The Swan's jukebox. "I jumped up and started doing this interpretive mime" recalled Justin, which prompted Dan to see his brother in a new light and as a potential frontman in their new project. "We formed the Darkness there and then," Justin later admitted to Mojo magazine.

LOCATION 342: just outside Beccles on the Suffolk and Norfolk county border on Loddon Road. Postcode: NR34 0LD

IPSWICH **ROCK GREATS AT THE GAUMONT**

Maybe due to its relative isolation as a large town in a vast rural area, Ipswich appears to have cornered the market in attracting just about every rock legend down the years. More recently renamed The Regent after years as the Gaumont, this grand venue has witnessed seminal gigs by a list that reads like the roll call of pop's seminal acts. Little Richard, Chuck Berry, Buddy Holly, Lonnie Donegan, The Stones, Dusty Springfield, The Kinks, The Beatles, The Byrds, Black Sabbath, Kiss, The Cure and Britpop pioneers Suede all trod the Gaumont's boards. There was even a Nineties Motown 'Dancing in the Streets' package tour which, unlike countless recent tribute shows, actually featured originals Martha Reeves, Edwin Starr and Freda Payne. You do get the feeling that if Elvis had ever come to England, this remarkable venue would have been his first port of call. This rather beautiful theatre even has its own biography, titled From Buddy to The Beatles: When the Regent Rocked, authored by BBC Suffolk's Stephen Foster with photographer David Kindred. An 18-year-old David volunteered to cover The Beatles' 1964 Ipswich press call and admits he made an expensive mistake. "The Beatles were only with us for a few minutes, they were polite but bored. My colleague had purchased two copies of A Hard Day's Night earlier in the day and took the opportunity to get

David Kindred

them both autographed. He gave one away to a girlfriend. In around 2005, my colleague sold his remaining album at Christie's, which sold for over £20,000. A couple of years later a "Bring Your Rock Memorabilia" day was held at a venue in Ipswich and they paid around £12,000 for an autographed copy of A Hard Day's Night from an Ipswich lady. I presume that was the second copy."

❛The photograph I took of children with The Byrds included a young girl holding a huge handbag, which no doubt belonged to her mother. The Gaumont manager organised competitions at the Saturday morning children's cinema the week before a "pop" show. The competition winners would meet the top band backstage before the show. This threw up a strange mix of young children and a bunch of rock stars who were taking something stronger than Smarties.❜ David Kindred

LOCATION 343: the town centre, 3 St Helen's Street, postcode IP4 1HE

Eastern England

SOUTHWOLD 'MORE THAN JUST A MUSIC FESTIVAL' AT LATITUDE

As their slogan suggests, Latitude is a festival where artists, comedians, poets, dancers and writers engage and entertain alongside a music bill that has seen Henham Park's picturesque setting secure Snow Patrol, Arcade Fire, Franz Ferdinand, the Pet Shop Boys and Florence + The Machine since the festival began in 2006. Old festival-going romantics might be forgiven for thinking they have been transported back to 1969 and Max Yasgur's farm in New York state: Latitude's woodland and lake form a backdrop creating a miniature Woodstock deep in the Suffolk countryside, five miles from Southwold.

Paul Wesley Griggs / Latitude Festival

LOCATION 344: Henham Park

is flanked by the A12 on its eastern perimeter and the A145 to the west. Postcode: NR34 8AN

The wooded, lakeside setting of the Latitude Festival

Born in Suffolk

Dina Carroll (b. 21 Aug 1968, Newmarket)
Alan Davey, bass, Hawkwind (b. 11 Sep 1963, Ipswich)
Brian Eno (b. 15 May 1948, Woodbridge)

Kate Jackson, Long Blondes (b. 16 Sep 1979, Bury)
Charlie Simpson, Busted (b. 7 Jun 1985, Woodbridge)
Tim Westwood, presenter (b. 3 Oct 1957, Lowestoft)

NORFOLK

Norfolk has Beatles and Nirvana for starters and is lyrically bracketed in the same line and league as Ibiza by David Bowie. Norfolk, or the "Norfolk Broads" as Bowie sang on 'Life On Mars', might be some kind of geographical rock extremity but never off the map when it comes to fondly remembered locations. Motörhead's giant mock-up Luftwaffe bomber stage set lies abandoned somewhere in Diss, The Stranglers like to be beside the seaside at Hunstanton, blue plaques abound in Norwich and the remote rock 'n' roll village of West Runton all contradict the notion that the Singing Postman and his Norfolk village of Stiffkey is the county's most iconic contribution to the music map of Britain. Unique as he was, the guitar-toting postie was actually born in Lancashire. The most famous current rock 'n' roll resident has to be Seasick Steve. If America's most celebrated blues hobo rents out a country cottage in the county and stays for more than a year, you know Norfolk has got something special.

HUNSTANTON
FUNK PHOTOCALL FOR THE MEN IN BLACK

The Stranglers named their 2004 album Norfolk Coast and were logically snapped by New York rock photographer Harrison Funk for the front cover, standing on Hunstanton beach.

LOCATION 345: the beach is west of the B1161 at the end of Hunstanton's Promenade, postcode PE36 5BF

NORWICH **NIRVANA AT THE ARTS CENTRE**

They would become reluctant Nineties superstars, but US grunge rockers Nirvana made an early impact in Norwich in 1989. Booked by the founder of the city's Wilde Club, Barry Newman, the band wowed a capacity 200-plus crowd at the Norwich Arts Centre a few months after the first release of their album Bleach. Norwich's rock fans had, in the main, turned out for Seattle band Tad that night, with the lesser known Nirvana (and Brain Drain 69) providing support. The Wilde Club can also point to early appearances by Oasis, Coldplay, Snow Patrol and

Muse. In 1991, the converted church was the setting for a dramatic gesture by Manic Street Preacher Richey Edwards when challenged by journalist Steve Lamacq about his music. The guitarist, grabbing a razor blade, cut the reply "4 Real" into his bare arm, an act that later required a hospital visit and 17 stitches.

LOCATION 346: Norwich Arts Centre is in the city centre at Reeves Yard, St Benedict's Street, in St Swithin's Church. Postcode: NR2 4PG

NORWICH **PERFECT TIMING FOR THE BEATLES' ONLY NORWICH GIG**

Seventeen-hundred lucky teenagers were present the day The Beatles made their only appearance in Norwich. On May 17th 1963, the Grosvenor Rooms were the setting for a concert timed perfectly by local promoters Ray Aldous and Peter Holmes. Securing a booking with a band who had yet to begin their run of chart-topping recordings, the two 33-year-olds were able to negotiate a pricey but affordable £250 fee with Beatles manager Brian Epstein. By the time The Beatles arrived in Norwich, they were No.1 in both the singles and albums charts and played two 20-minute sets to a delirious audience inside the former ballroom. Obviously on a tight schedule

and still tighter budget, John, Paul, George and Ringo man-handled all their own equipment on arrival, carried out a soundcheck and then watched a movie at the nearby ABC cinema before taking to the stage. Afterwards, there was no overnight stay in a hotel for them. Aldous and Holmes recall the four chatting with fans over a hurriedly consumed fish and chip supper at Valori's in Rose Lane before heading south to begin a third nationwide tour in Slough.

LOCATION 347: a plaque is all there is to mark this gig where the Grosvenor Rooms once stood in Prince of Wales Road in the city centre. Postcode: NR1 1NS

NORWICH **ORFORD CELLAR 'THE CAVERN FOR EAST ANGLIA'**

On March 6th 2010, a plaque was unveiled in Norwich to mark the spot where the city's underground venue, The Orford Cellar, once hosted gigs by the likes of Jimi Hendrix, Rod Stewart, Eric Clapton, David Bowie and Elton John. The unveiling was carried out by the lead singer of favourite local performers at the club, Lucas and The Emperors, who, together with the illustrious list above, were name checked on this Norwich Heritage and Economic Regeneration Trust (HEART for short) roll of honour. Lucas recalled playing the hot, sweaty club "every other

week" and one local fan who had campaigned for the plaque, Fred Agombar, described the place as "The Cavern for East Anglia". The Hendrix visit is perhaps remembered with most affection. According to one Cellar regular, January 25th 1967 saw a queue snaking back as far as the Bell Hotel at nearby Orford Hill. They had all turned up to see the new wild man of rock for the princely sum of seven shillings and sixpence.

LOCATION 348: the blue wall plaque is at 11 Orford Hill in Norwich city centre, postcode NR1 3QD

Eastern England

WEST RUNTON MOTORHEAD'S BOMBER AND ELVIS AT THE FAR PAVILION

Demolished in 1986, West Runton Pavilion was one of British rock's farthest flung outposts. A difficult enough journey for music fans from Norwich, the Pavilion nevertheless boasted a towering list of acts. As the blue plaque on West Runton's Village Inn describes, the Pavilion "hosted concerts by legendary pop, rock and punk artists from Chuck Berry, T.Rex and Black Sabbath [incorrectly as it turns out!] to the Sex Pistols and The Clash". This revered venue and the nearby Royal Links Pavilion at Cromer even have their own lovingly created book and website, What Flo Said, authored by Julie Fielder. Rarely visited by music paper scribes, West Runton village did however draw occasional visits from the NME's Ian Penman to report from "Norfolk's only hot hop", notably when Elvis Costello & The Attractions appeared in 1980. Some bands generously resisted the temptation to scale down their live show to fit the Pavilion's intimate surroundings. Motörhead famously included West Runton on their touring schedule in 1980. They even brought a version of the vast "Bomber" stage set, pictured on their No.1 album No Sleep 'til Hammersmith, to the Norfolk seaside venue. The 40ft framework representing a Luftwaffe bomber is, according to Motörhead's Lemmy in John Harris' excellent book Hail! Hail! Rock 'n' Roll, now "holding up a shed" [or is that "holed-up in a shed"?] in nearby Diss. Locals regale their friends with tales of visiting rock stars mingling with fans in The Village Inn. Some even managed a game of pool with Lemmy and John Otway, who once staged a rather hazardous gig in the corner by the dartboard.

❝There was a hearty cheer as the stage lights dimmed, the two propeller sets of lights from the Bomber rig (one set in each rear corner of the stage, at the top) lit up and began to revolve.❞
Brian R Tawn's review of the West Runton gig in a Motörhead fanzine

LOCATION 349: West Runton lies just north of the A149 on the North Norfolk coast. The plaque at The Village Inn (a short walk from the ex-Pavilion) is in Water Lane, postcode NR27 9QP. Website: www.whatflosaid.co.uk

Below: a packed West Runton Pavilion greets The Stranglers on March 2nd 1981 and a bird's eye view of the 1,400-capacity venue

John Lemon

The famous Pavilion logo atop a poster advertising a typically eclectic bunch of acts

West Runton Pavilion

FRIDAY MAR 2nd	OUR LATEST COUP......... THE PRETENDERS	ADM'N £1·20
SATURDAY MAR 3rd	FOR BEAUTIFUL REGGAE BROWN SUGAR	ADM'N £1·30
FRIDAY MAR 9th	THE ONLY ONES	ADM'N £1·20
SATURDAY MAR 10th	MORE JA REGGAE 90° INCLUSIVE	ADM'N £1·30
FRIDAY MAR 16th	PIERRE MOETLENS GONG DON'T MISS THIS MUSICAL EVENING	ADM'N £1·20
SATURDAY MAR 17th	JA BAND!! CULTURE	DON'T MISS THIS RARE OPPORTUNITY TO SEE THIS LEGENDARY JAMAICAN BAND
TUESDAY MAR 20th	ROCK AGAINST RACIALISM	
FRIDAY MAR 23rd	MOTORHEAD	

NORWICH PABLO FANQUE PLAQUE MARKS HIS PLACE IN SGT PEPPER'

A blue plaque honours an extraordinary Norwich citizen name checked by The Beatles in their Sgt Pepper's Lonely Hearts Club Band track 'Being For The Benefit Of Mr Kite'. Born in Norwich in 1796, Pablo Fanque was Britain's first black circus proprietor and the man responsible for hiring the Hendersons, an act also included in the song inspired by a 19th-century circus poster purchased in an antique shop by John Lennon. Fanque also enjoys a mention on 'Ritz', a 1974 Cockney Rebel track from their Top 10 album The Psychomodo.

LOCATION 350: the plaque is on the wall of the John Lewis building, All Saints Green, Norwich, postcode NR1 3LX

Born in Norfolk

Cathy Dennis, singer-songwriter (b. 25 Mar 1970, Norwich)
Ed Graham, drums, The Darkness (b. 20 Feb 1977, Great Yarmouth)
Myleene Klass (b. 6 Apr 1978, Gorleston)
Beth Orton (b. 14 Dec 1970, East Dereham)
Tony Sheridan, (b. 21 May 1940, Norwich)
Roger Taylor, drums, Queen (b. 26 Jul 1949, Dersingham)

ROCK ATLAS
The Midlands
UK and Ireland Edition

"Sandy Denny's cottage had remained largely untouched since she died. We heard the local shop had to wrap Sandy's copy of Vogue or her dog would devour it as it dropped through the letterbox!"

Andrew Batt, Sandy Denny expert and compiler of the late singer's 19CD box sety

East Midlands

NORTHAMPTONSHIRE

The county that gave birth to Radiohead's Thom Yorke was also where top music broadcasters 'Whispering' Bob Harris and Jo Whiley both uttered their first words. Here, deep in the Northamptonshire countryside, Britain's honey-voiced folk songstress Sandy Denny chose to live with her fellow Fairport Convention band member and husband Trevor Lucas. A reminder of Corby's industrial heritage is poignantly documented by Big Country's 'Steeltown' and Kettering can possibly claim to have some of the most excitable fans in pop history. In the autumn of 1972, fans of the Bay City Rollers caused what some reported as a riot eclipsing anything the local Granada had seen from earlier visits by pop's bad boys The Rolling Stones and Gene Vincent.

CORBY BIG COUNTRY'S 'STEELTOWN'

The town's population was boosted by the migration south of thousands of Glaswegians in the post-war Fifties. Corby was an iron and steel-making hotbed before decline in production and large scale unemployment in the Eighties. The band Big Country eloquently documented the promise of a new town and new life 'built on sand' by their fellow Scots on 'Steeltown', a track featured on the No.1 album of the same name in 1984.

LOCATION 351: an Asda supermarket now stands on the appropriately named Phoenix Parkway, the site where the steel works' blast furnaces once stood. Postcode: NN17 5DT

Eighties devastation for Corby: documented on Big Country's chart-topping album

BYFIELD SANDY DENNY'S COTTAGE

The first lady of British folk rock: Sandy Denny at her home in Byfield

The picture postcard cottage once shared by Sandy, Trevor, Georgia and Watson

This is the village where Sandy Denny, husband and fellow Fairport Convention band member Trevor Lucas, their daughter Georgia and Watson the Airedale Terrier lived in the mid-Seventies. Their Byfield home was affectionately known as The Twistle by Sandy's friends. The couple's orange and lime green VW Beetle and Rover cars were familiar sights around the local highways and byways and across the county boundary in the nearby Oxfordshire village of Cropredy, where the band's Dave Swarbrick and Dave Pegg had bought local properties. The large cottage in Byfield was where Sandy Denny lived and worked in the adjacent converted barn for the last four years of her troubled and frequently hedonistic life. Byfield Village Hall was the setting for her final public appearance in April 1978, shortly before her death later that same month.

LOCATION 352: Byfield is midway between Daventry and Banbury on the A361. The Village Hall location is The Green, postcode NN11 6UT

KETTERING ROLLERMANIA AT THE GRANADA

On October 25th 1974, the Bay City Rollers visited Kettering's art deco Granada cinema. "Fan behaviour unlike anything seen since the height of Beatlemania" was how Q magazine later listed this notorious appearance by a group who were, at the time, rocketing up the chart with their fifth consecutive Top 10 single, 'All Of Me Loves All Of You'. The fans who didn't faint that day (and there were many who did) mobbed the band, trapping them in the Granada manager's office before a rescue operation by Kettering's police force. In the two decades previously, the venue also played host to the likes of Gene Vincent and The Rolling Stones and featured as a destination on Dusty Springfield's first solo tour of Britain.

LOCATION 353: the building in Kettering's High Street still stands, but its purpose, like so many others, has changed. The Granada is now a bingo hall. Postcode: NN16 8ST

NORTHAMPTON 'UNCLE' LEN BOOKS THE BEATLES

The town's ABC cinema saw two visits by The Beatles in 1963, on March 27th (on a tour they were originally billed as supporting Americans Chris Montez and Tommy Roe before Beatlemania reversed the pecking order) and later that same year on November 6th, by which time they were undisputed headliners and chart-toppers with their first LP Please Please Me. The ABC was run by 'Uncle' Len Webster, as he was known, who cornered the market in Sixties beat groups as the town had no other music venues with any decent capacity at that time. The Stones, The Kinks and Marianne Faithfull all played the place.

LOCATION 354: at the busy Abington Square. The still magnificent art deco auditorium is currently the Northampton Jesus Centre, postcode NN1 4AE

Born in Northamptonshire

Daniel Ash, guitar, Bauhaus (b. 31 Jul 1957, Northampton)
Richard Coles, keyboards, The Communards (b. 23 Jun 1962, Northampton)
Bob Harris, broadcaster (b. 11 Apr 1946, Northampton)
David J. Haskins, Bauhaus (b. 24 Apr 1957, Northampton)
Kevin Haskins, drums, Bauhaus (b. 19 Jul 1960, Northampton)
Jim King, saxophone, Family (b. 5 May 1942, Kettering)
Peter Murphy, vocals, Bauhaus (b. 11 Jul 1957, Northampton)
Jo Whiley, broadcaster (b. 4 Jul 1965, Northampton)
Thom Yorke, vocals, Radiohead (b. 7 Oct 1968, Wellingborough)

LEICESTERSHIRE

The city of Leicester can be proud that it gave the world Family, one of the most distinctive sounding rock bands, featuring Roger Chapman's magnificent rasping vocals. More famously perhaps, the Human League's Phil Oakey was born here while Engelbert Humperdinck and Mark Morrison grew up in Leicester. From the city's southern outskirts, Blaby and Countesthorpe gave Kasabian to the world and Ashby-de-la-Zouch delivered up that tweedy trio Young Knives. The claims to rock fame keep coming with Stevie Wonder performing on his first visit to the UK as a 14-year-old and the wonderfully idiosyncratic Leicestershire creations that were Showaddywaddy and Cornershop. But it's the variety of live venues, big (De Montfort Hall) small (the Musician pub) and gone forever (The Charlotte), that best boost Leicester's rock CV.

LEICESTER THE ACCIDENTAL BIRTH OF SHOWADDYWADDY

Little changed since it was the Fosseway pub, the Indigo restaurant is the spot where Showaddywaddy were born. Ever wondered why there were so many band members? The eight glam rock Teddy Boys came into being one night in 1973 when the panic-stricken Fosseway landlord realised he had accidentally double-booked two bands. Both Choise and Golden Hammers were persuaded to play together and enjoyed themselves so much that they decided to team-up. As Showaddywaddy, they quickly sky-rocketed to success via TV show New Faces and a string of ten Top 10 hits beginning in 1974.

LOCATION 355: the Indigo at the Fosseway is at 432 Melton Road, three miles north of Leicester city centre, postcode LE4 7SN

East Midlands

LEICESTER
14-YEAR-OLD STEVIE WONDER AT THE ODEON

Fabulously restored to its original art deco glory as the Athena, the Odeon cinema once played host to the 1965 touring Tamla Motown Show. What struck 26-year-old local music fan Keith Dickens first was the excitement at seeing Martha and The Vandellas belting out their latest single 'Nowhere To Run', their debut on the UK Tamla Motown label. "But my most memorable recollection of the event was of seeing the fourteen-year-old, blind Stevie Wonder performing like an animated puppet." Surprisingly, the 21-date tour was considered a flop as attendances were low enough to necessitate Britain's own Georgie Fame being added to the show. But, as Dickens points out, "By the end of the 60s, any of the acts on that bill could have headlined their own show."

LOCATION 356: in the city centre at Queen Street, postcode LE1 1QD

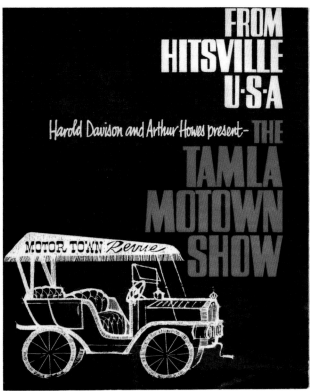

The Motown programme cover for the Leicester show featuring Stevie Wonder in 1965

LEICESTER INDOORS AND OUT AT DE MONTFORT HALL

Leicester's premier concert hall saw Sinatra, The Beatles, The Stones, The Jam, The Clash and Louis Armstrong appear in their heyday and a varied programme of visitors in 2010 included the likes of Henry Rollins, Joan Armatrading and Biffy Clyro. The growing British obsession with summer festivals has encouraged De Montfort Hall and Victoria Park to host June's folk orientated Big Session Festival and the Summer Sundae Weekender outdoor event every year since 2001.

LOCATION 357: the century-old concert hall is in Leicester city centre, 7 Granville Road, postcode LE1 7RU

LEICESTER THE PRINCESS CHARLOTTE: GONE BUT NOT FORGOTTEN

Noel Gallagher once lost a shoe escaping an over-enthusiastic crowd at The Princess Charlotte, Blur were filmed appearing here on the Starshaped DVD and Diesel Park West's John Butler referred to the place as "Leicester's version of [London's] Marquee Club". Gallagher nominated The Charlotte as the setting for his second favourite Oasis gig of all time. "It was that mental that I knew after the encore of 'I Am The Walrus' they were going to invade the stage," he said. "So, I put my guitar down and set the delay pedal going, then ran for my life. I ended up in the dressing room with one shoe." The much-loved pub on Oxford Street was successful partly due to its close proximity for students to the nearby De Montfort University. Many bands including Coldplay, Arctic Monkeys and local favourites Kasabian have good reason to thank The Charlotte for boosting their early careers, but future generations will only be able to read about the place as confirmation of its closure as a music venue came through in spring 2010.

❛The Charlotte is part of Leicester folklore.❜
John Butler (Diesel Park West)

LOCATION 358: if it still exists, you'll find it in Leicester city centre, 8 Oxford Street, postcode LE1 5XZ

LEICESTER **THE ULTIMA THULE 'WEIRD ROCK' EXPERIENCE**

Perhaps this is a rock pilgrimage best enjoyed in the mind. Despite the lack any longer of a physical presence in the city centre, this Leicester institution is still worth flagging up. "Purveyors of Progressive Music From Around the World", Conduit Street was once home to the imaginatively monikered Ultima Thule Record Shop. The owners of the shop were old-fashioned enough to encourage visitors to chat and first listen to the album they were about to consider purchasing. And where else could you possibly shop for progressive, psych, fusion, Krautrock, RIO, Zeuhl, Canterbury, Eurorock, weird, experimental and electronic rock? Now a mail-order operation only, manager Alan Freeman insists that the shop's name is a combination of several philosophical and mystical influences, but appropriately 'Ultima Thule' was also the title of an extremely rare Tangerine Dream single on Ohr Records from 1971.

LOCATION 359: recently relocated a mile or so south of the city centre at 21 Heather Road, postcode LE2 6DF. Now a mail-order operation with visitors by appointment. Website: www. ultimathulerecords.com

LEICESTER **AMERICANA ON CLYDE STREET**

Abandoned and derelict at the end of the 20th century, but on the back of a growing interest in roots music the Bakers Arms near Leicester city centre gradually transformed into The Musician. Hosting live music every night, the beautifully refurbished "Borderline of the Midlands" became Leicester's good news story. With so many music venues closing, local record label boss and gig promoter Darren Nockles turned his attention to filling the 220-capacity Americana-themed venue and bar and even enticing the likes of Ryan Adams to play the former back-street boozer.

❝ He had a classic rock and roll rider – a bottle of vodka and 40 Marlboro Lights. ❞
Darren Nockles persuades Ryan Adams to play The Musician

LOCATION 360: The Musician is close to the city centre in Clyde Street, postcode LE1 2DE. Website: www.themusicianpub.co.uk

Deep in the heart of Leicester: the Musician pub rocks to the sound of Ian Hunter in 2010

Paul Needham / Mohawk Visuals

Born in Leicestershire

Dave Bartram, vocals, Showaddywaddy, (b. 23 Mar 1952, Leicester)
Roger Chapman, vocals, Family (b. 8 Apr 1942, Leicester)
Brian Davison, drums, The Nice (b. 25 May 1942, Leicester, d. 15 Apr 2008)
John Deacon, bass, Queen (b. 19 Aug 1951, Oadby)

Chris Edwards, bass, Kasabian (b. 20 Dec 1980, Leicester)
Robert Gotobed, drums, Wire (b. 21 Apr 1952, Leicester)
Davey (Davy) Graham (b. 26 Nov 1940, Leicester, d. 15 Dec 2008)
John Illsley, bass, Dire Straits (b. 24 Jun 1949, Leicester)
Jon Lord, keyboards, Deep Purple (b.

9 Jun 1941, Leicester)
Tom Meighan, vocals, Kasabian (b. 11 Jan 1981, Leicester)
Philip Oakey, Human League (b. 2 Oct 1955, Leicester)
Viv Prince, drums, The Pretty Things (b. 9 Aug 1941, Loughborough)
Pick Withers, drums, Dire Straits (b. 4 Apr 1948, Leicester)

East Midlands

RUTLAND

Despite a population of just 35,000, Britain's smallest county delivers an excellent smattering of Rock Atlas entries from music heavyweights The Who, The Glitter Band, Geno Washington and Kasabian. The Seventies gave Rutland its most famous rock 'n' roll connection when Rutland Weekend Television and the best ever Beatles parody, The Rutles (both the fictitious creations of Neil Innes and Eric Idle) hit our TV screens.

EXTON **MARMALADE DOWN ON THE FARM**

The resourceful farm folk of Home Farm spotted a non-agricultural use for their two large, linked Dutch barns back in the Seventies. Hired out for barn dances, they went a stage further and coaxed a number of impressive chart acts to play down on the farm. Marmalade, who boasted eight Top 10 singles, and The Glitter Band, with six of their own, were "regularly on Top of the Pops and playing in front of hundreds of people on our farm," remembers farm manager's son Jamie Healey, who was 11 years old at the time.

LOCATION 361: Home Farm, Exton, north of the A606 between Oakham and Stamford, postcode LE15 8AZ

EXTON PARK & COTTESMORE **THE WHO RELAX IN RUTLAND**

Vernon Stokes

The Who were once regular visitors to Rutland during the period their tour manager Bob Pridden lived at Fort Henry in Exton Park. The band availed themselves of the local hospitality and were frequently spotted in the mid-Seventies rehearsing (Exton Village Hall), recording (Bob Pridden's Fort Henry studio) and drinking (The Sun Inn at Cottesmore).

When staying with Pridden at Fort Henry, local pub, The Sun Inn, was a particular favourite of Keith Moon. In 1975, teenage local music fan Vernon Stokes was star-struck on seeing Moon walk into the gents toilets at The Sun Inn. He remembered accidentally peeing down his own trouser leg, which led Moon to comment in an understanding kind of way, "Hey, that's rock

Favourite Who pub hang-out in the summer of '75, The Sun Inn at Cottesmore

'n' roll!", leaving the boy from Oakham with a memory he's never forgotten.

LOCATIONS 362 and **363:** Bob Pridden's Fort Henry is the mock-gothic folly on the Exton Park estate, postcode LE15 8AN. Website: www.extonpark.co.uk. The Sun Inn pub is at 25 Main Street, Cottesmore, postcode LE15 7DH

NORMANTON KASABIAN'S 'MASH-UP' FARM

Leicestershire's multi-award-winning band Kasabian seemingly escape to Rutland at any given opportunity. Aside from having a liking for the county's pubs (Oakham's Railway Inn is said to be a particular favourite), Normanton, near Rutland Water, has come to be the band's creative bolt-hole. Described by vocalist Tom Meighan as "our quiet, private place", the farm at Normanton was the location for a party the band were invited to attend before they hit big in 2004. They found the setting so much to their liking, they moved in and recorded debut album Kasabian there.

LOCATION 363: on the south-east shore of Rutland Water and south of the A606 between Oakham and Stamford. Postcode: LE15 8RP

❛ A big, psychedelic mash-up on a farm. ❜
Kasabian's Sergio Pizzorno describes the band's debut hit album, created at Normanton

STRETTON GENO WASHINGTON AND THE RAM JAM INN

Vernon Stokes

When Geno Washington left his native Indiana to travel from the UK as a member of the US Air Force, he managed to gain a reputation as a part-time soul singer. When discharged as an airman, Washington fronted Geno Washington and The Ram Jam Band, who promptly established themselves as mainstays of the live circuit and chart stars during 1966 and 67. The band were named after the Ram Jam Inn, situated on the A1 at Stretton, a handy stopping point for bands dragging themselves north and south up Britain's busiest road before the completion of the M1 motorway. Amazingly, Geno and his merry men never actually set foot in the place.

❛ In those days it was a pub-cum-restaurant with a petrol station next to it. We never stopped there but were looking for a name for the band and we went through about 2,000 names and none of them sounded right. We were coming down the A1 and just happened to see this place called Ram Jam and we started laughing about the name. We just thought it was a silly fucked-up name but by the time we got back to London we were still laughing at the name Ram Jam so we thought 'hey, if we are still

Still refreshing the parts other routes cannot reach: the Ram Jam Inn

laughing about some shit from two hours ago that must be a good name.' So we named ourselves The Ram Jam Band featuring Geno Washington. ❜
Geno Washington reveals all to Brian Southall in 2011

LOCATION 365: Great North Road, Stretton, postcode LE15 7QX

East Midlands

LINCOLNSHIRE

A county boasting two exceptional wordsmiths. Lyricist Bernie Taupin loved his Lincolnshire, living there and writing some of popular music's best-known lyrics from his times in Grimsby, Market Rasen, Owmby by Spital and, most importantly Tealby, where Britain's best-selling song was conceived. Rod Temperton is another lyrical Lincolnshire lad with a worldwide reputation. He has Michael Jackson's 'Thriller' among many songwriting credits to his name. Worthy of mention in passing is the fact that 'The Devil Went Down To Scunthorpe' by The Toy Dolls was a 1997 reworking of the Charlie Daniels Band smash hit, which had the horn-ed one originally visiting Georgia. The none more cockney British skiffle and rock 'n' roll pioneer Joe Brown was born in the county, in the village of Swarby, before moving south. Travelling in the other direction, Robert Wyatt has made the Lincolnshire town of Louth his home and recording base for more than two decades. And, best claim to fame of all: where would The Beatles have been without a significant Skegness incident?

MARKET RASEN
ELTON'S SATURDAY NIGHT ROCKER

The Aston Arms is where lyricist Bernie Taupin absorbed all his reference material for Elton John's classic rocker 'Saturday Night's Alright For Fighting'. As a teenager he visited Market Rasen to "get a little action in", as the song says, playing snooker, downing pints and watching the "aggravation" develop on a Saturday night. The track was included on Elton's double album Goodbye Yellow Brick Road, but the Aston Arms was pictured on the sleeve notes for follow-up LP Captain Fantastic And The Brown Dirt Cowboy. Another Lincolnshire location immortalised by Taupin was 'Grimsby', a love song on Caribou dedicated to the North Sea fishing port where a pub (not still standing, if it ever stood at all) called the Skinner's Arms gets a mention.

LOCATION 366: the Aston Arms, 18 Market Place, postcode LN8 3HL

SKEGNESS
TRIUMPH AND TRAGEDY: THE RORY STORM STORY

An important incident in the development of The Beatles took place in the bracing Lincolnshire seaside resort of Skegness. Merseyside rock 'n' roll outfit Rory Storm and The Hurricanes (with Richard Starkey, aka Ringo Starr on drums) had a season-long booking at the Butlins holiday camp back in 1962. During this summer residency, John Lennon and Paul McCartney drove from Liverpool to Skegness on August 15th to ask Starr to join The Beatles. Before their arrival, Starr had agreed to join Kingsize Taylor in Hamburg, as Taylor had suggested a £20 weekly pay packet. Lennon and McCartney offered £25 a week, which Starr accepted. Although revered in Liverpool and hugely popular at Butlins, the young Rory Storm was not bound for Ringo's glorious route to worldwide fame and died a tragic death aged just 33 in 1972.

❛Rory was very tall and slim, had bleached-blond hair – rare then – and used to run the mile race at the weekly [Butlins] sports day for a bit of fun. He made a pact with his mother saying that if he didn't emerge as the top Liverpool group he would take his own life. About ten years later, sadly, both him and his mother did this together. ❜
1962 summer season Butlins employee John Scholes, remembers Rory Storm

LOCATION 367: Skegness holiday resort, postcode PE25 1NU

OWMBY BY SPITAL BERNIE TAUPIN'S HOME VILLAGE

Born near the village of Anwick at Flatters, a farmhouse in the South Lincolnshire countryside, it was at the isolated village of Owmby-by-Spital where lyricist Bernie Taupin lived from the age of eight until his first marriage, to Maxine Feibelman, in 1971. Taupin's former bungalow home at Maltkiln Farm lies at the opposite end of Church Lane. He drew inspiration for his songwriting with Elton John through his affection for this remote area. Unconfirmed reports suggest he wrote 'Skyline Pigeon' for Elton's Empty Sky album from happy childhood memories of times spent exploring the village's Norman Church of St Peter and St Paul. The young Taupin would clamber up to the roof and its bell tower, with three bells dating back to 1687.

LOCATION 368: Owmby by Spital lies eight miles south of Lincoln. Both the bungalow (a private residence) and the church are in Church Lane, postcode LN8 2HN

TEALBY BRITAIN'S BEST-SELLING SINGLE WAS WRITTEN HERE

There is no plaque to mark the spot, but it was in this house, called affectionately "Piglet–in-the-Wild" by Bernie Taupin, that Elton John's songwriting partner wrote the original lyrics for 'Candle In The Wind', the song that would become Britain's biggest-selling single. First released on the 1973 Elton album Goodbye Yellow Brick Road, the song was reworked as a tribute to Diana, Princess of Wales in 1997, eventually selling 4.65 million copies in the UK and 33 million worldwide. Many more of Elton's hits that dominated the airwaves and charts in the Seventies were created under the roof of this little-changed cottage Taupin once shared with first wife Maxine.

LOCATION 369: south of the B1203 at Beck Hill, Tealby, postcode LN8 3. Status: private residence

Above: Elton John with Lincolnshire lyricist Bernie Taupin

Right: made in Lincolnshire, Britain's all-time best-seller

Left: Bernie Taupin's former cottage, Piglet-in-the-Wild in Tealby

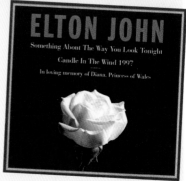

Born in Lincolnshire

Joe Brown (b. 13 May 1941, Swarby)
Raymond 'Boz' Burrell, bass, Bad Company (b. 1 Aug 1946, Lincoln, d. 21 Sep 2006)
Howard Devoto, vocals, Magazine (b. 15 Mar 1952, Scunthorpe)
Vince Eager, singer (b. 4 Jun 1940, Grantham)
Stephen Fretwell, singer-songwriter (b. 10 Nov 1981, Scunthorpe)

Tim Hart, guitar/vocals, Steeleye Span (b. 9 Jan 1948, Lincoln, d. 24 Dec 2009)
Graham Lewis, bass, Wire (b. 22 Feb 1953, Grantham)
Iain Matthews, vocals, Fairport Convention/Matthews' Southern Comfort (b. 16 Jun 1946, Scunthorpe)
Nicola Roberts, Girls Aloud (b. 5 Oct 1985, Stamford)

Martin Simpson, folk singer/guitarist (b. 5 May 1953, Scunthorpe)
Rodney Slater, multi-instrumentalist, Bonzo Dog Doo-Dah Band (b. 8 Nov 1941, Crowland)
Bernie Taupin, lyricist (b. 22 May 1950, Anwick)
Rod Temperton, songwriter/producer/musician (b. 15 Oct 1947, Cleethorpes)

East Midlands

NOTTINGHAMSHIRE

Nottingham University was the unannounced opening gig on Paul McCartney's first Wings tour back in 1972. Still in the seventies... no music related paragraph including the word 'Nottingham' can fail to feature Paper Lace. The band, that still includes one Carlo Santanna in their ranks and topped both the UK and US pop charts, even managed to join forces with Nottingham Forest football club and storm the chart with the men from the City Ground. Nottingham's other club, Notts County, had their own musical claim to fame in 1969 when hosting Britain's first footie stadium rock concert. One indoor venue that has worked hard to put the county on the map of rock 'n' roll worthiness is the star magnet that is Nottingham's Rock City and Retford's Porterhouse also gets more than a passing mention although now only, alas, in a historically gone-but-not-forgotten type of way.

NOTTINGHAM POP AND BLUES AT MEADOW LANE

Presented by Stirling Enterprises, Nottingham can claim to have staged the first outdoor rock gig in a football stadium. Notts County's Meadow Lane ground was the setting for the eleven-hour Pop & Blues Festival on May 10th 1969. Headline attractions were Fleetwood Mac, The Tremeloes and Marmalade, with up-and-coming Pink Floyd sandwiched further down the bill between The Move and Keef Hartley. Despite being headliners, Fleetwood Mac played an early set to enable themselves to fulfill a second booking later that day in Bangor, North Wales. Having reportedly printed 40,000 tickets, the organizer's enterprising but perhaps too eclectic bill attracted just 2,000 paying customers.

LOCATION 370: Notts County F.C., Meadow Lane, postcode NG2 3HJ

NOTTINGHAM BOWIE STARS, OZZY SLEEPS: ROCK CITY

This vibrant all-standing venue dates back to the Eighties and attracted bands of the eventual magnitude of Public Enemy, Nirvana, Pearl Jam and the Red Hot Chili Peppers to Nottingham. Once a bakery, then converted into a cabaret venue, this back-street location didn't make its debut as Rock City until 1980 when The Undertones and Shakin' Stevens entertained the rock-starved punters of Nottingham in the opening week. One memorable Rock City incident involved a no-show by Ozzy Osbourne, which caused a minor riot among waiting fans after the eccentric one failed to rise from his hotel bed. But the city centre venue's most famous moment came in 1997, when rock royalty in the shape of David Bowie did materialise for a visit as part of his Earthling tour, on August 5th.

LOCATION 371: 8 Talbot Street, postcode NG1 5GG. Website: www.rock-city.co.uk

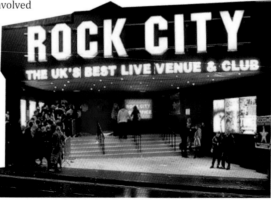

The Killers reportedly sold out Nottingham's rock mecca in 15 minutes

RETFORD NEW BEGINNINGS AT THE PORTERHOUSE

The Porterhouse was where Ultravox played one of their earliest gigs with Midge Ure, U2 got some vital Nottinghamshire feedback in 1980 and New Order began their live transformation from the dark end of Joy Division in 1981. Run by the now legendary Londoner Sammy Jackson, Motorhead and The Clash were among big names persuaded to stop by when heading north on their tour schedules. Jackson also booked AC/DC for only their second appearance on British soil back in May 1976.

LOCATION 372: no longer a music venue, the site of the Porterhouse is at 20 Carolgate, in the centre of Retford, postcode DN22 6BU

NOTTINGHAM
WINGS' SECRET UNIVERSITY GIG DEBUT

With no real definite idea where they were headed, Paul McCartney's new band Wings journeyed north looking for places to play in the early spring of 1972. Incredibly, the superstar ex-Beatle had originally fancied playing Ashby-de-la-Zouch as he liked the sound of the town's name, but their extraordinary journey in a van up the M1 eventually took them to the grand entrance of Nottingham University on February 8th. When an enquiry was made at the Student's Union asking whether Wings could play, the then social secretary, a disbelieving Elaine Woodhams, went outside little expecting to see Paul McCartney and family and band sitting patiently in their transit van. Arrangements were hurriedly made, some very basic advertising flyers pinned up and a 40 pence per ticket price agreed upon before 800 astonished fans watched the historic gig in the University's Portland Ballroom the next day. McCartney's first stage appearance since The Beatles continued with the eleven-gig tour in 15 days, eventually winding up at Oxford University on February 23rd.

❛The word went round like wildfire, just from the blackboard notice up in the bar.❜
Elaine Woodhams

LOCATION 373: a mile or two west of the city centre, the Portland Ballroom (now Portland Dining Room) is at University Park, postcode NG7 2RJ

Above: banned from the radio airwaves, 'Give Ireland Back To The Irish', the controversial first Wings single, which was released at the end of their February tour of universities. Left: promotional poster for the quirky first Wings tour

Born in Nottinghamshire

Rob B (Robert Birch), vocals, Stereo MC's (b. 11 Jun 1961, Ruddington)
David Boulter, keyboards, Tindersticks (b. 27 Feb 1965, Nottingham)
Mark Colwill, bass, Tindersticks (b. 12 May 1960, Nottingham)
Elton Dean, saxophonist (b. 28 Oct 1945, Nottingham, d. 11 Feb 2006)
Bruce Dickinson, vocals, Iron Maiden (b. 7 Aug 1958, Worksop)
Corinne Drewery, vocals, Swing Out Sister (b. 21 Sep 1959, Nottingham)
Andy Fletcher, keyboards, Depeche Mode (b. 8 Jul 1961, Nottingham)
Nick Hallam, DJ/producer, Stereo MC's (b. 11 Jun 1960, Nottingham)
Dickon Hinchliffe, violin/guitar, Tindersticks (b. 9 Jul 1967, Nottingham)
Simon Katz, guitar, Jamiroquai (b. 16 May 1971, Nottingham)
Alvin Lee, vocals/guitar, Ten Years After (b. 19 Dec 1944, Nottingham)
Al Macaulay, drums, Tindersticks (b. 2 Aug 1965, Nottingham)
Dave Manders, vocals/guitar, Paper Lace (b. 4 Aug 1947, Nottingham)
Ian Paice, drums, Deep Purple (b. 29 Jun 1948, Nottingham)
John Parr (b. 18 Nov 1954, Worksop)
Graham Russell, guitar/vocals, Air Supply (b. 11 Jun 1950, Nottingham)
Stuart Staples, vocals/guitar, Tindersticks (b. 14 Nov 1965, Nottingham)
Chris Urbanowicz, guitar, Editors (b. 22 Jun 1981, Aslockton)
Philip Wright, drums, Paper Lace (b. 9 Apr 1946, Nottingham)

DERBYSHIRE

A rocking great pub, a surreal Oasis photoshoot and Harry Webb's unveiling as Cliff Richard are three of the best Derbyshire rock spots. And, years after the famous Buxton Rock Festivals of 1973 and 74 when Rod Stewart andThe Faces and Chuck Berry came to strut their stuff in Derbyshire, sharing its site with the two neighbouring counties of Nottinghamshire and Leicestershire, is Donnington Park, host down the decades for the Monsters Of Rock then Download festivals.

CROMFORD A SURREAL OASIS PHOTOSHOOT

The quaint little grade II listed railway station buildings at Cromford were the location selected when Microdot art director Brian Cannon created the cover for what turned out to be the first No.1 single for Oasis in 1995. The surreal photographic sleeve for 'Some Might Say' featured Liam Gallagher waving from the railway bridge and Noel Gallagher dousing raincoat-wearing barmaid Carla Knox with water from a watering can on the platform. Others enlisted for the shoot included Cannon family members Brian Cannon Senior (with wheelbarrow) Helen Cannon (with mop) and assistant Matthew Sankey (begging for "Education Please").

LOCATION 374: just off Willersley Road, two miles south of Matlock. Cromford railway station, Lea Road, postcode DE4 5JJ. Status: currently advertised as The Waiting Room Holiday Cottage, available to rent as a holiday home. Website: www.cromfordstationwaitingroom.co.uk

❛**Noel [Gallagher] handed me a lyric sheet and said that he wanted all the lyrics represented in the image. That was a tough one. We came up with the concept of a disused railway station, because of the lyric, "Standing at the station/In need of education". We went driving around all over Derbyshire and the one we found in the end, near Matlock, was a masterpiece.**❜
Brian Cannon

Inset: then - the Gallagher brothers, Carla the barmaid, various members of art director Brian Cannon's family and his assistant pose for photographer Michael Spencer Jones' surreal photoshoot; now - the beautifully refurbished Cromford station as it is today

Peter Tarleton

DERBY THE VIC'S BEAT GOES ON

Recently spared demolition in a Derby city centre rejuvenation scheme, the Victoria Inn is an ordinary-looking pub with a passionate promoter and an exceptional list of performers. If you've been a regular at the Vic down the years you will probably have witnessed gigs by The Libertines, Kasabian and Snow Patrol. When the pub isn't reverberating to the next up-and-coming band, you can have a quiet drink gazing at the many rock-related photos, diary pages and posters pasted on the Vic's walls. DJ Micky Sheehan is the driving force behind this vital, 150-capacity venue that, after a struggle, appears to have won the fight to remain on the East Midlands live circuit.

❛ There's a touring route which goes from Scotland to the south and now Derby's on the route because I've worked hard to get good bands on. ❜ Victoria Inn promoter Micky Sheehan

LOCATION 375: opposite the train station at 12 Midland Place, postcode DE1 2RR. Website: www.thevictoriainnderby.co.uk

RIPLEY
HARRY WEBB MAKES HIS DEBUT AS CLIFF RICHARD

The Regal ballroom in Ripley played a huge part in Cliff Richard's personal musical history. On May 3rd 1958, having ditched real name Harry Webb, he performed for the first time under new name Cliff Richard. Billed as Cliff Richard and The Drifters' first appearance outside London and the group's home county of Hertfordshire, it was dance hall manager Harry Greatorex who was the catalyst in the name-change. Greatorex demanded an Elvis or Jerry Lee Lewis-like name for his posters, which resulted in a frantic discussion back in London to arrive at something that would excite Ripley's teenagers. A plaque marking the 50th anniversary of this historic gig was unveiled at the venue in 2008. The gig finished too late for the group to get a southbound train back to London, forcing Cliff and the boys to sleep on the ballroom's benches. However, band member Ian Samwell recalled the ballroom's proper stage with curtains unlike the cramped conditions they were familiar with back at Soho's 2i's club.

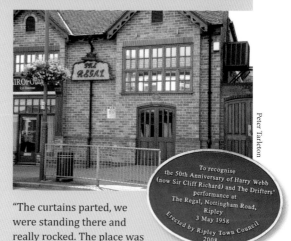

Peter Tarleton

To recognise the 50th Anniversary of Harry Webb (now Sir Cliff Richard) and The Drifters' performance at The Regal, Nottingham Road, Ripley 3 May 1958 Erected by Ripley Town Council 2008

"The curtains parted, we were standing there and really rocked. The place was absolutely jam-packed and the response was fantastic."

❛ I was so unused to the name that when I was introduced I was waiting for someone else to walk out on to the stage. ❜ Cliff Richard admits he wasn't ready for the switch from Harry to Cliff at Ripley

LOCATION 376: Ripley is midway between Derby and Mansfield and the ballroom is at 34 Nottingham Road, postcode DE5 3DJ. Current status: still advertising as an entertainment venue

Lovingly preserved: The Regal on Ripley's Nottingham Road

Born in Derbyshire

Martyn P. Casey, keyboards, Nick Cave and The Bad Seeds (b. 10 Jul 1960, Chesterfield)
Lloyd Cole, vocals/guitar, Lloyd Cole and The Commotions (b. 31 Jan 1961, Buxton)

Kevin Coyne, singer/guitarist (b. 27 Jan 1944, Derby)
Mark Shaw, vocals, Then Jerico (b. 10 Jun 1961, Chesterfield)
Dave Lee Travis, radio DJ (b. 25 May 1945, Buxton)

Mark Webber, guitar, Pulp (b. 14 Sep 1970, Chesterfield)
John Wetton, vocals/bass, Asia/King Crimson (b. 12 Jun 1949, Willington)

West Midlands

WARWICKSHIRE

The West Midlands Ocean Colour Scene boys get out and about in local public parks and gardens and the village of Tanworth-in-Arden is an idyllic mecca for Nick Drake fans. And, two-fifths of Britpop trail-blazers Suede were from the Warwickshire village of Tiddington.

LAPWORTH OCEAN COLOUR SCENE AMID THE TOPIARY

The cover of the 1999 album One From The Modern shows the boys relaxing at the delightful public gardens at Packwood House.

LOCATION 377: the Yew Garden, Packwood House, Lapworth, near Solihull, postcode B94 6AT

Ocean Colour Scene enjoy the topiary at Packwood House

LEAMINGTON SPA OCS SNAPPED AT THE JEPHSON MEMORIAL

Ocean Colour Scene's first hit album Moseley Shoals was 100% home-grown. Moseley Shoals was the Ladywood, Birmingham, studio where the band (three of whom were born in and around the Moseley district) recorded the 1996 release and made their base. The locally sourced album also featured a cover with the band snapped in front of the Jephson Memorial in nearby Leamington Spa's Jephson Gardens. Dr Henry Jephson was a Warwickshire doctor and philanthropist who died in 1878.

LOCATION 378: Moseley Shoals studio is in the Ladywood district of Birmingham and set for demolition. Jephson Gardens is a public park near the centre of Leamington Spa, accessed from The Parade. Postcode: CV32

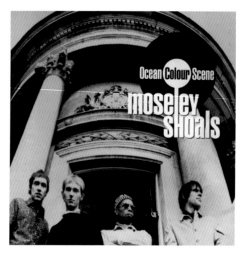

Shot in Leamington Spa: the album title was a play on words in homage to the Muscle Shoals recording studio in America's southern state of Alabama

TANWORTH-IN-ARDEN NICK DRAKE'S CHURCHYARD SHRINE

Largely overlooked by record-buyers when alive, Nick Drake is now pigeon-holed and revered as the shy genius of English songwriting. The three albums released in his lifetime have left a small but much-written-about canon of work. Suicide was the verdict of the coroner when Drake's short life ended in November 1974. Although born in Burma, Tanworth-in-Arden is the village where he spent his childhood at the family estate Far Leys. A short walk from the large Queen Anne house takes you to the village churchyard. Here, sheltered by an ancient oak tree, a gravestone marks the spot where Nick's ashes were interred under the oak's branches in this idyllic spot, much visited by a steady stream of "very sweet young people" as his sister, actress Gabrielle Drake, describes them. In accordance with the notice on the tree – "Fans are requested to pay their respects by leaving only small tokens or flowers." The area is often covered by all manner of tiny ephemera.

❛Now we arise. And we are Everywhere❜
Nick Drake's headstone epitaph, taken from his song 'From The Morning'

LOCATION 379: churchyard of the Church of St Mary Magdalene, Tanworth Green, East Side, postcode B94 5AL. Far Leys is situated in Bates Lane, a short distance west out of Tanworth-in-Arden: Status: private residence

Born in Warwickshire

Edgar Broughton, guitar/vocals, Edgar Broughton Band (b. 27 Oct 1947, Warwick)

Steve Broughton, drums, Edgar Broughton Band (b. 20 May 1950, Warwick)

Neil Codling, keyboards, Suede (b. 5 Dec 1973, Tiddington)

Nicholas 'Razzle' Dingley, drums, Hanoi Rocks (b. 2 Dec 1960, Royal Leamington Spa, d. 9 Dec 1984)

Simon Gilbert, drums, Suede (b. 23 May 1965, Tiddington)

Arthur Grant, bass guitar, Edgar Broughton Band (b. 14 May 1950, Leamington Spa)

June Tabor, folk singer (b. 31 Dec 1947, Warwick)

Simon Taylor-Davis, guitar, Klaxons (b. 18 Jun 1982, Warwick)

Justin Welch, drums, Elastica (b. 4 Dec 1972, Numeaton)

WORCESTERSHIRE

Cornering the market in locations linked to what most would agree to be among the top half dozen rock gods, Worcestershire has noteworthy Beatles, Elvis and Dylan connections and is the home county of Led Zeppelin's Robert Plant and John Bonham. The good Captain Beefheart once enjoyed high tea in Kidderminster and – astonishingly weird fact warning - Eric Clapton played a unique pub gig in front of four England cricket captains at The Crown pub in Martley.

BARNT GREEN ELVIS ON THE ROOF AT GRACELAND

No tourist trip to Worcestershire is complete without a trip to Graceland. A mile or so east of Barnt Green and you are on the Old Birmingham Road heading south towards the M42. Look out for Graceland Garage and the life-size guitar-playing Elvis Presley perched on the edge of the building's roof.

LOCATION 380: Graceland is at 283 Old Birmingham Road, postcode B60 1HQ

There's a guy works down the garage swears he's Elvis

KIDDERMINSTER CAPTAIN BEEFHEART AND MARC BOLAN AT FRANK'S

A plaque put in place by the town's Civic Society marks the spot where Frank Freeman's Dancing Club hosted gigs by rock legends Captain Beefheart, Tyrannosaurus Rex and Fleetwood Mac between 1968 and 1971. Together with his wife Wynn and DJ John Peel, who was a staunch supporter of this unlikely-named venue on his radio shows, the club gained a strong reputation across the Midlands and beyond. May 19th 1968 was the day Captain Beefheart and his Magic Band journeyed north to play this Kidderminster hotspot. Entertained to tea, cucumber sandwiches and cakes by Frank and Wynn and actually driven to the gig from London by John Peel, the good Captain enjoyed his short stay in Kidderminster, taking in the town's shoe shop and the next door Flamingo café where he relaxed over a few games played on the café's pinball machine.

❝ Frank's is the most amazing place. It's remarkable to find a club like this in the middle of nowhere. ❞
John Peel, interviewed by The Sun

LOCATION 381: look out for the extraordinary medieval-style door surrounded by blue tiled bricks in Lower Mill Street, postcode DY11 6UU

MARTLEY CLAPTON AT THE CROWN

Guitar God Eric Clapton played a bizarre gig as a result of losing a bet to his friend Ian Botham back in 1987. The result of the winning bet meant that the cricket legend was able to get Clapton to play for free at a gig of his choosing. Botham chose the wedding of the son of the landlord and landlady at his favourite pub, The Crown at Martley. Occurring on the eve of Worcestershire's County Championship match against Essex, it meant that both teams turned up at the Crown to witness Clapton's appearance. Supported by Chicken Shack guitarist Stan Webb, Clapton had the distinction of being cheered on by pub regulars, the wedding party and four former or future England cricket captains: Hussain, Gooch, Fletcher and a highly satisfied Botham.

LOCATION 382: deep in the Worcestershire countryside, approximately 10 miles north-west of Worcester on Berrow Green Road, postcode WR6 6PA. Website: www.crownatmartley.com

The pub where cricket fan Eric Clapton played in front of an audience that included four England captains

ERIC CLAPTON · BEHIND THE MASK

RUSHOCK JOHN BONHAM'S DRUMSTICK SHRINE

One of rock's greatest characters and drummers, John 'Bonzo' Bonham, is remembered by a headstone in the village churchyard, close to the Bonham family home at Old Hyde Farm. Bonham, who died in 1980, lived for eight years at the farm at Cutnall Green he bought from the proceeds of his extraordinary career with Led Zeppelin. Old Hyde Farm appears in scenes from the band's mid-Seventies movie, The Song Remains The Same. The prominent headstone at Rushock church is a regular place of pilgrimage for Bonham's legions of fans who, appropriately, bring drumsticks to add to the growing collection decorating the spot.

LOCATION 383: east of the A442, south of Kidderminster at St Michael's Parish Church, Rushock, Church Hill, postcode WR9 0NR

TENBURY WELLS THE BEATLES' £100 BOOKING AT THE BRIDGE INN

With a population that wouldn't fill half the Royal Albert Hall, the small market town of Tenbury Wells was nevertheless the location for a milestone gig for The Beatles. The visit coincided with the release of the Fab Four's first chart-topping single and they were booked for a £100 fee at The Bridge Hotel's Riverside Dancing Club well before they were nationally famous. However, the club committee's foresight, or luck, saw The Beatles take to the stage on April 15th 1963 at the same time as single 'From Me To You' and album Please Please Me were on their short climbs to No.1. The ballroom had already witnessed well received visits by Joe Brown and The Bruvvers, Johnny Kidd and The Pirates and Screaming Lord Sutch, but nothing could have prepared the organisers for the frenzied reception The Beatles enjoyed, stoked up by a fresh-in-the-memory TV appearance on ATV show Thank Your Lucky Stars. When John, Paul, George and Ringo took a pre-gig stroll down Teme Street, they experienced the growing hysteria that would soon become Beatlemania. They sneaked into local pub The Crow for a smoke and a drink only to be turfed out by a landlord who took exception to their long hair. A mini pub crawl developed and next stop was The Royal Oak before completing their tour of Tenbury at The Bridge Hotel, where at least one local was bought a pint of Wrekin bitter by George Harrison. Three days after the Bridge gig The Beatles were performing at London's Royal Albert Hall and confirmed as the best new music attraction in the country.

LOCATION 384: Tenbury Wells is 20 miles north west of Worcester. The Bridge Hotel is at 87 Teme Street, postcode WR15 8AE

❛ Looking back it was great that [The Beatles] did honour our booking, as by the time they came to Tenbury they were worth thousands. ❜
Dancing Club Committee member, Pat Lambert

Easter Monday 1963: The Beatles take a stroll in Tenbury Wells

Shropshire Star

WITLEY COURT DYLAN GOES GHOST HUNTING

Gutted by a fire in 1937, Witley Court was the setting for an extraordinary visit by Bob Dylan three decades later. The vast ruined, but still magnificent, mansion was the subject of a ghost-hunting expedition by Dylan and his on tour guitarist Robbie Robertson. Their guides for the night were Traffic band members Dave Mason and Jim Capaldi and local musician Kevyn Gammond. Dylan's vague recollections following this 1966 excursion suggest that Steve Winwood and his brother Muff Winwood were also present when he met his new friends one night at Birmingham club Elbow Room. They all drove the 25 miles from Birmingham to Witley Court in the early hours of the morning, but Dylan's presence was not enough to encourage any spooky activity, apparently. In 1967, Procol Harum's pre-video days film to accompany their smash hit 'A Whiter Shade Of Pale' was shot at Witley Court.

❛We went out to see a haunted house, where a man and his dog was to have burned up in the 13th century. Boy, that place was spooky. ❜
Bob Dylan recalls the trip to Witley Court in an interview with Rolling Stone

LOCATION 385: ten miles north of Worcester on the A443, postcode WR6 6JT. Status: open to the public

West Midlands

WEST MIDLANDS

Trying to avoid the sweeping generalisation that shy, sensitive folk singers are pretty thin on the ground and heavy strident rock predominates in Britain's second city is difficult. No shrinking violets these: made in Birmingham and world famous: The Moody Blues, The Move, ELO, Judas Priest, Black Sabbath, Slade, UB40, Duran Duran, Traffic, The Spencer Davis Group, Fine Young Cannibals and Steel Pulse have all contributed hugely to British music's timeline. Birmingham pays a Hollywood Boulevard-style tribute to some of these rock legends with its Walk of Stars, as does nearby Coventry, honouring its own with a Walk Of Fame and trail around the haunts associated with the city's distinctive 2-Tone movement, which is also the subject of its very own museum.

BIRMINGHAM
OZZY, NODDY AND TONY: STARS ON BROAD STREET

Birmingham's pavement tributes to local rock legends Ozzy Osbourne, Noddy Holder and Tony Iommi run the length of Broad Street. Recent additions to the Walk of Stars have been Bev Bevan, Beverley Knight and Joan Armatrading in what is an on-going process honouring local stars with stars.

❛ I'm so thrilled to have this star. It means more to me than the one I have in Hollywood. ❜
Ozzy Osbourne

LOCATION 386: Broad Street in Birmingham city centre. Noddy Holder's star is near the junction with Berkley Street, Ozzy Osbourne's is at Canal

Broad Street Business Improvement District

Presented to him by the city's mayor in front of a crowd of more than 1,500 fans, Ozzy Osbourne shows off his replica star in Birmingham

Bridge and the Tony Iommi star is outside Symphony Hall, postcode B1 2HF. For a complete guide to all the Walk of Stars locations download the Broad Street app or visit the website at www.broadstreet.co.uk

BIRMINGHAM
HOLE IN THE WALL BEGINNING FOR DURAN DURAN

The Hole In The Wall (now Saramoons) was the pub where Duran Duran were formed. One lunchtime back in 1978, John Taylor and Nick Rhodes met over a few drinks to plot the future of the band named after a character in the 1968 movie Barbarella, which also gave rise to the

name of city centre nightclub Barbarella's at that time. The duo then created their 'manifesto', as Nick Rhodes described it, at the Rum Runner, adding Simon Le Bon and making their chart debut in 1981.

LOCATION 387: Dale End, postcode B4 7LN

BIRMINGHAM
UB40 DOWN THE EAGLE & TUN

The Best of
UB40

Volume One

UB40 at the Eagle & Tun

Handily placed for a drink by the band, whose record label DEP International was close by in Digbeth, the Eagle & Tun pub has served more than one key role in UB40's history. Providing cover photos for the band's Best Of albums and the location for the filming of video 'Red Red Wine', the Victorian red brick building became the main meeting place for fans with the walls decked with UB40 photos. However, this popular community pub is currently closed and looks vulnerable to development.

LOCATION 388: 12 Banbury Street, postcode B5 5RH

COVENTRY
STARS ON THE WALK OF FAME

The Specials, The Selecter, Hazel O'Connor, Pete Waterman and Vince Hill are Coventry's musical sons and daughters honoured with a pavement star on the city's Walk of Fame.

LOCATION 389: the stars are arranged diagonally across Priory Place in Coventry city centre. Postcode CV1 5SQ

COVENTRY 2-TONE CENTRAL

Thanks to the fantastic work of local music expert Pete Chambers, the distinctive sound of 2-Tone music has its own museum. This homage to all things black and white was appropriately housed at Coventry University Students' Union until 2011 as this was the very spot that future Specials band members Jerry Dammers and Horace Panter first got acquainted and where fellow student, and soon to be Selecter front girl, Pauline Black regularly attended in the late Seventies. This location was also the setting for The Specials' 'Rat Race' video, shot back in 1980. All the fascinating 2-Tone memorabilia has now moved to a veritable 2-Tone village featuring Caribbean restaurant, 2-Tone café and even a scooter spares shop.

LOCATION 390: less than two miles east of the city centre, 2-Tone Central is at The Courtyard, 74-80 Walsgrave Road, CV2 4ED. For further details on the museum, an 11-plaque 2-Tone trail, accompanying book and app, visit the website: www.2tonecentral.co.uk

Founder of 2-Tone, Jerry Dammers, comes into contact with his earlier self at the 2-Tone Central museum in Coventry

John Coles

West Midlands

COVENTRY **LOCARNO TO LIBRARY CHART-TOPPERS**

Chuck Berry's biggest, although certainly not his best, hit single was recorded during a live performance at Coventry's Locarno on Smithford Way. Recorded at the Lancaster Arts Festival on February 3rd 1972, 'My Ding-A-Ling' became a novelty chart-topper later that same year, only prevented

from bagging the Christmas No.1 spot by the equally dubious 'Long Haired Lover From Liverpool' by Little Jimmy Osmond. Later that same decade, the Locano had a name change to Tiffany's, where another 'live' No.1 hit was recorded by The Specials. Some of the five tracks contributed to 'The

Special A.K.A. Live! EP', the band's first chart-topper, which hit the top spot in February 1980.

LOCATION 391: the Locarno ballroom at Smithford Way survived a name-change to Tiffany's and is now the city's Central Library, postcode CV1 1FY

COVENTRY **THE BIRTHPLACE OF 2-TONE**

A house on Albany Road was home to Specials founder Jerry Dammers and the general base and office for the 2-Tone record label. Here the band members would meet to perform DIY production line tasks, rubber-stamping the titles on the record sleeves of the first 2-Tone record releases. The building, which carries a plaque marking the birthplace of 2-Tone above the front bedroom window, is one of a number of locations included in a 2-Tone Trail featuring 11 distinctive black and white plaques dotted around the city. For more information on the Trail, which includes additional Rock Atlas entries at the University and Tiffany's, visit the www.2tonecentral.co.uk website.

❛Our office was a complete tip! Everything was run from this little bedroom at Jerry's house in Albany Road.❜
Lynval Golding of The Specials

LOCATION 392: the 2-Tone office was west of the city centre at 51 Albany Road, postcode CV5 6

The Specials' Lynval Golding and Coventry ambassador and plaque sponsor Pete Chambers outside the former 2-Tone bedroom office in Albany Road

The rubber stamp production line at Albany Road created these sleeves in the cramped bedroom at No.51

John Coles

HANDSWORTH
STEEL PULSE
REVOLUTION

A hotbed of reggae music, Handsworth was where Steel Pulse main man David Hinds grew up and formed the band while still at Handsworth Wood School. A milestone British reggae album release in 1978, Handsworth Revolution and its title track was a hopeful rallying cry to the black community in this vibrant inner city area of Birmingham.

❛ We feel comfortable there because there's a spirit down there, a sort of community spirit which we can't really find anywhere else. ❜
Steel Pulse keyboards man Selwyn Brown, talking to Sounds

LOCATION 393: three miles north-west of the city centre, postcode B21

WOLVERHAMPTON NORTHERN SOUL AT THE CATACOMBS

One of the least northerly of the legendary Northern Soul clubs, The Catacombs sounds like a subterranean system of tunnels but was actually a bare brick-walled first-floor club. Utilising the former lead smelting works furnace alcoves as the perfect atmospheric, dark and sweaty environment, the venue enjoyed a comparatively long existence from 1967 until its closure in 1974. Despite its fame as the epicentre of the Black Country's passionate soul community, the Catacombs also hosted the best underground rock groups such as Man and Caravan, and even David Bowie made an appearance back in 1969. As is frequently the case with iconic, much-loved music venues, it's hard to see how such a slab of a building can have meant so much to so many Northern Soul fans. Deserving of a plaque, it duly got one when the Wolverhampton Civic Society, who had previously limited its plaque budget to local dignitaries, created its 96th blue cast-iron memorial for the wall at the original Catacombs site in Temple Street.

LOCATION 394: the site of the original club and its plaque is in the centre of Wolverhampton on Temple Street, postcode WV2 4AQ

Original Northern Soul fans from the Sixties and Seventies congregate underneath the small plaque which marks the site of The Catacombs, or 'The Cats' as it was affectionately known

Born in the West Midlands

Kelli Ali (aka Kelli Dayton), vocals, Sneaker Pimps (b. 30 Jun 1974, Birmingham)
Astro (Terence Wilson), trumpet/vocals, UB40 (b. 24 Jun 1957, Birmingham)
Martin Barre, guitar, Jethro Tull (b. 17 Nov 1946, Birmingham)
Ritch Battersby, drums, The Wildhearts (b. 29 Jun 1968, Birmingham)

Blaze Bayley, vocals, Iron Maiden (b. 29 May 1963, Birmingham)
Bev Bevan, drums, The Move/Electric Light Orchestra (b. 24 Nov 1944, Birmingham)
John Bradbury, drums, The Specials (b. 1956, Coventry)
Jim Brown, drums, UB40 (b. 20 Nov 1957, Birmingham)
Trevor Burton, guitar,

The Move (b. 9 Mar 1949, Birmingham)
Terry 'Geezer' Butler, bass, Black Sabbath (b. 17 Jul 1949, Birmingham)
Ali Campbell, vocals, UB40 (b. 15 Feb 1959, Birmingham)
Robin Campbell, guitar, UB40 (b. 25 Dec 1954, Birmingham)
Rob Cieka, drums, The Boo Radleys (b. 4 Aug 1968, Birmingham)

Paul Clifford, bass, The Wonder Stuff (b. 23 Apr 1968, Birmingham)
Andy Cox, guitar, Fine Young Cannibals (b. 25 Jan 1956, Birmingham)
Graham Crabb, drums, Pop Will Eat Itself (b. 10 Oct 1964, Sutton Coldfield)
Steve Cradock, guitar/keyboards, Ocean Colour Scene (b. 22 Aug 1969, Birmingham)

West Midlands

Fyfe Dangerfield, vocals, Guillemots (b. 7 Jul 1980, Moseley)

'K.K.' Downing, guitar, Judas Priest (b. 27 Oct 1951, West Bromwich)

Earl Falconer, bass, UB40 (b. 23 Jan 1957, Birmingham)

Jem Finer, banjo, The Pogues (b. 25 Jul 1955, Stoke-on-Trent)

Simon Fowler, vocals, Ocean Colour Scene (b. 25 Apr 1965, Birmingham)

Steve Gibbons, vocals/guitar, The Uglys (b. 13 Jul 1941, Birmingham)

Roland Gift, vocals, Fine Young Cannibals (b. 28 May 1961, Birmingham)

Goldie (b. 19 Sep 1965, Walsall)

Kelly Groucutt, bass/vocals, Electric Light Orchestra (b. 8 Sep 1945, Coseley, d. 19 Feb 2009)

Rob Halford, vocals, Judas Priest (b. 25 Aug 1951, Sutton Coldfield)

Terry Hall, vocals, The Specials (b. 19 Mar 1959, Coventry)

Oscar Harrison, drums/keyboards, Ocean Colour Scene (b. 15 Apr 1965, Birmingham)

Norman Hassan, percussion, UB40 (b. 26 Jan 1958, Birmingham)

Ian Hill, bass, Judas Priest (b. 20 Jan 1951, West Bromwich)

Vince Hill (b. 16 Apr 1937, Coventry)

David Hinds, vocals/guitar, Steel Pulse (b. 15 Jun 1956, Birmingham)

Noddy Holder, vocals/guitar, Slade (b. 15 Jun 1946, Walsall)

Miles Hunt, vocals, The Wonder Stuff (b. 29 Jul 1966, Birmingham)

Frank Ifield (b. 30 Nov 1937, Coventry)

Tony Iommi, guitar, Black Sabbath (b. 19 Feb 1948, Birmingham)

Beverley Knight (b. 22 Mar 1973, Wolverhampton)

Jim Lea, bass/keyboards, Slade (b. 14 Jun 1949, Wolverhampton)

John Lodge, vocals/bass, The Moody Blues (b. 20 Jul 1943, Birmingham)

Jeff Lynne, The Move/Electric Light Orchestra/Traveling Wilburys (b. 30 Dec 1947, Birmingham)

Phil Lynott, vocals/bass, Thin Lizzy (b. 20 Aug 1949, West Bromwich, d. 4 Jan 1986)

Clinton Mansell, vocals, Pop Will Eat Itself (b. 7 Jan 1963, Coventry)

Tony Martin, vocals, Black Sabbath (b. 19 Apr 1957, Birmingham)

Nick Mason, drums, Pink Floyd (b. 27 Jan 1944, Birmingham)

Brian Matthew, radio presenter (b. 17 Sep 1928, Coventry)

Adam Mole, guitar, Pop Will Eat Itself (b. 8 Apr 1962, Stourbridge)

Hazel O'Connor (b. 16 May 1955, Coventry)

Ozzy Osbourne (b. 3 Dec 1948, Birmingham)

Carl Palmer, drums, Crazy World of Arthur Brown/Emerson, Lake & Palmer (b. 20 Mar 1950, Birmingham)

Dave Pegg, bass, Fairport Convention (b. 2 Nov 1947, Birmingham)

Brian Pendleton, guitar, The Pretty Things (b. 13 Apr 1944, Wolverhampton, d. 16 May 2001)

Jason Pierce, vocals/guitar, Spiritualized (b. 19 Nov 1965, Rugby)

Mike Pinder, keyboards/vocals, The Moody Blues (b. 27 Dec 1941, Birmingham)

Robert Plant (b. 20 Aug 1948, West Bromwich)

Don Powell, drums, Slade (b. 10 Sep 1946, Bilston)

Mathew Priest, drums, Dodgy (b. 3 Apr 1970, Birmingham)

Roddy Radiation (Roderick Byers), guitar, The Specials (b. 5 May 1955, Coventry)

Nick Rhodes, keyboards, Duran Duran (b. 8 Jun 1962, Moseley)

John Rostill, bass, The Shadows (b. 16 Jun 1942, Birmingham, d. 26 Nov 1973)

Kevin Rowland, vocals/guitar, Dexy's Midnight Runners (b. 17 Aug 1953, Wolverhampton)

Mike Skinner, The Streets (b. 27 Nov 1978, Birmingham)

Richard Tandy, keyboards, Electric Light Orchestra (b. 26 Mar 1948, Birmingham)

Roger Taylor, drums, Duran Duran (b. 26 Apr 1960, Birmingham)

Glenn Tipton, guitar, Judas Priest (b. 25 Oct 1947, Blackheath)

Richard 'Fuzz' Townshend, drums, Pop Will Eat Itself (b. 31 Jul 1964, Birmingham)

Brian Travers, saxophone, UB40 (b. 7 Feb 1959, Birmingham)

Stephen Vaughan, bass, PJ Harvey (b. 22 Jun 1962, Wolverhampton)

Mickey Virtue, keyboards, UB40 (b. 19 Jan 1957, Birmingham)

Johnnie Walker, radio presenter (b. 30 Mar 1945, Solihull)

Pete Waterman, producer (b. 15 Jan 1947, Coventry)

Peter Overend Watts, bass, Mott The Hoople (b. 13 May 1947, Birmingham)

Carl Wayne, vocals, The Move (b. 18 Aug 1943, Birmingham, d. 31 Aug 2004)

Toyah Willcox (b. 18 May 1958, Birmingham)

Mervyn 'Muff' Winwood, The Spencer Davis Group (b. 15 Jun 1943, Birmingham)

Steve Winwood, (b. 12 May 1948, Birmingham)

Chris Wood, flute/saxophone, Traffic (b. 24 Jun 1944, Birmingham, d. 12 Jul 1983)

Roy Wood (b. 8 Nov 1946, Birmingham)

STAFFORDSHIRE

Slash grew up in Blurton, Stoke-on-Trent, and recommends his grandmother's pies, his old chum Lemmy was born just down the road, and a third rock 'n' roll hellraiser, Ozzy Osbourne, bought a country retreat and tried manfully to settle down in the village of Ranton. Add to that a Hollywood Festival coming to Little Madeley and the mighty Northern Soul meccas The Golden Torch and the Heavy Steam Machine and you have a county brim full of legendary music locations. And, lest we forget, the name most likely to encourage local bigwigs to erect a plaque in his honour - there's even talk of a Robbie trail being created around these parts - would be the Port Vale F.C. loving Robbie Williams, who was born in Stoke and grew up in the cheery atmosphere of Burslem's Red Lion pub.

❝ My grandmother made great mince pies and my dad would take me for long walks in the countryside. I loved it. ❞
Slash expresses his fondness for Staffordshire in an interview with GQ

BURSLEM
ROBBIE'S CHILDHOOD HOME AT THE RED LION

Vacating their conventional three-bedroom semi in Burslem in 1976, the two-year-old Robert Williams and family moved to their new home farther along the same road. The Red Lion pub became the family home for a teenage Robbie Williams until mum and dad, landlady Jan and landlord Pete, separated. Burslem is one of Stoke-on-Trent's six towns in the Potteries, which also includes Tunstall, where Robbie subsequently lived with his mother and sister Sally in Greenbank Road. The singer's family connections to his local football club Port Vale are strong. His father was licensee at the football ground's Vale Park social club and Robbie is reported to have invested £240,000 in the club he has supported since he was a child living within sight of the stadium's floodlights at the Red Lion on Moorland Road.

❝ I've been a Port Vale fan all my life. When I was younger I was in the Railway Paddock and I used to dream about sitting in the chairman's box. ❞
Robbie Williams

LOCATION 395: the Red Lion, 3 Moorland Road, near to the crossroads with the main A50 in Burslem, postcode ST6 1DJ

A short walk from his home at the Red Lion pub would take the football-mad Robbie Williams up Hamil Road to watch his beloved Port Vale at Vale Park

West Midlands

LITTLE MADELEY
THE GRATEFUL DEAD COME TO HOLLYWOOD

On May 23rd 1970, American rock band The Grateful Dead played their first gig outside the US at the grandly-named Hollywood Rock Festival. On a stage adorned by a 20-foot-high red and gold-coloured phallic symbol, the festival line-up also featured a second West Coast band, The Flying Burrito Brothers, a career-defining performance by Mungo Jerry, strong sets from Traffic and Family and a special guest appearance from blind guitarist José Feliciano, who arrived in style on the festival site, chauffeur-driven in a Jaguar. Unsurprisingly, the local pubs in the area did fantastic business with almost 30,000 fans descending on the place. The Crewe Arms at Madeley Heath was particularly popular and was drunk completely dry within a few hours of opening.

LOCATION 396: the festival site is east of the village of Madeley, a short distance west of the M6 off the A525. Postcode: CW3 9JT

RANTON OZZY'S 'ATROCITY COTTAGE'

The delightfully named Bullrush Cottage is where Ozzy Osbourne lived with his equally delightfully named first wife Thelma Mayfair until the early 1980s. Here he would unwind from the rigours of rock stardom by firing off his shotgun and racing his motorbike and cars across the local fields and lanes. Not adverse to a bit of home improvement while at Bullrush Cottage, Ozzy organised the building of a home studio and turned his hand to creating the waterfall that feeds the front garden pond. Ozzy was a loyal supporter of local pub the Hand & Cleaver, where he spent almost as much time as he did back at 'Atrocity Cottage', as Ozzy and friends nicknamed his country home.

LOCATION 397: both the cottage and pub are a few miles west of Stafford in Butt Lane, Ranton, postcode ST18 9JZ. Status: Bullrush Cottage is a private residence

TUNSTALL
NORTHERN SOUL AT THE GOLDEN TORCH

This prominent building was purchased as the Regal cinema by new owner Chris Burton in 1965 and was christened as a music venue by Billy J Kramer and The Dakotas. The Golden Torch's popularity as a soul venue was first sparked by an enthusiastically received appearance by Inez and Charlie Foxx in 1967. Subsequent highlights, in Burton's opinion, included performances by Major Lance, Oscar Toney Jr, Junior Walker and The Stylistics. The Drifters and Edwin Starr also made it to Tunstall, where a record attendance was set in 1973 when 1,300 soul fans crammed in. A second Northern Soul hotbed could be found in the Potteries in Hanley, where the Heavy Steam Machine did good business without ever quite upstaging The Golden Torch.

LOCATION 398: sadly only the former site of The Golden Torch remains. The building is at Hose Street, Tunstall, postcode ST6 5AL

Born in Staffordshire

Mick Dyche, guitar, Sniff 'n' The Tears (b. 1951, Burton-upon-Trent)
Graeme Edge, drums, The Moody Blues (b. 30 Mar 1941, Rocester)
Richie Edwards, bass, The Darkness (b. 25 Sep 1974, Lichfield)
Mel Galley, guitar, Whitesnake (b. 8 Mar 1948, Cannock, d. 1 Jul 2008)
Fran Healy, vocals/guitar, Travis (b.

23 Jul 1973, Stafford)
Glenn Hughes, bass/vocals, Deep Purple/Black Sabbath/Trapeze/Black Country Communion (b. 21 Aug 1951, Cannock)
Joe Jackson (b. 11 Aug 1954, Burton-upon-Trent)
Lemmy (Ian Kilmister), vocals, Motörhead (b. 24 Dec 1945, Stoke)

Robert Lloyd, vocals, The Nightingales (b. 5 Jun 1959, Cannock)
Andy Moor, DJ (b. 16 Jan 1980, Stoke)
Jackie Trent (b. 6 Sep 1940, Newcastle-under-Lyme)
Jonathan Wilkes (b. 1 Aug 1978, Stoke-on-Trent)
Robbie Williams (b. 13 Feb 1974, Stoke-on-Trent)

SHROPSHIRE

The county of birth for proper rock legend Ian Hunter of Mott The Hoople. Shropshire's county town Shrewsbury was where DJ John Peel spent his somewhat reluctant school days and, additionally, was where the locals witnessed three appearances by The Beatles in less than five months. The second of these visits coincided with a particularly significant day in the life of Lennon and McCartney's song-writing partnership.

SHREWSBURY LENNON & McCARTNEY PEN THEIR FIRST NUMBER ONE

The Beatles made three visits to Shrewsbury, all in less than five months. December 14th 1962 saw them arrive for their first performance, at the town's Music Hall. Their third and final appearance was on April 26th 1963 at the same venue. However, the second Shrewsbury concert was to be the most significant - for them at least. Arriving in the back of their tour bus on the Helen Shapiro tour on February 28th 1963, as the coach transporting the group completed its journey from York to Shrewsbury's Granada cinema, John Lennon and Paul McCartney completed their latest composition, 'From Me To You'. A pivotal release in Beatles history, the song would register as the group's first number one hit and top the singles chart in the same week of their final visit to the town.

LOCATION 399: the Grade II listed building, once the Granada cinema now a bingo hall, is at 6 Castle Gates, postcode SY1 2AG

SHREWSBURY IAN HUNTER'S CHILDHOOD HOME

Before gravitating to London and before Mott The Hoople, Shrewsbury was where young Ian Hunter Patterson grew up. After the Mott The Hoople years, Ian Hunter, as he'd become by then, later released a steady stream of solo albums including the 1996 offering The Artful Dodger, which featured the autobiographical '23a Swan Hill'. His teenage address, the song paints a less than romantic picture of a place where it was always raining that he wanted a way out of.

LOCATION 400: 23a Swan Hill, town centre, postcode SY1 1NQ. Status: private residence

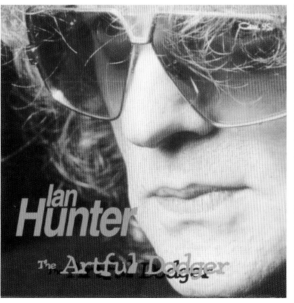

A rollicking crowd pleaser at Ian Hunter's solo gigs, the '23a Swan Hill' was featured on this 1996 album

Born in Shropshire

Michael Chetwood, keyboards, T'Pau (b. 26 Aug 1954, Telford)
Dick Heckstall-Smith, saxophonist (b. 16 Sep 1934, Ludlow, d. 17 Dec 2004)
Ian Hunter, vocals/guitar, Mott The Hoople (b. 3 Jun 1939, Oswestry)
Paul Jackson, bass, T'Pau (b. 8 Aug 1961, Telford)
Stephen Jones, Babybird (b. 16 Sep 1962, Telford)
Ronnie Rogers, guitar, T'Pau (b. 13 Mar 1959, Shrewsbury)

West Midlands

HEREFORDSHIRE

Just about every major act apart from The Beatles played Hereford's Hillside Ballroom back in the Sixties, but it's the interesting, less obvious venues at Grosmont Wood Barn and Hereford United football ground that are perhaps most noteworthy. And, Black Sabbath drummer Bill Ward's extraordinary and ingenious wrought iron homage to the band's track 'Paranoid' just begs the question why no other rock star mansions have followed suit. The county can claim to have also given us the majority of the line-ups for The Pretenders and Mott The Hoople, but it's Mike Oldfield's retreat to escape the pressures of stardom following Tubular Bells at Hergest Ridge that has to be the jewel in Herefordshire's rock crown.

CRADLEY THE BLACK SABBATH BLACKSMITH CALLS

It was near this upmarket Herefordshire village that Black Sabbath drummer Bill Ward commissioned the distinctive 'Paranoid'-themed entrance gates to his Summerville House home. Knowing that David Tangye was employed by Sabbath frontman Ozzy Osbourne but also a blacksmith by profession, Ward called on his craftsmanship to fashion the

iron gates displaying the opening musical notes to 'Paranoid', Black Sabbath's best known track. Tangye was a man of many talents: the Ozzy emissary and blacksmith also went on to co-author the Black Sabbath biography,

How Black Was Our Sabbath.

LOCATION 401:
Summerville House is on Bromyard Road, postcode WR13 5JL. Status: private residence

The rough sketch made by Black Sabbath blacksmith David Tangye for drummer Bill Ward's decorative gates to Summerville House

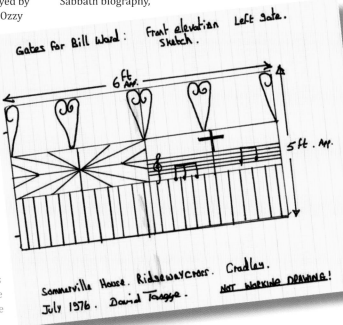

HEREFORD UNITED IN ROCK AT EDGAR STREET

Island Records' recording artists Mott The Hoople, Heads, Hands and Feet and Amazing Blondel formed the line-up for one of the earliest ever football stadium concerts at Hereford United's Edgar Street football ground. No Woodstock, the August Bank Holiday event in 1971 drew a crowd of more than 3,000 rock fans: still

substantially more than non-league United's attendances for football matches at the time, until their epic FA Cup giant-killing of Newcastle United the following winter.

LOCATION 402: the United football ground is in the centre of Hereford, at Edgar Street, postcode HR4 9JU

GROSMONT FLOYD, TULL AND MAC DOWN ON THE FARM

With no neighbours and a decent traffic-free route in, this location could have claimed to be the perfect rave venue, with police approval! Grosmont Wood Farm barn was the remote rural venue for some extraordinary rock concerts. The Gwent Constabulary Spring Bank Holiday Barn Dance in 1967 saw recent

chart debutants Pink Floyd performing while Jethro Tull, Fleetwood Mac and Arthur Brown played the place almost exactly two years later.

LOCATION 403: approximately two miles north-west off the B4521 at Cross Ash, postcode NP7 8LB. Status: private farm

KINGTON MIKE OLDFIELD UP ON THE RIDGE

Mike Oldfield's second massively popular album, Hergest Ridge, was named after the place where he created it. The elevated 1,000-foot-high ridge is a natural beauty spot with breathtaking views. The house where the 20-year-old Oldfield wrote the 1974 follow-up to Tubular Bells is The Beacon, close to the border between England and Wales at Kington. Oldfield's third studio album Ommadawn was also conceived and written at his former country retreat, which became a guesthouse.

❛ When [Mike Oldfield] was here, there was no road into The Beacon as such. He had to come along a lane to the common, and drag a grand piano 200 yards up the hillside, which he did, and then he couldn't get it through the door, so he took the windows out to get it in. ❜
Beacon owner Rob Pritchard, interviewed by BBC Hereford & Worcester

LOCATION 404: The Beacon, which has now reverted to a private residence, is on Bradnor Hill near Kington. Hergest Ridge can be visited by following the National Trail out of Kington, which is situated on the A44, postcode HR5

Mike Oldfield's Irish Wolfhound 'Bootleg' and his model glider decorate the Hergest Ridge album cover, photographed on the ridge by Trevor Key

Born in Herefordshire

Martin Chambers, drums, The Pretenders (b. 4 Sep 1951, Hereford)
Pete Farndon, bass, The Pretenders (b. 12 Jun 1952, Hereford, d. 14 Apr 1983)
Ellie Goulding (b. 30 Dec 1986, Hereford)
Dale 'Buffin' Griffin, drums, Mott The Hoople (b. 24 Oct 1948, Ross-on-Wye)
James Honeyman-Scott, guitar, The Pretenders (b. 4 Nov 1956, Hereford, d. 16 Jun 1982)
Albert Lee, guitar (b. 21 Dec 1943, Leominster)
Mick Ralphs, guitar, Bad Company/Mott The Hoople (b. 31 Mar 1944, Stoke Lacy)

Ellie Goulding hails from Herefordshire and still lives in the county

ROCK ATLAS
Wales

UK and Ireland Edition

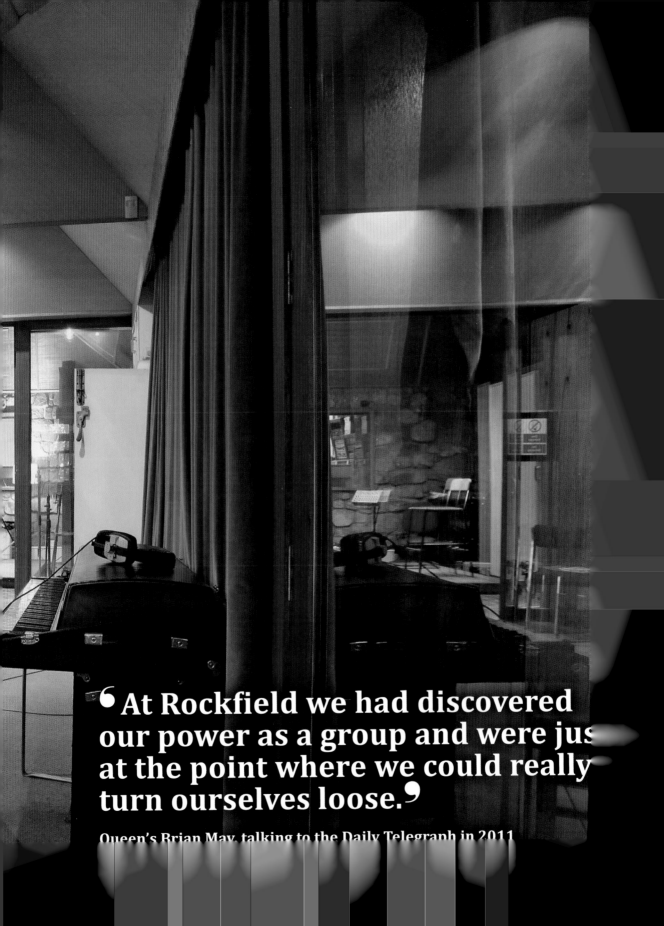

'At Rockfield we had discovered our power as a group and were jus[t] at the point where we could really turn ourselves loose.'

Queen's Brian May, talking to the Daily Telegraph in 2011

Wales

WALES

❝There are no proper roads between north and south Wales, and Beeching shut the railway down, so to travel from one end of the country to the other - either by rail or to get a proper road - you have to go through England. It's very political: divide and conquer and all that.❞ A geography lesson from Super Furry Animals singer Gruff Rhys from Ben Thompson's book Ways Of Hearing sets us up nicely for the journeys ahead.

There's immense pride in the principality at producing a steady stream of cutting-edge to comic Welsh rock from John Cale to Goldie Lookin Chain. A fact flow of stories tell of the survival of the world's oldest record shop, Jerry Hall dressing up as a mermaid for Bryan Ferry, Kurt Cobain failing to cough up £3 to enter a Newport nightspot, Page and Plant's cottage industry, Joe Strummer's Vultures, a Byrds Welsh mining song, the world's first residential recording studios in the village of Rockfield, a lovely trip to Bangor by The Beatles and the Fab Four's final concert on British soil.

❝The Welsh have voices sweeter than angels.❞ Robert Plant confirmed what we already knew in Ritchie Yorke's Led Zeppelin biography

ABERDARE & CWMAMAN
BIRTHPLACE OF THE STEREOPHONICS

On the day of former Stereophonics band member Stuart Cable's funeral in 2010, thousands of fans brought Aberdare to a standstill as family and friends packed into the drummer's local St Elvan's Church. A short stroll from the church takes you past the town's 600-seater Coliseum, where the band played an early breakthrough gig as Tragic Love Company. Throwing off the shackles of their existence under this less than memorable moniker, a name change and steady rise to success as the Stereophonics quickly followed. Just over two miles south of Aberdare lies the coal-mining village of Cwmaman, where the original line-up of Stereophonics met and went to school together: drummer Stuart Cable had lived in the same Cwmaman street where singer Kelly Jones lived. The nearby Workmen's & Social Club was the spot where the band made their earliest

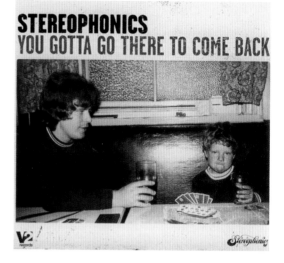

performance and it was here they returned on December 14th 2007 to play a one-off acoustic homecoming gig for a BBC Radio 1 Live Lounge programme presented by Jo Whiley.

LOCATION 405: Cwmaman Workmen's & Social Club is on Glanaman Road, postcode CF44 6LA

The band's 2003 No.1 album cover shows band member Kelly Jones' brother and dad enjoying some quality time at Cwmaman pub the Ivy Bush, where Kelly would later perform with an early incarnation of the Stereophonics

ABERGAVENNY JOHN LENNON'S
JUKE BOX JURY HELICOPTER DASH

The market town immortalised in the song 'Abergavenny', written and recorded by Marty Wilde in 1968, also hosted a newsworthy performance by The Beatles a few years earlier on June 22nd 1963. Not until 10.30pm did the Fab Four take to the Town Hall Ballroom stage as John Lennon arrived late after filming a TV appearance on the BBC show Juke Box Jury earlier in the day. Lennon was flown in by helicopter from London and touched down at the best available makeshift heliport Abergavenny could offer, the nearby Penypound football ground. The group's hour-long performance in front of 600 fans was followed by an untroubled overnight stay at the Angel Hotel.

LOCATIONS 406 and **407:** Abergavenny is on the Welsh/English border off the A40. The Town Hall (postcode NP7 5HD) and the Angel Hotel (postcode NP7 5EN) are both in Cross Street

BANGOR FLOWER POWER IN NORTH WALES: THE BEATLES BREAK COVER

Little had been seen of The Beatles since they quit concert performances in 1966. So, by 1967's 'Summer Of Love' when they made headlines with a trip to North Wales, all that pent-up Beatlemania was released once more on the largely bewildered seaside resort of Bangor. The purpose of the visit on August 25th was to take in the lectures of Maharishi Mahesh Yogi, leader of the Spiritual Regeneration Movement who was holding a conference at Normal College Bangor. Unimaginable today, but The Beatles entourage, including Mick Jagger and Marianne Faithfull, all travelled by train on the 3.15pm out of London's Euston Station, bound for Bangor. If the crowds of fans and reporters were enthusiastic to once again see the Fab Four at Euston they were in full hysterical mode by the time the train arrived in Bangor. Taxied without mishap to their spartan dormitory accommodation at the vacant University, The Beatles even managed to slip out for a late night meal at The Senior Chinese restaurant, but awoke the next morning to find the University gardens stripped of all the flowers by the growing hordes of flower power fans. The ten-day-long visit was cut short on August 27th when Paul McCartney took the telephone call that broke the news that Brian Epstein had been found dead. The extraordinary trip to North Wales had been the first The Beatles had undertaken without their manager.

❝Cyn [Cynthia] and I were thinking of going to Libya, until this came up. Libya or Bangor? Well, there was no choice, was there?❞ John Lennon

❝The Maharishi was **sitting in the darkened hall and he could see the teenagers looking through the windows. 'Let them all come in' he said. He was holding a dahlia in his hand and he slowly plucked off the petals. He couldn't quite pronounce 'dahlia' as we would and said 'A darrlia is a darrlia is a darrlia' and other mumbo jumbo.**❞ University Student Landlady Edna Pritchard recalls being a teenager again for one day

LOCATION 408: Hugh Owen Hall, Bangor University, Bangor, Gwynedd, LL57 2DG

Top: the University's framed plaque, and (above) Edna Pritchard attending the 40th anniversary reunion of The Beatles' two day trip to Bangor

Wales

BARAFUNDLE BAY GORKY'S PEMBROKESHIRE POSTCARD

The splendidly named but unfortunately now defunct Gorky's Zygotic Mynci hailed from Pembrokeshire and titled their 1997 album Barafundle after the beautiful bay and beach pictured on a postcard in the centre of the cover.

LOCATION 409: six miles south of Pembroke, closest postcode SA70

CARDIFF THE END OF THE ROAD FOR THE BEATLES AND KINKS

The Beatles' appearance at Cardiff's Capitol cinema on December 12th 1965 was the last on British soil in front of a paying audience. The Cardiff concerts – there were two 30-minute sets on the day – were the final date of the tour, on which they were supported by The Moody Blues and fellow Liverpool acts The Koobas and Beryl Marsden. Although 25,000 fans applied for tickets, only 5,000 were lucky enough to witness what would turn out to be a last chance to see The Beatles perform a regular concert in the UK. Two previous visits to the Capitol Cinema had already occurred when The Beatles toured with Roy Orbison and Gerry & The Pacemakers in May 1963 and again in November 1964, when Sounds Incorporated and Mary Wells were among the supporting bill. Similar hysterical receptions to those that greeted The Beatles at the Capitol were also experienced by early teen idols Bill Haley & His Comets in the Fifties and the Bay City Rollers in the Seventies. The venue also witnessed a famous on-stage bust-up that ended a bill-topping package tour by The Kinks in May 1965. So serious was the altercation between drummer Mick Avory and guitarist Dave Davies that Davies needed hospital treatment and the band failed to complete the remaining dates on the tour.

LOCATION 410: the Capitol cinema was demolished in 1983. A new Capitol Odeon was built at the Capitol shopping centre. Postcode: CF10 2HQ

BLACKWOOD MANIC STREET PREACHERS' 'HOME TOWN ECSTACY'

The local Miners' Institute was the venue for an extraordinary homecoming gig by the Manic Street Preachers on January 28th 2011. Twenty-five years since they last played their home town at the Blackwood Little Theatre, the band returned to a building where they recalled playing countless games of snooker as teenagers. The tiny Miners' Institute played host to an emotional appearance for both the Manics and 180 lucky fans, broadcast live on BBC Radio 2. A mile or so east of Blackwood, Oakdale Comprehensive School was where James Dean Bradfield, Richey Edwards, Nicky Wire and Sean Moore first forged friendships that would lead to the formation of the internationally famous band.

LOCATION 411: this former coal miners' meeting place

has been transformed into a now thriving community entertainment and local function centre. Blackwood is approximately 12 miles north of Newport and the M4 motorway. The Miners' Institute is in Blackwood High Street, postcode NP12 1BB

❝ It will be the smallest gig that we have played in a long time ... severe nerves, but hopefully a night of home town ecstasy. ❞
Nicky Wire looks forward to the Manics' return to Blackwood

❝ My opticians is still in Blackwood, I still go to Lui's Plaice now and again and I'm up to see my dad all the time. ❞

James Dean Bradfield explains to the South Wales Argus that the 2011 gig billing was, in one sense, a tad incongruous

CARDIFF
THE WORLD'S OLDEST RECORD SHOP

Founded in 1894 and still selling music, Spillers Records is the family business originally opened by Henry Spiller in Queen's Arcade, Cardiff. The world's oldest independent record shop moved to 'new' premises in the late 1940s and Spillers' current location is still in the Welsh capital's city centre. Threatened with almost certain closure in 2006, the shop's loyal supporters - most notably local band the Manic

Street Preachers campaigned successfully for its continued presence.

❝ We like records, tea, instores, and if you bring us biscuits from Wally's deli (in the arcade next to us) we'll like you a lot. ❞
The Spillers website staff biography

LOCATION 412: the city centre at 31 Morgan Arcade, postcode CF10 1AF. www.spillersrecords. co.uk

EWLOE **SECOND COMING DELAY BY THE STONE ROSES**

One of several locations booked for work on The Stone Roses' Second Coming album, the remote converted 12-room North Wales brewery base saw no conclusion to recordings during the band's two stays in 1992. It's supposed to be the difficult second album syndrome that most bands suffer from and The Stone Roses turned the whole business of creating one of the most eagerly-awaited albums in rock history into a media-infatuated marathon event. The Rolling Stones' mobile recording unit was hired, John Leckie tried to produce, but it would be a further two years until Second Coming finally arrived in record shops. Others sampling The Old Brewery's Angelshare Studios' hospitality who were more productive during their stays include John Martyn, Mansun, Roy Harper and The Farm.

LOCATION 413: on the B5125, Angelshare Studios no longer operate from The Old Brewery, Ewloe, postcode CH5 3BZ

MACHYNLLETH **PAGE AND PLANT AT BRON-YR-AUR**

The rewards from the relentless workload undertaken by Led Zeppelin for the band's first hectic three years of success were not only financial. By 1970 they had enough power to determine their own way forward away from the hurly-burly of the music business. Stepping off the treadmill of writing while touring, a period of time dedicated solely to creating new material began at this remote cottage up a bumpy mountain lane. Relaxing into their natural surroundings, Jimmy Page and Robert Plant wrote a number of songs that would end up on Led Zeppelin III (including the incorrectly spelt 'Bron-Y-Aur Stomp'), their fourth album and Physical Graffiti. Immortalised as an instrumental album track on Physical Graffiti, Bron-Yr-Aur was a cottage that Plant had remembered from childhood family holidays in North Wales. Page, accompanied by girlfriend Charlotte Martin, and Plant by wife Maureen, their baby daughter Carmen and Strider the family dog, shared their

Bernard Lewis

rustic environment with Led Zeppelin roadies Clive Coulson and Sandy MacGregor. With no running water or electricity, the luxury of a weekly bath was only achievable by visits to the local Glyndwr Hotel in Doll Street, Machynlleth.

LOCATION 414: leave the market town of Machynlleth heading north, turning left onto the A493 and then almost

Welsh Led Zeppelin hideaway Bron-Yr-Aur (translated from Welsh as 'Golden Hill')

immediately right up a lane that climbs towards Bron-Yr-Aur. Status: private residence. Postcode: SY20 8QA

❛ We took our guitars along and spent the evenings around log fires, with pokers being plunged into cider and that sort of thing. ❜
Jimmy Page talking to The Independent in 1991

Wales

PORTHMADOG ON THE BEACH: THE MANICS GO NORTH

Virtually an all-Welsh creation, Manic Street Preachers' 1998 No.1 album This Is My Truth Tell Me Yours was recorded at Monnow Valley and Rockfield Studios in Monmouth and the cover artwork was shot at Black Rock Sands. This North Wales beach created a breathtakingly dramatic location for the photoshoot, but it's a surprise perhaps that the South Wales trio and photographer didn't take the shorter journey to the equally photogenic Gower Peninsula.

LOCATION 415: head for Morfa Bychan two miles south-west of Porthmadog at Black Rock Sands Beach. Postcode: LL49 9YB

Quotation courtesy of Labour politician Aneurin Bevan, beach courtesy of Black Rock Sands

NEWPORT JOE STRUMMER'S VULTURES TAKE OFF AT PENTONVILLE

Newport was the place where Turkish-born Joe Strummer first picked up a guitar and began performing. It was in this second floor flat at Pentonville, Newport, that Strummer, known to all at the time as John "Woody" Mellor, lived in the early Seventies. Buying his first guitar for £12 and learning his first chords courtesy of fellow student Steve Richards, Strummer spent this period in Wales as a student and occasional performer at the students' union, along with frequent visits to absorb the West Indian music on offer at local open-mike club Silver Sands, in Pill. The Newport flat was the base where he formed his first band, The Vultures. Just over a month before his death in 2002, Strummer returned to Wales to play a gig with his band The Mescaleros at TJ's in Clarence Place. A plaque, unveiled by his widow Lucinda Tait, commemorates his time at the Pentonville flat where he took his first steps towards his life as a genuine rock legend in The Clash.

❛ Pat Gilbert's recently published biography tells a story that when Joe was living in his flat in Pentonville, in Newport, he recorded the first song that he ever wrote, 'Crumby Bum Blues'. ❜ Fellow student and housemate, Richard Frame

LOCATION 416: the flat and its plaque is close by Newport city centre, west of the River Usk at 12 Pentonville, postcode NP20 5HB. Status: private residence

MOLD THE BEATLES WANDER FREE IN NORTH WALES

Although by now gaining massively in popularity, The Beatles were still a few months away from registering their first No.1 single and album when they played Mold Assembly Rooms on January 24th 1963. Nevertheless, the sold-out 200-capacity venue was smaller than most they were playing at this point but did give enthusiastic fans an intimate view of the soon-to-be international superstars. The Fab Four were still relatively free to wander where they pleased and popped into the Y Pentan (then the Cross Keys pub) for a pre-gig drink. After the show, John Lennon, Paul McCartney and Ringo Starr visited Holywell's Beaufort Arms (back then the Talbot Hotel) to unwind: McCartney even spent half an hour entertaining the locals with an impromptu stint on the pub piano. Leaving immediately after the gig, George Harrison missed the late night pub visit, choosing instead to visit his auntie, who lived six miles away in Hawarden, on the way home.

LOCATIONS 417, 418 and 419: Mold Assembly Rooms in the High Street (postcode CH7 1AS) is now a bank: Y Pentan Bar & Restaurant is at 3 New Street, Mold, postcode CH7 1NY. The Beaufort Arms, now a residential building, is at 26 Well Street, Holywell, postcode CH8 7PL

HOLYHEAD
ROXY MUSIC'S SIREN OF THE SEA

Roxy Music's Bryan Ferry began dating Jerry Hall when she was chosen to model for the cover of Roxy's fifth album. The Texan was photographed as the Siren for the album of that name, released in late 1975. No digital fakery for this shoot: Jerry Hall, the photographer, make-up artist and Ferry all travelled to this wild spot for what proved to be one of rock's most memorable images.

LOCATION 420: north-west Anglesey at South Stack, reached by the A55. The exact location can be found by taking the bridge to the lighthouse and descending left to the rocks below. Postcode: LL65 1YH

Rock reference: the RSPB centre at Ellins Tower can be seen at the top of the cliffs

NEWPORT
KURT COBAIN GATECRASHES A HOLE GIG AT TJ'S

TJ's was the inspirational Newport venue owned and run by the mercurial John Sicolo. Although hosting a conveyor belt of up-and-coming bands such as Oasis, Green Day, The Offspring and Primal Scream, TJ's' stella moment involves a significant rock romance. It is said to be the place where Kurt Cobain proposed to Courtney Love when the couple visited the Newport nightspot where Courtney's band Hole were playing in 1991. Catatonia's 'Mulder And Scully' hit single video was shot at the venue in 1998 and one-time Newport resident Joe Strummer made one of his last stage appearances at TJ's before his death in 2002.

❝ Courtney Love's band, Hole, were playing and were sound checking just before the doors opened when this blond, straggly-haired geezer came up to the door. I said to him, 'If you're coming in, it'll be £3.' He said to me, 'No man, I'm here to see you Courtney; you see my accent?' I told him again it was three quid when Simon Phillips came rushing over going, 'No, no it's all right John, it's Kurt Cobain!' ❞
John Sicolo, owner and founder of TJ's, interviewed by BBC Wales

❝ The Seattle of the UK ❞
The New York Times describing Newport

LOCATION 421: in the city centre east of the River Usk at 14-18 Clarence Place, postcode NP19 0AE. TJ's closed after the death of John Sicolo, who passed away in 2010

The Newport Civic badge and coat of arms

NEWPORT
COAT OF ARMS LIFTED FOR STONE ROSES SINGLE

The bridge in Newport from where Houdini once famously jumped in 1913 was a point of artistic inspiration for Stone Roses guitarist John Squire. The band's long-awaited Second Coming album saw them spend a good deal of time in the nearby Rockfield recording studios, and when complete in 1994 Squire searched around for graphic imagery for the cover of the album's first single release 'Love Spreads'. The sleeve carries a photo of one of Newport Bridge's Newport coats of arms: the Civic Badge of Newport City Council, formerly the Coat of Arms of the former County Borough. The red chevron and cherub heraldry became so associated with the band at one point that Roses fans were reported removing the badges from the bridge.

LOCATION 423: Newport (or Town) Bridge is in the city centre, Clarence Place, on the B4591, postcode NP19 0AE

PRESTATYN
JAM FOR THE FAB FOUR AT THE ROYAL LIDO

They wouldn't feature on any list of all-time greatest band riders, but The Beatles were only just enjoying their first entry on the UK singles chart when they ordered Prestatyn's Royal Lido to bring them a pre-gig plateful of jam sandwiches. An informative circular record disc-styled plaque remembering John, Paul, George and Ringo's November 24th 1962 gig marks the spot where the Royal Lido (now renamed the Nova Centre) stood.

LOCATION 422: The Nova Centre, Central Beach, postcode LL19 7EY

Wales

PONTYPRIDD TOM JONES' GREEN, GREEN GRASS OF HOME

The Treforest Working Men's Club was where seventeen-year-old Tom Jones made his singing debut, but it wasn't until a gig at the Pontypridd YMCA six years later that he began to think he might make a career out of singing. Here in 1963, billed as Tommy Scott with a backing band called The Senators, he filled in for the actual Tommy Scott who had failed to appear for the night in question. After a few drinks as Dutch courage, paper mill worker Jones stepped in as "Tommy" at the request of The Senators to fulfil the booking and did a good enough job to stay as lead singer. In 2008, a demo tape of Jones recorded in the YMCA toilets (no doubt for the best possible acoustics) was auctioned at Christie's in London. The recording, which later sold for £2,500, was catalogued by the auction house as "a rare ¼-inch reel-to-reel master-tape recording of Tom Jones, 1962, on one reel of Emitape, featuring four un-released tracks, tracks comprise: 1 'Don't Pretend', 2 'Time Alone' 3 'What About Me', 4 'That's What Love Can Do'. Local working men's clubs in the mining villages were where 'Jones The Voice' gained a reputation for soulful singing, and at a 1964 performance at Cwmtillery's Top Hat he was 'discovered' by songwriter and Jones' future manager Gordon Mills. The Kingsland Terrace house in Treforest where Jones was born Thomas Jones Woodward still stands, as does his subsequent childhood home in Laura Street in the small village of Treforest, south-east of Pontypridd. When superstardom came calling, Jones moved to California and, recalling his teenage years phoning a stream of girlfriends, including his future wife, managed to purchase and ship the old red telephone box that stood at the end of Laura Street to his new L.A. home. To celebrate the singer's 65th birthday in 2005, a concert was held at nearby Ponty Park (Ynysangharad Park) at which he wowed a 20,000-strong crowd.

❛ I spent the first 24 years of my life in Wales and I loved it and have never really left. So I would want to be buried in Glyntaff Cemetery in Pontypridd – all of my forefathers are there. ❜
Tom Jones talking, to the Western Mail

LOCATIONS 424, 425 **and 426:** Pontypridd is due west off the A470. The YMCA is at Taff Street, postcode CF37 4TS. The house where Tom Jones was born is a mile south-east of Pontypridd in the village of Treforest at 57 Kingsland Terrace, postcode CF37 1RX. Less than a mile away is his childhood home at 44 Laura Street, postcode CF37 1NW. Status: private residences

The birthplace of Tom Jones, which, from its elevated position, looks out over the green, green grass of home

Young Tom featured on a mid-Sixties postcard

RHYL THE BEATLES MAKE THEIR WELSH DEBUT

In the summer of 1962, July 14th was the date of The Beatles' first paid gig on Welsh soil at the seaside resort of Rhyl. The town's Regent Dansette Ballroom was the venue for this historic appearance, a fact commemorated by an unusual artistic mosaic at Rhyl railway station created by the town's Youth Forum. Still performing at this time with Pete Best on drums, the band's Welsh debut was a few months short of their first chart entry and they took time out to tout for extra concert appearances. There is a report of them crossing the Foryd Bridge to the old Clwyd Hotel (now The Harbour) to unsuccessfully scrounge a cabaret appearance. Work was more plentiful a year later when John, Paul, George and now Ringo returned as UK chart-toppers for two more Rhyl gigs on consecutive nights. This time they played to an adoring, screaming audience at the now demolished Ritz Ballroom, with overnight luxury accommodation provided by Rhyl's Westminster Hotel bridal suite.

LOCATION 427: The Regent Dansette Ballroom, now converted to shops, is at 38 High Street, and the Westminster Hotel still dominates the seafront at 11-12 East Parade, postcode LL18 3AH

RHYMNEY THE STRIKING MINERS STORY BORROWED BY THE BYRDS

This Caerphilly village is the location name checked in one of the stand-out tracks on The Byrd's Mr Tambourine Man album released in 1965. The song which describes the General Strike in the spring of 1926 and its crippling effect on the local mining industry has been frequently covered by American folk artists and also North Wales band The Alarm, who included the song as a B-side to their 1984 hit single 'The Chant Has Just Begun'. The song's lyrics date back to a poem written by Rhymney-born former miner Idris Davies and the lines, first published in 1938, eventually attracted the attention of American protest singer Pete Seeger, who set the words to music. In addition to Rhymney's bells, those in Newport and Caerphilly, the brown bells of Merthyr, black bells of Rhondda, grim bells of Blaina, loud bells of Neath,

The Byrds added their own jingle-jangle to 'The Bells Of Rhymney' Below left: St David's Church

moist bells of Swansea, green bells of Cardiff and silver bells of Wye are all referred to in the song. In 2007, Welsh folk musician Huw Williams visited Pete Seeger in New York to research the origins of the song for a BBC documentary. The American folk legend had never seen Davies' original publication Gwalia Deserta, which included the poem, but had stumbled across a Dylan Thomas book which included 'The Bells Of Rhymney' in a chapter on Welsh poetry. Once Seeger had added his music, the song struck a chord with the American folk community. Before his time in The Byrds, Roger McGuinn had been turned on to the song while contributing arrangements and guitar parts to Judy Collins' 1963 album Judy Collins 3. This disc's tracks 'The Bells Of Rhymney' and 'Turn! Turn! Turn!' were adapted by McGuinn into the jingle-jangle style he was developing, and sparkled as key contributions to The Byrds' ground-breaking folk-rock album Mr Tambourine which appeared two years later.

❝ George [Harrison] had listened to The Byrds' version of 'The Bells Of Rhymney', the Pete Seeger song, and on it I had done the riff with the Rickenbacker going (de-de-de, de-de-de), so he took that and made the tune 'If I Needed Someone' out of it. ❞ Roger McGuinn describes how some musical cross pollination began with 'The Bells Of Rhymney' and resulted in a Beatles track on Rubber Soul

LOCATION 428: St David's Church, where the bells of Rhymney still chime, is situated in the village High Street of Rhymney which is on the B4257 east of Merthyr Tydfil. Postcode: NP22 5NG

Kevin Prosser

Wales

ROCKFIELD THE WORLD'S FIRST RESIDENTIAL RECORDING STUDIO

Rockfield claims to be the world's first residential recording studio. Since opening in 1965, artists as diverse as Del Shannon, Iggy Pop, Echo and The Bunnymen, The Undertones, Teenage Fanclub, Coldplay, KT Tunstall and Paolo Nutini have recorded there. And, you don't have to be in a band to stay at Rockfield. The complex offers bed and breakfast and self-catering accommodation for visiting this attractive corner of the Welsh countryside. Seasoned rock fans will associate Dave Edmunds most with the place; his 'I Hear You Knockin'' spent six consecutive weeks at the top of the singles chart in 1970 and helped put both the studio and the associated Rockfield label on the music map. Perhaps the studio's grandest moment came in 1975 when, while working on new album A Night At The Opera, Queen recorded 'Bohemian Rhapsody' there.

LOCATION 429: Rockfield Studios are less than two miles north-west of Monmouth on the B4233. Go left just before the village of Rockfield at Amberley Court, off Rockfield Road. Postcode: NP25 5ST. Website: www.rockfieldmusicgroup.com

❛ We were watching Marx Brothers movies at Rockfield, where we were recording, and

The main studio room at Rockfield, looking towards the control room in the Coach House Studio

we got a sense that they could go anywhere they wanted, they were so in control of their medium. And we felt the same sort of spirit: we had discovered our power as a group and were just at the point where we could really turn ourselves loose. ❜ Queen's Brian May, talking to The Daily Telegraph in 2011

WHITE GRIT RONNIE LANE SETTLES DOWN ON THE FARM

So nomadic was Faces rock star Ronnie Lane that it comes as a real compliment to the rolling hills of West Wales to have him settle down on a border farm here. Rock stars made a habit of escaping to the country during the Seventies, and the former Small Faces and Faces man did it in considerable style. Famed for his wonderfully conceived but ultimately financially draining The Passing Show, where he and Slim Chance toured the country circus style with big top, Lane's nomadic tendencies did at least lead to an idyllic home life based in the countryside. Here he became a sheep farmer with 100 acres, recording music in

Ronnie Lane down on Fishpool Farm

his mobile unit or even in the open air. Pete Townshend and Eric Clapton would visit, and the odd gig at local pubs, The Miner's Arms in Priestweston and the Drum & Monkey in Bromlow (now the Callow Inn) generously repaid the locals for the way in which London Eastender Lane was accepted by this rural community on the Welsh border with Shropshire.

LOCATION 430: just inside the Welsh border, close by the village of White Grit, Fishpool Farm is north of Bishops Castle on the A488, postcode SY5 0JN. Status: private residence

Born in Wales

Verden Allen, keyboards, Mott The Hoople (b. 26 May 1944, Crynant)

Shirley Bassey (b. 8 Jan 1937, Tiger Bay, Cardiff)

Andy Bell, guitar, Beady Eye/Oasis/Ride (b. 11 Aug 1970, Cardiff)

Tony Bourge, guitar/vocals, Budgie (b. 24 Nov 1948, Tiger Bay, Cardiff)

James Dean Bradfield, vocals/guitar, Manic Street Preachers (b. 21 Feb 1969, Pontypool)

Huw Bunford, guitar, Super Furry Animals (b. 15 Sep 1967, Cardiff)

Stuart Cable, drums, Stereophonics (b. 19 May 1970, Aberdare, d. 7 Jun 2010, Llwydcoed)

John Cale (b. 9 Mar 1942, Garnant)

Phil Campbell, guitar, Motörhead (b. 7 May 1961, Pontypridd)

Euros Childs, Gorky's Zygotic Mynci (b. 1975, Freshwater East)

Cian Ciaran, keyboards, Super Furry Animals (b. 16 Jun 1976, Bangor)

Julian Cope, vocals, The Teardrop Explodes (b. 21 Oct 1957, Deri)

Spencer Davis, guitar, The Spencer Davis Group (b. 17 Jul 1939, Swansea)

Duffy (b. 23 Jun 1984, Nefyn)

Dave Edmunds (b. 15 Apr 1944, Cardiff)

Richey Edwards, vocals/guitar, Manic Street Preachers (b. 22 Dec 1967, Blackwood, presumed dead 2008)

Sian Evans, vocals, Kosheen (b. 9 Oct 1973, Caerphilly)

Andy Fairweather Low (b. 2 Aug 1948, Ystrad Mynach)

James Frost, guitar, The Automatic (b. 22 Aug 1986, Cowbridge)

Green Gartside, Scritti Politti (b. 22 Jun 1955, Cardiff)

Mike Gibbins, drums, Badfinger (b. 12 Mar 1949, Swansea, d. 4 Oct 2005)

Roger Glover, bass, Deep Purple (b. 30 Nov 1945, Brecon)

Iwan Griffiths, drums, The Automatic (b. 4 Dec 1985, Cowbridge)

Ron Griffiths, bass, Badfinger (b. 2 Oct 1946, Swansea)

Pete Ham, guitar, Badfinger (b. 27 Apr 1947, Swansea, d. 24 Apr 1975)

Robin Hawkins, vocals/bass, The Automatic (b. 14 Dec 1986, Cardiff)

Mary Hopkin (b. 3 May 1950, Pontardawe)

Dafydd Ieuan, drums, Super Furry Animals (b. 1 Mar 1969, Bangor)

Katherine Jenkins (b. 29 Jun 1980, Neath)

Kelly Jones, vocals/guitar, Stereophonics (b. 3 June 1974, Cwmaman)

Paul Jones, bass, Catatonia (b. 5 Feb 1960, Colwyn Bay)

Richard Jones, bass, Stereophonics (b. 23 May 1974, Cwmaman)

Tom Jones (b. 7 Jun 1940, Treforest)

Jon Lee, drums, Feeder (b. 28 Mar 1968, Newport, d. 7 Jan 2002)

Deke Leonard, guitar, Man (b. 18 Dec 1944, Llanelli)

Eddie MacDonald, bass, The Alarm (b. 1 Nov 1959, St Asaph)

Cerys Matthews, vocals, Catatonia (b. 11 Apr 1969, Cardiff)

Donna Matthews, guitar/vocals, Elastica (b. 2 Dec 1971, Newport)

Sean Moore, drums, Manic Street Preachers (b. 30 Jul 1968, Pontypool)

Grant Nicholas, vocals/guitar, Feeder (b. 12 Nov 1967, Newport)

Owen If (Ian Rossiter), drums, Stereo MC's (b. 20 Mar 1959, Newport)

Mike Peters, vocals/guitar, The Alarm (b. 25 Feb 1959, Prestatyn)

Ray Phillips, drums, Budgie (b. 1 Mar 1949, Ely, Cardiff)

Guto Pryce, bass, Super Furry Animals (b. 4 Sep 1972, Cardiff)

Nigel Pulsford, guitar, Bush (b. 11 Apr 1963, Newport)

Gruff Rhys, vocals, Super Furry Animals (b. 18 Jul 1970, Haverfordwest)

Aled Richards, drums, Catatonia (b. 5 Jul 1969, Carmarthen)

Mark Roberts, guitar, Catatonia (b. 3 Nov 1969, Llanrwst)

Sasha, DJ/producer (b. 4 Sep 1969, Bangor)

Andy Scott, guitar, The Sweet (b. 30 Jun 1949, Wrexham)

Burke Shelley, vocals/bass, Budgie (b. 10 Apr 1947, Tiger Bay, Cardiff)

Rick Smith, keyboards, Underworld (b. 25 May 1959, Ammanford)

Shakin' Stevens (b. 4 Mar 1948, Ely, Cardiff)

Steve Strange, Visage (b. 28 Apr 1959, Newbridge)

Matt Tuck, vocals/guitar, Bullet For My Valentine (b. 20 Jan 1980, Bridgend)

Bonnie Tyler (b. 8 Jun 1951, Skewen)

Ricky Valance (b. 10 Apr 1939, Ynysddu)

Ian Watkins, vocals, Lostprophets (b. 30 Jul 1977, Pontypridd)

Nicky Wire, bass, Manic Street Preachers (b. 20 Jan 1969, Tredegar)

Paula Yates, presenter (b. 24 Apr 1959, Colwyn Bay, d. 17 Sep 2000)

ROCK ATLAS
North West England

UK and Ireland Edition

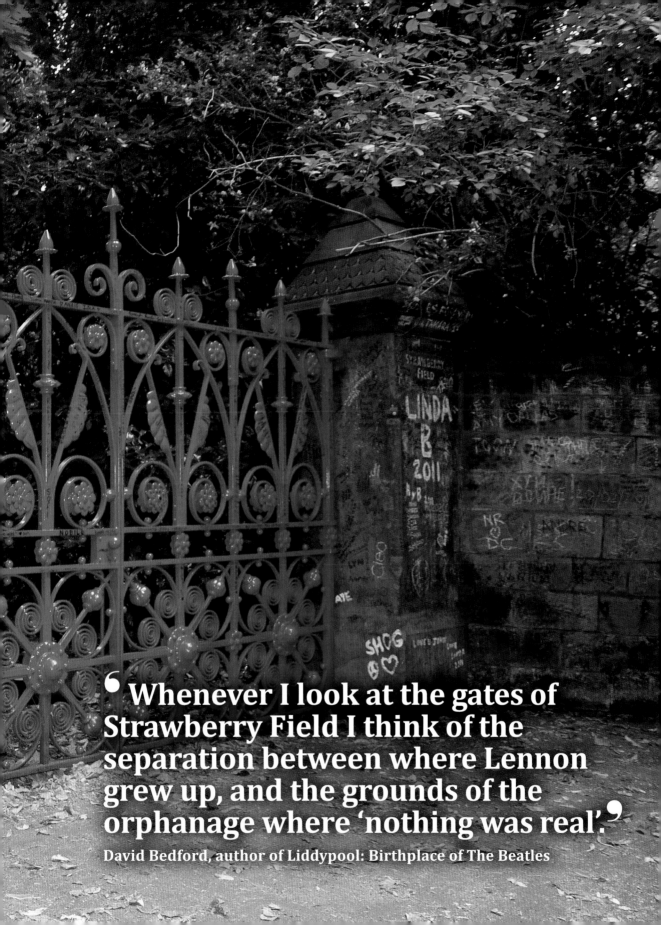

'Whenever I look at the gates of Strawberry Field I think of the separation between where Lennon grew up, and the grounds of the orphanage where 'nothing was real'.'

David Bedford, author of Liddypool: Birthplace of The Beatles

North West England

CHESHIRE

The county, famed for its footballer's Premier League palatial piles, gave birth to Gary Barlow and Ian Brown, has absorbed huge musical influences from nearby metropolis's Manchester and Liverpool, and come up with its own brooding bunch of rock locations. Cheshire is where Doves and Charlatans developed and prospered, Paul Simon and Elvis Costello were inspired to write some fine lyrics, Spike Island became the live event of the nineties and Ian Curtis lived and died.

NORTHWICH THE CHARLATANS' MELTING POT CAFÉ

Fondly remembered by The Charlatans as the place they first met after signing a recording deal with the Beggars Banquet label, the Weaverdale Café appears on the cover of the band's 1998 greatest hits album Melting Pot. Less than five miles north-east of Northwich, where The Charlatans were formed, lies Pickmere Lake, pictured on the band's 2004 album cover for Up At The Lake.

❛It's 18 miles south of Manchester, and 20 miles away from Liverpool. So I've had the most brilliant musical upbringing. ❜
Northwich Charlatan, Tim Burgess

LOCATION 431: Weaverdale Café is little changed at 96 Witton Street, near the centre of Northwich. Postcode: CW9 5AB

Meet me on the corner: The Charlatans' favourite café

SPIKE ISLAND THE STONE ROSES' FINEST HOUR

A former toxic waste site in Widnes was the location for one of the most memorable events in British rock. It was here on May 27th 1990 that the whole baggy, Madchester movement had its day in the sun when 28,000 mostly stoned Roses fans gathered for the biggest northern cool party of their lives. Due to the watery surroundings there were supposedly frogmen employed to rescue any fans who either accidentally or intentionally went for a swim. Despite the ramshackle nature of the organisation and the incredibly high consumption of fast food, lager, Ecstacy and dope, this giant rave recorded just four arrests for unruly behaviour. No doubt its legendary status as a key event in Britain's cultural history has grown out of all proportion due to the lack of much filmed evidence of what was The Stone Roses' finest hour.

❛Spike Island - that was the blueprint for my group. ❜
Noel Gallagher

❛I know some people have said there was a problem with chemicals in the air because the gig was next to a chemical plant, but I only know of a couple of people who were there who now have six fingers. ❜
Stone Roses tour manager Steve Adge, interviewed by The Observer

LOCATION 432: east off the A533 on the northern side of the River Mersey, postcode WA8 0DG

Michael Enkiri

MACCLESFIELD **THE BEGINNING AND END OF JOY DIVISION**

Fifteen miles south of the centre of Manchester lies the silk town of Macclesfield, where Joy Division singer Ian Curtis grew up and died. Born in Old Trafford, Manchester, Curtis' early childhood was spent in the family home at Balmoral Crescent, Hurdsfield, a short walk north-west of the centre of Macclesfield, before moving to a flat nearer the centre of town. A schoolboy at the town's King's School in Cumberland Street, along with future Joy Division drummer Stephen Morris, Curtis later married Deborah Woodruff at St. Thomas' village church, Henbury, west of Macclesfield. After two years living on the Manchester outskirts, the couple moved back to Macclesfield in 1977. Much of the Joy Division catalogue of songs was written at this time in the terraced house at No.77 Barton Street, Macclesfield. It was also the

setting for Curtis' tragic suicide. In the early hours of Sunday May 18th 1980, the day before the band were due to fly out of the UK bound for their first US tour, the 23-year-old singer hung himself in the kitchen. A memorial stone inscribed with the title of Joy Division's best-known song, 'Love Will Tear Us Apart', can be found at Macclesfield Crematorium. Pretty much a kerbstone, the small memorial to Curtis is usually decorated with fans' gifts and therefore relatively easy to find.

LOCATIONS 433, 434, 435, 436 and 437: Macclesfield is 15 miles south of Manchester: Balmoral Crescent (postcode SK10 2NP), The King's School is in Cumberland Street (SK10 1DA), St. Thomas', Henbury, three miles west of Macclesfield on the A537 (SK11 9NN), 77 Barton Street

The Barton Street house where Ian Curtis lived and tragically died

The Faber & Faber book authored by Ian Curtis' widow

Touching From a Distance
Ian Curtis & Joy Division
Deborah Curtis
ff

(SK11 6) and the memorial stone 87 Prestbury Road (SK10 3BU). A walking tour including some of these locations, plus Armitt Street Labour Exchange, where Curtis worked, and his favourite haunts, the Travellers Rest and Krumbles, have been included on a Joy Division tour, available by contacting the Macclesfield Tourist Information Centre

North West England

WIDNES PAUL SIMON WRITES 'HOMEWARD BOUND': BUT WHERE?

A thoroughly confusing story surrounds one of Britain's best-known music locations. While touring England's folk clubs in 1965, the American singer-songwriter apparently wrote 'Homeward Bound' on a Widnes railway station platform, but which one? Uncertainty about the spot comes from the man himself as to which railway station he was actually "sitting in", as the lyrics to the song says. Closed in 1994, Ditton railway station to the west of Widnes is the most likely location, although Simon may well have penned Simon and Garfunkel's first UK hit single as far away as Warrington Bank Quay station, seven miles east of Widnes. What *is* certain is that there is a plaque commemorating the Paul Simon connection situated in the ticket office on the Liverpool-bound platform of the main Widnes railway station and Simon was 'Homeward Bound' by train to girlfriend Kathy Chitty in London. So, the Widnes/Paul Simon association is certainly no rock myth. The station song-writing legend aside, he performed at Howff Folk Club, Geoff Speed's local club, in September 1965 and stayed several nights at Speed's parents' home in the town's Coroner's Lane.

LOCATION 438: Widnes station (and plaque) can be found north of the town centre at Victoria Avenue, postcode WA8 7TJ

Rob Newman

RUNCORN ELVIS COSTELLO'S INTER-CITY SONG

From Elvis Costello's 1977 debut album My Aim Is True, '(The Angels Wanna Wear My) Red Shoes' was a song written and stored in the Elvis memory banks during a train journey from Runcorn to Liverpool. A 20-minute section of the rail trip took the then 22-year-old songwriter north over the River Mersey and west to Lime Street station, Liverpool, before hastily returning home to safely capture the words and music.

❛I had to keep the song in my head until I got to my mother's house, where I kept an old Spanish guitar that I had had since I was a kid. ❜
Elvis Costello

LOCATION 439: to duplicate Elvis Costello's inspirational songwriting rail journey, board a Liverpool-bound train at Runcorn station, Shaw Street, Runcorn, postcode WA7 5UB

SPROSTON GREEN A CHARLATAN'S RAUNCHY ENCOUNTER

The final track on 1990 debut chart-topping Charlatans album Some Friendly, 'Sproston Green' is the nearby setting for a rather raunchy encounter put into song by the band's singer Tim Burgess. It's a biographical tale of seduction involving a Cheshire lass who seemingly got the better of the teenage Tim.

LOCATION 440: Sproston Green is a spot on the A54 six miles south-east of Northwich near the M6. Postcode: CW4 7LW

❛It's about a place in Northwich, where I had my first sexual encounter. ❜
Tim Burgess reveals the truth behind 'Sproston Green'

WILMSLOW DOVES KICK AGAINST THEIR ROOTS

Doves' 2005 atmospheric single 'Black And White Town' was written about this satellite town outside Manchester. The band's formation began when brothers Jez and Andy Williams met Jimi Goodwin at Wilmslow High School back in the mid-80s. Early gigging at the local leisure centre followed and eventually led to the formation of Sub Sub. A fire that destroyed the band's studio at nearby Ancoats forced a fresh start, and by 1998 Doves were born.

❛I think it's normal to be frustrated and resent where you're from. That's what the song 'Black And White Town' is about. It's something to kick against. ❜
Jimi Goodwin, talking to the Wilmslow Express in 2005

LOCATION 441: Wilmslow High School, Holly Road, postcode SK9 1LZ

Born in Cheshire

Gary Barlow (b. 20 Jan 1971, Frodsham)
Ian Brown, vocals, The Stone Roses/solo (b. 20 Feb 1963, Warrington)
Ben Byrne, drums, Starsailor (b. 8 Mar 1977, Warrington)
Chris Evans, presenter (b. 1 Apr 1966, Warrington)
Nigel Harrison, bass, Blondie (b. 24 Apr 1951, Stockport)
Robert Heaton, drums, New Model Army (b. 6 Jul 1961, Knutsford, d. 4 Nov 2004)
Steven Hewitt, drums, Placebo (b. 22 Mar 1971, Northwich)
Rupert Holmes, singer-songwriter (b. 24 Feb 1947, Northwich)
Stove King, bass, Mansun (b. 8 Jan 1975, Ellesmere Port)
John Mayall , guitar, Bluesbreakers (b. 29 Nov 1933, Macclesfield)
Jim Moray, folk singer-songwriter (b. 20 Aug 1981, Macclesfield)
Paul Morley, writer (b. 26 Mar 1957, Stockport)
Stephen Morris, drums, New Order/ Joy Division/The Other Two/Bad Lieutenant (b. 28 Oct 1957, Macclesfield)
Nemone (Nemone Metaxas), DJ (b. 3 Nov 1973, Chester)
Andie Rathbone, drums, Mansun (b. 8 Sep 1969, Blacon)
James Stelfox, bass, Starsailor (b. 23 Mar 1976, Warrington)

MERSEYSIDE

Despite The Beatles utter domination of this section of Rock Atlas, there are twenty-first-century bands that still epitomise what's so special about Merseyside. Take The Coral: absorbing all that's great from the history of the place and adding their own American West Coast take on things, they refuse to imagine a better base or recording location than their much-loved Wirral peninsula seaside town of Hoylake. Alongside The Farm, Cast, The Las and The Zutons, they add to the tradition of local bands naturally and defiantly singing with a Scouse accent. Across the world's most music-associated river this side of the Mississippi, American beat poet Allen Ginsberg pronounced Liverpool in 1965 "the centre of consciousness of the human universe", and music maverick Bill Drummond put forward the theory that a ley line of creative cosmic energy ran up the city's Mathew Street, linked to the thoroughfare's statue of psychologist Carl Jung. There is most definitely something in the Mersey water: Liverpool born and bred artists have conjured-up more than 50 No.1 singles since the chart began in 1952 and the city has had its fair share of hits written about it. Little Jimmy Osmond's 'Long Haired Lover From Liverpool, (No.1) Liverpool F.C.'s 'Anfield Rap' (No.3), The Scaffold's 'Liverpool Lou' (No.7) and Gerry and The Pacemakers' 'Ferry 'Cross The Mersey' (No.8) all fit the smash-hit category, with less well remembered but really rather good releases 'In Liverpool' by Suzanne Vega and 'Going Down To Liverpool' by The Bangles propping up the nether regions of the chart. But, indisputedly top of the pops, it is The Beatles for which the area is so hugely famous. Thanks to John Lennon, Paul McCartney, George Harrison and Ringo Starr, nowhere else in Britain can boast such a tightly-packed plethora of iconic locations worthy of rock pilgrimage.

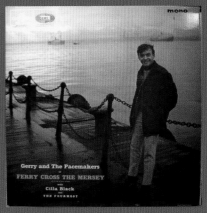

The soundtrack album to the Ferry 'Cross the Mersey movie from Gerry and The Pacemakers, the first British act to achieve three No.1 singles with their first three releases

North West England

Colin Unwin

Tommy Steele's Eleanor Rigby statue

LIVERPOOL 1 THE ELEANOR RIGBY STATUE

Set back from the road in Stanley Street sits a statue of the character from The Beatles' saddest song, 'Eleanor Rigby'. The figure of Eleanor Rigby was the subject of a project by actor, artist and rock 'n' roller Tommy Steele, who created the sculpture. It is dedicated to "all the lonely people", a line from the lyrics written by Paul McCartney, who was reportedly influenced in choosing a name for his song when acting with Eleanor Bron in the movie Help! But, there was an Eleanor Rigby buried in a nearby churchyard, a place McCartney and John Lennon would visit for sunbathing when teenagers, which points to a rather more obvious influence. At 34 Stanley Street stands the Eleanor Rigby Hotel. The former scullery maid, who died aged 44 in 1939, could hardly have imagined leaving such a powerful legacy. The music shops where The Beatles bought their early instruments were situated close by. No.60 Stanley Street was the location where Hessy's Music Centre famously sold a 1958 Hofner Senator guitar to John Lennon's Aunt Mimi. On July 31st 1960, she paid a £17 deposit followed by further instalments of £13 and nine shillings to provide John with the guitar he would later take with him to Hamburg. The Beatles were also customers at Rushworths Music House, a short distance away in Whitechapel.

LOCATION 442: Stanley Street, postcode L1 6AL

LIVERPOOL 1 BILL HARRY'S MERSEY BEAT HQ

Created in 1961 to report on the extraordinary beat boom that occurred in Liverpool, the Mersey Beat music paper was devised and put together by Bill Harry and his girlfriend Virginia Sowry from premises in Renshaw Street.

❛We initially moved into a tiny attic room at the top of 81a Renshaw Street, bringing a desk, typewriter and a couple of chairs. My girlfriend Virginia and I ran the entire fortnightly newspaper. [Brian] Epstein ordered 144 copies of issue No.2 in which the entire front cover story was of The Beatles recording in Hamburg, which led him to ask me to arrange for him to visit The Cavern to see The Beatles. The Beatles used to come into the office to help Virginia out while I was interviewing and I began publishing John Lennon's writings in the first issue. As it was such an innovative publication it soon sold out each issue and we were able to move into two large rooms on the first floor. ❜
Bill Harry

LOCATION 443: 81a Renshaw Street, postcode L1 4EN. Website: www.merseybeat.com

LIVERPOOL 1 LENNON'S PEACE & HARMONY SCULPTURE

On the 70th anniversary of John Lennon's birthday, a sculpture was unveiled in the centre of Liverpool as a shrine where people are encouraged to pay tribute to the city's famous son. The unveiling ceremony on October 9th 2010 by Lennon's son Julian and first wife Cynthia revealed the 18-foot-high artwork created by American artist Lauren Voiers. Entitled "Peace & Harmony", incorporated in the monument's design are musical notes and a guitar, topped off by a dove of peace and a white feather.

LOCATION 444: in the heart of the city at Chavasse Park, close by the Liverpool Hilton Hotel and Liverpool ONE shopping centre, postcode L1 8LW

LIVERPOOL 2 THE 'CRADLE OF MERSEY BEAT' AT THE IRON DOOR

A short walk north of The Cavern is the site where Liverpool's second most popular venue for beat music attracted crowds of more than 1,000. The Iron Door was a particular favourite of Cilla Black and The Searchers during its short four-year life.

❛I was talking with Paul McCartney the other day about The Iron Door. We used to have all-night sessions that started at 8 o'clock – and I'm only 15 years of age, maybe 16 – started at 8 o'clock and finished at 8 the following morning. And we'd all be tumbling out and pinching bottles of milk off the doorstep because we'd been singing all night. ❜
Cilla Black

LOCATION 445: the Iron Door plaque sits proudly among the swanky new office blocks at 13 Temple Street, postcode L2 5RH

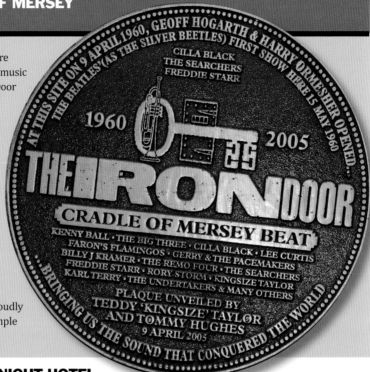

Peter Tarleton

LIVERPOOL 2 THE HARD DAYS NIGHT HOTEL

With Beatles-themed bars, a restaurant, lounge and bedrooms, the Hard Days Night Hotel provides luxurious 4-star accommodation in its grade II listed city centre building. Open to 'day trippers' as well as residents, Blake's Bar - named after Sir Peter Blake who designed the Sgt Pepper's Lonely Hearts Club Band album cover - and BarFour are suitably decorated to reflect the different eras of Beatles history. Visitors wishing to enjoy an 'Imagine'-themed night's sleep can book the Lennon Suite, which comes complete with white furnishings and white piano. The grand exterior of the hotel includes four individual statues by sculptor Dave Webster of each Beatle. The hotel is very well placed for Beatles tours, being situated at the end of Mathew Street.

The Lennon Suite at the Hard Days Night Hotel

LOCATION 446: North John Street, postcode L2 6RR. www.harddaysnighthotel.com

North West England

LIVERPOOL 2 THE WALLS OF FAME

Two Walls of Fame are situated in the street opposite The Cavern Club, paying tribute to Liverpool's music heritage. Building bricks are engraved with the names of the many performers who have graced the stage of The Cavern. This commemorative display is joined by a second display of more than 50 discs, one for each act that has achieved a British No.1 hit single since the chart began in 1952.

LOCATION 447: opposite the Cavern Club entrance, Mathew Street, postcode L2 6RE

Colin Unwin

John Lennon watches the tourists in Mathew Street

LIVERPOOL 2 THE MATHEW STREET LENNON STATUE

This statue is one of two solo figures commemorating John Lennon, the second is at John Lennon Airport. The Mathew Street fibreglass sculpture is the work of Dave Webster and captures the young Lennon perfectly, casually leaning against the wall gazing at the teenagers headed for The Cavern.

LOCATION 448: at the north end of Mathew Street, postcode L2 6RE

LIVERPOOL 2 ARTHUR DOOLEY'S BEATLE STREET SCULPTURE

Looking down from the wall of Mathew Street opposite Cavern Walks is the unconventional sculpture by Liverpool artist Arthur Dooley titled "Beatle Street", with the slogan "Four Lads That Shook The World". Constructed from wood, bronze and plastic dolls, it depicts Paul McCartney, George Harrison and Ringo Starr as three cherubs in the arms of the Madonna (or Mother Liverpool) with John Lennon represented as another small cherub to the right. At various points down the years, since it was first created in 1974, the original McCartney cherub has disappeared (a fact acknowledged by a plaque reading "Paul has taken wings and flown") and a new Lennon cherub has been added following his death in 1980 with another plaque reading "Lennon Lives".

LOCATION 449: Mathew Street, postcode L2 6RE

LIVERPOOL 2 JOHN DOUBLEDAY'S BRONZE BEATLES

A statue of all four Beatles playing guitars and drums greets visitors to the ground floor of the Cavern Walks shopping arcade. Created by Essex sculptor John Doubleday, this bronze representation was officially unveiled in 1984 by Paul McCartney's brother Mike. Apparently, he was none too impressed and reportedly had difficulty recognising which of the four figures was his brother. Other Beatles-related artwork includes terracotta relief dove and rose imagery on the walls of the centre, designed by Cynthia Lennon in memory of husband John.

LOCATION 450: in Cavern Walks shopping centre, Mathew Street, postcode L2 6RE

LIVERPOOL 2 A MEMBERS ONLY PUNK PARADISE AT ERIC'S

With an entrance opposite Merseyside music mecca The Cavern, Eric's became a new venue for a new wave of music when it opened for the first time on October 1st 1976. Like its famous neighbour, Eric's was a basement club with jazz connections and co-owner Roger Eagle named the new venture he started with Ken Testi and Pete Fulwell after L.A.-born jazz musician Eric Dolphy. A membership only club, Eric's benefited from a wider fanbase than the Merseybeat-based Cavern had done, attracting bands and members from way beyond the Liverpool city limits. Punk and new wave acts The Teardrop Explodes, OMD, Elvis Costello, Dead or Alive and Echo and The Bunnymen were local regulars with visits from nationally hot bands The Clash, Buzzcocks, Joy Division and Simple Minds. Visual memories of the club's heyday inevitably feature the extraordinary Big in Japan, comprising the shaven-headed Jayne Casey, Scotsman Bill Drummond, Holly Johnson, Ian Broudie, Budgie and Dave

Balfe, who all became famous for doing other things beyond the cramped but exciting walls of Eric's. Will Sergeant of Echo and The Bunnymen vividly remembers sharing a Christmas bill with Iggy Pop in 1979. When Iggy was prevented from completing his trademark walk over a packed crowd of 600, he was forced to crawl across the heads of punters because the ceiling was so low. The club closed in March 1980 when the subject of a drugs raid by police, but the building has continued as a music venue under other names into the twenty-first-century, re-opening as Erics in 2011 thanks to the efforts of new owner John Lynch. Erics' enduring appeal has been the subject of both a musical' Erics - The Musical, (2008) and a book, All The Best Clubs Are Downstairs, Everybody Knows That (2009).

❛It turned my head upside-down. I was so overawed I just sat there and smiled.❜
Julian Cope recalls his first visit to Eric's

Above: an original Eric's membership card belonging to The Accelerators' drummer Brian Damage

Below left: original Eric's member and Mudkiss online fanzine editor Melanie Smith visits the club's dressing room before work began on re-vamping the place in 2011

Right: Melanie Smith back in the day with Glen Matlock when The Rich Kids played Eric's

Far left: Eric's regular Vanessa Pimblett shares a truly rock 'n' roll moment with The Clash's Mick Jones

❛People talk about The Cavern or The Marquee or CBGB's – these seminal, catalytic environments. Eric's was one of those places, for a very strong generation of musicians.❜
Andy McCluskey, whose OMD first came into being at Eric's

❛It's all being recreated in the image of the original, so for anyone who used to go to Eric's it will be like stepping back in time.❜
John Lynch

LOCATION 451: 9 Mathew Street, postcode L2 6RE. Website: www.ericsclub.co.uk

Phil King

North West England

LIVERPOOL 2 THE 'FROM US TO YOU' SCULPTURE

Above the entrance to a shop devoted to all things Beatle-related is a sculpture erected in 1984 of all four Beatles by David Hughes. The local sculptor's bronze carries the inscription "From Us To You" and was funded by fans from around the world through the initiative of the shop's owner, Ian Wallace.

LOCATION 452: 31 Mathew Street, postcode L2 6RE. www. thebeatleshop.co.uk

LIVERPOOL 2 THE GRAPES: A BEATLES BOLT-HOLE

The famous Grapes pub is where Sixties Merseybeat groups escaped to in between performances at the nearby Cavern Club. The pub has been updated but still retains the backroom area where The Beatles sat to enjoy a beer and a smoke. In the early Sixties The Cavern was unlicenced, so The Grapes was an attractive bolt hole for performers wanting something stronger. On the wall of the snug, marking the location of The Beatles' favourite table, is a photograph of the four of them in the pub and a preserved piece of Sixties wallpaper that appears in the photo behind them. The Grapes was the first place Pete Best headed for, to drown his sorrows, when informed by manager Brian Epstein that he'd been replaced by Ringo Starr.

LOCATION 453: 25 Mathew Street, postcode L2 6RE. Website: www. liverpool0151.co.uk/ grapes

LIVERPOOL 2 THE CAVERN CLUB

Opened originally as a jazz club in 1957, The Beatles played their first of 292 bookings at The Cavern on February 9th 1961. The Beatles' association with the Mathew Street club goes back even earlier when proto-Beatles, The Quarry Men, played the famous basement as a skiffle group in 1957. When local bands in the early Sixties performed their rock 'n' roll (often at lunchtime), the venue attracted capacity crowds of almost 1,000 fans. If you climb down the 30 steps off Mathew Street it's hard to imagine how such a small damp warehouse cellar could accommodate so many people and generate so much excitement. With nowhere for the stench of sweat and cigarette smoke to escape, the walls dripped with perspiration and were frequently washed down with bleach, which gave The Cavern a unique aroma that fans who were present fifty years ago remember to this day. Doorman Paddy Delaney, resident DJ Bob Wooler and owner Ray McFall were the men that ran the club in its heyday, witnessing the birth of the Mersey beat sound and the group that would go on to make Liverpool famous worldwide for its music. The current Cavern Club is a faithfully reconstructed 1982 version of the the real thing using much of the same area and more than 15,000 of the original bricks. Situated 15 yards away from its old entrance near Cavern Walks, the present site is still a great place for a drink and venue for great music. Paul McCartney returned here in 1999 to perform a special ground-breaking

The world famous Cavern is open from 10.30am until after midnight, seven days a week

internet broadcast gig. In many ways The Cavern was just as significant a venue for The Hollies as it was for The Beatles. It was here in January 1963 that the Manchester group were 'discovered' by EMI producer Ron Richards, which led to their Parlophone signing.

LOCATION 454: 10 Mathew Street, postcode L2 6RE. Website: www.cavernclub.co.uk

LIVERPOOL 3 THE BEATLES STORY VISITOR ATTRACTION

Located within Liverpool's Albert Dock, The Beatles Story will transport you into the life, times, culture and music of the Fab Four. Open seven days a week, it is now on two sites – the second a short distance north at the Mersey Ferries terminal at Pier Head.

LOCATION 455: Britannia Vaults, Albert Dock, postcode L3 4AD

LIVERPOOL 3 THE LIVER BUILDING

The Liver Building, with the rather fanciful addition of Mersey surfer Ian Broudie, features on the cover of The Lightning Seeds' 1997 album Like You Do... Best Of The Lightning Seeds.

LOCATION 456: Royal Liver Building, Pier Head, postcode L3 1HT

Eddie Evans

> Charismatic live performer, songwriter, animal lover and gentle man.
>
> Some of the words on the plaque at the foot of Billy Fury's statue

LIVERPOOL 3 THE BILLY FURY STATUE

A few steps from the River Mersey stands a striking likeness of Billy Fury sculpted by Tom Murphy. It depicts a Liverpool rock 'n' roller who had already enjoyed 13 hit singles before The Beatles first charted in 1962. But as Jack Good, the man responsible for 50s pop TV shows Oh Boy! and Six-Five Special, said when unveiling the statue in 2003, there was another reason Billy was so special: "Billy was the first one of that stature to write his own songs. People say that it all started with The Beatles, but it was Billy Fury who did it first," said Good, as quoted in Spencer Leigh's book Wondrous Face.

LOCATION 457: situated on a patch of grass next to the Piermaster's House, on the banks of the River Mersey at Albert Dock, postcode L3 4AN

LIVERPOOL 3 JOHN AND CYNTHIA'S MOUNT PLEASANT WEDDING

The Georgian building at No.64 was the registry office where John Lennon married Cynthia Powell on August 23rd 1962. The small wedding party consisted of Cynthia's brother Tony, John's best man, Brian Epstein, Paul McCartney and George Harrison.

LOCATION 458: 64 Mount Pleasant is east of the city centre. The building is no longer a registry office. Postcode: L3 5SD

LIVERPOOL 7 PERCY PHILLIPS' RECORDING STUDIOS

An unassuming red-bricked house at 38 Kensington was the family home and business address for record producer Percy Phillips. Harmonising and playing into one microphone in Phillips' tiny studio, The Quarry Men recorded two songs straight to vinyl, but not before each group member had stumped-up the three shillings and sixpence demanded by Phillips in advance. This 1958 session featured John Lennon, Paul McCartney, George Harrison, John Lowe and Colin Hanton, recording Buddy Holly's 'That'll Be The Day' and a McCartney/Harrison composition, 'In Spite Of All The Danger'. This remarkable location displays a glass image to commemorate these Kensington recordings above the front door where five excited young musicians passed through on that day in 1958. Other local clients included Billy Fury, The Swinging Blue Jeans, Ken Dodd and Brian Epstein.

LOCATION 459: a mile east of the city centre on the A57, 38 Kensington, postcode L7 8. Status: private residence

Colin Unwin

LIVERPOOL 8
RINGO'S BIRTHPLACE

Richard Starkey was born at this house in Madryn Street on July 7th 1940. At 10 shillings a week, the rent on the property was just too expensive and the family were forced to move the short distance to a more modest, affordable house in Admiral Grove.

LOCATION 460: 9 Madryn Street, Toxteth, postcode L8 3TT. Status: private residence and the subject of much speculation about its future

LIVERPOOL 8
RINGO'S CHILDHOOD HOME

When Ringo was a young boy, his family split up. As a result, he and his mother moved a short distance from his birthplace to a smaller property in Admiral Grove when he was five. Richard Starkey suffered poor health, accompanied by frequent hospital visits, and was mostly schooled at home. As a teenager he was visited here by a friend, who would, like himself, go on to find fame with a name change from Priscilla White to Cilla Black. Ringo celebrated his 21st birthday and prepared for his wedding at Admiral Grove, the house that remained his Liverpool base until The Beatles became chart-toppers for the first time in 1963.

LOCATION 461: 10 Admiral Grove, postcode L8 8BH. Status: private residence

Still standing: the Starkey family's local pub

LIVERPOOL 8 A SENTIMENTAL JOURNEY TO THE EMPRESS PUB

Between the Liverpool districts of Toxteth and Dingle stands the Empress pub - a two-minute walk from Ringo Starr's former homes in Madryn Street and Admiral Grove. The distinctive tall, thin pub is immortalised on the cover of Ringo's first solo album Sentimental Journey, a fact tastefully engraved into the glass below the stone arch in the centre of the building.

LOCATION 462: 93 High Park Street, Toxteth, L8 3UF

LIVERPOOL 8
CENTRAL RESERVATION INSPIRATION FOR HOLLY JOHNSON

One of the most memorable and controversial No.1 singles in pop history began as a rhyme made up by local lad Holly Johnson as he hurried along Princes Avenue, Toxteth, to a Frankie Goes to Hollywood rehearsal. On arrival at the rehearsal, Johnson immediately laid down a vocal on to a one-note bass line from bass guitarist Mark O'Toole and drummer Peter Gill and 'Relax' was on its two-year journey to the top of the UK chart in 1984.

❝One day in the winter of 1982, I was late for rehearsals, walking very quickly along the central reservation, and I made up this little rhyme in my head, which was 'Relax, don't do it.'❞
Holly Johnson

LOCATION 463: two miles south east of the city centre on Princes Avenue, Toxteth, postcode L8 2UP

LIVERPOOL 12 CASBAH QUEUES IN THE SUBURBS

The extraordinary basement Casbah club in a Victorian house in the West Derby area of Liverpool carries a very strong Beatles imprint. The house and club, owned by the family of Pete Best, the early Beatles' drummer, was not only a music venue for all the various early Quarry Men and Silver Beatles line-ups, it also contains (even today) artistic interior decoration painted by John Lennon and Paul McCartney. John painted the Aztec pattern on the ceiling and carved his name on the wall while Paul painted a room with rainbows. A giant spider decorated another wall, while the remaining band members set about painting stars across ceilings and the tiny bar. On August 29th 1959, the Casbah opened its doors for the first time as a coffee bar. Performances by all the latest Liverpool groups brought long queues down the road, attracted by the novelty of rock 'n' roll music, sandwiches, coffee and Coca-Cola laid on by Pete Best's mother Mona.

LOCATION 464: the Best family run tours of the Casbah which can only be booked in advance by contacting Liverpool telephone number 0151 280 3519. Reached by taking the A5089 West Derby Road east out of the city centre at 8 Hayman's Green, postcode L12 5

LIVERPOOL 18 McCARTNEY'S CHILDHOOD HOME

Colin Unwin

Paul McCartney's childhood home at Forthlin Road

The McCartney family home in Forthlin Road was where Paul and his brother Michael were raised by their father after their mother tragically died in 1956, the year after they moved in. Now maintained in all its quaint 1950s glory by the National Trust, the small terraced house is a visitor attraction open to the public. 'Let It Be', for Paul's mother Mary, 'When I'm Sixty-Four', about his father Jim, 'Love Me Do' and 'I Saw Her Standing There' were just some of more than one-hundred songs written by the teenage Lennon and McCartney in the tiny front room. The two would sometimes bunk off school and enter the empty house during the day. As Paul had no key he would make for the back of the house, climb up the drainpipe and enter through the open toilet window, before running downstairs to let John carry in their guitars. Paul's bedroom was situated above the front door. From this window, years later, he would witness the growing number of fans arriving to try to catch a glimpse of a Beatle. They would camp out all night and take mementos - even a wing mirror from Paul's car - and by 1964 the McCartney family were forced to move to a spot 25 miles away from Forthlin Road which has continued to be a pilgrimage point for fans from all over the world.

LOCATION 465: 20 Forthlin Road, Allerton, postcode L18 9TN. Status: open to public visits. www.nationaltrust.org.uk/main/w-20forthlinroadallerton for further details

LIVERPOOL 15
A TOUR OF PENNY LANE

The extended Penny Lane area of Liverpool was the childhood haunt of John Lennon and Paul McCartney and title and subject of The Beatles' 1967 single. This area of Liverpool is best experienced sound-tracked by the song on your MP3 player as you visit each of the places name checked by the song, a guided tour with lyrics of mostly McCartney's memories. The shelter in the middle of the roundabout where the pretty nurse sells her poppies is directly linked to the roundabout at the top of Penny Lane, where the building in the middle was a bus shelter, waiting room and public convenience. On the corners at the roundabout are where both the barber and the banker were described in 'Penny Lane'. The fireman referred to in the lyrics of the song no doubt worked in the fire station where Allerton Road meets Mather Avenue. Even though this was half a mile from Penny Lane itself, it was on the bus route Paul McCartney would take to school every day when heading towards Penny Lane roundabout from his home in Forthlin Road. Bordered on one side of Penny Lane is St Barnabas Church, where the young McCartney was a member of the choir. Paul was best man at his brother Mike's wedding here in 1982, a ceremony that attracted sizeable crowds to get a glimpse of the returning Beatle.

LOCATION 466: Tony Slavin's barber shop is at 11 Smithdown Place off Penny Lane, and on the same block is the original bank (now a doctor's surgery). Begin your tour from here and head south for the full effect. Postcode: L15 9EH

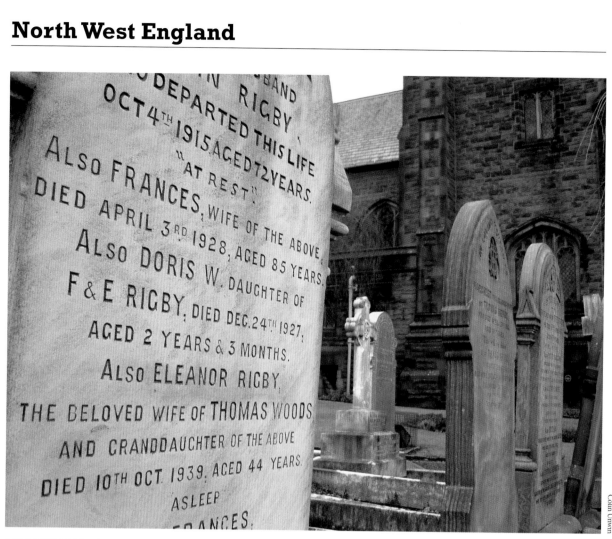

Colin Unwin

LIVERPOOL 25 ELEANOR RIGBY'S GRAVE

To paraphrase the Beatles song, Eleanor Rigby did indeed die and was buried along with her name, and St Peter's Church graveyard is the resting place of the real Eleanor Rigby, a former scullery maid who died in 1939. As the song describes, Eleanor's final years may possibly have been lonely, but earlier she had lived a relatively normal life and was married at one time to a railway foreman. She was born in the street behind Menlove Avenue, where John Lennon grew up, and this church location was familiar to both Lennon and McCartney during their formative years. John was a member of the St Peter's Church Youth Club, sang in the choir and attended Sunday school here. The facts behind the song's creation (predominantly written by Paul) are less than clear. What is certain is that both John and Paul first met each other in the nearby church field and were introduced to each other in the church hall. They were also frequent visitors to the graveyard in their youth, especially when the weather was hot enough for

The Eleanor Rigby headstone in St Peter's churchyard: much visited by Lennon and McCartney in their youth and by Beatles fans more than half a century later

a spot of summer sunbathing. Reports suggest John would sit in front of Eleanor Rigby's headstone fascinated by the word "ASLEEP", which is inscribed in the lower half of the impressive stone work. Weirdly, just two rows away from Eleanor Rigby's headstone lies the body of a John McKenzie, possibly a subconscious connection to the song's "Father McKenzie" character who also featured in McCartney's lyrics.

LOCATION 467: St Peter's Church, Church Road, postcode L25 5JF

LIVERPOOL 24 "ABOVE US ONLY SKY" AT JOHN LENNON AIRPORT

Liverpool's largest Beatles monument is Liverpool John Lennon Airport. The gateway to tourists arriving in the city, the airport name is aptly branded with the additional slogan "above us only sky", a line from Lennon's solo No.1 hit, 'Imagine'. The airport adopted Lennon's name in 2002 at a ceremony attended by Yoko Ono, when she unveiled the statue of her late husband by local sculptor Tom Murphy. The seven-foot-tall bronze overlooks the check-in hall on the first floor. The walls of the airport buildings are decorated with Beatles images and display cases of the group's clothing. Outside the terminal building is a giant Yellow Submarine. This 25-tonne model stands on the traffic island at the airport entrance. The 16-metre-long sculpture, representing the underwater craft featured in the song and movie Yellow Submarine, was built originally in 1984 for Liverpool's International Garden Festival by a group of 80 apprentices from the world-famous Cammell Laird shipyard.

❛Other airports have the Concorde, we have the Yellow Submarine.❜
Airport Managing Director, Neil Pakey

LOCATION 468: seven miles south-east of the city, in Speke, postcode L24 1

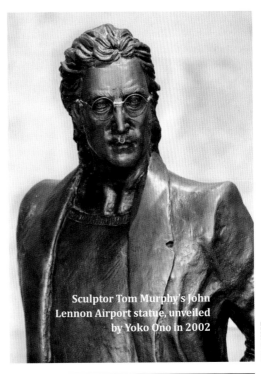

Sculptor Tom Murphy's John Lennon Airport statue, unveiled by Yoko Ono in 2002

Eddie Evans

LIVERPOOL 25 LENNON AND McCARTNEY'S FIRST MEETING

A significant performance by local skiffle group The Quarry Men occurred in the field outside St Peter's Parish Church on July 6th 1957. The occasion was a fete to mark the crowning of the local Rose Queen, which involved decorated floats, stalls, a police dog display and live music by The Quarry Men. In the audience to watch John Lennon and his mates perform was budding musician Paul McCartney. A short walk south from the church down Church Road brings you to the mecca for all fans of The Beatles, as this is the spot where, later that same day, 16-year-old John Lennon was first introduced to 15-year-old Paul McCartney. The introduction was made by Ivan Vaughan, a member of The Quarry Men, and noticing that John (taught by his mother Julia) played banjo chords on his guitar, Paul wasted no time in showcasing his skills with the guitar in front of the impressed group members. He played versions of Eddie Cochran's 'Twenty Flight Rock' and Little Richard's 'Long Tall Sally' and sometime soon after was asked to join The Quarry Men. Within a month or two, he was playing in the band (taking over from banjo player Rod Davies, who was leaving anyway) and taking the stage at St Peter's Church Hall. The building, though modernised, stands as it did in 1957 and the stage has been rescued by Liverpool City Council to be displayed in the new Museum of Liverpool. The hall's outside wall carries a commemorative plaque to mark the day that John first met Paul.

❛We were there playing when Paul arrives on his bike from Allerton and meets Ivan Vaughan – another kid from the Sunday school in Woolton and Ivan wanted to show him his friend John Lennon and his group. Paul remembers that we were playing 'Come Go With Me'. Paul thought this was really rather cool – this guy with the check shirt up front looked pretty good. At some stage later Paul said he picked up a guitar and played 'Twenty Flight Rock'. Here was McCartney, not only did he know 'Twenty Flight Rock', not only could he sing all the words, not only could he play proper guitar chords, he could even play them upside down. Later that evening Pete [Shotton] and John were strolling home and John said to Pete, 'What do you think of that friend of Ivan's? Why don't we have him in the group?' ❜
Quarry Men banjo player Rod Davies

LOCATION 469: St Peter's Church Hall, Church Road, postcode L25 5JF

North West England

LIVERPOOL 25 MENDIPS: JOHN LENNON'S CHILDHOOD HOME

Mendips, the house belonging to John Lennon's Aunt Mimi and Uncle George, was where he came to stay after his parents separated when John was just five years old. The suburban semi on Menlove Avenue was his home from 1945 until 1963. With all the fixtures and fittings that decorated the place in Lennon's time there, the house is now a beautifully restored shrine owned by the National Trust and open to the public. Underlining the Oasis obsession with their hero John Lennon, the Britpop band's single 'Live Forever' pictured Mendips on its front cover and many similarly enthusiastic Beatles fans, including Bob Dylan, have enjoyed the house tour, experiencing an insight into the lifestyle of the young Lennon. John's small bedroom was where, along with Paul McCartney, he sat and wrote future Beatles songs including 'Please, Please Me'. His bedroom was above the house's front porch, an area the boys would use to play their guitars, directed to go there by Mimi, who was not fond of the noise the two generated inside Mendips. Menlove Avenue was also the spot where Mimi's sister and John's mother Julia was killed when knocked down by a car when hurrying to catch a bus at the Menlove Avenue bus stop on July 15th 1958.

❛Last May [2009], a guided group arrived by bus, and I saw that Bob Dylan was among them. I paused for a moment, then I simply started my patter: "Welcome to Mendips, the childhood home of John Lennon..." Later, when we reached John's bedroom, Bob Dylan spotted the volume of Just William, which was one of John's favourite books. Dylan was fascinated by the book, and I remember thinking, "I'm standing in John Lennon's bedroom with Bob Dylan." It was a totally surreal moment.❜

Mendips' custodian, Colin Hall

LOCATION 470: 251 Menlove Avenue, postcode L25 7SA. Status: open to public visits. www.nationaltrust.org.uk/main/w-mendips for further details

John Lennon's home: where he lived as a schoolboy, art student and Beatle until 1963

Colin Unwin

LIVERPOOL 25 LENNON'S ESCAPE TO STRAWBERRY FIELD

Salvation Army

Colin Unwin

All that remains structurally from the childhood days when John Lennon would play in the grounds of the children's orphanage are the still iconic red Strawberry Field gates and wall signs and an overgrown area of bushes and brambles. But there is a real sense of atmosphere about the place even now. The Salvation Army property was demolished and rebuilt but now lies vacant in the large rambling fields that once backed on to John's home at Mendips. He would squeeze through the hedge at the bottom of Aunt Mimi's garden and play in the area around the Victorian orphanage at Strawberry Field. This was a magical place for the young Lennon, where his imagination later conjured up The Beatles' earliest psychedelic song 'Strawberry Fields Forever'. Like everyone else who is haunted by the song's lyrics, Lennon's widow Yoko and son Sean paid a visit to the children at the Strawberry Field Orphanage and grounds in 1984.

Strawberry Field orphanage as it was back in the days of John Lennon's childhood

The original gates in 2010, shortly before they were replaced by a new set

LOCATION 471: Beaconsfield Road, Woolton, postcode L25

LIVERPOOL 15 GEORGE HARRISON'S CHILDHOOD HOME

George Harrison grew up in a small terraced house, the youngest of three brothers and one sister. When George was a boy, the rent was 10 shillings per week, and before his father Harold landed a job as a bus conductor the family were forced to rely on welfare payments. Harold also spent a period in the Navy and brought some interesting records home. One vivid memory George recalled from his childhood at Arnold Grove was listening to 'One Meat Ball' by American Josh White.

LOCATION 472: 12 Arnold Grove, postcode L15 8HP. Status: private residence

North West England

Born on Merseyside

Jacqui Abbott, vocals, The Beautiful South (b. 10 Nov 1973, St Helens)

Marc Almond (b. 9 Jul 1957, Southport)

Ian Astbury, vocals, The Cult (b. 14 May 1962, Heswall)

Rick Astley (b. 6 Feb 1966, Newton-le-Willows)

Cilla Black (b. 27 May 1943, Liverpool)

Roy Boulter, drums, The Farm (b. 2 Jul 1964, Liverpool)

Ian Broudie, The Lightning Seeds (b. 4 Aug 1958, Liverpool)

Tim Brown, bass, The Boo Radleys (b. 26 Feb 1969, Wallasey)

Mel C (Melanie Chisholm), Spice Girls (b. 12 Jan 1974, Whiston)

Les Chadwick, bass, Gerry & The Pacemakers (b. 11 May 1943, Liverpool)

Paul Draper, vocals/guitar, Mansun (b. 26 Sep 1970, Liverpool)

Aynsley Dunbar, drummer (b. 10 Jan 1946, Liverpool)

Brian Epstein, manager (b. 19 Sep 1934, Liverpool, d. 27 Aug 1967)

Tom Evans, singer-songwriter, Badfinger (b. 5 Jun 1947, Liverpool, d. 19 Nov 1983)

Billy Fury (b. 17 Apr 1940, Liverpool, d. 28 Jan 1983)

Peter 'Ped' Gill, drums, Frankie Goes to Hollywood (b. 8 Mar 1964, Liverpool)

Franny Griffiths, keyboards, Space (b. 1 Jul 1970, Liverpool)

Steve Grimes, guitar, The Farm (b. 4 Jun 1957, Liverpool)

George Harrison (b. 25 Feb 1943, Liverpool, d. 29 Nov 2001)

Paul Heaton, vocals, The Housemartins/The Beautiful South (b. 9 May 1962, Bromborough)

Michael Holliday, singer (b. 26 Nov 1924, Liverpool, d. 29 Oct 1963)

Peter Hooton, vocals, The Farm (b. 28 Sep 1962, Liverpool)

Carl Hunter, bass, The Farm (b. 22 Apr 1965, Bootle)

Tony Jackson, vocals/bass, The Searchers (b. 16 Jul 1938, Liverpool, d. 18 Aug 2003)

Holly Johnson, vocals, Frankie Goes to Hollywood (b. 9 Feb 1960, Liverpool)

Simon Jones, bass, The Verve (b. 29 May 1972, Wigan)

Billy J. Kramer (b. 19 Aug 1943, Bootle)

Ben Leach, keyboards, The Farm (b. 2 May 1969, Liverpool)

John Lennon (b. 9 Oct 1940, Liverpool, d. 8 Dec 1980)

Dave McCabe, vocals, The Zutons (b. 1980, Liverpool)

Nick McCabe, guitar, The Verve (b. 14 Jul 1971, St Helens)

Paul McCartney (b. 18 Jun 1942, Liverpool)

Jim McCarty, drums, The Yardbirds (b. 25 Jul 1943, Liverpool)

Andy McCluskey, vocals/guitar, Orchestral Manoeuvres in the Dark (b. 24 Jun 1959, Heswall)

Ian McCulloch, vocals, Echo & The Bunnymen (b. 5 May 1959, Liverpool)

Ian McNabb, vocals, The Icicle Works (b. 3 Nov 1960, Liverpool)

John McNally, guitar, The Searchers (b. 30 Aug 1941, Liverpool)

Stuart Maconie, broadcaster (b. 13 Aug 1961, Whiston)

Les Maguire, piano, Gerry & The Pacemakers (b. 27 Dec 1941, Wallasey)

Freddie Marsden, drums, Gerry & The Pacemakers (b. 23 Nov 1940, Liverpool)

Gerry Marsden, vocals, Gerry & The Pacemakers (b. 24 Sep 1942, Liverpool)

Lee Mavers, vocals, The La's (b. 2 Aug 1962, Liverpool)

Damon Minchella, bass, Ocean Colour Scene (b. 1 Jun 1969, Liverpool)

Joey Molland, guitar, Badfinger (b. 21 Jun 1947, Liverpool)

Brian 'Nasher' Nash, guitar, Frankie Goes to Hollywood (b. 20 May 1963, Liverpool)

Nigel Olsson, drums, Elton John Band (b. 10 Feb 1949, Wallasey)

Keith O'Neill, drums, Cast (b. 18 Feb 1969, Liverpool)

Mark O'Toole, bass, Frankie Goes to Hollywood (b. 6 Jan 1964, Liverpool)

David 'Yorkie' Palmer, bass, Space (b. 7 Apr 1965, Liverpool)

Sean Payne, drums, The Zutons (b. 1978, Liverpool)

John Peel, broadcaster (b. 30 Aug 1939, Heswall, d. 25 Oct 2004)

Mike Pender, vocals, The Searchers (b. 3 Mar 1942, Liverpool)

John Power, vocals, Cast/The La's (b. 14 Sep 1967, Liverpool)

Russell Pritchard, guitar, The Zutons (b. 22 May 1979, Liverpool)

Heidi Range, Sugababes (b. 23 May 1983, Liverpool)

Paul Rutherford, vocals, Frankie Goes to Hollywood (b. 8 Dec 1959, Liverpool)

Will Sergeant, guitar, Echo & The Bunnymen (b. 12 Apr 1958, Liverpool)

Chris Sharrock, drums, The Icicle Works (b. 30 May 1964, Bebington)

James Skelly, guitar/vocals, The Coral (b. 1980, Birkenhead)

Sice (Sice Rowbottom), vocals, The Boo Radleys (b. 18 Jun 1969, Wallasey)

Ringo Starr (b. 7 Jul 1940, Liverpool)

Liam 'Skin' Tyson, guitar, Cast (b. 7 Sep 1969, Liverpool)

Peter Wilkinson, bass, Cast (b. 9 May 1969, Liverpool)

GREATER MANCHESTER

Rock pilgrimages to Greater Manchester should be enjoyed while listening to The Beautiful South's 'Manchester'. The track from their 2006 album Superbi pulls no punches when describing it in all its rainy glory, but it's done optimistically in a 'never mind' sort of way while namechecking just about everywhere from Altrincham to Wythenshawe. Elbow, Doves, The Smiths and even Take That also bring Manchester locations into songs with the delightful Bury, the M62, Whalley Range, Rusholme and the Mancunian Way as a backdrop, and who can blame them for their emotional attachment to the city and its surrounding area that gave birth to Manc exports ranging from Herman's Hermits to Oasis. Few places have as rich a small community feel in such a vast area, throwing up classic soap opera song stories like The Freshies' 'I'm In Love With The Girl On A Certain Manchester Megastore Check-Out Desk' and some of the best comic rock from that band's Chris Sievey, creator of the Timperley papier-mache-headed troubadour Frank Sidebottom.

The Grateful Dead's Jerry Garcia and Ron 'Pigpen' McKernan brave the elements at Bickershaw

Chris Hewitt www.tractor-ozit.com

BICKERSHAW **THE FESTIVAL THAT INSPIRED JOE AND ELVIS**

The promoter and driving force behind the epic Bickershaw Festival in 1972 was Jeremy Beadle. The professional practical joker and broadcaster persuaded 40,000 rock fans to attend what many present agree was one of the best and also one of the wettest outdoor music gatherings of the Seventies. The tiny village of Bickershaw played host to The Grateful Dead, who played for five hours, and the extraordinary Captain Beefheart. Among the soggy gathering excited and inspired by what they saw over the three days from May 5th to 7th were two young fans who would later make their own revered music, Joe Strummer and Elvis Costello.

LOCATION 473: the often waterlogged fields used for the festival still remain pretty much as they did in the Seventies, just off the B5237 where it joins Bolton House Road, approximately five miles south-east of Wigan. Postcode: WN2 4XU

North West England

MANCHESTER 1 THE WORLD FAMOUS HACIENDA

Now rebuilt as a block of apartments still carrying the Hacienda name, the site of this former yacht showroom and Bollywood cinema on Whitworth Street became a focal point for Greater Manchester's music fans during its heyday in the late 1980s. The facilities on offer included a dance floor, DJ balcony, downstairs cocktail bar, conventional bar and café, kitted out in the strikingly memorable yellow and black-striped hazard warning décor. Financed by Factory Records and therefore primarily by Factory's biggest earners and stakeholders New Order, it finally closed for business following a drugs raid in 1997. The building was demolished in 2002 and some fixtures and fittings, artefacts and posters, including items from Rob Gretton's Hacienda collection, are now at the Manchester Museum of Science & Industry. Despite the club's strong association with the Madchester music and fashion scene, its international fame was fanned by an appearance on the cover of influential American magazine Newsweek and an early appearance by the relatively unknown Madonna in 1983.

❛The most famous nightclub ever, in my opinion.❜
Clint Boon (Inspiral Carpets)

LOCATION 474 and 475: a short walk south west of Manchester city centre, Hacienda apartments, on Whitworth Street West, on the south side of the canal. Postcode: M1 5DE. The Manchester Museum of Science & Industry is at Liverpool Road, Castlefield, postcode M3 4FP

Chris Hewitt/www.tractor-ozit.com

A specially made bass guitar, partly constructed from the original wooden dance floor at the Hacienda, was presented to Peter Hook (right), by the man behind the idea, Chris Hewitt (left), and guitar-maker Brian Eastwood

BOLTON DANCING ALL NIGHT AT VA-VA

Spanish for "Go-Go", Va-Va was perhaps the best appointed and most modern of all the Northern Soul clubs. Offering "All-Nighters Every Friday of the Year", the club was regularly packed to its 400 capacity with fans from all over the north of England. Lavishly designed with Perspex and tiles, Va-Va tended to overshadow three equally worthy Bolton locations for rare soul aficionados: the Cromwellian, the Bolton Palais, and Troggs in nearby Farnworth.

LOCATION 476: the original site is close to the job centre, Elizabeth House, just off Great Moor Street, in the centre of Bolton. Postcode: BL1 1TP

HAIGH THE VERVE'S HAIGH HALL HOMECOMING

Guaranteed to reach fever pitch, homecoming gigs by world-conquering heroes almost always hit the spot and few have been bigger and better than The Verve's at Haigh Hall in 1998. The Wigan band's May 24th appearance drew 33,000 fans to the country parkland six months after their third hit album Urban Hymns had topped the UK chart.

LOCATION 477: about three miles north of Wigan, accessed from the B5239 near the village of Haigh, Haigh Hall Country Park is open to the public, postcode WN2 1PE

BURY GUY GARVEY'S WEDDING BUS RIDE

'Great Expectations', from the 2005 Elbow album Leaders Of The Free World, is vocalist Guy Garvey's charming imagined wedding story set on a bus between Manchester and Bury.

❛I got married once on the 135 bus to Bury. It was such a low-key affair that even the bride didn't know. Stockport supporters club kindly supplied us a choir. ❜
Guy Garvey explains 'Great Expectations'

LOCATION 478: the 135 bus route to Bury, north of Manchester. Postcode: Bury BL9

Mark Makin/Retna

MANCHESTER 2 JEERS AND "JUDAS" FOR DYLAN AT THE FREE TRADE HALL

One of British music history's most controversial concerts occurred on May 17th 1966 when Bob Dylan and The Hawks took to the Free Trade Hall stage and launched into 'Like A Rolling Stone'. It wasn't Dylan's first appearance at the grand old venue more familiar to fans of the Halle Orchestra. Just over a year earlier he had performed solo and acoustic to the delight of Manchester's folk fraternity. But in 1966 he ditched his acoustic guitar and plugged in a Stratocaster and introduced a whole new loud, electric take on his revered folk back catalogue. Not all the audience that night disapproved, but one among the dissenters did become audibly vocal among the jeers and slow handclaps. Recordings of the concert include Keith Butler yelling out rock music's most famous heckle. "Judas!" was the damning one-word criticism shouted out by the young Keele University student during Dylan's regeneration from folk minstrel to rock star. Less well reported but equally disgruntled was the

❝I shot 36 pictures on the night on 400 asa film. I thought no more about the pics for almost 30 years when I started to see them on the internet. It took me several years and £10,000 to establish my copyright! I was the only one to take pictures as Barry Feinstein had the night off. ❞
Mark Makin

demonstration by one female fan who had drawn lots with her friends to determine who would make the long walk down the aisle to the Free Trade Hall stage to deliver a scribbled note to Bob requesting he unplug and tell his band to go home. Also in the audience was 17-year-old Mark Makin, who captured the historic gig for posterity on his camera.

LOCATION 479: now a hotel, the imposing Manchester Free Trade Hall is situated in the city centre on Peter Street, postcode M2 5GP

North West England

MANCHESTER 2 SEX PISTOLS INSPIRE AND SHOCK YOUNG MANCHESTER

The Lesser Free Trade Hall was the venue for the now legendary Sex Pistols gig on June 4th 1976. When Bolton college students Pete McNeish (later Pete Shelley) and Howard Trafford (later Howard Devoto) failed to persuade the powers that be at Bolton Institute of Technology that they should play host to the Pistols, they audaciously booked one of Manchester's grandest cultural venues. Where Dylan had controversially played in the main hall a decade earlier, the Sex Pistols played in front of a crowd estimated at no more than 40 in the smaller, upstairs, Lesser Free Trade Hall. This gig, along with a much better attended second appearance on July 20th, saw the then little-known punk outfit from London create an indelibly strong impression on an impressionable Manchester audience of budding musicians. "Expecting a band in silver trousers, like Iggy Pop or the New York Dolls" was how Penetration fanzine editor Paul Welsh put it. What the crowd witnessed was "...ugly bastards in strategically ripped charity shop clothing". But, the Pistols' loud, stripped-down, aggressive bunch of Stooges and Mod cover versions and a few of their own songs struck a chord with a group of local music fans present at the birth of a new genre of music. Aside from

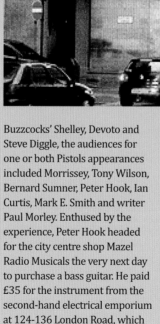

Buzzcocks' Shelley, Devoto and Steve Diggle, the audiences for one or both Pistols appearances included Morrissey, Tony Wilson, Bernard Sumner, Peter Hook, Ian Curtis, Mark E. Smith and writer Paul Morley. Enthused by the experience, Peter Hook headed for the city centre shop Mazel Radio Musicals the very next day to purchase a bass guitar. He paid £35 for the instrument from the second-hand electrical emporium at 124-136 London Road, which has long since disappeared.

6It was the most shocking thing I've ever seen in my life.9
Peter Hook on the Lesser Free Trade Hall gig quoted from Bernard Sumner: Confusion by David Nolan

LOCATION 480: now a hotel, the still imposing Manchester Free Trade Hall is situated in the city centre on Peter Street, postcode M2 5GP

LESSER FREE TRADE HA
MANCHESTER

SLAUGHTE
& THE DOG
PRESENTED BY R. & B.

THE SEX PISTOLS
PRESENTED BY MALCOLM McLAREN

PLUS SUPPORT

TUES. 20th JULY 1976
from 7.30 p.m.

TICKETS £1.00
obtainable from the Box Office, or pay at the door.

HEYWOOD THE JOHN PEEL-FUNDED TRACTOR SOUND STUDIOS

A plaque marks the place where John Peel financed a Heywood recording studio after the DJ had struck up a friendship with local band Tractor, who sent him a demo tape in 1973. The area was already familiar to Peel. The town was his home and Rochdale's Townhead cotton mill his place of work during a happy six months prior to his life-changing trip to the US and debut as a radio DJ in the Sixties.

LOCATION 481: 58 Market Street, Rochdale, postcode, 0L10 1UK

MANCHESTER 1 PICCADILLY RAVES, ELBOW, GOMEZ AND MC TUNES

The station, or area of the city centre called Piccadilly, gets namechecked in the Elbow track 'Station Approach' and 'Whippin' Piccadilly' by Gomez, with Piccadilly Gardens pictured on the cover of MC Tunes' The North At Its Heights album. The rear of Piccadilly station in Fairfield Street was where Manchester's first warehouse rave 'happened', starring The Stone Roses in the summer of 1985.

LOCATION 482: Piccadilly station at Station Approach, postcode M1 2PA

MANCHESTER 15 THE JOY DIVISION BRIDGE

THE BEST OF
JOY DIVISION

One of a series of Joy Division photos shot one winter's day in 1979 appears on the cover of the band's Best Of album. Photographed by Kevin Cummins, Ian Curtis, Bernard Sumner, Peter Hook and Stephen Morris are pictured on the Epping Walk Bridge in Hulme, an area packed full of locations familiar to the band. On a route leading to the site of the Hacienda, the bridge is also close to the Russell Club in Royce Road where Joy Division played some of their earliest gigs. Also nearby are TJ Davidson's rehearsal rooms, the Boardwalk club and Tony Wilson's former flat, making the bridge in Hulme the perfect memorial to the late Ian Curtis. A petition to have the structure named after the singer was set up in 2010.

❛It's the photograph that sums the band's sound up because of the sparseness, space and bleakness. ❜
Kevin Cummins, talking to the Manchester Evening News

LOCATION 483: the footbridge is over the A5103 Princess Road leading to Princess Parkway, south of Manchester city centre. The bridge is best accessed from Poynton Street on the eastern side. Postcode: M15 6PN

MANCHESTER 1 EARLY SOUL AND CREAM AT THE TWISTED WHEEL

The city's Twisted Wheel club claims to be the only surviving soul club still spinning Sixties R'n'B classic vinyl in the original club building. Prior to its location in Whitworth Street as pivotal purveyor of Northern Soul, The Twisted Wheel began life as a rhythm and blues venue in 1963 at Brazennose Street. The club was founded by Ivor Abadi and soon provided The Small Faces with their first public appearance. In 1965, the club relocated to nearby Whitworth Street, where a second notable debut took place when rock supergroup Cream played their first gig. The trio played The Twisted Wheel on July 29th 1966 as a warm-up gig for their formally advertised debut at the National Jazz & Blues Festival back down south in Windsor two days later.

❛The first concert we did was at the Twisted Wheel in Manchester. It was just called Cream. It wasn't advertised. Somebody had pulled out of the gig and we just took the gig up as a practice the day before doing the Windsor Jazz Festival. That was our first official concert.❜
Jack Bruce (Cream)

LOCATION 484: the London Road end of Whitworth Street at No.6, postcode M1 3QW. Website: www. thetwistedwheel.com

North West England

MANCHESTER 20 SIFTERS OASIS' 'SHAKERMAKER' RECORD SHOP

A regular haunt of the Gallagher brothers in their teenage years, Sifters second-hand record shop also made an appearance in Oasis' 1994 hit single 'Shakermaker'. The reference to "Mr Sifter" in the song was a line apparently hurriedly created to complete the lyrics en route to the recording studio. The Gallaghers taxi stopped at some traffic lights outside Sifters and Noel quickly added the lines to polish off another hit, with Mr Sifter, traffic lights and all.

LOCATION 485: south of Manchester city centre, Sifters is still 'selling songs' at 177 Fog Lane, Burnage, postcode M20 6FJ

Bernd Kugnow/losteuropaphotography.co.uk

The shop where Mr Sifter sold his songs to the 16-year-old Noel Gallagher

MANCHESTER 8 THE FALL'S 'CHEETHAM HILL'

The Manchester area known as Cheetham Hill was the inspiration for the song of the same name that appeared on The Fall's 1996 album The Light User Syndrome. According to the band's Broughton-born frontman Mark E. Smith, Cheetham Hill, formerly a run-down and dangerous place, isn't what it once was when he was a street gang lad. Ah, those were the days!

LOCATION 486: Cheetham Hill Road runs from south to north in north Manchester, a short distance from Prestwich, where The Fall's Mark E. Smith grew up as a child. Postcode: M8 8

MANCHESTER 13 JOHNNY CASH AT THE ASTORIA IRISH CLUB

On October 10th 1963, three years before he undertook his first full UK tour, Johnny Cash played a one-night stand at Manchester's Astoria Irish Club. Popular with the packed audience, who had no doubt enjoyed Cash's 1961 recording of his Irish song 'Forty Shades Of Green', he was supported on his live UK concert debut by his backing group The Tennessee Three. The venue, later named the Carousel, Sloskys and International 2, was where Noel and Liam Gallagher's mother and father first met and it has hosted a variety of acts from The Pogues to Public Enemy.

LOCATION 487: 210 Plymouth Grove, Longsight, postcode M13 0AS

MANCHESTER 14 'RUSHOLME RUFFIANS' AND TOP OF THE POPS

Home to Manchester's famously tasty Curry Mile of restaurants, Rusholme has appeared in at least two hit songs and was home to BBC's Top of the Pops shows for over a decade. The Smiths' 'Rusholme Ruffians' appeared on their 1985 album Meat Is Murder and the cleverly-titled 'From Rusholme With Love' was included on Mint Royale's 1999 debut On The Ropes. The former church and then film studio on Dickenson Road was where the BBC first began broadcasting Top of the Pops from January 1964, with Jimmy Savile presenting the very first show.

LOCATION 488: Rusholme is two miles south of the city centre. The Top Of The Pops studio in the converted Wesleyan Church is on the western end of Dickenson Road and is remembered by a green plaque. Postcode M14 5AT

MANCHESTER 13 'FROM ATLANTA GEORGIA TO LONGSIGHT MANCHESTER'

The Stone Roses' spiritual heartland appears to be located in this edgy region of south-east Manchester. Famous for all the wrong reasons in the Nineties with its weekly news headlines of guns, gangs and drugs, the place gets a mention in Roses track 'Daybreak' ('from Atlanta, Georgia to Longsight, Manchester') and 'Longsight M13' was the opener on Roses vocalist Ian Brown's Solarized solo album. The Madchester movement had its roots in places like Longsight and Moss Side, where, alongside gang graffiti for local footie giants United and City, baggy hieroglyphics for the Roses, Happy Mondays and Inspiral Carpets sat side-by-side.

LOCATION 489: about three miles out of Manchester city centre on the A6 at postcode M13

MANCHESTER 15 TJ DAVIDSON'S

It's the long, shabby, bare brick room in this converted warehouse that was the setting for Joy Division's performance in the 'Love Will Tear Us Apart' video. The recording and rehearsal business was run by Tony Davidson, son of the owner of well-known Manchester jeweller Davidson's on Oldham Street.

LOCATION 490: was at 35 Little Peter Street, Knott Mill, until demolition in the 80s, postcode M15 4QJ

The Savoy Picture House had, by the late 1950s when the Gibb brothers made their debut there, become the Gaumont, before closing in 1962. Below: a Co-op funeral directors now occupies the site

MANCHESTER 21 **THE BEE GEES' GAUMONT DEBUT**

Born on the Isle of Man, Keppel Road, Chorlton-cum-Hardy became home to the brothers Gibb until the family left to build a new life in Australia in the late Fifties. During their eight years at Keppel Road, Barry, Robin and Maurice began singing three-part harmony before their teenage years, performing live as The Rattlesnakes. The location of their singing debut was at the Gaumont cinema on Manchester Road East, a few minutes walk from their home.

LOCATIONS 491 and **492:** the Bee Gees, home still stands at 51 Keppel Road, postcode M21 0BP. You can trace the footsteps of the three brothers as they ran to their live singing debut at the Gaumont (now Co-operative Funerals) on Manchester Road East (postcode M21 9PN) by turning out of Keppel Road into Selborne Road and then crossing Manchester Road East.

MANCHESTER 15 **YELLOW AND SMILEY AT THE BOARDWALK**

A yellow smiley face beams out from the traditional blue plaque that marks the spot where famous Madchester venue and nightclub The Boardwalk operated between 1984 and 1999. The club's last seven years saw the popular Yellow night provide a unique atmosphere offering the very best in house, soul, disco and funk. The building also provided Oasis with their first proper rehearsal space in the below ground level area behind the glass tiles, which are still evident today on the swanky, upmarket structure, now converted to offices.

❛Very Manchester; a brilliant mix of black and white, students, single mothers from Sale and Droylsden, dental nurses from Chorlton, Cheshire girls, Moss Side boys. You get that kind of club once in a generation.❜
Yellow/Boardwalk DJ Dave Haslam describes the Boardwalk audience on his website www.davehaslam.com

LOCATION 493: close to Deansgate train station, Manchester city centre, at 21 Little Peter Street, postcode M15 4PS

North West England

MANCHESTER 16
CHORLTONVILLE: HOME OF THE BLUES

On a typically damp south Manchester day in 1964, an ambitious Granada TV production was filmed and broadcast featuring American blues legends Muddy Waters, Sister Rosetta Tharpe and Sonny Terry and Brownie McGhee. An astonishing makeover of Alexandra Park station by Granada saw the platform and station buildings transform into a typical railroad scene from the southern states of America. Station platform signs were substituted to read 'Chorltonville' in keeping with the American theme, and it was also the name of the nearby 20th-century garden village.

LOCATION 494: the railway line still runs through what was Alexandra Park station at the end of Athol Road, Chorlton-cum-Hardy, about 3 miles south of Manchester city centre. Postcode: M16 8QW

"Is Steven in?" The house where it all started back in 1982

MANCHESTER 32 MARR CALLS ON MORRISSEY

Sandwiched between the railway line and Longford Park in Stretford is the house where Smiths vocalist Morrissey lived as a teenager. The red-bricked semi-detached house on Kings Road is where The Smiths first came into being in 1982 when John Maher (later Johnny Marr) first arrived to discuss the forming of a band that May with Steven Patrick Morrissey. Almost two years after this meeting The Smiths released their eponymous debut album including 'Still Ill', a song that refers to the iron bridge on Kings Road next to house number 502.

LOCATION 495: about three miles south-west of Manchester city centre at 384 Kings Road, postcode M32 8GW

MANCHESTER 60
STRANGEWAYS WARNING BY THE SMITHS

A category A correctional facility familiar to all Mancunians, Strangeways Prison was renamed HM Prison Manchester in the 1990s. But it is as the former weirdly-named institution that attracted songwriters and included singer Ian Brown as an inmate following his conviction on an 'air rage' charge in the late Nineties. Deep Purple's 1987 album The House Of Blue Light carried a 'Strangeways' track, but it is The Smiths' final album, Strangeways, Here We Come, that gives the "Victorian monstrosity of a prison", as Smiths singer Morrissey put it, its biggest claim to fame.

❝I was always intrigued by the word Strangeways. I remember as a kid, when I first heard that the prison was really called that, I wondered had it not occurred to anybody to change the name?❞
Johnny Marr (The Smiths)

LOCATION 496: north of Manchester city centre at 1 Southall Street, postcode M60 9AH

MANCHESTER 19 THE GALLAGHER FAMILY HOME

In 1972, the Gallagher family moved home from Longsight to a cul-de-sac in Burnage. This three-bedroomed house was home to Tommy and Peggy Gallagher and their three boys Paul, Noel and Liam. Here Noel began to write a steady stream of songs, some that would appear on Oasis albums in the Nineties. The teenage Noel scrawled words and notes on what he called his 'wonderwall' in the small bedroom he shared with younger brother Liam.

LOCATION 497: Ashburn Avenue, Burnage, postcode M19 IDQ

ROCHDALE 24 HOUR PARTY PEOPLE AT CARGO STUDIOS

Home to Tractor Music, Cargo Studios and Suite 16 down the years, this location played a vital role in the development of some of the north-west's ground-breaking bands. Closely linked to the place, bass guitarist Peter Hook participated in Joy Division's first Factory Records recordings at Cargo Studios and later owned the building when named Suite 16. Architecturally rather nondescript, 16 Kenion Street nevertheless made an authentic appearance as itself in music movie 24 Hour Party People and was awarded a plaque in 2009.

❝Watching The Stone Roses, Happy Mondays, The Chameleons, The Charlatans, oh my god the list is endless, walk through those [Cargo Studios] doors, the effect it had on Rochdale and the north-west music scene is immeasurable, much as Ian Curtis had on Macclesfield.❞
Peter Hook

LOCATION 498: 16 Kenion Street, postcode OL16 1SJ

ROCHDALE MIKE HARDING'S WILD NORTH WEST

The wild north-west was the subject for comedian and folkie Mike Harding's 1975 hit single. Expressing how difficult it was to attach spurs to clogs, 'Rochdale Cowboy' put Rochdale on the map much as songstress Gracie Fields had done decades earlier. Harding was born in the nearby town of Crumpsall.

LOCATION 499: to search for the song's local "pie and pea saloon", head for the town centre, postcode OL16 1LR

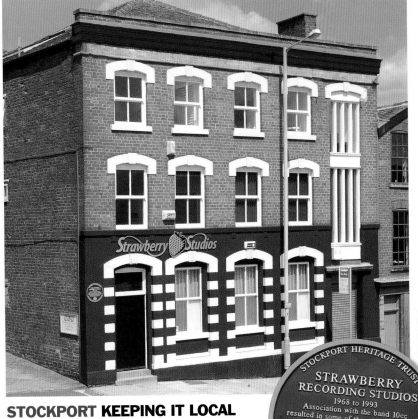

Peter Tarleton

STOCKPORT HERITAGE TRUST
STRAWBERRY RECORDING STUDIOS
1968 to 1993
Association with the band 10cc resulted in some of the most memorable music being produced at these Studios. Paul McCartney, Neil Sedaka, Stone Roses, The Syd Lawrence Orchestra and many others also recorded here.
THE METROPOLITAN BOROUGH OF STOCKPORT

STOCKPORT KEEPING IT LOCAL AT STRAWBERRY STUDIOS

Opened in 1967 by former Sixties beat groups road manager Peter Tattersall and Mindbenders band member Eric Stewart back in the days when recording studios outside London were uncommon. The duo named their new business venture after the current Beatles track 'Strawberry Fields Forever' and support from another investor, Graham Gouldman, and session help from local musicians Kevin Godley and Lol Creme quickly established the studios as a thriving concern. Aside from recording artists including Neil Sedaka, the team behind Strawberry Studios recorded themselves as Hotlegs and eventually in 1972 began a run of massively successful singles and albums as 10cc. By the late Seventies, an association with local producer Martin Hannett opened up a whole new wave of talent hungry to make a recording, and a second cut-price facility at Strawberry Studios South, welcomed The Durutti Column, Joy Division and The Stone Roses. Other local bands making good use of the recording facilities on their doorstep included Buzzcocks, Simply Red, James and New Order. A plaque marks the spot of this recording and mixing activity.

LOCATION 500: Strawberry Studios ended its association with Stockport in 1993. The original site has private offices that still retain the name at 3 Waterloo Road, Stockport: postcode SK1 3BD

Chris Hewitt/www.tractor-ozit.com

ROCHDALE **THE DEEPLY VALE FREE FESTIVALS**

The crowd awaits the arrival on stage of Steve Hillage in 1978

Fondness for the Deeply Vale mid-to late, Seventies series of free festivals set in an idyllic valley on the moors outside Rochdale has spawned a hugely informative website, its own T-shirts and a lovingly put-together DVD released in 2007. Drawing inspiration from the success of the neighbouring, earlier Bickershaw Festival, Deeply Vale began tentatively, drawing just a few hundred fans in 1976. Popularity accelerated sharply until, in 1978, 20,000 hippies and punk fans flooded into the site to camp and groove to the sounds of Steve Hillage, The Fall, The Durutti Column and a young, flame-haired Mick Hucknall fronting The Frantic Elevators. Deeply Vale provided the inspiration for a new generation of musicians in the north-west. Making up the audience were Ian Brown, future Wedding Present band member Dave Gedge, future Smiths bass guitarist Andy Rourke, assorted members of The Mock Turtles and an eight-year-old Jimi Goodwin, who would find success with Doves two decades later. One of the few events to combine the great outdoors with new wave music, Deeply Vale still attracts a few punk era pilgrims rambling through the valley in search of the site of this locally produced success story.

❝It was far more organised than early Glastonburys. My day job was running musical events indoor and outdoor – so we took some of the chaos out of the stage arrangements that happened at Stonehenge and early Glastos - things ran to a timetable and all types of bands were welcome.❞
Deeply Vale stage manager and co-organiser Chris Hewitt

LOCATION 501: the festival site lies in a moorland valley and can be reached easily by heading west out of Rochdale on the A680 and turning left on to Ashworth Road just as the A680 reaches Ashworth Moor Reservoir. Postcode OL11 5UN. Website: www.deeplyvale.com

SALFORD SMITHS PHOTOSHOOT PUTS THE LADS CLUB ON THE MAP

Opened in 1904 by Boy Scouts leader Robert Baden-Powell, Salford Lads Club became a location worthy of pilgrimage for thousands of Smiths fans when the red brick building formed a backdrop for an iconic group photo in 1986. The famous inside cover picture for the band's fourth hit album The Queen Is Dead became the archetypal bedroom wall poster at the time. In 2005 photographer Stephen Wright's famous image was accepted into the National Portrait Gallery collection. There's a Smiths room at the club that acts as a focal point and shrine to visitors. A film featuring Smiths vocalist Morrissey cycling round Salford and revisiting the club's front doorway a year later was shot for the intended video 'Stop Me If You Think You've Heard This One Before', but the release's airplay was banned by the BBC due to the song's "plan a mass murder" line in the wake of the infamous Hungerford massacre. Former members of Salford Lads Club include Joy Division and New Order's Peter Hook. Graham Nash and Allan Clarke also used the club for early Hollies band rehearsals.

❝We started the session at the Salford Lads Club at Morrissey's request. The rotten light and the casual pose help the photo have a relaxed nature. ❞
Photographer Stephen Wright

LOCATION 502: Salford Lads Club is roughly a mile west of Manchester city centre, on the corner of the 'real' Coronation Street, Salford, M5 3RS

Salford Lads Club and The Smiths: in the National Portrait Gallery collection

Stephen Wright/smithsphotos.com

North West England

SALFORD
EWAN MacCOLL'S 'DIRTY OLD TOWN'

The city of Salford is the subject of Ewan MacColl's song 'Dirty Old Town'. Most familiar versions of the gritty description of the large chunk of urban Greater Manchester are by The Pogues, The Dubliners and The Clancy Brothers, which has led to a case of mistaken identity. The assumption that the song had been written about an Irish location is wide of the mark. Folk musician MacColl was born and grew up in the Broughton area of Salford, vividly bringing to life the canal, gas works, factory and docks in 'Dirty Old Town', which he wrote in his early thirties in 1949. Local band Doves followed in MacColl's footsteps, painting an equally moody industrial picture on 'Shadows Of Salford', a track from their 2005 chart-topping album Some Cities.

LOCATION 503: Ewan MacColl was born in Heath Avenue, Lower Broughton, postcode M7 1

WIGAN 'THE WORLD'S BEST DISCO'

Hardly worthy of a visit today, the site where hoards of nationwide Northern Soul fans trekked to in the Seventies has latterly become a shopping centre and car park. That said, Wigan's Casino was Britain's best known and most popular venue for a music and fashion movement that escaped the mainstream in pop's nearest thing to a secret society. The Casino's all-nighters ran from 1973 to 1981, and if the present-day websites, books and internet forums are any indication, the teenagers that attended back then still continue to celebrate what American music magazine Billboard voted the 'World's best disco' in 1974.

LOCATION 504: the site of the former Casino Club is at Station Road, Wigan, postcode WN1 1

Born in Greater Manchester

Stuart Adamson, vocals, Big Country (b. 11 Apr 1958, Manchester, d. 16 Dec 2001)

Paul 'Bonehead' Arthurs, guitar, Oasis (b. 23 Jun 1965, Burnage, Manchester)

Richard Ashcroft, vocals, The Verve/solo (b. 11 Sep 1971, Wigan)

Bez (Mark Berry), percussion, Black Grape/Happy Mondays (b. 18 Apr 1964, Salford)

Clint Boon, vocals/keyboards, Inspiral Carpets (b. 28 Jun 1959, Oldham)

Elkie Brooks (b. 25 Feb 1945, Salford)

Tim Burgess, vocals, The Charlatans (b. 30 May 1967, Salford)

Dean Butterworth, drums, Good Charlotte (b. 26 Sep 1976, Rochdale)

Allan Clarke, vocals, The Hollies (b. 5 Apr 1942, Salford)

John Cooper Clarke (b. 25 Jan 1949, Salford)

Lol Creme, guitar/vocals, 10cc (b. 19 Sep 1947, Prestwich)

Chris Curtis, drums, The Searchers (b. 26 Aug 1941, Oldham, d. 28 Feb 2005)

Ian Curtis, vocals, Joy Division (b. 15 Jul 1956, Stretford, d. 18 May 1980)

Saul Davies, guitar/violin, James (b. 28 Jun 1965, Oldham)

Paul Davis, keyboards, Happy Mondays (b. 7 Mar 1966, Swinton)

Mark Day, guitar, Happy Mondays (b. 29 Dec 1961, Manchester)

Steve Diggle, guitar/vocals, Buzzcocks (b. 7 May 1955, Manchester)

Howard Donald, Take That (b. 28 Apr 1968, Droylsden)

Billy Duffy, guitar, The Cult (b. 12 May 1961, Hulme, Manchester)

Georgie Fame (b. 26 Jun 1943, Leigh)

James Fearnley, accordion, The Pogues (b. 9 Oct 1954, Worsley)

Martin Fry, vocals, ABC (b. 9 Mar 1958, Stockport)

Liam Gallagher, vocals, Oasis/Beady Eye (b. 21 Sep 1972, Burnage, Manchester)

Noel Gallagher, guitar/vocals, Oasis/Noel Gallagher's High Flying Birds (b. 29 May 1967, Longsight, Manchester)

Freddie Garrity, vocals, Freddie and The Dreamers (b. 14 Nov 1936, Manchester, d. 19 May 2006)

Guy Garvey, vocals/guitar, Elbow (b. 6 Mar 1974, Bury)

Andy Gibb (b. 5 Mar 1958, Manchester, d. 10 Mar 1988)

Gillian Gilbert, keyboards/vocals, New Order (b. 27 Jan 1961, Whalley Range, Manchester)

Craig Gill, drums, Inspiral Carpets (b. 5 Dec 1971, Salford)

Kevin Godley, drums/vocals, 10cc (b. 7 Oct 1945, Prestwich)

Jimi Goodwin, vocals/guitar, Doves (b. 28 May 1970, Manchester)

Larry Gott, guitar, James (b. 24 Jul 1957, Manchester)

Graham Gouldman, bass/vocals, 10cc (b. 10 May 1946, Salford)

Karl Green, bass, Herman's Hermits (b. 31 Jul 1947, Davyhulme)

Martin Hannett, record producer (b. 31 May 1948, Miles Platting, Manchester, d. 18 Apr 1991)

Mike Harding, folk singer-songwriter/broadcaster (b. 23 Oct 1944, Crumpsall, Manchester)

Roy Harper, singer-songwriter/guitarist (b. 12 Jun 1941, Rusholme, Manchester)

Les Holroyd, bass/vocals, Barclay James Harvest (b. 12 Mar 1948, Oldham)

Peter Hook, bass, Joy Division/New Order (b. 13 Feb 1956, Salford)

Dominic Howard, drums, Muse (b. 7 Dec 1977, Stockport)

Mick Hucknall, vocals, Simply Red (b. 8 Jun 1960, Denton)

Davy Jones, vocals, The Monkees (b. 30 Dec 1945, Manchester)

Mike Joyce, drums, The Smiths (b. 1 Jun 1963, Fallowfield, Manchester)

Richard Jupp, drums, Elbow (b. Bury)

Jay Kay (Jason Cheetham), vocals, Jamiroquai (b. 30 Dec 1969, Stretford)

Andy Kershaw, presenter (b. 9 Nov 1959, Rochdale)

Liz Kershaw, presenter (b. 30 Jul 1958, Rochdale)

Graham Lambert, guitar, Inspiral Carpets (b. 10 Jul 1964, Oldham)

John Lees, guitar/vocals, Barclay James Harvest (b. 13 Jan 1947, Oldham)

Paul 'Kermit' Leveridge, vocals, Black Grape (b. 10 Nov 1969, Manchester)

Ewan MacColl, singer-songwriter (b. 25 Jan 1915, Salford, d. 22 Oct 1989)

Paul 'Guigsy' McGuigan, bass, Oasis (b. 9 May 1971, Manchester)

Johnny Marr, guitar, The Smiths/ Electronic/The The/Modest Mouse/ The Cribs (b. 31 Oct 1963, Ardwick, Manchester)

Graham Massey, keyboards, 808 State (b. 4 Aug 1960, Manchester)

Morrissey (b. 22 May 1959, Davyhulme, Trafford)

Gary 'Mani' Mounfield, bass, Primal Scream/The Stone Roses (b. 16 Nov 1962, Crumpsall, Manchester)

Martin Noble, guitar, British Sea Power (b. 28 Jan 1986, Bury)

Peter Noone, vocals, Herman's Hermits (b. 5 Nov 1947, Davyhulme, Trafford)

Jason Orange, Take That (b. 10 Jul 1970, Crumpsall, Manchester)

Mark Owen, Take That (b. 27 Jan 1972, Oldham)

Lyn Paul, The New Seekers (b. 16 Feb 1949, Wythenshawe, Manchester)

Craig Potter, guitar, Elbow (b. Bury)

Mark Potter, keyboards, Elbow (b. Bury)

Mel Pritchard, drums, Barclay James Harvest (b. 20 Jan 1948, Oldham, d. 28 Jan 2004)

Mark Radcliffe, broadcaster (b. 29 Jun 1958, Bolton)

Mike Read, broadcaster (b. 1 Mar 1947, Manchester)

Andy Rourke, bass, The Smiths (b. 17 Jan 1964, Manchester)

Paul Ryder, bass, Happy Mondays (b. 24 Apr 1964, Manchester)

Shaun Ryder, vocals, Black Grape/ Happy Mondays (b. 23 Aug 1962, Salford)

Dave Sharp, guitar, The Alarm (b. 28 Jan 1959, Salford)

Pete Shelley, guitar/vocals, Buzzcocks (b. 17 Apr 1955, Leigh)

Mark E. Smith, vocals, The Fall (b. 5 Mar 1957, Salford)

John Squire, guitar, The Stone Roses/ The Seahorses (b. 24 Nov 1962, Altrincham)

Lisa Stansfield (b. 11 Apr 1966, Rochdale)

Eric Stewart, guitar/vocals, 10cc (b. 20 Jan 1945, Droylsden)

Bernard Sumner, vocals/guitar, Joy Division/New Order/Electronic/Bad Lieutenant (b. 4 Jan 1956, Salford)

Simon Tong, guitar/keyboards, The Verve (b. 9 Jul 1972, Wigan)

Pete Turner, bass, Elbow (b. 28 Aug 1974, Bury)

Nigel Twist, drums, The Alarm (b. 18 Jul 1958, Manchester)

Paul 'Wags' Wagstaff, guitar, Black Grape (b. 28 Dec 1964, Stockport)

Martyn Walsh, bass, Inspiral Carpets (b. 3 Jul 1968, Rusholme, Manchester)

Barry Westhead, keyboards, Starsailor (b. 13 May 1977, Wigan)

Gary Whelan, drums, Happy Mondays (b. 12 Feb 1966, Manchester)

Katie White, vocals, The Ting Tings (b. 3 Mar 1983, Wigan)

Andy Williams, vocals/drums, Doves (b. 22 Feb 1970, Manchester)

Jez Williams, vocals/guitar, Doves (b. 22 Feb 1970, Manchester)

Tony Wilson, record label owner/ presenter (b. 20 Feb 1950, Salford, d. 10 Aug 2007)

Stewart 'Woolly' Wolstenholme, vocals/keyboards, Barclay James Harvest (b. 15 Apr 1947, Chadderton, d. 13 Dec 2010)

Alan 'Reni' Wren, drums, The Stone Roses (b. 10 Apr 1964, Manchester)

UK and US Chart-topping Manchester exports, Freddie and The Dreamers

LANCASHIRE

Tragically, a good deal of Lancashire's great rock heritage has been demolished. Nelson's incredible Imperial Ballroom, which attracted just about every major Sixties act to the small mill town has long since burned to the ground, Blackpool's Northern Soul mecca succumbed to the wrecking ball in 2009 and Ribchester's location for major punk bands, the Lodestar, has an uncertain future. Despite demolition and uncertainty, there are still stories to tell and plenty of Lancashire locations worthy of pilgrimage that have survived the years and in one case the centuries. Black Sabbath's Heysham graves date back to the eleventh century, the Blackpool church hall where Jethro Tull began life still stands, and the town's magnificent Empress Ballroom has experienced extraordinary scenes involving The Rolling Stones, The Stone Roses and The White Stripes while Blackburn's Reidy's music store is a magnet for musos even if the town's 4,000 holes are best avoided.

FAR&NEAR
The holes in our roads

THERE are 4,000 holes in the road in Blackburn, Lancashire, or one twenty-sixth of a hole per person, according to a council survey.

If Blackburn is typical there are two million holes in Britain's roads and 300,000 in London.

£225,0000 sea defence scheme for Felixstowe is being urged on the Government by East Suffolk River Board.

1,000 ratepayers in Harrow, Middlesex, said the Exchequer

The 1967 story that Lennon included in 'A Day In The Life'

Ian Anderson returns to his roots with flute

News & Pictures North

BLACKPOOL CHURCH HALL DEBUT FOR THE EMBRYONIC TULL

A plaque at Blackpool's Holy Family Church Hall has been erected in honour of Jethro Tull. In 1964, local teenagers Ian Anderson, Jeffrey Hammond and John Evan, then playing as The Blades, performed their first gig and one of Britain's most enduring rock bands was born.

❝I don't even think there was a stage here at the time and, in my memory, it was so much bigger. To us at the time it was like playing Madison Square Gardens in New York.❞
Ian Anderson, speaking to Blackpool paper The Gazette at the plaque unveiling in 2010

LOCATION 505: Holy Family Church Hall, Links Road, North Shore, postcode FY1 2RU

BLACKBURN THE FOUR PENNIES AT REIDY'S

The town's chart-toppers, The Four Pennies, named themselves after Penny Street in Blackburn town centre. The street's music store, Reidy's, was where the group bought all their gear and they were at the grand opening of the new store in 1964, the same year their biggest hit 'Juliet' made No.1. Quite the men about town, the band even played at Ewood Park in front of thousands of football fans.

LOCATION 506: Reidy's 'home of music' is at 9-13 Penny Street, Blackburn, postcode BB1 6HJ

BLACKBURN LENNON'S 4,000 LANCASHIRE POTHOLES

A national newspaper article that caught the eye of John Lennon was responsible for the legendary lyric line in The Beatles 'A Day In The Life', recorded in 1967. The story about 4,000 holes in Blackburn found its way into the Sgt Pepper's album track following a Daily Mail feature about the state of the potholed roads in the Lancashire town. The same edition of the paper also carried an account of the death in a car crash of Tara Browne, heir to the Guinness fortune. This prompted Lennon to include the line "he blew his mind out in a car" in, one of the last true Lennon and McCartney compositions.

LOCATION 507: Blackburn lies 25 miles north of Manchester, just off the M65 motorway. Postcode: BB1 5AF

BLACKPOOL
THE MECCA FOR SEASIDE SOUL AND SUN

Demolished in 2009, the Blackpool Mecca hosted Northern Soul nights from 1971 to 1979. Without an all-night licence to compete with Wigan's Casino - the restricted fun only lasted from 8pm to 2am - Blackpool Mecca still packed in soul enthusiasts at its Highland Room thanks to dedicated, expert DJs Ian Levine and Colin Curtis. Fans of the venue were given the opportunity to own their own tiny piece of the much-loved venue when it was pulled down. Small sections of the wooden dance floor went on sale at £10.

❝The rivalry between Blackpool Mecca and Wigan Casino was tribal, like two football clubs who hate each other. ❞ DJ Colin Curtis, who kept the punters happy during the Mecca's heyday

LOCATION 508: was situated on Central Drive, postcode FY1 5

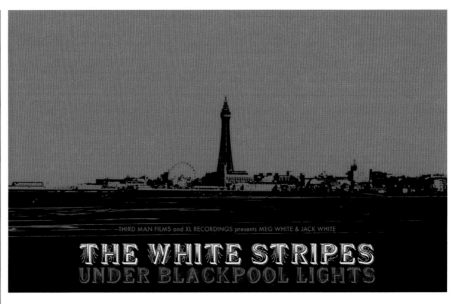

THIRD MAN FILMS and XL RECORDINGS presents MEG WHITE & JACK WHITE
THE WHITE STRIPES
UNDER BLACKPOOL LIGHTS

BLACKPOOL STONES, ROSES AND STRIPES AT THE EMPRESS BALLROOM

Commonly hired as a genteel dancing venue, or for trade fairs and conferences, the Empress Ballroom was the setting for a Rolling Stones riot and the first really big gig The Stone Roses performed. The Rolling Stones' visit in 1964 saw the band forced to exit the stage when fans began throwing bottles, smashing the ballroom chandeliers and wrecking a Steinway piano. The aggressive behaviour of some of the 7,000 crowd squeezed into the ballroom on July 24th, and the injuries to 50 teenage fans requiring hospital treatment, led to the band being barred from ever returning to Blackpool's grandest venue. Twenty-five years later, The Stone Roses, by comparison, were greeted almost reverentially by at least 4,000 of their followers who descended on the town one hot August day in 1989 and witnessed what many observers reckoned to be the band's finest moment. Fortunately The Stone Roses filmed their Empress Ballroom appearances and The White Stripes chose this popular venue to create their first DVD, Under Blackpool Lights, in 2004.

LOCATION 509: a short walk from the promenade seafront at the Winter Gardens, Church Street, postcode FY1 1HU

RIBCHESTER PISTOLS AND RATS AT THE LODESTAR

With bookings impossible to get in and around London, Irish new-wavers The Boomtown Rats hit the provinces to make their mark. The Lodestar Hotel was the setting for the band's first UK gig on May 6th 1977. Bob Geldof recalled only 12 people being there that night but 180 rammed into the place when they returned later that August. Geldof and co stayed overnight at the Victoria Hotel in nearby Clitheroe. The Lodestar must have developed a reputation for harbouring punk and new wave waifs and strays as this remote venue had previously played host to the Sex Pistols on August 18th 1976. Remarkably, this came after their legendary appearances at Manchester's Lesser Free Trade Hall in the same year.

LOCATIONS 510 and **511:** on the B6245 a few yards north of the Ribchester Bridge over the River Ribble lies the currently unoccupied building (summer 2011) that back in 1977 was the Lodestar Hotel, more recently renamed De Tabley Arms. Postcode: PR3 3ZQ. Clitheroe's Victoria Hotel is on the corner of King Street and York Street, postcode BB7 2BZ

North West England

NELSON SMALL TOWN, HUGE STARS AT 'THE IMP'

This book doesn't generally resort to lists to emphasise a point, but in Nelson's case we will make an exception. The Imperial Ballroom in a town with a population of less than 30,000 is a venue that has attracted The Beatles, The Rolling Stones, The Who, Jimi Hendrix, The Small Faces, The Kinks, Otis Redding, Smokey Robinson, The Animals, Pink Floyd, Ike and Tina Turner, Cream, Free, Stevie Wonder, Bo Diddley and Little Richard. The man responsible for booking so many household names was Bob Caine, the extraordinarily successful manager of the venue affectionately known as The Imp. Shortly after changing its name to The Column, this imposing building was destroyed by fire. The ballroom's legacy of hosting the cream of 60s and 70s pop acts lives on. Imperial Gardens – a sheltered housing development – occupies the spot where Lennon and Hendrix strutted their stuff.

LOCATION 512: the Imperial Ballroom stood on the lower side of the canal bridge in Carr Road where Imperial Gardens stands today. Postcode BB9 7TG. Memories of The Imp linger on at website www.lankybeat.com and Steve Chapples excellent book Goin' Down Th' Imp

The Nelson Leader

THE BEST OF
BLACK SABBATH

The eleventh-century graves overlooking Morecambe Bay

HEYSHAM BLACK SABBATH'S ROCK GRAVES

The ruins of St Patrick's Chapel at Lower Heysham provided the atmospheric cover for Black Sabbath's Best Of album in 2000. The row of six stone graves, which are said to date from the eleventh century, are located in a timeless, windswept spot overlooking the coast at Morecambe Bay. The graves' original contents and stone covers disappeared centuries ago.

LOCATION 513: easily accessed in a beautiful location, the row of graves at St Patrick's Chapel are next to the small church of St Peter's village of Heysham, postcode LA3 2RW

Born in Lancashire

Chris Acland, drums, Lush (b. 7 Sep 1966, Lancaster, d. 17 Oct 1996)
Jon Anderson, vocals, Yes (b. 25 Oct 1944, Accrington)
Neil Arthur, vocals, Blancmange (b. 15 Jun 1958, Darwen)
Tony Ashton, keyboards, Ashton, Gardner & Dyke (b. 1 Mar 1946, Blackburn, d. 28 May 2001)
Dave Ball, Soft Cell (b. 3 May 1959, Blackpool)
Bobby Elliott, drums, The Hollies (b. 8 Dec 1941, Burnley)
John Foxx, vocals, Ultravox (b. 26 Sep 1947, Chorley)
Keef Hartley, drummer (b. 8 Apr 1944, Preston)
Eric Haydock, bass, The Hollies (b. 3 Feb 1942, Burnley)
Victoria Hesketh (aka Little Boots) (b. 4 May 1984, Blackpool)
Tony Hicks, guitar, The Hollies (b. 16 Dec 1945, Nelson)
Chris Lowe, keyboards, Pet Shop Boys (b. 4 Oct 1959, Blackpool)
Nicholas McCarthy, guitar/keyboards, Franz Ferdinand (b. 13 Dec 1974, Blackpool)
Sarah Martin, violin/vocals, Belle & Sebastian (b. 12 Feb 1974, Blackburn)
Lionel Morton, guitar/vocals, The Four Pennies (b. 14 Aug 1941, Blackburn)
Graham Nash, Crosby, Stills, Nash & Young/The Hollies (b. 2 Feb 1942, Blackpool)
Ken Nicol, guitar, Steeleye Span (b. 27 May 1951, Preston)
Danbert Nobacon, Chumbawamba (b. 16 Jan 1962, Burnley)
Les Pattinson, bass, Echo & The Bunnymen (b. 18 Apr 1958, Ormskirk)
Mike Pickering, musician/DJ/record (b. 24 Feb 1958, Accrington)
Maddy Prior, vocals, Steeleye Span (b. 14 Aug 1947, Blackpool)
Robert Smith, vocals, The Cure (b. 21 Apr 1959, Blackpool)
Andy Summers, guitar, The Police (b. 31 Dec 1942, Poulton-le-Fylde)
Diana Vickers (b. 30 Jul 1991, Blackburn)
John Waite, vocals, The Babys (b. 4 Jul 1952, Lancaster)
James Walsh, vocals/guitar, Starsailor (b. 9 Jun 1980, Chorley)

CUMBRIA

England's third largest county was where Spooky Tooth and British Sea Power were rooted, but not since The Beatles played Carlisle has there been as rocktastic an event as that which saw Lady Gaga arrive on stage in a coffin at BBC's travelling circus, the Radio 1 Big Weekend, in front of 20,000 damp fans in a field in Cumbria in May 2011. Those aforementioned Beatles made two newsworthy appearances in Carlisle that saw them ejected then feted in the Sixties, and Black Sabbath paid their dues at Carlisle's Cosmo. Then there's Maryport's beat boom mecca and, more recently, the seriously funny Half Man Half Biscuit, honouring Ambleside by selecting the Lake District town to appear on an album cover.

❛Just put your paws up, coz you were born this way Carlisle!❜
Lady Gaga addresses her fans at the 2011 Radio 1 Big Weekend

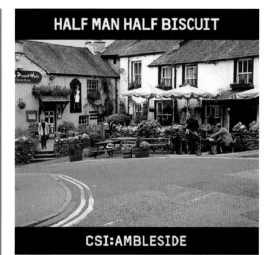

AMBLESIDE THE HALF MAN HALF BISCUIT CSI FRANCHISE

The Half Man Half Biscuit album cover for the band's 2008 release CSI: Ambleside pictures the Lake District town's Church Street and the Priest Hole restaurant.

LOCATION 514: Church Street in the centre of Ambleside, postcode LA22 0BU

CARLISLE SABBATH RETURN

When local band Earth played an end of school year dance for £40 in Carlisle and promised to return for a second booking a year later, the student organisers reasoned that with the December 15th 1970 date approaching they might have a no-show on their hands. In the period between the two bookings, Earth had gone through a line-up change down in Birmingham and turned into album chart-toppers Black Sabbath. But the 1970 school dance wasn't disappointed when the band and truck duly rolled into the Cosmopolitan venue car park and performed to the hall's capacity crowd for the agreed £70 fee. The Who, Pink Floyd and The Moody Blues also played more conventional gigs at the Cosmo and, no doubt, for certainly more money than the honourable Sabbath.

LOCATION 515: the Cosmopolitan dance hall, first derelict then due for demolition, was situated in Central Avenue, Harraby, south-east of the centre of Carlisle, sandwiched between the A6 and M6. Postcode: CA4

CARLISLE BEATLES EJECTED THEN FETED

The Beatles made two memorable visits to Carlisle. The first came just a few days before their first recording sessions for debut album Please Please Me when they managed to get themselves ejected from the Crown & Mitre Hotel ballroom on February 8th 1963. On tour supporting Helen Shapiro, both the band and the 16-year-old chart starlet were in the hotel bar next to where Carlisle Golf Club's annual dinner dance was in full swing in the ballroom. They were invited to join in by one local lad, but when the club chairman spotted the four leather-clad Beatles sampling the buffet and twisting on the dance floor with Shapiro he asked them all to leave. The Beatles were clearly not too upset by their treatment, although Helen Shapiro was "mortified" by a Daily Express story about the incident. They returned later that year on November 21st as chart-toppers to an ecstatic reception from fans, who in some cases had queued for 36 hours for a chance to get a ticket. The ABC cinema where The Beatles performed on both occasions became Lonsdale City and despite the art deco building's inactivity as a music venue, or indeed a cinema, it still stands today in Warwick Road.

LOCATION 516 and **517:** the Crown & Mitre Hotel still stands in the centre of Carlisle at 4 English Street, postcode CA3 8HZ. The old ABC cinema is a few minutes' walk away on Warwick Road, postcode CA1 1DN

North West England

MARYPORT BEAT BOOM STARS AT THE PALACE

Built on the site of an old brewery and opened in 1934, the Palace Ballroom was one of British music's significant outposts on the beat boom tour circuit. The Hollies, Manfred Mann, The Animals and The Small Faces were among the hugely popular chart stars that headed to Cumbria's east coast.

LOCATION 518: off the A596 north-west of the Lake District, on the coast at Maryport, Lower Church Street. More recently known as the Civic Hall, the building was demolished to make way for housing in 2009. Postcode: CA15 6LE

Born in Cumbria

Glen Cornick, bass, Jethro Tull (b. 23 Apr 1947, Barrow)
Mike Harrison, vocals, Spooky Tooth (b. 30 Sep 1942, Carlisle)
Steve Hogarth, vocals, Marillion (b. 14 May 1959, Kendal)
Greg Ridley, bass, Humble Pie (b. 23 Oct 1942, Aspatria)
Matthew Wood, drums, British Sea Power (b. Kendal)
Neil Hamilton Wilkinson, vocals/bass, British Sea Power (b. Kendal)
Yan Scott Wilkinson, vocals, British Sea Power (b. Kendal)

ISLE OF MAN

The island's chief rockular claim to fame is as the birthplace of the Bee Gees. Justifiably proud of the Gibb brothers, the place has set about honouring the trio in a number of ways. They have even been the subject of a set of stamps. By happy coincidence, their mother once worked behind the counter at the local Post Office. The island's Ballroom was a favourite stopping off point for chart acts in the Sixties. The Stones appeared twice in August 1964 and September 1965, and The Who's Pete Townshend even wrote a song set on the Isle of Man following a gig in 1966. That August's visit inspired 'Happy Jack', their 1967 No.3 smash hit written about a man who "lived in the sand at the Isle of Man". By the time Mott The Hoople played their last UK gig here, at the Ballroom in 1974, the island's booming tourist years were in decline and the rock and pop visits declined with them.

The Douglas-born Gibb Brothers get the Isle of Man stamp of approval

DOUGLAS BIRTHPLACE OF THE BEE GEES

Bee Gees Barry, Robin and Maurice were all born in the island's capital Douglas. In 1999, on the 50th anniversary of Robin and Maurice's birthday, the brothers were honoured in a unique way. Six sets of postage stamps, each themed around a Bee Gees song, were issued by the Isle of Man Post Office in recognition of the world-famous trio's achievements, with a second philatelic tribute in 2009. In 2010, the two surviving brothers, Barry and Robin, returned to Douglas where they were honoured as freemen of their home borough in a ceremony at the town hall: Maurice Gibb was also honoured posthumously. Home to the brothers had been a spacious three-bedroomed semi-detached at 50 St Catherines Drive. By 1952, the family had moved to 43 Snaefell Road on the Willaston estate and in 1955 they left the island for Manchester.

LOCATION 519: St Catherines Drive is a short walk east of the seafront at Douglas, postcode IM1 4BF. Snaefell Road is north of the town centre, postcode IM2 6

DOUGLAS UNHAPPY STONES SQUEEZE IN A GIG AT THE LIDO

Sandwiched between a lengthy spell of recording in Hollywood, California, and a tour of Germany, The Rolling Stones tried unsuccessfully to get their gig in Douglas on September 8th 1965 cancelled. A telegram from Mick, Keith and Andy [Andrew Oldham] failed to prevent their appearance at the Palace Lido despite their "It's impossible" plea. The Stones' flying visit (a year after their only other performance on the island) did allow one night at the Castle Mona Hotel, next door to the venue. The obligatory band photocall was staged on the hotel balcony with screaming fans below. Amid all the hysteria, Mick, Keith, Brian, Bill and Charlie were forced to make their entrance to the venue via the Ballroom's toilet window. Despite their seeming reluctance to fulfil their contracted booking, they put on a storming show.

❛The island's only police dog Rex and his handler Henry Corlett were up on stage as a deterrent to stop people climbing up to join The Stones. Girls who fainted were lifted up by the crowd and passed up on to the stage to be revived by the first-aiders. As the night went on I noticed people around me had brown faces,

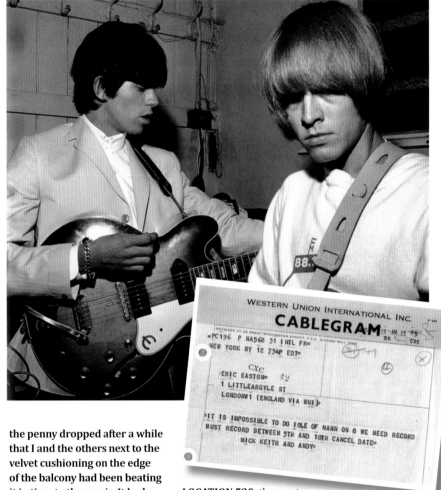

the penny dropped after a while that I and the others next to the velvet cushioning on the edge of the balcony had been beating it in time to the music. It had obviously never been beaten so hard and the dust of many years was rising into the air and sticking on the sweaty hands and faces.❜
15-year-old schoolboy Andy Sykes recalls The Rolling Stones' first of two visits to the Isle of Man in August 1964

LOCATION 520: the ornate Palace Ballroom, later called the Lido, was said to be the largest in Europe at one time. Demolished to extend the casino, this imposing structure stood next to the once magnificent, and still standing, Castle Mona Hotel on The Promenade, Douglas, postcode IM2 4LY

Brian Jones (note the IOM radio station T-shirt) and Keith Richards practise for their show at the Ballroom

---

Born on the Isle Of Man

Christine Collister, singer-songwriter (b. 28 Dec 1961, Douglas)
Barry Gibb (b. 1 Sep 1946, Douglas)

Maurice Gibb (b. 22 Dec 1949, Douglas, d. 12 Jan 2003)
Robin Gibb (b. 22 Dec 1949, Douglas)
Davy Knowles, guitarist/vocalist (b. 1987, Port St Mary)

ROCK ATLAS
Yorkshire and Humber
UK and Ireland Edition

‘Eric Clapton came to visit my father in Ovenden, John Lee Hooker and BB King also visited and Dad loved to cook gumbo, red beans with rice and black-eyed peas with fish which everyone loved.’

Champion Jack Dupree's daughter, Georgiana

EAST RIDING OF YORKSHIRE

The ceremonial county that includes the former Humberside city of Kingston-upon-Hull has pirates, Housemartins, The Beautiful South and the folk family Waterson to commend it. The nucleus of Bowie's Spiders From Mars (Mick Ronson and Trevor Bolder) was hatched in Hull and vocalist Lene Lovich and Fine Young Cannibals frontman Roland Gift grew up here, but sadly most of the venues that saw The Rolling Stones, Buddy Holly and many other ground-breaking rock acts visit The East Riding are long gone, including Hull's two Beatles locations, which saw the Fab Four arrive in 1962 and 1963 to play the Majestic Ballroom, returning again in 63 and 64 to play the ABC Cinema.

HULL 'THE RISING OF GRAFTON STREET'

London 0 Hull 4 was the title of The Housemartins' 1986 album, a title prompted by the band's propensity to rate their live gigs in terms of football scorelines. A key figure in The Housemartins' growing success story, Merseyside-born singer-songwriter Paul Heaton moved to Hull in 1983 and made the city his base for the next 20 years. The spiritual home for first The Housemartins, then Heaton's commercially massive The Beautiful South was No.87 Grafton Street. 'The Rising Of Grafton Street' was the cheerfully upbeat instrumental track on The Beautiful South's 1990 album Choke.

❝ My favourite winter pub would be The Grafton on Grafton Street in Hull. It's just great on a rainy day to hear dominoes and the old characters who are really entertaining. ❞
Paul Heaton

LOCATION 521: Grafton Street is about three miles north of the city centre, west of the A1079. Postcode: HU5 2NP

Hull 2 Rest of the World 2: of this line-up, only Dave Hemingway (left) and Stan Cullimore (right) were actually born in Hull. The remaining two fledgling Housemartins were Norman Cook (born Surrey) and Paul Heaton (born Cheshire)

BRIDLINGTON BAY
PIRATE DJS BRAVE THE OCEAN WAVES

The choppy sea off the Yorkshire coast was home to the DJs of Radio 270 for 18 exciting months before government legislation outlawed their broadcasts in 1967. Dutch vessel Oceaan V11 had more than its fair share of choppy seas, and even the ship's final day farewell party was a let-down when a North Sea storm prevented a number of staff members getting aboard for the sad goodbye. DJ Paul Burnett, who clearly never quite acclimatized to life on the ocean waves, once reportedly chucked-up his breakfast live on air during the reading of a Radio 270 commercial break for bacon! Aside from the physical discomfort experienced, those aboard also suffered a bomb threat which happily and fortunately turned out to be a hoax.

LOCATION 522: in the North Sea approximately three miles east of Bridlington's Esplanade, which is at postcode YO15 2PB

Born in The East Riding

Trevor Bolder, bass, Uriah Heep/Spiders From Mars (b. 9 Jun 1950, Hull)

Stan Cullimore, guitar, The Housemartins (b. 6 May 1962, Hull)

Dave Hemingway, The Beautiful South/The Housemartins (b. 20 Sep 1960, Hull)

Graham Jones, guitar, Haircut 100 (b. 8 Jul 1961, Bridlington)

Mick Ronson, guitar (b. 26 May 1946, Hull, d. 29 Apr 1993)

Dave Rotheray, guitar, The Beautiful South (b. 9 Feb 1963, Hull)

Lal Waterson, folk singer (b. 15 Feb 1943, Hull, d. 4 Sep 1998)

Mike Waterson, folk singer (b. 16 Jan 1941, Hull, d. 22 Jun 2011)

Norma Waterson, folk singer (b. 15 Aug 1939, Hull)

SOUTH YORKSHIRE

There's a very real pride in the city of Sheffield that consumes the more thoughtful, local, musical wordsmiths Richard Hawley and Jarvis Cocker. The latter's poetry is literally writ large on the wall of a student hall while Hawley is a walking Sheffield Information Centre, name-checking the place in album titles and lyrics and once appropriately recording live in the city's Hawleys Tyre & Exhaust centre on Bridge Road. There's even a Hawley Street close by in a city centre crammed full of great clubs (The Leadmill, The Boardwalk) and great pubs, (The Grapes and The Pack Horse) that have witnessed the birth of The Clash through to the Arctic Monkeys. Northern Soul, electronica and Britpop all owe Sheffield a debt of gratitude for boosting their profiles and even the memories left by legendary but demolished music meccas The Limit and The Mojo linger on powerfully thanks to online forums. If you like your legends of the rock variety, Sheffield does too. The first two acts to be accorded the honour of a star on the city's Walk Of Fame were Joe Cocker and Def Leppard.

DONCASTER
NEVER MIND THE SEX PISTOLS, HERE'S THE TAX EXILES

The Sex Pistols' first Doncaster appearance in 1976 was an event met with a good deal of indifference. On August 24th 1977 the Pistols' return to The Outlook club was only possible when the band changed their name to The Tax Exiles to avoid the ban that was widespread in British venues at the time. Despised nationwide by local authorities, but with three Top 40 singles under their belt, the band were still almost three months away from their Never Mind The Bollocks Here's The Sex Pistols album release, which would enter the chart at No.1 on November 12th. But as life-changing experiences go there was one particular gig at The Outlook during 1977's 'Summer Of Hate' that Sheffield music fans still rave about today. A 75 pence ticket bought them a night to remember when The Ramones laid waste to The Outlook supported by Talking Heads.

LOCATION 423: depressingly demolished, The Outlook was on Trafford Way, postcode DN1

HIGH GREEN
CHAMPAGNE CHART RUNDOWN AT THE PACK HORSE

This is the pub where the Arctic Monkeys, and as many of their fans who could squeeze in with them, first heard the news they had made their chart debut at No.1. On a Sunday in October 2005, requesting the landlord to switch on the chart rundown on the pub radio, the band settled down to toast their success at whichever point 'I Bet You Look Good On The Dancefloor' entered the Top 40. The noisy gathering were not disappointed.

❝ I think the Sugababes had a big tune out the same week and we just thought, "There's no way this is gonna happen. It's great if we even got Top 10." And then they played the Sugababes tune at No.2 and everyone cheered. People were jumping on pool tables, and it were all champagne and nonsense. ❞
Monkey Alex Turner talking to Mojo magazine

LOCATION 524: the northernmost part of suburban Sheffield. The Pack Horse Inn is at 23 Pack Horse Lane, High Green, postcode S35 3HY

SHEFFIELD 1 THE ONE-TIME NATIONAL CENTRE FOR POP

The Nigel Coates-designed four-drum steel structure for Sheffield's National Centre for Popular Music was a gem, but the project it housed failed little more than a year after its spectacular opening in 1999. The structure is now The Hubs and houses the local students' union.

LOCATION 525: a short walk from the railway station and the city centre at Paternoster Row, postcode S1 2QQ

Architectural gem and failed National Centre for Popular Music

SHEFFIELD 1
GRAPES PUB DEBUT FOR THE ARCTIC MONKEYS

Friday the 13th was the date of the Arctic Monkeys' first gig back in June 2003. The band had been playing together for 18 months prior to this subsequently historic booking but had no master plan mapped out to climb the slippery pole of rock stardom. But, confidence boosted by this and a second Grapes gig quickly led to the first Arctic Monkeys demo recordings. By October 2005 they were the nation's favourites, when 'I Bet You Look Good On The Dancefloor' hit the top of the singles chart.

❝ That was our first [gig], in this little function room of a pub called The Grapes in Sheffield. About 30 people there, in this very tiny room. There's bigger bathrooms than that room. ❞
Monkey frontman Alex Turner talking to Mojo

LOCATION 526: the 60-capacity upstairs venue is at The Grapes pub, 80 Trippet Lane, in the city centre, postcode S1 4EL

Early Monkeys starting point: Friday the 13th didn't prove unlucky for the Arctic Monkeys

Peter Tarleton

SHEFFIELD 1 JOE COCKER AND DEF LEPPARD ARE TOWN HALL LEGENDS

Nominated by the city's residents and honoured with a pavement plaque are two world famous music legends. Former gas fitter Joe Cocker, who was born in Sheffield and grew up at 38 Tasker Road, Crookes, has one and Sheffield's hard-rocking exports Def Leppard have the other. Both can be visited at the Sheffield Legends Walk of Fame, outside the Town Hall.

LOCATION 527: Pinstone Street in the city centre, postcode S1 2HH

Joe Cocker: Sheffield star

SHEFFIELD 1
DARK, STICKY AND GLORIOUS: THE LIMIT

Sheffield had a certain number of nightclub licences, and for one to open another had to close. It's thought that was the inspiration for the appropriately named The Limit. From 1978, this small basement club played an essential part in the development of early Eighties synth pop and also hosted gigs from eventual legends Simple Minds, U2, local turned national favourites Cabaret Voltaire, Pulp and the Human League. Genre specific nights, such as reggae on Wednesdays, saw The Limit create a healthily broad booking policy with Aswad, Steel Pulse and UB40 plus ska acts The Specials and The Beat. On big nights the capacity of 330 was dangerously trebled and the variety of music played and watched live meant that the club experienced its fair share of tribal violence from mods, goths, skinheads and punks all mingling together. Despite this, and the unbelievably beer-sticky carpet flooring, The Limit, along with its handily-placed next door pie and chip shop, was for many Sheffield music fans the perfect location for a night out. Neil Anderson's book Take It To The Limit gives the full, sometimes gory, but always glorious story of the club's 13-year existence.

LOCATION 528: the building where The Limit stood is no more, replaced by the current apartment block at 70 West Street, near the junction with Carver Street in the city centre, postcode S1 4DZ

SHEFFIELD 1 "SWEAT AND LEATHER" AT THE LEADMILL

Gaining a reputation, according to NME, as a cross between a thrifty working men's club and Manchester's Hacienda, The Leadmill has enjoyed a starry three decades since first opening for business in 1980. Despite failing to book Madonna when offered the emerging superstar in 1983, the venue has established itself on the back of thousands of appearances by cool bands and staunch supporters. When Mel C made her solo debut at the club, she was cheered on by an appreciative crowd that included the remaining Spice Girls and David Beckham. Gil Scott-Heron, the Bay City Rollers, Rose Royce, the Sugarhill Gang with Grandmaster Melle Mel and just about every indie guitar band under the sun have all graced the former flour mill.

LOCATION 529: a short stroll south of the city centre at 6 Leadmill Road, postcode S1 4SE

❛ A heady cocktail of sweat, leather, sound and fury, beer and vodka and limes. ❜
ABC's Martin Fry describes The Leadmill

Neon and stone: the distinctive signage at The Leadmill

Peter Tarleton

SHEFFIELD 2 SOUL CENTRAL AT SAMANTHA'S

While Wigan had its Casino and Stoke had The Torch, Sheffield's Northern Soul hot spot was a long upstairs room above the city's Silver Blades ice skating rink. Catering for a wide cross-section of dance fans, Samantha's reigned supreme from 1973 to 1977 in the building now operating as Stars Party Suite.

LOCATION 530: Samantha's (now Stars) is on the main A61 south out of the city centre on Queens Road, postcode S2 4DF

SHEFFIELD 2 and 6 DEF LEPPARD CONNECTIONS

Made in Sheffield, Def Leppard rehearsed for the first time in a redundant spoon factory for a £5 weekly rental, a stone's throw from Sheffield United's Bramall Lane football ground. The location holds special memories for the band's bass player Rick Savage, who came close to making a career in football playing for Sheffield United, despite supporting Sheffield Wednesday, the club located at Hillsborough, which in turn was the birthplace of their now deceased

guitarist Steve Clark, buried in the nearby Wisewood Cemetery.

LOCATIONS 531 and **532:** Stag Works (the former spoon factory turned music rehearsal facility) is at 84 John Street where the road meets Bramall Lane, postcode S2 4QU. Steve Clark's black granite gravestone is easily found at plot 1697, section D, just inside the entrance of Wisewood Cemetery, Loxley Road, Sheffield S6 4TD

SHEFFIELD 1,3 and 8 RICHARD HAWLEY'S STEEL CITY GUIDE

Postal districts 1, 3 and 8 don't cover the half of it, as can be seen from this section's introduction. Born in Sheffield, raised in the city suburbs of Pitsmor and Kelham Island, musician and producer Richard Hawley takes every opportunity to reference local place names in the titles of his record releases. First came Lowedges (2003), then Coles Corner (2005), Lady's Bridge (2007) and Truelove's Gutter (2009). Even his 2001 album, Late Night Final, a title that echoed the cry of Sheffield newspaper vendors, carried a cover image of Hawley devouring the local paper in Castle Market's Sharon's Café.

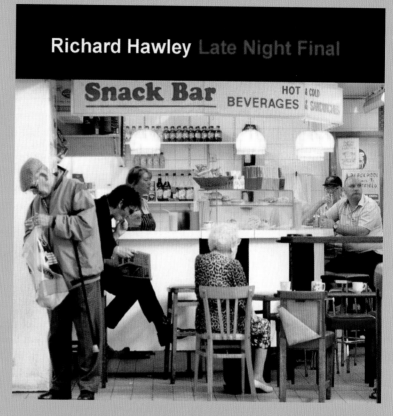

❝ Sheffield's couples, lovers, friends, mums and dads or whatever, would meet [there]. I've always found it quite a romantic notion - how many kids in Sheffield are knocking about as a result of a meeting at Coles Corner? ❞
Richard Hawley

❝ It's a really ancient fording point. It was originally built out of wood in 1140 by a Norman Prince, and it was rebuilt after the great Sheffield floods of the 1840s. The title is a metaphor too; it's about leaving the past behind. ❞
Richard Hawley describes Lady's Bridge for Uncut magazine

❝ I'm into local history and I was looking through manuscripts from the 1700s when I saw that street name - Truelove's Gutter, opposite where you once had a pub The

Black Swan. The Sex Pistols played there and it's now called The Boardwalk. So while I wasn't looking for the album title, it just appeared. ❞**
Richard Hawley interviewed by Mojo magazine

LOCATIONS 533, 534, 535, 536 and 537: Lowedges is a residential area around six miles south west of the city centre, postcode S8 7. Cole's Corner was named after the sight of the old Cole Brothers department store in the city centre where Fargate meets Church Street, postcode S1 2HE. The city's

Richard Hawley in Sharon's Café, which is in the same Castle Market where a young Jarvis Cocker manned the fresh fish stall

Lady's Bridge spans the River Don, postcode S3 8LB. Truelove's Gutter was named after the 18th century publican Thomas Truelove, whose drains, according to historians, ran into the gutter of Castle Street, postcode S3 8LT. Sharon's Café is at 133 Castle Market in the city centre, postcode S1 2AF

SHEFFIELD 2 JARVIS COCKER'S WALL OF WORDS

Born and brought up in the Intake area of the city, Jarvis Cocker was asked to create a poem to appear on the side of the new halls of residence building for students situated south of the city centre. Excavations for the site had unearthed an old forge and the powers that be had requested he write something about the forge and the local steel industry. The result is 14 lines of Jarvis' handy-work fashioned in shiny steel lettering.

LOCATION 538: on the wall of The Forge, roughly one mile

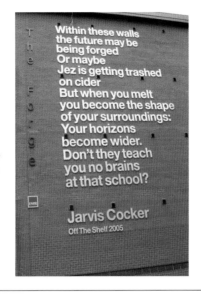

Within these walls
the future may be
being forged
Or maybe
Jez is getting trashed
on cider
But when you melt
you become the shape
of your surroundings:
Your horizons
become wider.
Don't they teach
you no brains
at that school?

The Forge

Jarvis Cocker
Off The Shelf 2005

Showing off and being inappropriate: Jarvis Cocker's poem in Boston Street

south of the city centre at 2 Boston Street, almost opposite the junction with Hermitage Street, postcode S2 4QG

❛ **The show off in me really wanted to have something on the side of a building but then the proper Sheffielder thought is this really right? So what I thought I'd do was I'd write something that I thought was inappropriate. So I wrote this poem and they liked it!** ❜
Jarvis Cocker talking on BBC Radio 2 documentary Jarvis Cocker's Musical Map Of Sheffield

SHEFFIELD 3 BLACK SWAN DEBUT FOR THE CLASH

Tucked away in a corner of the city centre, thus far safe from the developers' wrecking ball, is a music venue that has attracted Genesis, AC/DC, and, for their one and only Sheffield gig, the Sex Pistols. The Pistols' appearance coincided with The Black Swan's biggest claim to fame as the venue for The Clash's debut on July 4th 1976, with the Pistols as their support act. Now The Boardwalk, this lively venue's name went through earlier identities as the aforementioned Black Swan and The Mucky Duck for a period. During its half-century existence, the place has rolled with the times, successfully staying in business as it staged gigs by everyone from local boy-made-rock-superstar Joe Cocker to dynamic glam rockers The Sweet and, more recently, the likes of David Gray and Seasick Steve.

LOCATION 539: at the corner of Bank Street and Snig Hill near the city centre. Postcode: S3 8NA. Website www.theboardwalklive.co.uk

The Boardwalk still carries a visual reminder of its heyday in the Seventies, when it was regularly packed to the rafters as The Black Swan

Peter Tarleton

Yorkshire and Humberside

SHEFFIELD 3 SOUL AND HENDRIX AT STRINGFELLOW'S MOJO

Soul music's Sixties popularity coincided with the opening of a new club catering for the very American style of music in a quiet road north of the city centre. The Mojo club (or King Mojo) was situated in a Victorian bow-window-fronted house run by local youngster Peter Stringfellow, who later became the internationally famous celebrity night-club owner. Stringfellow and his two brothers would advertise a records-only night once a week and hype up the playlist in the local paper. When hosting live acts, the place boasted Edwin Starr's first UK appearance and attracted the cream of US soul and R&B to this innovative new venture, which made its debut in 1964. Soon attracting a dedicated and enthusiastic mod clientele, the Mojo hosted The Who, The Kinks and The Small Faces at the out-of-town address in Pitsmoor Road. Much like Liverpool's Casbah Club, this residential road venue was decorated inside with pop art wall murals and posters, and when the psychedelic era arrived Stringfellow switched the musical emphasis, renaming the place The Beautiful King Mojo. Shortly after booking Jimi Hendrix, who was the subject of a botched drugs raid by the local constabulary, the club closed in February 1967 when some neighbours campaigned against the noise and nuisance caused by a hugely exciting venture in a rather inappropriate suburban location.

❝ It was one bus into town, from town to the Wicker, another bus up Pitsmoor Road, maybe even another bus! You had to really want to go to the Mojo club! ❞
Peter Stringfellow

LOCATION 540: Pitsmoor Road is two miles north of the city centre but the Pitsmoor Road junction with Roe Lane, where the Mojo club house once stood, is now a white-painted housing block, postcode S3 9AU

SHEFFIELD 10 VINYL HEAVEN ON FULWOOD ROAD

Sheffield band Little Man Tate bigged-up their local record shop by featuring it on the cover of their 2007 debut album About What You Know. The photoshoot captured the quartet rummaging in the vinyl half of Record Collector.

LOCATION 541: Record Collector can be visited on the A57, a couple of miles west of the city centre at 233 Fulwood Road, postcode S10 3BA

Vinyl heaven at Record Collector

Born in South Yorkshire

Rick Allen, drums, Def Leppard (b. 1 Nov 1963, Sheffield)
Nick Banks, drums, Pulp (b. 28 Jul 1965, Rotherham)
Paul Carrack (b. 22 Apr 1951, Sheffield)
Joanne Catherall, vocals Human League (b. 18 Sep 1962, Sheffield)
Jarvis Cocker (b. 19 Sep 1963, Sheffield)
Joe Cocker (b. 20 May 1944, Sheffield)

Jamie Cook, guitar, Arctic Monkeys (b. 8 Jul 1985, High Green, Sheffield)
Joe Elliott, Def Leppard (b. 1 Aug 1959, Sheffield)
Glenn Gregory, Heaven 17 (b. 16 May 1958, Sheffield)
Richard Hawley (b. 17 Jan 1967, Sheffield)
Matt Helders, drums, Arctic Monkeys/Mongrel (b. 7 May 1986, Sheffield)
Jon McClure, Reverend and The Makers (b. 1981,

Sheffield)
Steve Mackey, bass, Pulp (b. 10 Nov 1966, Sheffield)
Adrian McNally, The Unthanks (b. 28 May 1975, Chapeltown, Sheffield)
Ian Craig Marsh, Heaven 17 (b. 11 Nov 1956, Sheffield)
Nick O'Malley, bass guitar, Arctic Monkeys (b. 5 Jul 1985, Sheffield)
Steve Rothery, Marillion (b. 25 Nov 1959, Brampton)
Kate Rusby (b. 4 Dec 1973,

Penistone)
Rick Savage, bass, Def Leppard (b. 2 Dec 1960, Sheffield)
Russell Senior, guitar, Pulp (b. 18 May 1961, Sheffield)
Stephen Singleton, saxophone, ABC (b. 16 Apr 1969, Sheffield)
Jon Stewart, guitar, Sleeper (b. 12 Sep 1966, Sheffield)
Peter Stringfellow(b. 17 Oct 1940, Sheffield)
Susanne Sulley, vocals,

SHEFFIELD 11
THE HUMAN LEAGUE DEBUT AT THE WHAM BAR

Based at Hallam University's Psalter Lane campus, the Wham Bar (also known as Bar 2) was where local synthpop legends the Human League performed live for the first time on June 12th 1978.

LOCATION 542: Psalter Lane Campus was the smallest of three Hallam University campus locations at Brincliffe, a couple of miles south-west of the city centre. Postcode: S11 9BG. Status: site currently under redevelopment

Human League (b. 22 Mar 1963, Sheffield)
Alex Turner, Arctic Monkeys (b. 6 Jan 1986, High Green, Sheffield)
Martyn Ware, Heaven 17 (b. 19 May 1956, Sheffield)
Mark White, guitar/keyboards, ABC (b. 1 Apr 1961, Sheffield)
Mick Whitnall, Babyshambles (b. 7 Nov 1968, Doncaster)
Chris Wolstenholme, bass, Muse (b. 2 Dec 1978, Rotherham)

WEST YORKSHIRE

West Yorkshire seems to have a strong attraction for American blues legends. Big Bill Broonzy and Champion Jack Dupree are remembered with fondness by the good folk of Glasshoughton and Ovenden, while BB King visited Dupree in Halifax, Sonny Terry and Brownie McGhee performed in the same town and Louis Armstrong played Batley. Then there's the story of Kurt Cobain and the Duchess of York's sofa, a beer named in honour of a visit to Ilkley by Jimi Hendrix, a fruit-loving Michael Jackson in Halifax, the rain-lashed Krumlin Festival and the setting for the recording of one of rock's greatest live album in Leeds. Halifax was the location for Dusty Springfield's first solo debut, and it was local boy Don Lang who sang the theme tune to 50s BBC TV's ground-breaking show for teens, Six-Five Special. The Cribs have been honoured by a Hollywood-style star in Wakefield, Wintersett is something of a spiritual home for The Unthanks, and the county currently hosts one of Britain's best-attended festivals, which has seen Radiohead, Kings of Leon and just about every other act that you might describe as the world's biggest band play Bramham Park in recent years.

BRAMHAM PARK
HOME OF THE LEEDS FESTIVAL

Held on the same weekend in August as the annual Reading Festival and sharing the same bill, the Leeds Festival has been held at Bramham Park since 2003. It consistently attracts the best-known headline acts in the world and gets some heavyweight endorsement from rock's biggest names...

LOCATION 543: the festival site is approximately five miles south of Wetherby at Bramham Park, accessed by leaving junction 45 of the A1M. Postcode: LS23 6ND

❛ If the Manic Street Preachers have a spiritual festival home then it is the Leeds Festival. They have the most knowledgeable fans of rock music and an instinctive appreciation of intelligent music and entertainment. ❜
Nicky Wire, Manic Street Preachers

❛ There's something about Leeds that always brings out the best in us. ❜
Lars Ulrich of Metallica praises the annual Leeds Festival

GLASSHOUGHTON
BIG BILL BROONZY AT THE COSY CINEMA

In a small West Yorkshire town on the outskirts of Castleford, local music fans had an unexpected injection of the blues one Saturday night in June 1956 when the American blues legend Big Bill Broonzy played a one-off show at the Cosy Cinema, Glasshoughton. This unusual personal appearance occurred when the cinema owner called in a favour from a showbiz impresario friend. Broonzy, the Arkansas-raised grandson of a cotton-picking slave, had recently played a Leeds jazz club and was dispatched by the impresario from Leeds to the outskirts of Castleford, at Glasshoughton, to repay the favour.

LOCATION 544: following its closure, the Cosy Cinema became part of the Castletex textile factory before disappearing completely to make way for flats at Lagentium Plaza, Leeds Road, Glasshoughton. Postcode: WF10 4PP

Yorkshire and Humberside

HALIFAX MICHAEL JACKSON COMES TO TOWN

www.smalltownsaturdaynight.co.uk

When The Jacksons played the Civic Theatre, on February 19th 1979, Michael Jackson was already a solo superstar with five UK Top 10 singles and two US No.1s behind him. By all accounts his ego was very much under control on his visit to Halifax, only shyly requesting a bowl of fruit for the dressing room. Not so the rest of his brothers, two of whom had fallen out on the journey to the venue. The disharmony led to them allegedly refusing to perform until theatre manager Robbie Robinson read the riot act and the shame-faced

The Jacksons' security guards insisted on "no pictures" during their Halifax visit: this shot of Michael backstage was the unique exception

Jacksons took to the stage and were, according to assistant manager Les Milner, "superb". Despite the management's problems that day, The Jacksons paved the way for more appearances by Motown and soul acts at the Civic with Martha Reeves, Freda Payne, The Supremes and Smokey Robinson all heading for this West Yorkshire pop hotspot.

LOCATION 545: in the town centre, the Civic Theatre, now renamed the Victoria Theatre, still stands at 2 Fountain Street, postcode HX11BP

HALIFAX
DUSTY'S DEBUT ON BROAD STREET

Already nationally famous as one-third of hit trio The Springfields and a panellist on BBC TV's Juke Box Jury, Dusty Springfield made her solo debut at the Odeon Cinema on November 8th 1963. A "special guest star" addition to a bill featuring Freddie & The Dreamers, Brian Poole & The Tremeloes and The Searchers, the nervous Dusty performed what would become her first solo chart hit, 'I Only Want To Be With You'.

❝ **I have never been so scared in all my life.** ❞

So said Dusty on making her world debut as a solo performer in Halifax

LOCATION 546: the striking art deco cinema still stands (now a bingo hall) on the corner of Broad Street and Orange Street in the centre of Halifax, postcode HX1 1YA

A rare picture of Dusty in Halifax

www.smalltownsaturdaynight.co.uk

HOLMFIELD BEATLES, SMALL FACES AND R.E.M. AT HOLDSWORTH HOUSE

At the height of Beatlemania, and amid enormous security, the four Beatles and manager Brian Epstein celebrated John Lennon's 24th birthday here in the opulent surroundings of Holdsworth House Hotel. On the evening of October 9th 1964, the 17th century Jacobean manor house, then known as the Cavalier Country Club, was the first overnight stop on The Beatles' first bill-topping tour. Earlier that day, they had opened the nationwide shows at the Bradford Gaumont, before heading out of the city to this country retreat, aided by a road block and accompanied by a police escort. Despite suffering a bout of toothache, Lennon, by all accounts, enjoyed his celebration meal before retiring to bed. He and Ringo Starr slept in a bedroom which is now one of the hotel's offices, while Paul McCartney and George Harrison were given the Ayrton Room, which these days is used for conferences. A popular haunt for rock stars and celebrities, the hotel's reputation and Beatles connection spread as far as Athens, Georgia, with R.E.M. booking in as guests during the American band's Yorkshire visit to play two £1.6 million-grossing gigs at Huddersfield's McAlpine Stadium in July 1995. On learning that the landlord of the local pub, The Ivy House, was a big R.E.M. fan, Michael Stipe and the rest of

the band paid him a surprise visit. Later that same week hotel staff were astonished when a "so glad you are feeling better" fax came through from US President Bill Clinton and wife Hillary for bass player Mike Mills, who had recently undergone abdominal surgery. And the stories of rock royalty at Holdsworth House don't stop there. In the Sixties, John Lee Hooker and Cliff Richard both enjoyed stays and current owner Gail Moss (then a teenager) recalls The Small Faces checking-in and giving her a lift to school the next morning on their way to Halifax to do a spot of shopping.

LOCATION 547: Holdsworth House Hotel & Restaurant, near Holmfield, is three miles north of Halifax and seven miles west

The Beatles arrive at Holdsworth House. The bill for two rooms, bed and breakfast and a slap-up birthday dinner for John Lennon was £42

of Bradford east of the A467. Postcode: HX2 9TG. Website: www.holdsworthhouse.co.uk

❛ Although I wasn't a huge music fan I knew the band were just about the biggest in the world at the time, so imagine my son Nicholas' reaction when I rang him at boarding school to tell him the news that E.R.M. [sic] are coming to stay!❜
Gail Moss

Yorkshire and Humberside

KRUMLIN THE MOTHER OF ALL RAIN-LASHED FESTIVALS

It must have seemed like a great idea at the time. Pick August, traditionally the hottest month, find a peaceful piece of Yorkshire and find an equally hot line-up of established and up-and-coming acts. However, this storm-ravaged three-day festival in a moorland valley suffered power failures, a ramshackle running order and medical treatment was required for hundreds of fans suffering from exposure. The Yorkshire Folk, Blues & Jazz Festival, to give it its proper name, did set out to provide a varied bill of acts as the name suggests, although how many of the 30 or so artists showed up or finished performances is debatable. Well-received gutsy sets by Elton John and Georgie Fame helped save the first day following a hugely frustrating five-hour wait by fans for the festival to begin. Day two started promisingly enough with The Groundhogs, Alexis Korner and Graham Bond mentioned in dispatches for some classic British blues before the weather turned particularly nasty as Zoot Money and Alan Price brought proceedings to an inclement close on Saturday. The driving rain turned the site into a freezing mudbath overnight and when many of the big names advertised failed to appear or bailed out at the eleventh hour, the final Sunday line-up of acts was literally washed away.

❛ **Ginger Baker in fact turned up on the Sunday to play free of charge, not even asking for his expenses, but by that time the festival had been abandoned.** ❜
Walter Lloyd, Chairman of Civil Aid, who looked after the welfare of the 15,000 fans

LOCATION 548: Krumlin, near Barkisland, approximately six miles south-west of Halifax, postcode HX4 0AT

Right: British R&B legend Alexis Korner arrives backstage at Krumlin. Below: before the storm: The Groundhogs on stage at the Yorkshire Folk, Blues & Jazz Festival

www.smalltownsaturdaynight.co.uk

ILKLEY HENDRIX GIG HALTED AT THE TROUTBECK

The spa town of Ilkley was the unlikely final stopping point on a 1967 UK tour by the Jimi Hendrix Experience. On March 12th they played to a packed audience at the Troutbeck Hotel, but the trio had barely got into their psychedelic stride when the local police force made a decision to halt the show. In an early act of health and safety enforcement, the trio and 400-strong crowd were forced to file out into the cold evening air. Although subsequent Daily Express "riot" headlines were wide of the mark, some of the more disgruntled fans who had squeezed in to see their heroes did damage some hotel furnishings. In 2008, the nearby Crescent Hotel named a beer "Jimi's", created by brewer Moorhouse's, to commemorate the

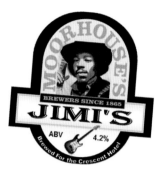

I'll have a pint of Jimi's please!

guitarist's stay at the hotel while in town to play the Troutbeck.

❛ My recollection of Jimi was that he was quiet, polite, friendly and funny - and he enjoyed a nice cup of tea. ❜
Danny Pollock, who booked Jimi Hendrix for the Troutbeck Hotel, Ilkley

LOCATION 549 and 550: a nursing home now occupies the buildings where the Troutbeck Hotel once booked the Jimi Hendrix Experience at Crossbeck Road, postcode LS29 9JP. The Crescent Hotel, where they once served Jimi's, is in Ilkley town centre on Brook Street, postcode LS29 8DG

LEEDS THE WHO RECORD THE GREATEST LIVE ALBUM OF ALL-TIME

A blue plaque on the wall of the Leeds University Refectory marks the spot where The Who recorded what the commemorative disc says was "the most celebrated live album of its generation". And they're not exaggerating; Live At Leeds topped Q magazine's list of greatest live albums and even the New York Times weighed-in with a "best ever" accolade. Despite the fact that The Who had to plug in to the refectory's kitchen electricity power point, the performance on February 14th 1970 at the 2,000-capacity art deco dining hall also charted in Q's list of loudest gigs. Reports suggest the band were even louder when they returned to Leeds to reprise their performance in 2006, although this time the kitchen plug sockets were not required.

❛ I have never taken drugs but I think I now know what a 'high' must be like. Colleagues suggest that I will have calmed down by Christmas and I simply ask 'which Christmas?' ❜
John Standerline, Leeds University Entertainments team member and student electrician on witnessing The Who's 1970 gig

LOCATION 551: the plaque, unveiled by The Who when they returned to perform Live At Leeds Again, is left of the entrance doors to the refectory building, Cromer Road, postcode LS1 1UH

LEEDS KURT COBAIN AND THE DUCHESS OF YORK'S SOFA

Sandwiched between two John Peel sessions for the BBC, Nirvana played a gig on October 25th 1989 at the Duchess of York pub in Leeds city centre. The Seattle band's visit to Leeds gained legendary status when singer Kurt Cobain crashed out in the upstairs dressing room after the gig and slept the night on a piece of furniture that has since enjoyed an extended life as the most famous rock 'n' roll sofa in the world. The extended life was prolonged by Cobain's use of the rather tatty settee that had already attracted the autographs of many musicians relaxing on it in the pre-and post-performance gigging hours at the pub. Originally purchased at auction for £6 by promoter John Keenan, the sofa's increasing fame and value as a national treasure was

acknowledged by Sheffield's National Centre for Popular Music, who snapped it up for its collection. The Duchess, much loved for its patronage of emerging bands from all over the UK, closed for music business on March 26th 2000. Fittingly Chumbawamba, billed with their famous lyric line "I Get Knocked Down" on tickets, were the last act to play the Duchess before renovations saw the building transformed into a branch of a well-known fashion store.

LOCATION 552: despite the Duchess of York's demise, it's still possible to cast your eyes upwards to the first floor of what is now the Leeds branch of Hugo Boss and imagine Kurt Cobain curled up on that sofa at 71 Vicar Lane. Postcode: LS1 6QA

Yorkshire and Humberside

OVENDEN A BLUES LEGEND SETTLES IN YORKSHIRE

The New Orleans-born bluesman Champion Jack Dupree settled in Britain permanently in 1959 and lived in this village on the outskirts of Halifax after meeting and marrying Yorkshire lass Shirley Harrison. In 2003, a wall plaque was unveiled in memory of the pianist who attracted a good few celebrity music pilgrims to make the trip to Ovenden.

LOCATION 553: Champion Jack Dupree's home was at 173 Ovenden Way, a couple of miles north of Halifax on the A629. The plaque is mounted on the wall at the Dean Clough complex in the reception area, near the cafe for the Viaduct Theatre, postcode HX3 5AX. Website: www. smalltownsaturdaynight.co.uk

❛ Eric Clapton came to visit us in Ovenden. John Lee Hooker and BB King also visited us among loads of other people and dad loved to cook. He would do gumbo, red beans with rice and black eyed peas with fish, which everyone loved. ❜
Champion Jack Dupree's daughter Georgiana, quoted from Trevor Simpson's Small Town Saturday Night books

❛ I'll always remember the first time I saw him in George Street [Halifax] sometime in the mid-Sixties. He was getting out of his American station wagon with lace curtains in the back and his name 'Champion Jack Dupree – Blues Pianist – of New Orleans - LA - USA' emblazoned on each of two side doors in big gold leaf letters. He never locked the car before he strolled across the road into The Griffin pub and he left most people in the street open-mouthed and staring at the car in disbelief at what they had just seen. It was highly unusual to see a black guy at the time. ❜
Small Town Saturday Night author Trevor Simpson

Above: The Champion Jack Dupree plaque, unveiled 11 years after his death in 1992

Left: The son of a French black man and Cherokee Indian mother, the internationally acclaimed Champion Jack Dupree entertains members of the Halifax Women's Institute

LEEDS **PABLO FANQUE'S GRAVESTONE**

In St George's Field cemetery there's an inscription on a gravestone for Pablo Fanque, the nineteenth-century circus promoter whose name headed a now famous poster inspiring John Lennon to write a track for Sgt Pepper's Lonely Hearts Club Band. The Beatle spotted and bought the travelling circus poster including Fanque's name in an antique shop and wrote the song 'Being For The Benefit Of Mr Kite!', one of the acts billed on the poster. Fanque, aka. William Darby, died in 1871 and was buried next to his wife Susannah, who died when the Fanque Circus big top collapsed on her in a tragic accident in 1848.

LOCATION 554: partly hidden within the campus of the university, the Leeds General Cemetery Company's site is at St George's Field, postcode LS2 9JT

WAKEFIELD **HOME TOWN PLAQUE FOR THE CRIBS**

In 2011, The Cribs and their fans got the news that the local council were to honour the Wakefield band with a commemorative plaque in their home town. The band voiced their Wakefield pride most obviously on the 2005 track 'The Wrong Way To Be' and were immortalised in a Hollywood-style pavement plaque in the city centre for their contribution to the local music scene.

LOCATION 555: the star plaque is at the Bull Ring, just outside the Tourist Information Centre in the heart of Wakefield, postcode WF1 1HB

The star-struck Jarman brothers, who became The Cribs in 2001

Wakefield Council

Yorkshire and Humberside

WINTERSETT
EARLY INSPIRATION FOR THE UNTHANKS

The reservoir at Wintersett was the inspiration for the band name Rachel Unthank & The Winterset. The folk group's songwriter, producer and band member (and Rachel Unthank's husband) Adrian McNally grew up a couple of miles south of the West Yorkshire reservoir in the mining village of South Hiendley. In 2009, the band name was shortened to The Unthanks but Wintersett - note the place name's spelling with three 't's - still draws McNally and fellow Unthanks band member Chris Price back to the area where they both enjoyed a childhood living three doors apart on the same street in South Hiendly.

Max McNally

❝ There's a tiny real ale pub [near Wintersett] that Chris and I drink in whenever we're home to see our parents called the Angler's Retreat. ❞
Adrian McNally (The Unthanks)

LOCATION 556:
six miles south-east of Wakefield, the Angler's Retreat public house is a short walk from the reservoir at Ferry Top Lane, Wintersett, postcode WF4 2EB

Above: "A photo that rather captures the place which my dad took years ago," says Adrian McNally. "It's infinitely better than any other picture I've seen of Wintersett"

Born in West Yorkshire

Craig Adams, bass, The Mission (b. 4 Apr 1962, Otley)

Tasmin Archer, (b. 3 Aug 1963, Bradford)

Mel B (Melanie Brown) (b. 29 May 1975, Leeds)

Tom Bailey, vocals/keyboards, Thompson Twins (b. 18 Jan 1954, Halifax)

Corinne Bailey Rae (b. 26 Feb 1979, Leeds)

Nick "Peanut" Baines, keyboards, Kaiser Chiefs (b. 21 Mar 1978, Leeds)

Sarah Blackwood, vocals, Dubstar (b. 6 May 1971, Halifax)

Tim Booth, vocals, James (b. 4 Feb 1960)

Billy Currie, Ultravox (b. 1 Apr 1950, Huddersfield)

Kiki Dee (b. 6 Mar 1947, Bradford)

Keith Emerson, keyboards, The Nice/Emerson, Lake and Palmer (b. 2 Nov 1944, Todmorden)

David Gedge, vocals, The Wedding Present (b. 23 Apr 1960, Leeds)

Robert Hardy, bass, Franz Ferdinand (b. 16 Aug 1980, Dewsbury)

John Helliwell, saxophone, Supertramp (b. 15 Feb 1945, Todmorden)

Nick Hodgson, drums, Kaiser Chiefs (b. 20 Oct 1977, Leeds)

Gary Jarman, bass/vocals, The Cribs (b. 20 Oct 1980, Wakefield)

Ross Jarman, drums, The Cribs (b. 22 Sep 1984, Wakefield)

Ryan Jarman, guitar/vocals, The Cribs (b. 20 Oct 1980, Wakefield)

Don Lang, vocals, Don Lang & His Furious Five (b. 19 Jan 1925, Halifax, d. 3 Aug 1992)

Derek Leckenby, guitar, Herman's Hermits (b. 14 May 1943, Leeds, d. 4 Jun 1994)

Chris Moyles, radio DJ (b. 22 Feb 1974, Leeds)

Danny McNamara, vocals, Embrace (b. 31 Dec 1970, Bailiff Bridge, Brighouse)

Richard McNamara, guitar (b. 23 Oct, 1972 Bailiff Bridge, Brighouse)

Bill Nelson, guitar, vocals, solo and Be-Bop Deluxe (b. 18 Dec 1948, Wakefield)

Robert Palmer (b. 19 Jan 1949, Batley, d. 26 Sep 2003)

Rhianna (b. 7 Jan 1983, Leeds)

Simon Rix, bass, Kaiser Chiefs (b. 18 Oct 1977, Leeds)

Shutty, drums, Terrorvision (b. David Shuttleworth, 20 Mar 1967, Keighley)

Dave Stead, drums, The Beautiful South (b. 15 Oct 1966, Huddersfield)

Kimberley Walsh, Girls Aloud (b. 20 Nov 1981, Bradford)

Andrew "Whitey" White, guitar, Kaiser Chiefs (b. 28 Aug 1974, Leeds)

Ricky Wilson, vocals, Kaiser Chiefs (b. 17 Jan 1978, Keighley)

NORTH YORKSHIRE

Rock legends Arthur Brown, David Coverdale, Chris Rea and Paul Rodgers all hail from England's largest rural county. It's the setting for busloads of fans descending on a remote Hendrix gig, The Rolling Stones first show outside Greater London, Paul Simon's Scarborough Fair folk education, Welsh rock band Man's gloomy song story and album cover shoots for The Cure and Richard Hawley. All that plus a gem of a record shop and the hang-out of those Stainsby Girls.

BOLTON ABBEY PORL THOMPSON'S CURE COVER

A barely recognisable fog-shrouded image of Bolton Priory provides the cover of The Cure's 1981 album Faith. Musician and painter Porl Thompson (who had been an original member of The Cure in the late Seventies) was the cover designer for Faith. He subsequently re-joined the band in 1983.

LOCATION 557: seven miles east of Skipton, north of the A59, postcode BD23 6EX. www.boltonabbey.com

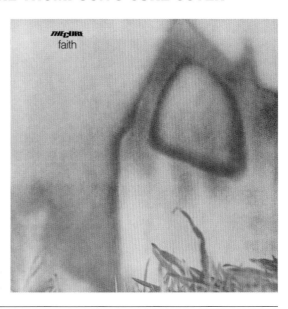

A suitably gloomy day at Bolton Priory

KIRKLEVINGTON HENDRIX AT THE KIRK COUNTRY CLUB

A former petrol station and garage workshop was the setting for a remote haven for music fans near the small village of Kirklevington. Converted into a dance hall, Kirklevington Country Club did have one advantage: the main A19 ran right past it, providing easy access for teenagers who poured out of Middlesbrough at weekends to enjoy gigs by some of the UK's biggest names in the Sixties, Seventies and Eighties. Biggest of all perhaps was the appearance of Jimi Hendrix in January 1967. The legendary guitarist journeyed north to play The Kirk the day before a three-day booking in London's Mayfair and a memorable appearance on BBC TV's Top Of The Pops.

❛ The night Hendrix came I can remember loads of double-decker buses coming from Stockton and Middlesbrough packed with people. ❜
Son of the club's owner, Tom Reay

LOCATION 558: now residential housing, the site of the Kirklevington Country Club was on the old A19. Postcode: TS15

MIDDLESBROUGH THE ROLLING STONES HEAD NORTH TO THE ALCOVE

The Outlook was Middlesbrough's answer to London's Marquee Club, seemingly showcasing every national act seconds before they became megastars. On July 13th 1963, local legend John McCoy booked a double bill featuring "Top Twenty Stars from Manchester The Hollies" and "From London – The Rolling Stones". It was the first time The Stones had ventured outside their native Greater London concert circuit, with McCoy, the man later credited with hiring out the nearby Kirklevington Country Club, securing the band for a £65 fee, which also included subbing their then leader, Brian Jones, for three packets of the band's favourite Player's cigarettes.

Stevie Wonder and The Who were other inspired acquisitions for the basement venue below teenage fashion shop Young Outlook, which McCoy dubbed The Alcove to give it a separate identity. In addition to the club on Corporation Road, the Corporation Hotel was where the Stones stayed overnight on their first exploration north, and also the location of the much-loved Hamilton's record shop.

LOCATION 559: in the town centre, The Outlook (52 - 60 Corporation Road) no longer exists as a club and the Corporation Hotel, where The Stones and many other Outlook-booked groups once stayed, is now Middlesbrough's tallest skyscraper. Postcode: TS1 2

Yorkshire and Humberside

MIDDLESBROUGH
CHRIS REA "FELL IN LOVE WITH A STAINSBY GIRL"

His biggest hit up to 1985, Chris Rea's 'Stainsby Girls' was the vocalist/guitarist's tribute to his wife Joan. Stainsby Girls, according to the song's lyrics, weren't the type who loved horses or stayed at home, but loved The Rolling Stones, which obviously met with the approval of Rea, born and bred in Middlesbrough. The Stainsby referred to in the song was Stainsby Secondary Modern School, now renamed Acklam Grange Secondary School.

LOCATION 560 the renamed school, which educated all those Stainsby girls, including Chris Rea's future wife Joan, is two miles south-west of the centre of Middlesbrough at Lodore Grove, Acklam, postcode, TS5 8PB

CHRIS · REA
STAINSBY · GIRLS

STOCKTON-ON-TEES VINYL SURVIVES AT SOUND IT OUT

Teeside's last remaining vinyl record shop survives and is the revered subject of a movie documentary made by local film-maker Jeanie Finlay. Sound It Out's vast range of "Abba to Zappa" sleeves can be thumbed in the wonderfully ramshackle shop surroundings in the back streets of Stockton.

LOCATION 562: the shop is situated in Stockton town centre, 15a Yarm Street, postcode TS18 3DR. Website: www.sounditoutrecords.co.uk

SCARBOROUGH MARTIN CARTHY'S FOLK LESSON TO PAUL SIMON

Once a medieval fair for tradespeople and now a more modest entertainment-based celebration, Scarborough Fair was the inspiration for a folk song made internationally famous by Simon and Garfunkel. Paul Simon first learned the old ballad on his folk exploration of Britain in the Sixties, when introduced to the song by London folk club regular Martin Carthy. It was Carthy's 20th-century arrangement of the traditional ballad the American duo used when recording the track, which appeared first on their 1966 album Parsley, Sage, Rosemary and Thyme, then The Graduate film soundtrack LP in 1968. Covers and variations of the song run into the hundreds, including Bob Dylan's take on Carthy's arrangement of the traditional 'Scarborough Fair', which he recorded as 'Girl From The North Country' in 1963.

LOCATION 561: on the North Sea coast, Scarborough is Yorkshire's largest holiday resort. The present day Scarborough Fair celebrations take place in the town in the month of September. Postcode: YO11 1JW

SCOTCH CORNER MAN'S TURTLE TRIPPING CAFÉ ENCOUNTER

'Scotch Corner' is a nine-minute plus track on Welsh band Man's most successful album Rhinos, Winos + Lunatics. According to the 1974 album's liner notes, the song was inspired by the band's encounter at the Scotch Corner transport café with a man who looked like a turtle who was on his way to the Lake District to commit suicide.

❢ It was a psychedelic experience. We were on our way back from Scotland and all tripping. We called in at the cafe on Scotch Corner. It was all a bit shabby. We noticed a guy who looked like a turtle. So it was inspired by being there but nothing actually happened. ❡
Deke Leonard, Man guitarist and songwriter

LOCATION 563: an important refuelling point on the A1, Scotch Corner is approximately seven miles south of Darlington. Postcode: DL10 6NP

SCARBOROUGH MADE IN SHEFFIELD, SHOT IN SCARBOROUGH

The Stephen Joseph Theatre appears on the cover of Richard Hawley's Coles Corner album. The real lovers' meeting place was actually in Sheffield, but Scarborough's town centre theatre was an ideal 21st-century substitute for the photoshoot.

LOCATION 564: in the centre of Scarborough at the junction of Westborough and Northway, postcode YO11 1JW

Sheffield lovers' location photographed in Scarborough

Born in North Yorkshire

Paul Banks, guitar, Shed Seven (b. 6 Jul 1973, York)
John Barry, film score composer (b. 3 Nov 1933, York, d. 30 Jan, 2011)
Arthur Brown (b. 24 Jun 1942, Whitby)
Chris Corner, Sneaker Pimps/IAMX (b. Middlesbrough)
David Coverdale, vocals, Whitesnake (b. 22 Sep 1951, Saltburn-by-the-Sea)
Stuart Fletcher, bass, The Seahorses (b. 16 Jan 1976, York)
Vin Garbutt, folk singer (b. 20 Nov

1947, Middlesbrough)
Alistair Griffin, singer-songwriter (b. 1 Nov 1977, Middlesbrough)
Chris Helme, vocals, The Seahorses (b. 22 Jul 1971, York)
Mik Kaminski, violin, ELO (b. 2 Sep 1951, Harrogate)
Richard March, bass, Pop Will Eat Itself (b. 4 Mar 1965, York)
Micky Moody, guitar, Juicy Lucy/ Whitesnake (b. 30 Aug 1950, Middlesbrough)
Chris Norman, vocals, Smokie (b. 25 Oct 1950, Redcar)

Charles O'Connor, Horslips (b. 7 Sep 1948, Middlesbrough)
Chris Rea (b. 4 Mar 1951, Middlesbrough)
Paul Rodgers, vocals/guitar, Bad Company/Free (b. 17 Dec 1949, Middlesbrough)
Pete Trewavas, bass, Marillion (b. 15 Jan 1959, Middlesbrough)
Charlie Whitney, guitar, Family (b. 24 Jun 1944, Skipton)
Pete York, drums, The Spencer Davis Group (b. 15 Aug 1942, Redcar)

ROCK ATLAS
North East England
UK and Ireland Edition

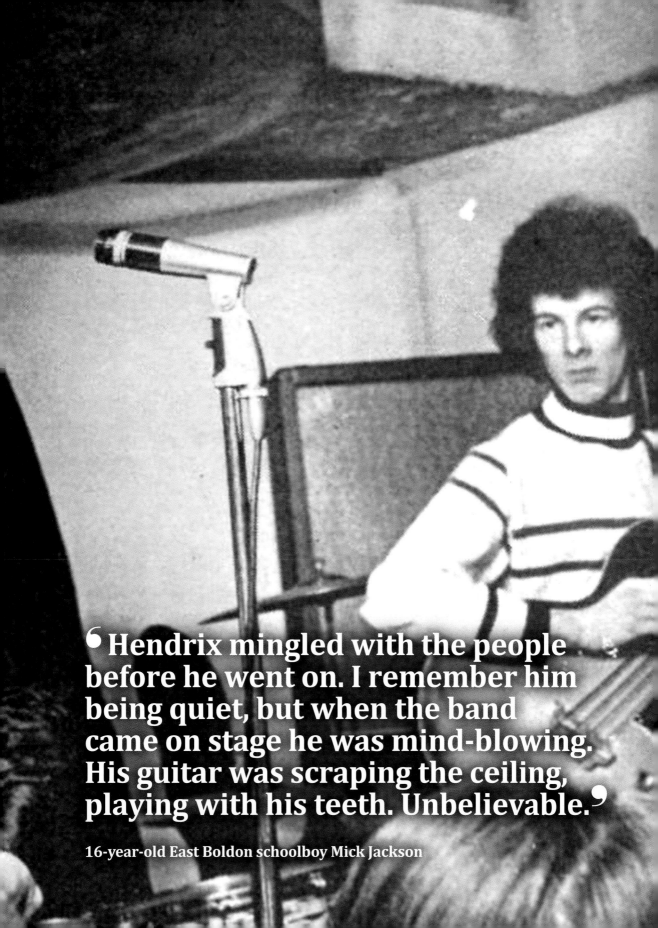

‘Hendrix mingled with the people before he went on. I remember him being quiet, but when the band came on stage he was mind-blowing. His guitar was scraping the ceiling, playing with his teeth. Unbelievable.’

16-year-old East Boldon schoolboy Mick Jackson

North-East of England

COUNTY DURHAM

Roger Whittaker's 1969 debut hit 'Durham Town (The Leavin')' maybe the most obvious county connection, but dig deeper and there's a varied bunch of locations awaiting rock pilgrimage. Worthy sons and daughters of County Durham include singer / songwriter Lesley Duncan, Prefab Sprout's McAloon brothers and singer Susan Maughan. There's a Peterlee pub that booked Led Zeppelin, the aforementioned Sprouts' Langley Park, a visit by The Beatles to Stockton touched by tragedy and a visually memorable album cover photoshoot for The Who at Easington.

EASINGTON COLLIERY
THE WHO'S NEXT ALBUM COVER

Easington is the colliery that made headlines in 1951 when 83 men lost their lives in a tragic mining disaster. It was here that The Who assembled in 1971 for photographer Ethan A Russell to snap them for the sleeve of Who's Next. The album that would become the band's first chart-topper featured the front cover image of a huge man-made monolith rising from the barren slag heap landscape. They say the camera never lies but the photo shoot concept that Pete Townshend, Roger Daltrey, John Entwistle and Keith Moon had evidently just relieved themselves on the concrete structure was not completely authentic. At least a couple of the band members couldn't 'go', so rain water from an empty film canister was splashed against the concrete to get the desired effect.

LOCATION 565: the colliery, which ceased mining in 1994, is between Easington village and the sea on Seaside Lane, postcode SR8 3

The end result of Ethan A Russell's Easington Colliery photoshoot

PETERLEE LED ZEPPELIN AT THE ARGUS BUTTERFLY

This pub, named after an endangered local butterfly, once played host to a few of rock's biggest attractions. March 23rd 1969 saw Led Zeppelin perform for a £100 fee a fortnight before their debut album scorched into the chart. Deep Purple, Family, Jethro Tull, Taste and Ten Years After also appeared at the tiny venue billed as Peterlee Jazz Club. Joint promoters Brian Stoker and David Richards had the knack of booking big names on the verge of superstardom. Typically, Free appeared at the pub just a week before 'All Right Now' rocketed to No.2 in the singles chart.

❛ I said 'what are you doing next month?' and [Jimmy Page] said they were playing the Hollywood Bowl, so that was the last we saw of [Led Zeppelin]. ❜
Promoter Brian Stoker interviewed by the Hartlepool Mail in 2008

LOCATION 566: Peterlee is between the A19 and the coast. The Argus Butterfly is on York Road, postcode SR8 2DP

STOCKTON-ON-TEES A SAD NIGHT AS THE BEATLES PLAY THE GLOBE

Although the Fab Four played Stockton's Globe Theatre on October 15th 1964 at the height of Beatlemania, it was their earlier visit on November 22nd 1963 that would be most powerfully etched in the minds of the young fans that day. As those present at the first of two shows that evening left and fans for the second show filed into the Globe, news began filtering through that President John F Kennedy had been assassinated in Dallas, Texas. Other superstar visits to the Globe included Buddy Holly, Chuck Berry, The Everly Brothers and Cliff Richard and The Shadows. One number sure to have been played live at the Globe when The Shadows (featuring local Stockton boy Hank Marvin) appeared was their 'Wonderful Land' B-side 'Stars Fell On Stockton'. Status Quo were the last rock group to play the Globe in 1974 before it closed completely in 1996. It seems extraordinary that such an impressive structure should be allowed to decay and local public pressure will surely see this grand entertainment centre restored to its former glory sometime soon.

LOCATION 567: at 101 High Street, postcode TS18 1BD

LANGLEY PARK
PREFAB SPROUT'S SEARCH FOR EXCITEMENT

Prefab Sprout actually hailed from the neighbouring village of Witton Gilbert, but maybe Witton Gilbert To Memphis lacked the more obvious geographical connection of From Langley Park To Memphis, the group's third and highest charting studio album release. The final track, 'The Venus Of The Soup Kitchen', also namechecks the 1988 album's title.

❛ Langley Park is a small village in County Durham where I come from in the north of England. Nowhere seemed more exotic to someone from there than a place like Memphis where Presley came from, so really it's about looking across the sea from where you live and thinking the rest of the world is much more exciting. ❜
Prefab Sprout's Paddy McAloon (1988)

LOCATION 568: south of the A691 about five miles east of Durham. Postcode: DH7

Born in County Durham

Gem Archer, guitar, Oasis (b. 7 Dec 1966, Durham)
Eds Chesters, drums, The Bluetones (b. 24 Oct 1970, Bishop Auckland, Darlington)
Lesley Duncan, singer/songwriter (b. 12 Aug 1943, Stockton-on-Tees, d. 12 Mar 2010)
Keith Gregory, bass, The Wedding Present (b. 2 Jan 1963, Darlington)
Claire Hamill, singer/songwriter (b. 4 Aug 1954, Port Clarence, Stockton-on-Tees)
Liam Howe, Sneaker Pimps (b. 1974, Elwick, Hartlepool)
Susan Maughan, Sixties singer (b. 1 Jul 1938, Consett)
Martin McAloon, bass, Prefab Sprout (b. 4 Jan 1962, Durham)
Paddy McAloon, vocals, Prefab Sprout (b. 7 Jun 1957, Consett)
Wendy Smith, vocals, Prefab Sprout (b. 31 May 1963, Durham)
Alan White, drums, Yes (b. 14 Jun 1949, Pelton, Chester-le-Street)

TYNE AND WEAR

The first beat boom sensation to come out of the North-East, The Animals were so inextricably in thrall to the music of America's southern states that in the mind of vocalist Eric Burdon the River Tyne became the Mississippi. They covered Timmy Shaw's R&B hit 'Gonna Send You Back To Georgia', tailoring it to namecheck a local suburb of Newcastle on 'Gonna Send You Back To Walker'. Bizarrely, the Walker version, only a B-Side in the UK, was an A-Side hit single in the US. Not surprisingly, the band's bass player Chas Chandler's association with Jimi Hendrix sees him dominate Tyne and Wear's Rock Atlas entries based on the legendary guitarist's six extraordinary appearances in the area. Then there's the discovery of Sting in Gosforth, the Police man's debut at the canny new community music centre The Sage in Gateshead, and the South Shields shenanigans of the Angelic Upstarts. The region also gave stage debuts to Tommy Steele and Nirvana and created the necessary romantic grittiness to inspire modern-day folk songs about the Tyne, Corstophine Town, Jarrow and Spanish City, from Lindisfarne, The Nice, Splinter, Alan Price and Dire Straits respectively.

❛ Those walks, which were many - on my way home from Ville Carre Jazz Club -the River Tyne in my mind became the Mississippi and I was convinced I was already there. I was already in New Orleans before I'd ever left my home town. ❜
Eric Burdon

NEWCASTLE A UK DEBUT FOR NIRVANA AT THE RIVERSIDE

The Riverside was the first venue on Nirvana's first tour of the UK. The October 23rd 1989 gig was typical of the far-sighted management at The Riverside, who also managed to book early appearances by Pearl Jam, Red Hot Chili Peppers, The Smashing Pumpkins and Nine Inch Nails. The place seems to have anecdotes to burn, with Buster Bloodvessel once causing a complete power outage when shooting lager over the audience and soaking the electrics at a Bad Manners gig. Then there was the abandoned Oasis performance due to fighting and, years before Glastonbury went in for this sort of thing, a hugely popular appearance by student cult hero Rolf Harris. Proud of its heritage, The Riverside is decorated with an array of iconic pictures on the walls.

LOCATION 569: The Close, Quayside, postcode NE1 3RQ

North-East of England

GATESHEAD THE SAGE: THE NORTH EAST'S COMMUNITY MUSIC CENTRE

Granted, The Sage may not have much rock heritage to speak of, but the sci-fi-like structure built on post-industrial wasteland next to the River Tyne is worthy of a mention for its stunning architectural contribution alone. The Norman Foster-designed live music and music education centre was opened in 2004 and fittingly celebrated its fifth birthday with a concert featuring two of the North-East's most accomplished recording artists, rock star Sting and traditional musician Kathryn Tickell. Performers at The Sage tend to be at the more cerebral end of the rock music spectrum with Elbow, Morrissey, Robert Plant, Goldfrapp, Herbie Hancock, David Crosby and Graham Nash all playing the 1,640-seat venue since its opening by the Queen. It's unlikely you will find Metallica or AC/DC shaking The Sage anytime soon. Aside from the concert hall, this remarkable building's library of music, access to rehearsals, listening posts and internet access is open to the public daily, free of charge.

Mark Savage

❛I'm from Wallsend, which is the posh part of Tyneside.❜ Proud to be making his debut at The Sage in 2009, Sting jokes about his roots

LOCATION 570: on the south bank of the River Tyne at St Mary's Square, Gateshead Quays, postcode NE8 2JR. Website: www.thesagegateshead.org

Above: The Sage viewed from the River Tyne's Millennium Bridge

Above left: Kathryn Tickell and Sting blend together the ancient and modern music of their native North-East at the Sage birthday bash

GOSFORTH STING 'DISCOVERED' AT THE GOSFORTH HOTEL

It was while working as a Virgin Records PR man that Andy Worrall 'discovered' Sting in the upstairs performance room in this small blue-tiled traditional pub in Gosforth. Locally famous as the place where the first copies of the comic Viz were sold, The Gosforth Hotel hosted folk and jazz nights, and on the night in question in 1976 Sting was playing with jazz, pop band Last Exit. Impressed by the bass player from nearby Wallsend,

Worrall approached Sting and the band's manager, Sting's first wife Frances Tomelty to find out where he might bring his head of A&R to see them again. Although that gig did not result in a recording contract - not commercial enough according to Virgin - Sting did subsequently get offered and sign his publishing over to Virgin. Not long after this The Police were formed and in 1978 their first hit 'Can't Stand Losing You', entered the singles chart.

❛A few years later I was again involved with Sting when, in a dispute between him and Virgin regarding his publishing, I was called to London to attend a court hearing to recount the beginnings of this story. The case was settled out of court. So The Gosforth Hotel is a landmark in Sting's career.❜ Andy Worrall

LOCATION 571: Gosforth Hotel, Salters Road, postcode NE3 1DH

NEWCASTLE 'WILD' ANIMALS A'GOGO

Local R&B chart stars The Animals got their big break (and their name due to their "wild" stage antics) at the Club A'GoGo when they began a residency at the city centre Percy Street venue in 1963. By this time the club had already established itself in North-East folklore hosting performances by a number of emerging acts from London including The Rolling Stones. Local youngsters Bryan Ferry, AC/DC's Brian Johnson, Lindisfarne's Rod Clements, Jimmy Nail and Sting were frequent fans of the venue and the many blues rock bands that played the A'GoGo. Brian Ferry would go on to play there with his band The Gas Board. On March 10th 1967, the Jimi Hendrix Experience made their first Newcastle appearance, playing two sets at the club's linked venues The Young Set and then the Jazz Lounge. Hendrix repeated his ceiling-puncturing act from a recent South Shields performance, this time spectacularly leaving his guitar hanging from the roof at the climax of the gig.

❛ I lay in my bed that night with my ears ringing and my world view significantly altered. ❜
Sting's memory of the Hendrix gig at the A'GoGo in March 1967

LOCATION 572: the club buildings were demolished in 1983 and replaced by the Eldon Garden shopping centre, postcode NE1 7RA

HEATON CHAS CHANDLER AND JIMI HENDRIX AT SECOND AVENUE

Animals founder member Chas Chandler grew up in Heaton, and despite moving to London when success beckoned as a pop star and then a manager, he returned frequently to the solid-looking terraced house on Second Avenue. His most famous client as a manager was Jimi Hendrix, and when the wild man of rock played in the North-East in 1967 Chandler, saving money on hotel bills, took Hendrix home to stay at his parents' flat at No.35, where a plaque marks the spot. Without a home telephone, Chandler would walk to the local public call box to make contact with London. It was here he discovered his client was on his way to massive popularity when he got the news that 'Hey Joe' had rocketed up to No.6 in the singles chart. In addition to enjoying Mrs Chandler's hospitality, unsubstantiated reports suggest that Hendrix also took to the streets to complete a spot of busking on nearby Chillingham Road.

LOCATION 573: the plaque at 35 Second Avenue, Heaton, is two miles north-east of Newcastle city centre. Postcode: NE6 5XT. For a great deal more information on this and other Hendrix stories, visit www. hendrixnortheast.pwp.blueyonder.co.uk

JARROW ALAN PRICE'S HOME TOWN SONG

Alan Price's fourth Top 10 single was his stirring account of the Jarrow March of 1936. 'Jarrow Song' was his hurriedly-written tribute to the 200 protesters who marched more than 280 miles from Jarrow to Westminster to lobby Parliament over the North-East's unemployment and poverty during the depression.

❛ The director who made the television documentary for Omnibus said: 'You have to write a song about the Jarrow March.' I said I didn't want to because it was just after the miners' strike in the Seventies and it would get me into trouble politically. But he took me to the George pub in Fatfield where my father used to drink and I sat down and wrote it in five minutes. ❜

❛ If I ever get a bit of time up [in the North East] I have a wander around Jarrow. Where I used to live in Russell Street is the start of the Tyne Tunnel now. And I sometimes go to visit Fatfield where I was born. ❜
Alan Price interviewed by NorthEastLife

LOCATION 574: Alan Price's former Jarrow home on Russell Street is six miles east of Newcastle on the A19, south of the River Tyne. Postcode: NE32 3AW

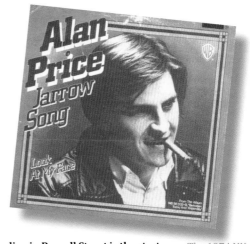

The 1974 UK No.6 hit single that told the story of the astonishing protest march in 1936

North-East of England

NEWCASTLE LINDISFARNE'S FOG ON THE TYNE

The song 'Fog On The Tyne', included on the album of the same name that featured a 19th-century illustrated view of the river and city, became a Geordie theme tune in the mid-Seventies. It gave local band Lindisfarne (named after the nearby Northumberland Island) national fame when the album shot to No.1, becoming the top-seller in 1972 by any UK act. The song was 'revisited' when Lindisfarne and Geordie footballing hero Paul Gascoigne teamed-up to release a new version in World Cup year, 1990. Promoted this time by a video set in Geordieland, the single made No.2 in the chart but thankfully didn't herald a new career in pop for the irrepressible Gazza.

LOCATION 575: the Gazza and Lindisfarne 'Fog On The Tyne (Revisited)' video was shot on the banks of the River Tyne around the Tyne Bridge, postcode NE1 3

NEWCASTLE FIVE NICE BRIDGES ON A NICE ALBUM

A dramatic river's-eye view of the Tyne Bridge decorates the cover of Five Bridges, The Nice's most successful album, released in 1970. Peaking at No.2 in the UK chart, and recorded with a full orchestra, this creation in five movements is synchronized to what were, at the time, the city's five bridges and was commissioned for the Newcastle Arts Festival.

LOCATION 576: the five bridges spanning the Tyne at the time of the release of Five Bridges were the Tyne Bridge, Swing Bridge, High Level Bridge, King Edward VII Bridge and Scotswood Bridge. The Tyne Bridge postcode: NE1 3

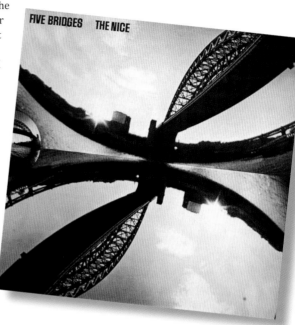

SOUTH SHIELDS SPLINTER'S COSTAFINE TOWN

'Costafine Town' provided South Shields duo Splinter (Bill Elliott and Bobby Purvis) with their only hit single. The place they sang about is actually spelt 'Corstorphine Town' and is little more than a short stretch of road near the banks of the River Tyne. The track, which features guitar work and production by George Harrison, evokes days gone by when this area was commercially busy and the local pub, the Commercial Hotel, was thriving.

LOCATION 577: south of the centre of South Shields, postcode NE33 1SQ

SUNDERLAND TOMMY STEELE DEBUTS AT THE EMPIRE

The Empire Theatre was the location for Tommy Steele's debut on November 5th 1956 as part of a variety bill that gave the Sunderland public their first taste of the rock 'n' roll phenomenon. So new was this exciting craze that the electric guitars and amplifiers used that night attracted the attention of the local fire brigade, who threatened to prevent Steele performing. The go-ahead was only given with the proviso that a fireman sit on stage armed with a blanket and fire bucket to prevent the band bursting into flames. Steele's famously thrilling debut was thankfully fire free, attracting six curtain calls. The Empire witnessed a second sensational rock 'n' roll debut a year later when Marty Wilde made his bow. By the time The Beatles played the Empire in 1963 variety was pretty much dead, but happily this striking century-old building is still open for business.

LOCATION 578: 4-5 High Street West on the corner of Garden Place in the city centre. Postcode: SR1 3EX

SOUTH SHIELDS HENDRIX IN THE CELLAR

With its low ceiling and revolving stage, the New Cellar Club was one of the North-East's most passionately supported music venues. When this enterprising club moved from Beach Road to Thomas Street, Cream were booked for the grand opening. But it was the appearance of the Jimi Hendrix Experience two months later on February 1st 1967 that local rock fans still rave about to this day. According to the Experience's bass guitarist Noel Redding, they were just about to launch into opening number 'Foxy Lady' when Hendrix's 200-watt amp blew-up. But despite the resulting frantic unplugging and plugging in, the trio went down a storm. In the confined space, Hendrix managed to shove his guitar through the ceiling and then narrowly avoid crashing into the Cellar wall when the revolving stage was activated to remove the band from view at the end of a sensational gig witnessed by under 100 fans.

LOCATION 579: now a dental clinic, The New Cellar Club (later renamed The Chelsea Cat and The Wave) was at 8 Thomas Street, postcode NE33 1PU. Visit www.hendrixnortheast.pwp. blueyonder.co.uk/hendrix for detailed info on all Hendrix's gigs in the North-East

6 Sounds which had never been heard on this earth before, it was all very amazing, a new breed of music had been born. I remember departing the club quite literally gob-smacked. 9
21-year-old engineer Graham Cook

6 My one main outstanding memory was of [Hendrix], on his own, kicking off an absolutely killer version of Muddy Waters' 'Catfish Blues', a slow, sensual, lascivious, wicked blues with guitar licks the like of which the world had never heard up to that point (or so it seemed to us). 9
19-year-old Dave Bainbridge, guitarist with local support band that night, The Bond

6 Hendrix mingled with the people before he went on. I remember him being quiet, but when the band came on stage he was mind-blowing. His guitar was scraping the ceiling, playing with his teeth. Unbelievable. After that we followed him till he died. 9
16-year-old East Boldon schoolboy Mick Jackson

Fietschers Fotos

Sensational value for money: The Jimi Hendrix Experience play the New Cellar Club for £71 and five shillings

North-East of England

WHITLEY BAY
SPANISH CITY INSPIRATION FOR DIRE STRAITS

The dome atop the Empress Theatre and Ballroom still stands as a reminder of the hugely popular Spanish City fairground featured in Dire Straits' 1981 hit single 'Tunnel Of Love'. The fairground provided the young Mark Knopfler with his first exposure to loud rock 'n' roll music. The song, which also namechecks the nearby town of Cullercoats, is not the only locally connected composition by songwriter Knopfler, who grew up in nearby Blyth. His 'Going Home' theme from the Local Hero soundtrack is played at the start of every Newcastle United home match at their St James' Park football ground.

❛ It was just a little fun fair on the coast, but to us it was infused with all kinds of things. ❜
Mark Knopfler

LOCATION 580: Whitley Bay is about ten miles north-east of Newcastle city centre, postcode NE26. The mostly demolished fairground site where Spanish City once stood is near the junction of Marine Avenue and the Promenade, postcode NE26 1LX

SOUTH SHIELDS
A PIG'S HEAD FLIES AT BOLINGBROKE HALL

They don't play gigs like this one at Bolingbroke Hall anymore. The 21st-century health and safety police would have had a field day at venues booking the Angelic Upstarts. On a snowy Friday night in March 1978, the Northumbrian agitators made another of their increasingly headline-grabbing performances. Creating an indelible impression on the punk memory banks, the South Shields audience witnessed a performance of the provocative Upstarts favourite 'Police Oppression'. During the song they were accompanied on stage by their manager Keith Bell, who held a pig's head aloft, which eventually got booted into the steaming hot crowd.

LOCATION 581: in the centre of South Shields, in Bolingbroke Street, postcode NE33 2SS

Born in Tyne and Wear

Michael Algar, aka 'Olga', vocals/guitar, The Toy Dolls (b. 21 Sep 1962, South Shields)
Ruth-Ann Boyle, vocals, Olive (b. 26 Apr 1970, Sunderland)
Eric Burdon (b. 11 May 1941, Walker, Newcastle upon Tyne)
Chas Chandler (b. 18 Dec 1938, Heaton, Newcastle upon Tyne, d. 17 Jul 1996)
Rod Clements, bass, Lindisfarne (b. 17 Nov 1947, North Shields)
Cheryl Cole, Girls Aloud (b. 30 Jun 1983, Newcastle upon Tyne)
Simon Cowe, guitar, Lindisfarne (b. 1 Apr 1948, Jesmond Dene, Newcastle upon Tyne)
Bryan Ferry (b. 26 Sep 1945, Washington)
Ginger (David Walls), vocals, The Wildhearts (b. 17 Dec 1964, South Shields)
Trevor Horn, producer (b. 15 Jul 1949, Houghton-le-Spring)

Alan Hull, Lindisfarne (b. 20 Feb 1945, Newcastle upon Tyne, d. 17 Nov 1995)
Lee Jackson, bass/vocals, The Nice (b. 8 Jan 1943, Newcastle upon Tyne)
Ray Jackson, Lindisfarne (b. 12 Dec 1948, Wallsend)
Brian Johnson, vocals, AC/DC (b. 5 Oct 1947, Dunston, Gateshead)
Ray Laidlaw, drums, Lindisfarne (b. 28 May 1948, North Shields)
Lauren Laverne, Kenickie/ TV and radio presenter (b. 28 Apr 1978, Sunderland)
Danny McCormack, bass, The Wildhearts (b. 28 Feb 1972, South Shields)
Hank Marvin, guitar, The Shadows (b. 28 Oct 1941, Newcastle upon Tyne)
Ross Millard, guitar/vocals, The Futureheads (b. 22 Jul 1982, Sunderland)

Jimmy Nail (b. 16 Mar 1954, Benton, Newcastle upon Tyne)
Alan Price, keyboards, The Animals/solo (b. 19 Apr 1942, Fatfield)
John Steel, drums, The Animals (b. 4 Feb 1941, Gateshead)
Dave Stewart, musician/producer, Eurythmics, Tourists (b. 9 Sep 1952, Sunderland)
Sting (b. 2 Oct 1951, Wallsend)
Andy Taylor, Duran Duran (b. 16 Feb 1961, Cullercoats)
Neil Tennant, Pet Shop Boys (b. 10 Jul 1954, North Shields)
Becky Unthank (b. 9 Sep 1985, Ryton, Gateshead)
Rachel Unthank (b. 1 Sep 1977, Gateshead)
Hilton Valentine, guitar, The Animals (b. 21 May 1943, North Shields)
Chris Wilkie, guitar, Dubstar (b. 25 Jan 1973, Gateshead)

NORTHUMBERLAND

With the lowest density population of any English county, rural Northumberland is unsurprisingly a tad thin on the ground when it comes to rock locations or venues. Nevertheless, the inspirational landscape has created a region of great folk tradition steeped in the unique music of the small pipes and other local instruments played by expert exponent Kathryn Tickell, who, on her many side projects, has recorded and performed with North-East rock star Sting. Although born a few miles down the road in Newcastle, Sting taught the secondary school children of Cramlington in Northumberland before a career in The Police beckoned. Out at sea, the island tourist attraction that is Lindisfarne inspired the name of one of Britain's much-loved folk rock bands and Hexham was the birthplace of Libertines and Babyshambles rock idol Pete Doherty.

Northumberland's best-known female musician, Kathryn Tickell

GS Studios

HOLY ISLAND
THE BRETHREN BECOME LINDISFARNE

In 635 AD, Saint Aidan journeyed from Scotland and founded a monastery on this island, which became an evangelical base for the Christian faith. When Newcastle folk-rock group The Brethren chose Lindisfarne as their new name, they became more famous than the island from which they took their name when their Fog On The Tyne album topped the UK chart in 1972.

❛ We chose the name Lindisfarne after the small tidal island off Newcastle – it's completely cut off at high tide; consequently the pubs stay open all day without fear of police action. ❜
Lindisfarne's Ray Jackson, interviewed by Record Mirror (1972)

LOCATION 582: five miles east of the A1 at Beal. Take the Lindisfarne Causeway to the island. Postcode: TD15 2SH. The island, its priory and craggy hilltop castle are only accessible when the tide permits. Website: www.lindisfarne.org.uk

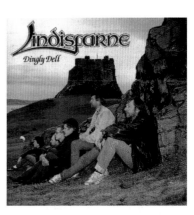

Stranded on Lindisfarne: the band wait for low tide and contemplate a visit to the island pub

Born in Northumberland

Dave Cliff, jazz guitar (b. 25 Jun 1944, Hexham)
Pete Doherty (b. 12 Mar 1979, Hexham)
Robson Green, actor/singer, Robson & Jerome (b. 18 Dec 1964, Hexham)
Kathryn Tickell (b. 8 Jun 1967, Walk on Tyne)

ROCK ATLAS
Scotland

UK and Ireland Edition

'At first, the father of the American family I babysat for just said that there was a VIP coming in. When he told me it was Elvis I could hardly believe it.'

16-year-old Elvis fan Anne Murphy, on walking out at Prestwick Airport to see Elvis Presley in 1960

Scotland

SCOTLAND

"Dripping in atmosphere" was how Madonna described the remote beauty of Scotland at the time of her Highland wedding to Guy Ritchie. The remoter corners of the Highlands have certainly drawn admiring visits from the most legendary rock stars. Lennon, McCartney, Page and Dylan have all holidayed, recuperated and rejuvenated themselves (or bought into the Highland lifestyle) and a small part of Prestwick has almost become hallowed ground as the only spot in Britain to have witnessed an appearance by Elvis Presley. But it's a matter of fact that indicates the country's passion for music. Outside of central London, statistics prove that the good folk of Inverness are Britain's most avid music fans. When it comes to shopping for albums, the Entertainment Retailers Association proved that the inhabitants of the Highland city bought, on average, three times the number of albums purchased by the apparently less fanatical music fans of places such as Wigan and Wolverhampton down south. There's no reduction in fanaticism where the actual music created by the country's musicians is concerned, either. Few groups have added "mania" to their moniker in the way Edinburgh's Bay City Rollers matched The Beatles after a year-long residency at the city's Top Storey Club set them on their way and gave the rest of the world Rollermania. And give it up for Glasgow, where rock extrovert Alex Harvey, Postcard Records and Belle & Sebastian all contributed to their own hugely inspirational little worlds. From the tenement blocks of the Gorbals to the rugged quiet of Kintyre, Scotland oozes an eccentric mix of music stories exemplified by Alex Harvey's obsession and recorded investigation to undercover the truth about the Loch Ness Monster...

ABERDEEN WHOLE LOTTA SOUL AT THE MUSIC HALL

Northern Soul didn't get much more northern than Aberdeen and the passion for it in the Granite City has endured for five decades. Formerly the Assembly Rooms, Aberdeen's Music Hall was a favourite venue for devoted soul fans who would travel extreme distances to dance to the right records. The place also attracted rock's finest. When Led Zeppelin visited in 1973, the council neglected to lay on the wherewithal for the required light show. Despite the lack of visual entertainment, the boisterous audience got good value for their £1 tickets. Zeppelin put on a gutsy performance one would expect from a band at the height of their powers. The rock Gods may no longer visit Scotland's third largest city, but the Music Hall still attracts rock, pop and blues acts alongside classical music and comedy.

LOCATION 583: the Music Hall is still open for business on Union Street, in the city centre, postcode AB10 1QS

ABERDEEN BALLROOM BEATLES

The Beatles' 1963 tour of Scotland wound up here at the art deco seafront Beach Ballroom on January 6th. Snow and freezing temperatures characterized the mini tour, which ended just after the band's first hit 'Love Me Do' hit its chart peak of No.17. In 1967, The Who arrived at the Ballroom but the venue would soon be too parochial for the rock age with the likes of Pete Townshend, Roger Daltrey, Keith Moon and John Entwistle taking on the world at Monterey, Woodstock and the Isle of Wight.

LOCATION 584: Beach Promenade, postcode AB24 5NR

ALLOA UNIDENTIFIED BEATLES MAKE THEIR SCOTTISH DEBUT

The Town Hall in Alloa was the venue for the early Beatles' first date on a Scottish tour backing Decca heartthrob Johnny Gentle. Unidentified on adverts for the gig, the then named Silver Beatles line-up was John Lennon, Paul McCartney, George Harrison, Stuart Sutcliffe and Tommy Moore, and this booking gave the band their first taste of life as professional musicians, earning a wage of £18 each for the week-long tour. The opening night in Alloa also billed support act Alex Harvey (who would later front The Sensational Alex Harvey Band), as "Scotland's Own Tommy Steele". After Alloa, the Johnny Gentle/Silver Beetles tour travelled north to Inverness, Fraserburgh, Keith, Forres and Nairn, ending in Peterhead.

LOCATION 585: Alloa is roughly 30 miles north of both Glasgow and Edinburgh. Looking much as it did back in 1960, the imposing Town Hall is in the centre of Alloa at Marshill, postcode FK10 1AB

BALADO T IN THE PARK: SCOTLAND'S FIFTH BIGGEST TOWN

Growing rapidly since its debut at Strathclyde Country Park in 1994, T in the Park these days turns this Kinross-shire spot into Scotland's fifth biggest town when the annual festival arrives at Balado Park. Aside from attracting rock's biggest names, the festival has seen some exciting live collaborations down the years. In 2002, Noel Gallagher joined with Paul Weller and 2005 saw Brandon Flowers guest with New Order. The airfield site attracts 85,000 music fans per day over the weekend each summer and is famous for its stunning sunsets over the Ochil Hills. In 2010, Madness even paused mid set and invited the crowd to turn round and admire the view.

LOCATION 586: Balado Park is accessed off the A91 near Kinross, postcode KY13 www.balado.co.uk and www. tinthepark.com

Above: T in the Park: Scotland's fifth largest town every July

Left: 2010 T in the Park headliners Kasabian experience the Balado sunset effect

Scotland

CAMPBELTOWN PAUL McCARTNEY'S KINTYRE HIDEAWAYS

Purchased in 1966, High Park Farm was a hugely important location in Paul McCartney's life and music. It was here, while still a Beatle, he wrote 'The Long And Winding Road', said by some to have been inspired by the long and winding B842 in Kintyre that led to his farm. When post-Beatles depression set in he would escape to Scotland, but despite the farm's isolation the media were hungry to find out what the McCartney was up to. He didn't take kindly to invasions of privacy from the media and one over-zealous photographer from Life magazine who made it all the way to the farm had a bucket thrown at him by the exasperated McCartney. By the fag end of 1970 and the beginning of 1971, McCartney made the secluded, dilapidated, two-bedroom farmhouse his family home. A corrugated iron-roofed farmhouse extension was used to rehearse and record McCartney's new songwriting projects that would show up on albums Ram (credited to Paul and Linda McCartney) and Wild Life (his first album credited to Wings). A hand-drawn sign, "Rude Studio", over the door was the only indication that this was where McCartney, refreshed by his detachment from city life, was restoring his confidence and enthusiasm for songwriting after the dark, demoralising end days of The Beatles. After leaving his new home to tour with Wings, McCartney returned to High Park in 1973 and set about writing Band On The Run. This time rehearsals were undertaken in the barn over the hill at Lower Ranachan, a second farm purchased by Paul and Linda, who would ride horseback the short distance to work each morning. In 1977, the area's best known claim to fame arrived in the shape of Paul McCartney's biggest hit record, 'Mull Of Kintyre'. A lasting memorial to Linda, who died from cancer in 1998, can be found in the form of a statue in Campbeltown, marking the happy times the McCartney family spent on this isolated but beautiful peninsula.

LOCATIONS 587, 588 and 589: the Linda McCartney statue is in the Memorial Garden in the library and museum grounds at Campbeltown, best found by taking the back gate from Shore Street, postcode PA28 6. The farms at High Park and Lower Ranachan are four miles out of Campbeltown just north of the A83, postcode PA28 6NY. The Carskiey Estate, photographed on the cover of the 'Mull Of Kintyre' single, is east of Campbeltown, postcode PA28 6RU

6 Hiding away in the mists, there was a lot of that. 9
Paul McCartney

Pictured above:
The Campbeltown statue of Linda McCartney by sculptor Jane Robbins and the cover of Paul McCartney's best-selling single, featuring Davaar Island viewed from the Carskiey Estate, Mull of Kintyre

CALLANISH ULTRAVOX AND COPE COVER SHOTS

The ancient Callanish Stones are pictured on covers for Ultravox's 1984 Top 10 album Lament and Julian Cope's 1995 Top 20 offering Jehovahkill. Both show illustrations of what archaeologists specifically name Callanish I to identify the group of stones among others in the local area. Callanish I and Callanish III were also locations for the wintry filming of an Ultravox video featuring the band freezing to death while miming to 1984 hit single 'One Small Day'.

LOCATION 590: the village of Callanish (Calanais in Gaelic) and the stones are on the Isle of Lewis in the Western Isles, postcode HS2 9DY. www. callanishvisitorcentre.co.uk

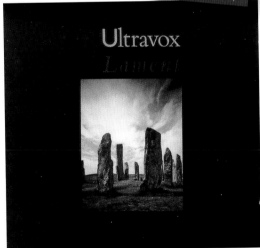

DINGWALL 19 FANS AT THE BEATLES' REMOTEST GIG

Arguably the Fab Four's most remote gig occurred at Dingwall Town Hall as part of their Scottish mini tour on January 4th 1963. According to Ken McNab's excellent The Beatles In Scotland, only 19 people turned out for their appearance. So sparsely attended was the gig that The Beatles packed up their gear early and journeyed five miles west with most of the audience (two Beatles by van, two on the bus) to a late night dance at Strathpeffer Pavilion. Here at the Strath, local band The Chessmen were supporting Irish show band The Mel-Tones, attracting about 1,000 more punters than The Beatles had managed in Dingwall. Despite the poor attendance, John, Paul, George and Ringo appeared to enjoy their stay in the small town, bed and breakfasting in the National Hotel and partaking in a pre-gig beer or two at the Commercial Bar.

LOCATION 591: Dingwall is at the head of the Cromarty Firth. The Town Hall, Commercial Hotel and National Hotel are all in the High Street, postcode IV15 9RU

DORNOCH MADONNA'S SECRET SERVICE AT SKIBO CASTLE

Under the cloak of secrecy, Jon Bon Jovi, Bryan Adams, Celine Dion and Sting all travelled to Sutherland for the rock wedding of the decade when Madonna married Guy Ritchie at Skibo Castle. The magnificent luxury hotel and estate was the setting for the wedding on December 22nd 2000 and nearby Dornoch Cathedral saw the couple's son Rocco's christening a day earlier.

LOCATION 592: forty miles north of Inverness on the A9, Skibo Castle is accessible to Carnegie Club members only. Postcode: IV25 3. Dornoch Cathedral is about 7 miles east of the castle in the High Street

❛ Well first of all, Scotland is dripping in atmosphere. It is so beautiful. ❜
Madonna talks wedding venues

CAIRNHOLY COPE'S INTERPRETER

Although partly inspired by Berkshire's Newbury by-pass protests in the mid-Nineties, the setting for the dramatic cover of Julian Cope's 1996 album Interpreter is the group of standing stones known as Cairnholy I in south-west Scotland. As can be seen from the Callanish entry, Cope, a keen archaeologist, has also released albums with standing stone cover images from the Isle of Lewis.

LOCATION 593: near the village of Creetown (postcode DG8 7JH), Dumfries and Galloway, signposted from the A75 down a single track road

Scotland

DUNDEE **A NIGHT AT THE OPERA WITH QUEEN AT CAIRD HALL**

Caird Hall's architectural magnificence has rock heritage to match. This imposing Grade A listed building, with its Doric columned frontage, has seen the likes of Frank Sinatra, The Beatles, Led Zeppelin, Elton John, and David Bowie take the stage. One of Caird Hall's best nights, and certainly one of the best-timed gigs, was Queen's appearance on December 13th 1975 when their Night At The Opera Tour came to Dundee. Two weeks previously the band had topped the UK singles chart for the first time with 'Bohemian Rhapsody', a run that would continue that winter for nine weeks in total. The emerging superstars celebrated by tossing red roses into the crowd during the encore, but were soon brought back down to earth with a bump when their tour bus broke down and the AA were called to fix it.

❝ **We're in cake!** ❞
All four Beatles' response to a TV reporter's question when asked whether they knew where they were when playing Dundee in 1964

LOCATION 594: the City Square, postcode, DD1 3BB

Grade A listed and still packing in the crowds: the magnificent Caird Hall

DUNBAR **SCOTLAND'S OWN RADIO PIRATES**

Scotland's very own pirate radio station was anchored off the south-east coast. Debuting during the final seconds of New Year's Eve in 1965, the 61-year-old former Irish lightship, The Comet, was home to Radio Scotland 242 until government legislation signalled the end just 20 months later. Owing to a weak broadcasting signal, The Comet moved north from the Dunbar coast to first the west coast waters off Troon, then Ballywalter off County Down, before returning once more to Dunbar. Despite a two- million fan petition to the government, it ceased broadcasting in the summer of 1967.

LOCATION 595: less than four miles off the coast from the East Lothian town of Dunbar, postcode EH42 1

ELGIN **CHART STARS HEAD NORTH TO THE TWO RED SHOES BALLROOM**

The Beatles played their most northerly UK gig on January 3rd 1963 when they took the stage at the Two Red Shoes Ballroom in the Grampian region of Scotland. The scheduled gig a day earlier, 15 miles south-east of Elgin in Keith, had been cancelled due to heavy snow and the Two Red Shoes Ballroom's Thursday night Elgin Folk Music Club hosted the Fab Four, although John Lennon almost missed the performance having dashed back south for a day. By October the place had another non-folk injection of excitement when Alex Harvey and His Soul Band came to town, and then the venue became a regular northern outpost on tours by chart stars The Four Pennies, The Honeycombs, The Moody Blues, The Nashville Teens and The Animals. Despite being great for dancing, the ballroom's 'L'-shaped floor layout was inconvenient for pop fans wanting a clear view of their idols on the frequent occasions the place was packed out. By July 1967, psychedelia came to Elgin with the venue grooving to the sounds and light show of The Pink Floyd, who performed their then current No.6 chart smash hit 'See Emily Play'.

LOCATION 596: the ballroom still stands and, until recently, was continuing in the entertainment business as the Red Shoes Theatre, 4-8 South College Street, postcode IV30 1EP

DURNESS JOHN LENNON'S NOSTALGIC RETURN TO SANGO BAY

The most north-westerly village on the British mainland is where the young John Lennon was packed off to enjoy summer holidays with his relatives in a croft overlooking Sango Bay. In 1969 he returned with his own children, Julian and Kyoko, and wife Yoko, full of nostalgia for this quiet corner of Scotland. Amazingly, the trip north from Surrey was undertaken with Lennon at the wheel of a hired Mini, stopping en-route at bed and breakfast accommodation in an attempt to normalise his family life. But, by the time they had made it to Edinburgh, the burnt out Mini's gearbox meant that a replacement car was called for. A far worse motoring disaster followed on arrival in Durness, before the vacation had hardly begun. While touring the Sutherland villages of Tongue and Loch Eriboll, the holiday came to an abrupt end when Lennon crashed the family's Austin Maxi on a narrow stretch of road near the Kyle of Tongue. The accident led to a five-day stay in the nearby Lawson Memorial Hospital for both John and Yoko. The couple made the most of the peace and quiet afforded them as a result of their injuries, which required numerous stitches due to the impact of the crash. While the rest of the world tuned in to hear the duo's new hit 'Give Peace A Chance', John and Yoko escaped the media excitement surrounding the Plastic Ono Band's debut and gratefully accepted their enforced relaxation. On July 6th, John, Yoko and Kyoko were airlifted by helicopter to Inverness Airport before flying back to London in a private jet. Unhurt by the crash, Julian was collected earlier by his mother Cynthia. Surprisingly, the wrecked Austin Maxi was eventually shipped back south to the Lennon family home, Tittenhurst Park, where the car lay in the grounds as a souvenir sculpture of their Highland holiday and a reminder of John's appalling driving. More recently, a ceremony to mark the unveiling of three standing stones as a memorial to John Lennon's visits to Durness was attended by his cousin Stan Parkes, who once shared those childhood holidays in Durness.

Press Association

LOCATIONS 597 and **598:** the croft where Lennon spent his childhood summers is marked by a blue plaque at 56 Sangomore, found by following the A838 east out of the centre of Durness. When the road turns south away from the sea, look for the white croft on the hill underneath the transmitter tower. Postcode: IV27 4PZ. The John Lennon memorial stones are to be found in the community garden in the centre of the village, overlooking the beach where Lennon played as a boy. Postcode: IV27 4PZ. The Lawson Memorial Hospital lies on Station Road, just north of the A9 in Golspie, postcode KW10 6SS

❛ I am a crippled family who need som mony to git out of Scotland, a few hundred will do. - Jack McCripple (ex seamen). ❜
John Lennon's 1969 holiday postcard to Beatles Press Officer Derek Taylor

The Lennon family enjoy their Durness holiday, with Julian and Kyoko sporting tartan outfits purchased from Scotch House in Princes Street during the family's Edinburgh stopover

Scotland

EDINBURGH NIRVANA IN SECRET AT THE SOUTHERN

A charity gig featuring "very, very, special American guests" (note the two "verys") was fly-posted as happening at this Edinburgh bar on December 1st 1991. The Southern was packed to bursting amid rumours that grunge gods Nirvana, who were touring Glasgow and Edinburgh, were in town and about to take the stage of this tiny bar and music venue. At the time the band were riding high in the album chart courtesy of Nevermind, with single 'Smells Like Teen Spirit' released just days earlier. No-one was too surprised when a spokesman stood up amid The Southern's expectant punters to explain that a rumour was all it was and Nirvana would not be performing. But when the announcement had eventually succeeded in reducing the crowd to 20 an hour later, the remaining fans' disappointment turned to amazement as Nirvana's Kurt Cobain and Dave Grohl wandered in and took to the stage for an extraordinary acoustic performance.

Kai Monk

The rumours turned out to be true: Dave Grohl and Kurt Cobain play The Southern

LOCATION 599: a mile south of the city centre on the A7 at 22-26 South Clerk Street, Newington, postcode EH8 9PR

FINDHORN
WATERBOY MIKE SCOTT'S MORAYSHIRE SANCTUARY '

The Waterboys' 2003 album Universal Hall is named after the venue where the band have performed some of their most memorable gigs and where this album was recorded in the studio under the hall itself. The studio and the Findhorn Foundation spiritual sanctuary have seen The Waterboys' Mike Scott return regularly to this extraordinary coastal community. Scott has been a member of the local wedding band, ceilidh band and jazz band and performed regular solo spots at this unique eco village which he now calls home.

LOCATION 600: Universal Hall is off the B9011 near Findhorn Village, County Moray, postcode IV36 3TZ. Website www.findhorn.org

More than 400 fans, some travelling from as far away as eastern Europe, packed Universal Hall in 2002 to see The Waterboys perform in this remote spot

EDINBURGH MARILLION'S 'HEART OF LOTHIAN'

Marillion's song 'Heart Of Lothian' refers to Edinburgh's Royal Mile in the lyrics and the stone mosaic Heart of Midlothian embedded in the pavement on this famous street running through the city. Local superstition dictates that to spit on the heart mosaic brings good luck. 'Heart of Lothian' appears on Marillion's 1985 concept album Misplaced Childhood.

LOCATION 601: the cobblestone heart is on the Royal Mile, outside the west door of St Giles' Cathedral. Postcode: EH1 1RE

FOYERS JIMMY PAGE'S SINISTER LOCH NESS RETREAT

On the eastern shore of Loch Ness lies the property once inhabited by Jimmy Page. The Led Zeppelin guitarist purchased and lived in a few noteworthy homes, but the secluded Boleskine House was acquired due to its connection with former owner Aleister Crowley. The notorious occultist and magician, who had lived in the house from 1899 to 1913, was a source of fascination for Page, who believed the man billed by the early 20th-century press as "The Wickedest Man in the World" was a misunderstood genius. Having bought the house in the early Seventies, Page locked into the mysterious atmosphere of the estate when filming a night-time full moon fantasy sequence on December 10th and 11th 1973 for the Led Zeppelin movie The Song Remains The Same. Satanist Charles Pace was commissioned by Page to recreate the Crowley décor by painting a series of murals in Boleskine House, but what had been little more than an infrequent retreat was vacated entirely by the rock star in 1991.

❝ The house was built on the site of a kirk dating from around the 10th century that had burned down with all of its congregation inside. Nobody wanted it. It was in such a state of decay. I hadn't originally intended to buy it, but it was so fascinating. It's not an unfriendly place when you walk into it. It just seems to have this thing... ❞
Jimmy Page, talking to Melody Maker in 1974

LOCATION 602: midway between the villages of Foyers and Inverfarigaig, Inverness, above the B852 loch side road, Boleskine House (with cemetery on the opposite side of the road) is a private residence. Postcode: IV2 6XT

Boleskine House: Jimmy Page's former home, overlooking Loch Ness

GLASGOW ALEX HARVEY'S "HOUSE OF MUSIC"

The south side of Glasgow's River Clyde was once the impoverished Gorbals birthplace of one of Scotland's greatest rock legends. Famed for his extrovert blending of American blues and British musical hall and his trademark black and white hooped T-shirts, Alex Harvey was born on Govan Road in 1935. Later the family moved the short distance to Durham Street, where his younger brother Leslie formed The Kinning Park Ramblers with girlfriend Maggie Bell. Someone once chalked, "This is the house of music" on the wall and for good reason as Alex would eventually form The Sensational Alex Harvey Band and Maggie and Leslie would find fame of their own when creating blues rock band Stone The Crows. In the mid-Seventies, around the same time Alex Harvey's fame was peaking with his first appearance on TV's Top Of The Pops at the age of 40, the rough neighbourhood of his childhood was disappearing. Redeveloped or demolished, his wartime homes made way for new, improved living conditions and the building of Glasgow's M8 motorway.

LOCATION 603: Alex Harvey's birthplace at 49 Govan Road is no longer standing and Durham Street is barely recognisable from the days of his youth. The old Harvey childhood locations are sandwiched between the River Clyde and the M8 south of the centre of Glasgow. Postcode: G51 1JL

Scotland

GLASGOW BOWIE CATCHES A FALLING STAR AT BARROWLAND

Barrowland Ballroom is a family affair. After fire gutted the first ballroom, built by the indomitable millionairess Maggie McIver, her family re-opened the new structure in 1960 with Maggie's grandson still running the business. With its iconic neon-signed frontage and 1,950 standing capacity floor space, the Barrowland Ballroom is a Glasgow institution favoured by touring bands from Arcade Fire to The Zutons. In 1997, one performing superstar took away a fragment of Barrowland history. When David Bowie played the ballroom, the venue's manager Tom Joyes remembered him stopping during a pre-gig soundcheck when a porcelain star fell off the ballroom ceiling, narrowly missing his head. Without complaining, Bowie bent down, picked up the star and slid it into his pocket.

LOCATION 604: in the city centre at 244 Gallowgate, postcode G4 OTS. Website: www.glasgow-barrowland.com

Same as it ever was: the famous ballroom has remained largely unchanged since the Sixties

INVERMORISTON ALEX HARVEY'S MONSTER INVESTIGATIONS

Even the most sceptical scientist can't say with any certainty that the Loch Ness Monster doesn't exist, and when Scottish music legend Alex Harvey has something to say on the subject, one is inclined to listen. So enthralled in the mystery was he that he recorded an album investigating the monster legend, which included his interviews with the Loch-side villagers of Invermoriston. Buy the album and draw your own conclusions!

LOCATION 605: Invermoriston lies seven miles north of Fort Augustus on the northern side of Loch Ness where the A82 meets the A887. Postcode: IV63 7YA

❛ Now I'm nae telling you whether I've seen it or not but there's a water bailiff up there who's consulted about the movement of fish by experts all around the world and he's seen it 18 or 20 times. ❜
Alex Harvey, interviewed by Sounds in 1977

Alex Harvey's 1977 side project

GLASGOW
BELLE & SEBASTIAN SNAPPED AT TCHAI-OVNA

The cover photograph for Belle & Sebastian's 2003 album Dear Catastrophe Waitress was shot at the extraordinary Tchai-Ovna in Glasgow's West End. Inspired by the tea houses of the Czech Republic, Tchai-Ovna offers 80 varieties of tea, vegetarian food, hookah pipes and live music. Aside from Belle & Sebastian's obvious love of the place, fellow Glasgow indie bands Franz Ferdinand and Camera Obscura have also enjoyed a cuppa there.

❛ It's a real hub for right-thinking poets, and wrong-playing jazzers. It's the closest we got to real Boho, man! ❜
Stuart Murdoch, Belle & Sebastian

LOCATION 606: a short walk from the university, Tchai-Ovna is at 42 Otago Lane, postcode G11 9PB

Refreshments all round at the Tchai-Ovna tea house

GLASGOW POSTCARD RECORDS' HQ AT WEST PRINCES STREET

Founded in 1979 by 19-year-old student Alan Horne, Postcard Records was a tiny, short-lived inspiration underpinned by the line "The Sound of Young Scotland", the motto printed on every record label. Like most great labels, its personality was determined by the person that ran it. The analogy describing Horne as Glasgow's Andy Warhol running the city's equivalent of Factory Records was about right. A larger than life character, he operated from a wardrobe in a small tenement apartment on West Princes Street. Up the stairs to the second floor trudged The Go-Betweens, Aztec Camera, Josef K and Orange Juice, the four bands that helped make a sea change in the rest of the UK's perception of Scottish pop music. After two short years, Postcard Records closed for business. Horne, who was headhunted by London Records, had been unable to capitalise on the musical change he had helped to develop. A&R scouts were beating a path north in large numbers, signing virtually any Scot clutching a guitar, and Postcard was brushed aside. The iconic label's disappearance was not forgotten by a stream of new bands years later, who revelled in the memory of what had been a golden period in the timeline of Scottish pop.

LOCATION 607: the flat was on the second floor at 185 West Princes Street, West End, Glasgow, postcode G4 9BZ

From the bedroom wardrobe: an original Postcard single sleeve

❛ I remember the wardrobe, the singles were there. That was where Alan [Horne] kept the stock. He used the bedroom as an office and the phone was in the hall. People would phone to arrange to collect the singles and the artwork and all of that. ❜
Edwyn Collins, former Orange Juice member, interviewed in the Herald, 2009

GLASGOW OASIS WOW ALAN McGEE AT KING TUT'S

"Quite possibly the finest small venue in the world" says the NME. This lively basement copied the name King Tut's Wah Wah Hut from a New York club when it opened in Glasgow city centre in 1990. Despite its limited space for only 300 punters, King Tut's importance has continually exceeded its capacity, attracting exciting, emerging bands on the cusp of greatness. Scottish acts Travis, Texas, Biffy Clyro and Franz Ferdinand have all played significant gigs in their development as major music attractions at King Tut's. But it was the Oasis performance on May 31st 1993 that helped give the place its legendary status and provided a crucial turning point for the unknown, unsigned Manchester band. In the audience that day, checking out Scottish band 18 Wheeler, was record label boss Alan McGee, who was so excited by the five-song set by Oasis that he decided to sign them up for his Creation Records set-up by the end of song three.

LOCATION 608: city centre, 272 St Vincent Street, postcode G2 5RL. www.kingtuts.co.uk

Scotland

GLASGOW SIMPLE MINDS' RESIDENCY AT THE MARS BAR

During most of 1978, Simple Minds were the resident Sunday night band at the Mars Bar. The tiny L-shaped club was the launchpad for the Glasgow band's burgeoning career as stadium rockers. While most live gigging at the time was of the high-energy post-punk or new wave variety, Simple Minds were all melodic melodrama, featuring Jim Kerr pushing a few Glasgow club boundaries by taking to the tiny stage in white jacket and make-up. It was at the Mars Bar that they would perfect the ten songs that would form their 1979 debut album Life In A Day.

Their focused vision of what they wanted to achieve on a larger scale was evident by employing their own lighting and sound engineer, even at this early stage. The club, a popular meeting place for mod revivalists, was also forced into calling itself Countdown: the manufacturers of the famous chocolate bar were not happy, apparently.

LOCATION 609: the club burnt down but was once the centre of the universe for young Glasgow music fans at Howard Street, just off St Enoch Square, postcode G1 4

KIRRIEMUIR BON SCOTT'S HOME TOWN MEMORIAL

Kirriemuir is the small town where AC/DC front-man Bon Scott was born and spent the first six years of his life before emigrating to Australia. In May 2006, a Caithness stone memorial to the singer, who died in 1980, was unveiled in the town, watched by 500 of Scott's fans. The work of acclaimed local sculptor Bruce Walker, the stone pavement plaque lies in the town's Cumberland Close. Nearby is Bon Scott Place, a residential road in memory of the man who sported a "Scotland Forever" tattoo on his arm. Enhancing his

Scottish folk hero credentials, he played the bagpipes on 1975's T.N.T. album track 'It's A Long Way To The Top, (If You Wanna Rock 'N' Roll)' and was once voted rock's greatest frontman in Classic Rock magazine.

LOCATIONS 610 and **611:** Kirriemuir is in eastern Scotland about 20 miles north of Dundee. The memorial stone is at Cumberland Close, postcode DD8 4EF, and Bon Scott Place is at postcode DD8 4LD

Bon Scott's pavement plaque

LOCHEARNHEAD THE BONNIE WEE STUDIOS

In 1986, Simple Minds' success led them to invest in Dalkenneth House, a property on the banks of Loch Earn in Perthshire. Their retreat became the perfect bolt-hole for the band and work began on a purpose-built recording studio. The refreshing isolation created the ideal environment for writing and recording tracks for albums Street Fighting Years, Real Life and Good News From The Next World. The Bonnie Wee Studios got their name following a question posed by Jon Bon Jovi to Simple Minds' Jim Kerr about where the drums were recorded on tracks he'd heard: "In the bonnie wee studios" was Kerr's instant description, and from then on the name of the striking hexagonal building, designed and built by Gaia Architects, stuck. Architect Howard Liddell's final flourish on completion of the timber structure was to erect a "Simple Winds" weather vane.

❝ Loch Earn is not far east of Loch Lomond, but it feels worlds away — it's dark and peaty and sort of mystical. My son James used to ask me if there was a monster in it, like Loch Ness, and I'd say yes — these lochs were so deep that they all link together. I think I half believed it myself. ❞
Jim Kerr

LOCATION 612: Dalkenneth House is on the north side of Loch Earn. Status: now a private residence. Postcode: FK19 8PZ

NETHY BRIDGE
BOB DYLAN'S HIGHLAND HOME

In 2007, Bob Dylan added property owner to his existing Scottish connection of honorary degree at the University of St Andrews. The music icon spent a week in the spring of 2006 enjoying the five-star bed and breakfast country comforts of Aultmore House in the Cairngorms. So delighted was he with the experience that he purchased the woodland estate and house, along with his brother, for £2.2 million. The ten-bedroom house's interior had previously been the location for BBC TV drama Monarch of

Bob Dylan's Aultmore House, the perfect spot for hiking, biking, fishing and water sports

the Glen. Since purchasing the place, sightings of Bob Dylan have been harder to come by than a glimpse of the elusive local ospreys and capercaillie.

LOCATION 613: about 30 miles south-east of Inverness, Nethy Bridge is two miles east of the A95. Follow the B970 north out of Nethy Bridge. Postcode: PH25 3ED

LEITH BIRTHPLACE OF THE PROCLAIMERS

Sunshine On Leith is the album and album track released by local duo The Proclaimers in 1988. The identical twin brothers Charlie and Craig Reid are the most Scottish-sounding of rock stars and enthusiastic supporters of their local Edinburgh football club Hibernian, where 'Sunshine On Leith' is blasted out on match days as something of a local anthem. Sunshine On Leith - the musical, infused with the brothers' socialist ideology but not featuring the twins themselves, played to packed houses across Scotland in the Noughties.

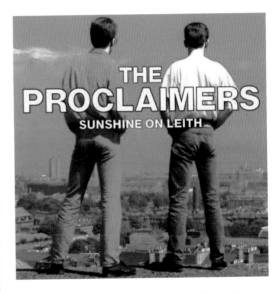

LOCATION 614: Leith is the waterside port area of Edinburgh, postcode EH6

The Leith-born Reid twins survey their local manor

LOCH LOMOND ON THE BONNIE BANKS WITH RUNRIG

The most sung-about of all Scotland's beauty spots, 'Loch Lomond' became the closing song at gigs by Celtic rock ambassadors Runrig. It gave them their biggest hit when their 2007 version raised funds for BBC TV's Children In Need, making No.9 in the singles chart. Revised and retitled

down the years, this traditional folk song has been covered by Bill Haley & His Comets, AC/DC and Marillion, among others. The bonnie banks of Loch Lomond were also the setting for what ranks as the band's favourite concert, when close to 50,000 turned out to see them in the

grounds of Balloch Castle in 1991.

LOCATION 615: Balloch Castle, on the banks of Loch Lomond in West Dunbartonshire, was the setting for Runrig's big Loch Lomond bash. Status: public country park, postcode G83

Scotland

PRESTWICK ELVIS PRESLEY'S ONLY VISIT TO BRITAIN

The 'secret' visit may only have lasted 80 minutes, but when the aircraft carrying Elvis Presley touched down at Prestwick Airport it was, as it turned out, a deeply significant moment. March 3rd 1960 was the day music's greatest star made his first visit to Britain, which duly became the singer's only stay on British soil. The brief encounter was not a planned meet and greet the fans visit, more born out of practicality, made possible due to Elvis' period in the military. Back in 1960, aged 25, he was a serving Sergeant in the US Army, travelling from Germany to be demobbed back home and return to civilian life and his career in music and films. The flying visit to this small Scottish airport was simply for aircraft refuelling on the long journey home but Elvis did nevertheless enjoy a brief experience of Scottish hospitality. After a few polite words with reporters, he sped away in a chauffeured limo to the NCO's mess and youth club on the US air base. This gave those teenagers lucky enough to be present that day the opportunity to thrust an autograph book or scrap of paper over the airport's chicken wire fence. Some of the screaming fans even got to hold hands and one or two of the more excitable girls even claimed they had managed to kiss their idol. Proud of the associated limelight that Elvis Presley brought to Prestwick, the airport has marked his visit with a plaque on the terminal building floor and the creation of an Elvis tribute bar in the departure lounge.

❛ At first, the father of the American family I babysat for just said that there was a VIP coming in that evening. When he told me it was Elvis I could hardly believe it and told my other Elvis-mad friend to dress American and we walked out to the airport. ❜
16-year-old Elvis fan Anne Murphy

❛ Ah kind of like the idea of Scotland. ❜
Elvis sums up his brief visit before flying home

LOCATION 616: despite being 32 miles from Glasgow city centre on Scotland's west coast, the airport is now known as Glasgow Prestwick Airport at Graceland (nice touch) Arcade. Postcode: KA9 2PL

Prestwick is the only place in the United Kingdom visited by 'The King' of Rock and Roll. Sergeant Presley was greeted by screaming fans on 3 March 1960 when his aircraft stopped to refuel.

Left: Elvis' short, enforced stay in Scotland was a closely guarded secret, but these teenagers mobbed the air base once rumours started circulating locally

Below: the Elvis star in the main concourse and the plaque, with a DJ from West Sound Radio, an Elvis impersonator and airport Chief Executive, Iain Cochrane

3 March 1960, twenty-five year old Sergeant Elvis Presley flew into what then a US Air Force base at Prestwick on a brief re-fuelling stop, en-route from Germany to the USA. Sergeant Presley was on his way home after two years military service.

PAISLEY
STEALERS WHEEL'S FERGUSLIE PARK

The title of Stealers Wheel's 1974 album Ferguslie Park came from a deprived area of Paisley where musical duo Gerry Rafferty and Joe Egan were born and raised. The housing estate has, with considerable investment, improved its reputation down the years. Don't try reading too much into the decision-making behind the album title; according to Egan it was "just a name we thought sounded good".

LOCATION 617: north-west of Paisley, north of the A761. Postcode: PA3 1DW

Just a name that sounded good: the cover of Ferguslie Park

STENNESS
VAN MORRISON'S PHILOSOPHER'S STONE

A trawl through the Van Morrison archives, his 1998 Top 20 album The Philosopher's Stone depicts the standing stones of Stenness on the cover. The 19-foot-tall megaliths are off the north-east tip of Scotland on the Orkney mainland.

LOCATION 618: Stenness village, Orkney, postcode KW17

Scotland

Born in Scotland

James Allan, vocals/guitar, Glasvegas (b. 21 Sep 1979, Dalmarnock, Glasgow)

Ian Anderson, vocals, Jethro Tull (b. 10 Aug 1947, Dunfermline)

Colin Angus, vocals/guitar, The Shamen (b. 24 Aug 1961, Aberdeen)

Roger Ball, saxophone, Average White Band (b. 4 Jun 1944, Broughty Ferry, Dundee)

Maggie Bell, solo/Stone The Crows (b. 12 Jan 1945, Maryhill, Glasgow)

Robert Bell, keyboards, The Blue Nile (b. 22 Aug 1952, Glasgow)

Guy Berryman, bass, Coldplay (b. 12 Apr 1978, Kirkcaldy)

Norman Blake, vocals/guitar, Teenage Fanclub (b. 20 Oct 1965, Glasgow)

Edith Bowman, DJ/presenter (b. 15 Jan 1974, Anstruther, Fife)

Stuart Braithwaite, guitar, Mogwai (b. 10 May 1976, Dalserf, South Lanarkshire)

Steve Bronski, keyboards, Bronski Beat (b. 7 Feb 1960, Glasgow)

Jack Bruce, bass/vocals, Cream (b. 14 May 1943, Bishopbriggs, East Dunbartonshire)

Paul Buchanan, vocals, The Blue Nile (b. 16 Apr 1956, Edinburgh)

Martin Bulloch, drums, Mogwai (b. 14 Aug 1974, Bellshill, Glasgow)

Charlie Burchill, guitar, Simple Minds (b. 27 Nov 1959, Glasgow)

David Byrne, vocals/guitar, Talking Heads (b. 14 May 1952, Dumbarton)

Isobel Campbell, cello/keyboards, Belle & Sebastian/solo (b. 27 Apr 1976, Glasgow)

Martin Carr, guitar, The Boo Radleys (b. 29 Nov 1968, Thurso)

Zal Cleminson, guitar, The Sensational Alex Harvey Band (b. 4 May 1949, Glasgow)

Richard Colburn, drums, Belle & Sebastian (b. 25 Jul 1970, Perth)

Edwyn Collins (b. 23 Aug 1959, Edinburgh)

Brian Connolly, vocals, The Sweet (b. 5 Oct 1945, Hamilton, d. 9 Feb 1997)

Mick Cooke, brass, Belle & Sebastian (b. 15 Dec 1973, Dundee)

Tommy Cunningham, drums, Wet Wet Wet (b. 22 Jun 1964, Drumchapel, Glasgow)

Justin Currie, vocals/bass, Del Amitri (b. 11 Dec 1964, Glasgow)

Stuart David, bass, Belle & Sebastian (b. Glasgow)

Barbara Dickson (b. 27 Sep 1947, Dunfermline)

Lonnie Donegan (b. 29 Apr 1931, Glasgow, d. 3 Nov 2002)

Donovan (b. 10 May 1946, Glasgow)

Eddy Duffy, bass, Simple Minds (b. 30 Dec 1969, Glasgow)

Malcolm 'Molly' Duncan, saxophone, Average White Band (b. 24 Aug 1945, Montrose)

Andy Dunlop, guitar, Travis (b. 16 Mar 1972, Lenzie, East Dunbartonshire)

Sheena Easton (b. 27 Apr 1959, Bellshill, Glasgow)

Joe Egan, Stealers Wheel (b. 18 Oct 1946, Paisley)

Eric Faulkner, guitar, Bay City Rollers (b. 21 Oct 1953, Edinburgh)

Fish, vocals, Marillion (b. 25 Apr 1958, Dalkeith, Midlothian)

Roddy Frame (b. 29 Jan 1964, East Kilbride)

Elizabeth Fraser, vocals, Cocteau Twins (b. 29 Aug 1963, Grangemouth)

Barry Fratelli (Barry Wallace), guitar, The Fratellis (b. 23 Apr 1979, Glasgow)

Jon Fratelli (John Lawler), vocals, The Fratellis (b. 4 Mar 1979, Cumbernauld)

Mince Fratelli (Gordon McRory), drums, The Fratellis (b. 16 May 1983, Glasgow)

Benny Gallagher, Gallagher & Lyle (b. 10 Jun 1945, Largs, Ayrshire)

Chris Geddes, keyboards, Belle & Sebastian (b. 15 Oct 1975, Dalry, Ayrshire)

Bobby Gillespie, vocals, Primal Scream/drums, The Jesus and Mary Chain (b. 22 Jun 1962, Glasgow)

Alan Gorrie, bass/vocals, Average White Band (b. 19 Jul 1946, Perth)

Clare Grogan, vocals, Altered Images (b. 17 Mar 1962, Glasgow)

Robin Guthrie, multi-instrumentalist, Cocteau Twins (b. 4 Jan 1962, Grangemouth)

Calvin Harris (b. 17 Jan 1984, Dumfries)

Alex Harvey (b. 5 Feb 1935, Glasgow, d. 4 Feb 1982)

Les Harvey, guitar, Stone The Crows (b. 13 Sep 1944, Glasgow, d. 3 May 1972)

Iain Harvie, guitar, Del Amitri (b. 19 May 1962, Glasgow)

Colin Hay, vocals, Men At Work (b. 29 Jun 1953, Kilwinning, Ayrshire)

Mike Heron, vocals, The Incredible String Band (b. 27 Dec 1942, Edinburgh)

Richard Hynd, drums, Texas (b. 17 Jun 1965, Aberdeen)

Stevie Jackson, guitar, Belle & Sebastian (b. 16 Jan 1969, Glasgow)

Bert Jansch, guitar, Pentangle (b. 3 Nov 1943, Glasgow)

Richard Jobson, vocals, The Skids/TV presenter (b. 6 Oct 1960, Dunfermline)

Ben Johnston, drums/vocals, Biffy Clyro (b. 25 Apr 1980, Kilmarnock)

James Johnston, bass/vocals, Biffy Clyro (b. 25 Apr 1980, Kilmarnock)

Malcolm Jones, guitar/pipes, Runrig (b. 12 Jul 1959, Inverness)

Graeme Kelling, guitar, Deacon Blue (b. 4 Apr 1957, Paisley, d. 10 Jun 2004)

Jim Kerr (b. 9 Jul 1959, Glasgow)

David Knopfler, guitar, Dire Straits (b. 27 Dec 1952, Glasgow)

Mark Knopfler, guitar, Dire Straits (b. 12 Aug 1949, Glasgow)

Annie Lennox (b. 25 Dec 1954, Aberdeen)

Alan Longmuir, bass, Bay City Rollers (b. 20 Jun 1948, Edinburgh)

Derek Longmuir, drums, Bay City Rollers (b. 19 Mar 1951, Edinburgh)

Gerard Love, bass/vocals, Teenage Fanclub (b. 31 Aug 1967, Motherwell)

Lulu (b. 3 Nov 1948, Lennoxtown, East Dunbartonshire)

Graham Lyle, Gallagher & Lyle (b. 11 Mar 1944, Bellshill, Glasgow)

Calum Macdonald, vocals/drums, Runrig (b. 12 Nov 1953, Lochmaddy, North Uist)

Rory Macdonald, vocals, Runrig (b. 27 Jul 1949, Dornoch, Western Isles)

Billy Mackenzie, vocals, Associates (b. 27 Mar 1957, Dundee, d. 22 Jan 1997)

Dan McCafferty, vocals, Nazareth (b. 14 Oct 1946, Dunfermline)

Jimmy McCulloch, guitar, Wings (b. 4 Jun 1953, Dumbarton, d. 27 Sep 1979)

Chas McDevitt (b. 4 Dec 1934, Eaglesham, Glasgow)

Johnny McElhone, guitar, Altered Images/bass, Texas (b. 21 Apr 1963, Bearsden, East Dunbartonshire)

Ally McErlaine, guitar, Texas (b. 31 Oct 1968, Glasgow)

Alan McGee, record label boss/manager (b. 29 Sep 1960, East Kilbride)

John McGeoch, guitar/saxophone, Magazine (b. 25 Aug 1955, Greenock, Renfrewshire, d. 4 Mar 2004)

Raymond McGinley, guitar/vocals, Teenage Fanclub (b. 3 Jan 1964, Glasgow)

Lorraine McIntosh, vocals, Deacon Blue (b. 13 May 1964, Glasgow)

Robbie McIntosh, drums, Average White Band (b. 6 May 1950, Dundee, d. 23 Sep 1974)

Onnie McIntyre, guitar, Average White Band (b. 25 Sep 1945, Lennoxtown, East Dunbartonshire)

Les McKeown, vocals, Bay City Rollers (b. 12 Nov 1955, Edinburgh)

Shirley Manson, vocals, Garbage (b. 26 Aug 1966, Edinburgh)

Paul Joseph Moore, keyboards, The Blue Nile (b. Glasgow)

Donnie Munro, vocals/guitar, Runrig (b. 2 Aug 1953, Uig, Isle of Skye)

Stuart Murdoch, vocals, Belle & Sebastian (b. 25 Aug 1968, Ayr)

Simon Neil, vocals/guitar, Biffy Clyro (b. 31 Aug 1979, Irvine, North Ayrshire)

Paolo Nutini (b. 9 Jan 1987, Paisley)

Brendan O'Hare, drums, Teenage Fanclub (b. 16 Jan 1970, Cambuslang, Glasgow)

Dougie Payne, bass, Travis (b. 14 Nov 1972, Glasgow)

Marti Pellow, vocals, Wet Wet Wet (b. 23 Mar 1965, Clydebank)

Frankie Poullain, bass, The Darkness (b. 15 Apr 1967, Edinburgh)

James "Optimus" Prime, keyboards, Deacon Blue (b. 3 Nov 1960, Kilmarnock)

Neil Primrose, drums, Travis (b. 20 Feb 1972, Cumbernauld)

Finley Quaye (b. 25 Mar 1974, Edinburgh)

Gerry Rafferty (b. 16 Apr 1947, Paisley, d. 4 Jan 2011)

Eddi Reader, vocals, Fairground Attraction (b. 29 Aug 1959, Glasgow)

Charlie Reid, The Proclaimers (b. 5 Mar 1962, Leith)

Craig Reid, The Proclaimers (b. 5 Mar 1962, Leith)

Jim Reid, vocals, The Jesus and Mary Chain (b. 29 Dec 1961, Glasgow)

William Reid, guitar/vocals, The Jesus and Mary Chain (b. 28 Oct 1958, Glasgow)

Brian Robertson, guitar, Thin Lizzy (b. 12 Sep 1956, Clarkston, Glasgow)

Ricky Ross, vocals, Deacon Blue (b. 22 Dec 1957, Dundee)

Bon Scott, vocals, AC/DC (b. 9 Jul 1946, Kirriemuir, d. 19 Feb 1980)

Mike Scott, The Waterboys (b. 14 Dec 1958, Edinburgh)

Tom Simpson, keyboards, Snow Patrol (b. 7 Jan 1972, Angus)

Jimmy Somerville, vocals, Bronski Beat/The Communards (b. 22 Jun 1961, Glasgow)

Sharleen Spiteri, vocals, Texas (b. 7 Nov 1967, Bellshill, Glasgow)

Al Stewart (b. 5 Sep 1945, Glasgow)

Hamish Stuart, vocals/guitar, Average White Band (b. 8 Oct 1949, Glasgow)

Stuart Sutcliffe, bass, The Beatles (b. 23 Jun 1940, Edinburgh, d. 10 Apr 1962)

Gavin Sutherland, bass/vocals, Sutherland Brothers and Quiver (b. 6 Oct 1951, Peterhead)

Iain Sutherland, guitar/vocals, Sutherland Brothers and Quiver (b. 17 Nov 1948, Ellon, Aberdeenshire)

Dougie Thomson, bass, Supertramp (b. 24 Mar 1951, Glasgow)

Paul Thomson, drums, Franz Ferdinand (b. 15 Sep 1976, Glasgow)

Len Tuckey, guitar, Suzi Quatro Band/The Nashville Teens (b. 15 Dec 1947, Aberdeen)

KT Tunstall (b. 23 June 1975, St Andrews, Fife)

Midge Ure (b. 10 Oct 1953, Cambuslang, Glasgow)

Ewen Vernal, bass, Deacon Blue (b. 27 Feb 1964, Glasgow)

Nancy Whiskey (b. 4 Mar 1935, Bridgeton, Glasgow, d. 1 Feb 2003)

Robin Williamson, vocals, The Incredible String Band (b. 24 Nov 1943, Edinburgh)

Paul Wilson, bass, Snow Patrol (b. 20 Oct 1978, Kinlochleven, Scottish Highlands)

Pete Wishart, keyboards, Runrig (b. 9 Mar 1962, Dunfermline)

Stuart 'Woody' Wood, guitar, Bay City Rollers (b. 25 Feb 1957, Edinburgh)

Angus Young, guitar, AC/DC (b. 31 March 1955, Glasgow)

Malcolm Young, guitar, AC/DC (b. 6 Jan 1953, Glasgow)

ROCK ATLAS

Ireland

(Republic and Northern)

UK and Ireland Edition

Photo: Diarmud O'Sullivan

‘**Mitch Mitchell performed in the De Barra folk club with Noel [Redding], which was as close as many of us here got to seeing the Jimi Hendrix Experience.**’

Ray Blackwell, De Barra's manager

Northern Ireland

Whether it be 'The Troubles', local hero George Best or simply the atmosphere of the place, Belfast has a lengthy back catalogue of songs featuring the city in the title. Simple Minds' 'Belfast Child', Don Fardon's football favourite 'Belfast Boy', Boney M's 'Belfast' are three of the most enduring hits. And Orbital duo Paul and Phil Hartnoll were inspired to name their instrumental hit 'Belfast' after playing the demo at 4am on a car stereo driving home from a gig in the city. No-one does a better job at eulogising the province generally than Van Morrison, whose deep-seated attachment to places discovered in his youth reveal themselves in beautiful lyrics narrated on Van tracks like 'Cyprus Avenue' and 'Coney Island.' There's a classic Led Zep cover shoot on the rugged coast, the tale of Pearly Spencer, The Beatles' best attended UK gig and the scandalous lack of a plaque to commemorate the Derry location that enabled The Undertones to shake the world. But, we begin with one location that rightly and recently did bag a plaque.

BELFAST THEM ARE BIG NEWS AT THE MARITIME HOTEL

The Ulster History Circle's blue plaque is a constant reminder to everyone that the city's Maritime Hotel was the focal point responsible for nurturing not just local bands but an entire music genre. Back in 1964, it begat Belfast's own Celtic take on rhythm and blues and the distinctive sound of local boys Them, featuring the young Van Morrison. The opening of the Maritime as a music venue coincided with the new band's unveiling in a now legendary Belfast newspaper ad campaign: 'Who Are? What Are? THEM', immediately followed by a debut appearance at Maritime's new Club Rado. Formerly a police station and a seaman's hostel, the city centre building's new role as Belfast's equivalent to Liverpool's Cavern saw a stream of increasingly confident young bands converge on the 200-capacity club, which soon began to pack twice that number in when queues stretched around the block. Bands with no previous place to play, or those enthusiastically assembled overnight in the beat boom, included The Aztecs, The Mad Lads, The Fugitives, The Few, Five By Five, The Method, The Deltones, The Lovin' Kind and The Alleykatz.

The plaque at College Square North was unveiled in April 2010

❝ Them lived and died on the stage at The Maritime Hotel. ❞
Van Morrison

LOCATION 619: the inspirational Maritime Hotel once stood in College Square North. Its position is marked by a shiny blue plaque on an uninspiring brick wall opposite the junction with Hamill Street and Killen Street. Postcode: BT1 6

BELFAST
STONES AND LED ZEP DRAMA AT THE ULSTER HALL

Built in 1859, Ulster Hall's foundations were tested to the limit when The Rolling Stones made their first visit to Northern Ireland on July 31st 1964. The 1,200-capacity venue was wildly oversubscribed as 3,000 fans packed the hall, causing suffocating panic and forcing the termination of The Stones' performance after just 12 minutes. No surprise, then, that when Mick, Keith, Brian, Bill and Charlie returned in January and September a year later Ulster Hall was out of bounds for a group whose shows were igniting mass states of hysteria among fans throughout Britain. Their 1965 appearances were made at the ABC Theatre and although hysteria was contained some fans queued for two days and nights to be sure of bagging tickets to see their idols. Rioting of a much more serious kind coincided with an equally memorable visit by Led Zeppelin on March 5th 1971. Rock fans who braved a particularly bad night of sectarian unrest on the surrounding streets witnessed Jimmy Page's live introduction of the famous double-necked Gibson guitar and the debut performance of 'Stairway To Heaven', almost nine months ahead of its release on their fourth album. As you enter the hall look out for a plaque, inside the main doors, in memory of Belfast's Fifties' chart star Ruby Murray.

❝ [The Stones] made The Beatles look like the Old Time Music Hall. ❞
Belfast Telegraph, 1964

LOCATION 620: in Belfast city centre at 1-7 Bedford Street, postcode BT2 7

BELFAST STREETS AND AVENUES OF VAN MORRISON'S CHILDHOOD

A small brass plaque to the right of the door of No.125 Hyndford Street discreetly indicates that this was the home of the young Van Morrison from 1945 until he was 16. Years before the plaque, fans of Them, Morrison's hugely popular Belfast R'n'B export to the world in the Sixties, would chalk the walls of the small terraced home with their own mark of appreciation: "Them's House". Fond of evoking places and activities from his youth in song, there's no better example than Morrison's narration on the track 'On Hyndford Street' from his 1991 No.5 album Hymns To The Silence. His childhood home is pictured on the back of the album cover and the track takes the listener on a journey to nearby Abetta Parade, Cyprus Avenue (the title of another Van track), Fusco's ice-cream parlour (on Woodstock Road), Orangefield (his secondary

school), St Donard's church (on Bloomfield Road) and a little further afield to Beechie River, Cherryvalley, North Road Bridge the Castlereagh Hills, Cregagh Glen and Holywood (a bus journey for the young Morrison north-east of the city on the coast). One of Van's most popular tracks, 'Cyprus Avenue' appears on his 1968 album Astral Weeks. This mature tree-lined avenue is a short stroll from his modest Hyndford Street home but a world away in property prices and was a mystical, romantic place for Van the budding songwriter to escape to.

LOCATION 621, 622 and 623: 125 Hyndford Street (postcode: BT5 5) is about one mile south-east of the city centre. Most of the other locations namechecked by Van Morrison in song are within walking distance of his childhood home, including Cyprus Avenue,

Van the (young) man: Them would congregate at Van's Hyndford Street home, on the right beyond the telegraph pole

postcode BT5 5NT. Fusco's is still serving ice-cream at 369 Woodstock Road, postcode BT6 8PU

❝ We lived in a pretty funky neighbourhood. ❞
Van Morrison, talking to Rolling Stone in 1970

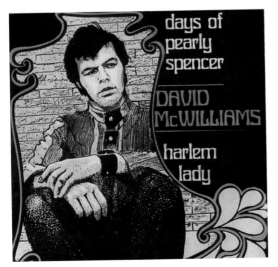

BALLYMENA
THE HOMELESS PEARLY SPENCER

Although familiar and much loved by anyone who possessed a pair of ears in the Sixties, 'The Days Of Pearly Spencer' was inexplicably never a UK hit for David McWilliams when released as a single in 1967, despite topping the French hit parade at the time. Sensitive to the plight of society's disadvantaged, McWilliams wrote the song about one particular homeless man he encountered in his home

town of Ballymena, where he grew up on the Rectory Estate. The poignant tale of an impoverished life in County Antrim was covered in some style in 1992 by Yorkshireman Marc Almond, and this time McWilliams' song shot to No.4 in the UK singles chart.

LOCATION 624: the Rectory Estate is less than a mile north of the centre of Ballymena, postcode BT43

Northern Ireland

BELFAST **THE BELFAST MUSIC EXHIBITION**

A hub of the city's music activity, the Oh Yeah music centre, named after the 1996 Ash hit single 'Oh Yeah', is housed in a three-storey warehouse that includes the Belfast Music Exhibition. Highlights of this visitor attraction include Ash frontman Tim Wheeler's Flying V guitar and the Fender guitar on which Snow Patrol's Gary Lightbody wrote 'Run' and 'Chasing Cars'. Gone but thankfully not forgotten is one of the city's key historic music venues, The Maritime Hotel. The place is heavily featured in the exhibition through memorabilia recalling the days when the place provided a haven for jazz, rhythm and blues and rock to flourish in the Sixties.

LOCATION 625: in the heart of Belfast at the Oh Yeah music centre, 15-22 Gordon Street, postcode BT1 2LG

Tim Wheeler with his Golden Gibson Flying V, which is now a popular exhibit at the Oh Yeah music centre

Carrie Davenport

BELFAST **SIMPLE MINDS' 'BELFAST CHILD'**

The 1989 Simple Minds single 'Belfast Child' was based on the traditional Irish folk tune 'She Moves Through The Fair'. With lyrics by the band's Glasgow-born singer Jim Kerr, the chart-topper was a poignant updating of the ballad, prompted by the recent escalation of violence during 'The Troubles' in the province at the time. Where most late Eighties pop promo videos were selling records using exotic Caribbean locations as backdrops, the 'Belfast Child' video was soberly filmed in and around the city's derelict and disappearing landscape. Shot in black and white, Simple Minds perform the song against the backdrop of the once thriving Harland and Wolff shipyard and on top of a Belfast rubbish dump, interspersed with glimpses of depressingly decaying streets and the Stormont Parliament Buildings.

LOCATION 626: the increasingly redundant shipyard area is a short distance north-east of the city centre, postcode BT3 9DU

❛ Enniskillen was, I think, the catalyst to the song. ❜
Jim Kerr

BELFAST **VAN MORRISON AT THE OPERA HOUSE**

First released in 1984, Live At The Grand Opera House Belfast was an album of tracks selected from the best of four sell-out shows Van Morrison played a year earlier. Pictured on the cover is the famed theatrical architect Frank Matcham's building opened in 1895, restored in 1980, bombed twice in the 1990s and extended in 2006.

LOCATION 627: in the city centre, 2 Victoria Street, postcode BT2 7

Matcham's masterpiece of a building that hosted four Van Morrison shows in 1983

BELFAST **THE WALLS OF FAME**

When attending the city centre's twin music venues The Limelight and the Spring & Airbrake, check out the signed photo Walls of Fame.

LOCATION 628: the walls lining the lobby of The Limelight and the entrance to its sister venue the Spring & Airbrake, 15-17 Ormeau Avenue, postcode BT2 8HD

BELFAST 'TEENAGE KICKS' AT WIZARD SOUND STUDIOS

The Undertones recorded their career-defining hit 'Teenage Kicks' at Wizard Sound Studios, a short walk from Belfast city centre. On June 16th 1978, they recorded a 4-track EP's worth of material for the £108 it cost to hire the tiny studio. Belfast record label Good Vibrations in Great Victoria Street was where the band, along with other young outfits the Moondogs and The Outcasts were signed. Where these bands once popped in and out of the Good Vibrations office, Belfast folk now book holidays and rent cars at the newly erected Norwood House, where the label and record shop once did its business. If accessing the city by using the M3 motorway, look out for the mural featuring The Undertones' "Teenage Kicks all through the Night" lyric line, which spans the wall beneath the flyover at Bridge End to the east of the city.

LOCATION 629, 630 and 631: Wizard Sound Studios were at Exchange Place, off Lower Donegall Street, postcode BT1 2. Slightly south of the city centre was where the Good Vibrations label operated from a record shop (now demolished) at 102 Great Victoria Street, postcode BT2 7BE. The M3 Teenage Kicks... flyover mural is less than a mile east of the city at Bridge End, postcode BT5 4

BELFAST KING'S HALL SETS RECORD BEATLES ATTENDANCE

While the Ritz Cinema at Fisherwick Place was the first to host a concert by them in 1963 (demolished and now Jurys Inn hotel), the King's Hall is Northern Ireland's only venue still standing that played host to The Beatles. Reassuringly, the cavernous King's Hall looks much the same from the outside as it did back on November 2nd 1964 when the Fab Four made the second of only two visits to Northern Ireland. The King's Hall provided enough space for The Beatles to attract their largest British concert audience when 17,500 fans, no doubt excited by the summer release of the A Hard Day's Night movie and LP, crammed into the venue for two capacity attendances of 8,750, witnessing an early and late evening show. All four Beatles tucked into The King's Hall's catering, scoffing a selection of north Irish bread and a pot of tea served by waitress Susy Crymble, who was treated to their impromptu rendition of the Everly Brothers hit 'Wake Up Little Susie'.

Also working for the catering company that day was May Majury, who, despite getting John, Paul, George, Ringo and manager Brian Epstein's autographs, was dismayed that they didn't pay their half crown (12 pence) bill. May eventually got over her indignation at the incident when, years later, the signatures realised an astronomical value unthinkable at the time.

❛ **A local paper had run an article that the boys liked jelly babies and Lennon and McCartney were playfully ducking to and fro trying to avoid the downpour of jelly babies thrown by their adoring fans.** ❜
Belfast Beatles fan Ed McCann remembers attending the late evening show at The King's Hall

LOCATION 632: about three miles south-west of the city centre on Lisburn Road, postcode BT9 6GW

Pictured below: the cavernous King's Hall, where 17,500 Beatles fans attended the two shows on November 2nd 1964

Programme cover for The Beatles' record-breaking King's Hall date in 1964 and fourteen-year-old Ritchie McLardy's ticket to The Beatles' second show

Pete Nash

Northern Ireland

PORTBALLINTRAE HOUSES OF THE HOLY AT THE GIANT'S CAUSEWAY

The Giant's Causeway is an extraordinary rock formation and World Heritage site situated on the northern coastline of Northern Ireland, a place that captured the imagination of graphic artists Hipgnosis when creating a new album cover for Led Zeppelin in 1973. Remarkably, in the days before effortless photo montaging on screen in a comfy design studio, creative types (and their models) actually braved all-weathers to snap the best images for covers, like this superb sci-fi landscape for the band's Houses Of The Holy album.

❛ **The photo for the cover of Led Zeppelin's Houses Of The Holy was taken at the Giant's Causeway in Northern Ireland. At 4am every morning for a week, three adults and two children were sprayed silver and gold from head to toe and driven to the location to await a glorious sunrise that never happened. ❜**
Storm Thorgerson (Hipgnosis)

LOCATION 633: less than four miles by road north-east of Portballintrae in County Antrim, on the B147 at 44a Causeway Road, postcode BT57 8SU

Inspired by Arthur C. Clarke's book Childhood's End, Hipgnosis designer Aubrey 'Po' Powell hand-tinted the black and white photo and used cutouts of the children to make a collage for the finished result

BELFAST THE RUBY MURRAY MURAL

Moltke Street and Benburb Street were where the young Ruby Murray grew up. Britain's top chart star in 1955, Ruby's achievement of five hit singles in one week's Top 20 that year is a record unsurpassed by any female singer to this day. The shy girl who made her TV debut aged just 12 is immortalised off the Donegall Road by an informative biographical mural in nearby Maldon Street.

LOCATION 634: Ruby Murray's original homes in Moltke Street then 49 Benburb Street are no longer standing. The mural is opposite the Methodist church in Maldon Street. All three locations join the Donegall Road in an area a mile or so south-west of the city centre. Postcode: BT12 6

Ruby's Maldon Street wall mural

CONEY ISLAND VAN THE DAY TRIPPER

A biographical spoken word poem set to a sweeping orchestral accompaniment, 'Coney Island' first featured on Van Morrison's 1989 album Avalon Sunset. Not an island at all but a small group of seaside bungalows and a beach on the County Down coast, Coney Island is one destination on the frequently made journeys out of his home city of Belfast in which Van namechecks the day trip destinations of his youth. Downpatrick, St John's Point, Strangford Lough, Shrigley, Killyleagh, Lecale District and Ardglass all get a mention as his narration recalls favourite pastimes: birdwatching, reading the Sunday papers and snacking on mussels and potted herring.

LOCATION 635: Van Morrison's Coney Island is 30 miles south east of Belfast. To emulate Van's car trips to the seaside, head for Downpatrick and then follow the A2 coastal road round to Coney Island. Postcode: BT30 7UQ

LONDONDERRY
EARLY UNDERTONES AT BULL PARK AND THE CASBAH

The Undertones' five members came together to form a band in Derry in 1975, and three years later they had broadened their horizons and caught the punk epidemic, marking their recording debut with 'Teenage Kicks' in Belfast's Wizard Sound Studios. Closer to home, two important locations of activity for the band were Derry's now demolished Casbah, little more than a portacabin on a bomb site, and Bull Park, where the five friends once played football as kids. The park was the setting for a group photo taken for the cover of their first LP and where they played an outdoor gig in 1978. Surprisingly, there is still no plaque on the walls of the Foyleside shopping centre, where the mighty Casbah once helped five lads from Derry to shake the world.

LOCATIONS 636 and **637:** the north wall of Bull Park is the spot where the band were photographed for their debut album sleeve. The park is on the B524 Lonemore Road near the city centre, postcode BT48 9. The Casbah was at the top of Orchard Street, where it turns left at Bridge Street at the junction

❛ For us getting up on stage at the Casbah on a Friday night, slightly bombed on three pints of beer, it was pure, utter escapism. Our audience, i.e. our mates, didn't really need us on a Friday night to get up and lecture them about what was politically and socially going on around them. For them it was the same thing, three pints of Guinness and hallelujah here comes Saturday morning. ❜
Feargal Sharkey

The Undertones at Bull Park line up for the cover of their debut album

Born in Northern Ireland

Derek Bell, multi-instrumentalist, The Chieftains (b. 21 Oct 1935, Belfast, d. 17 Oct 2002)

Eric Bell, guitar, Thin Lizzy (b. 3 Sep 1947, Belfast)

Michael Bradley, bass, The Undertones (b. 13 Aug 1959, Londonderry)

Jake Burns, vocals/guitar, Stiff Little Fingers (b. 21 Feb 1958, Belfast)

Andy Cairns, vocals/guitar, Therapy? (b. 22 Sep 1965, Ballyclare, Co. Antrim)

Vivian Campbell, guitar, Def Leppard (b. 25 Aug 1962, Belfast)

Henry Cluney, guitar, Stiff Little Fingers (b. 4 Aug 1957, Belfast)

Nathan Connolly, guitar, Snow Patrol (b. 20 Jan 1981, Belfast)

Phil Coulter, songwriter (b. 19 Feb 1942, Londonderry)

Nadine Coyle, Girls Aloud (b. 15 Jun 1985, Londonderry)

Peter Cunnah, vocals, D:Ream (b. 30 Aug 1966, Londonderry)

Billy Doherty, drums, The Undertones (b. 10 Jul 1958, Enniskillen)

Candida Doyle, keyboards, Pulp (b. 25 Aug 1963, Belfast)

Fyfe Ewing, drums, Therapy? (b. 1 Nov 1970, Larne, Co. Antrim)

Mark Hamilton, bass, Ash (b. 21 Mar 1977, Lisburn)

Neil Hannon, The Divine Comedy (b. 7 Nov 1970, Londonderry)

David Holmes, DJ/producer (b. 14 Feb 1969, Belfast)

Bobby Kildea, bass, Belle &

Sebastian (b. 14 Mar 1972, Bangor)

Gary Lightbody, vocals/guitar, Snow Patrol (b. 15 Jun 1976, Bangor)

Mark McClelland, bass guitar, Snow Patrol (b. 30 Mar 1976, Belfast)

Henry McCullough, guitar, Spooky Tooth/Wings (b. 21 Jul 1943, Portstewart)

Michael McKeegan, bass, Therapy? (b. 23 Mar 1971, Larne, Co. Antrim)

Ali McMordie, bass, Stiff Little Fingers (b. 31 Mar 1959, Belfast)

Rick McMurray, drums, Ash (b. 11 Jul 1975, Downpatrick)

David McWilliams, singer/songwriter (b. 4 Jul 1945, Belfast, d. 8 Jan 2002)

Gary Moore, guitar (b. 4 Apr 1952, Belfast, d. 6 Feb 2011)

Van Morrison (b. 31 Aug 1945, Belfast)

Ruby Murray (b. 29 Mar 1935, Belfast, d. 17 Dec 1996)

Damian O'Neill, guitar, The Undertones (b. 15 Jan 1961, Londonderry)

John O'Neill, guitar, The Undertones (b. 26 Aug 1957, Londonderry)

Jonny Quinn, drums, Snow Patrol (b. 26 Feb 1972, Bangor)

Clodagh Rodgers (b. 5 Mar 1947, Ballymena)

Feargal Sharkey (b. 13 Aug 1958, Londonderry)

Tim Wheeler, vocals/guitar, Ash (b. 4 Jan 1977, Downpatrick)

Eric Wrixon, Them/Thin Lizzy/The People (b. 29 Jun 1947, Belfast)

Republic of Ireland

If Dublin is the logical homing-in point for music fans who congregate in tourist-friendly Temple Bar, there are plenty of music venues punching above their weight farther afield, particularly in Clonakilty, Limerick and a proper rock pilgrimage point at Slane Castle. When County Clare's Lisdoonvarna Festival (so good Christy Moore wrote a song about it) halted, Slane Castle began to dominate the festival scene; thus began U2's castle connections, supporting Thin Lizzy at Slane in 1981 and famously using Moydrum and Carrigogunnell for cover album shots. A late developer, Ireland's rock heritage had its legacy based in the folk and highly successful showband culture, but the country would appear to be streets ahead of the UK when it comes to honouring its own. Phil Lynott, Joe Dolan and Rory Gallagher are all remembered by their statues. 'Foreigners' Noel Redding and Ronnie Wood came to live, The Rolling Stones came to tea and The Beatles paid a flying visit, with John Lennon returning to buy an island off the west coast. Then there's Horslips' haunted house, Sebadoh's Harmacy, Van the Mans Veedon Fleece cover, The Waterboys' inspirational base on Galway Bay, a Script video, US West Coast obsessives The Thrills and a plethora of U2 locations in keeping with the adoration afforded one of the world's biggest rock acts.

ATHLONE UNFORGETTABLE FIRE AT MOYDRUM CASTLE

Built in the 17th century, the ruined Moydrum Castle provided the spectacular landscape featured on the cover of U2's 1984 album The Unforgettable Fire. The cover shoot for what would become the band's second No.1 album includes Bono, The Edge, Larry Mullen, Jr and Adam Clayton in the foreground of the ivy covered structure photographed by Anton Corbijn. A second ruin, Carrigogunnell Castle, is pictured on the vinyl album back cover and in the CD booklet.

LOCATION 638: Athlone is in County West Meath in the centre of Ireland. On the Athlone by-pass (N6), head east and turn left after the next junction after the town centre turn off. Then turn right again, following a sign to Mount Temple. After more than two miles, turn right at the junction just before two red brick properties. Continue up the hill to the next corner. The castle is on the right. Carrigogunnell Castle is a mile north of Clarina, off the N69 west of Limerick

A symbol of British power, Moydrum Castle was the target for an Irish Republican Army attack when set on fire in 1921

BLACKROCK
EAST IRELAND TO WEST COAST FOR THE THRILLS

Thrills band members Conor Deasy and Daniel Ryan were born next door to each other in the east coast town of Blackrock. The nucleus of the band and friends famously decamped to California in their late teens, seeking out the roots of their obsession with US West Coast musical heroes. The resulting formation of The Thrills and release of their debut album So Much For The City in 2003 led to one in six homes in Ireland owning a copy.

LOCATION 639: Blackrock, County Dublin, is six miles south of the centre of Dublin, found by taking the N11 then N31 out of the city

BALLINCOLLIG
RORY GALLAGHER'S SUNBURST HEADSTONE

St Oliver's Cemetery at Ballincollig is where guitarist Rory Gallagher was buried following his death in 1995, aged just 47. The unusual sunburst-style headstone is shaped to mimic the 1972 award he received for International Guitarist of the Year. Before the funeral at this peaceful place outside the city where he lived, crowds numbering 15,000 lined the streets of Cork for the funeral procession to pay their last respects to a true Irish rock legend.

LOCATION 640: Ballincollig is west of Cork city. The cemetery is signposted on Model Farm Road. As you enter, go past the little house on the left and turn right.

ARDFIELD
NOEL REDDING: COUNTY CORK'S ADOPTED SON

When Noel Redding moved to Ardfield in 1973 he didn't lead the archetypal rock reclusive lifestyle - he thoroughly embraced everything the local community had to offer. The former Jimi Hendrix Experience bass guitarist purchased Dunowen House, a farmhouse built in 1771, located a short stroll from the sea, and helped support a thriving music scene in the local area. The villagers' fondness for the rock star born in Folkestone, Kent, was illustrated by the Ardfield plaque they erected in his memory after his death in 2003. Redding's funeral service was held at the Catholic church in nearby Clonakilty and his ashes were scattered in the gardens at his Dunowen home.

LOCATION 641: Ardfield, County Cork, is a small hamlet on the Atlantic coast, five miles south of Clonakilty. The Noel Redding memorial plaque is set in a wall outside O'Mahoney's pub

BRAY
DR STRANGELY STRANGE'S RIVER DARGLE 'GARDEN OF EDEN'

A tranquil spot where the local angling club is based is the setting for the cover of Dr Strangely Strange's Kip Of The Serenes album. Produced by Joe Boyd, the psychedelic folk group's 1969 debut release came in a sleeve picturing the band assembled in the trickling waters of the River Dargle, a spot well known for producing some of Ireland's biggest sea trout.

❛ **Us three kids spent our days in this Garden of Eden on the banks of a Guinness-brown torrent in winter and a stately trickle in the summer.** ❜
Dr Strangely Strange band member Tim Goulding recalls his childhood on the River Dargle

LOCATION 642: The River Dargle and Dargle Valley are near Bray, County Wicklow

River Dargle: folk on the rocks

BALLYSHANNON RORY GALLAGHER'S BIRTHPLACE AND STATUE

Although blues rock guitar hero Rory Gallagher's childhood (from the age of three) was spent in Derry and then Cork, where he formed Taste, Ballyshannon was his birthplace. Although he never had the chance to return and perform in the town once he became internationally famous, Ballyshannon's favourite son is immortalised in a life-size statue in the town centre. What is said to be the oldest town in Ireland has hosted the Rory Gallagher Festival annually for many years, attracting thousands of music fans to this west Ireland spot. In another memorial to the great

man, the building where his mother both sang and acted for The Abbey Players was renamed the Rory Gallagher Theatre in his honour.

LOCATION 643: Ballyshannon is close to Ireland's west coast in County Donegal. The statue is positioned in the town centre where Main Street and Market Street fork

The intense stage pose of Rory Gallagher captured brilliantly by sculptor David Annand

Republic of Ireland

CORK U2 PHOTOSHOOT AT THE MONTENOTTE

It would be more than a year before U2 would enjoy their first UK chart entry, but in February 1980 the quartet were already registering their second Irish chart-topper. On the 4th of this month they played Cork City's Country Club Hotel (now the Montenotte Hotel) and were snapped in front of the Cork City skyline by NME freelance photographer David Corio on the building's roof. Corio's pictures of the fresh-faced future rock legends are now displayed in the hotel's lobby, but the most memorable shot was used to great effect years later on the book cover U2 by U2 and greatest hits album and DVD U218 Singles, published and released in 2006.

LOCATION 644: on Middle Glanmire Road, north-east of the city centre

David Corio had never heard of U2 when dispatched for his first overseas photoshoot for NME in 1980

CASTLEMARTYR THE ROLLING STONES STOP FOR TEA

The quiet village of Castlemartyr played host to the world's most controversial pop stars when The Rolling Stones broke their journey on route to Cork on January 8th 1965. The Austin Princess ferrying them to two evening performances at Cork's Savoy Theatre stopped outside what is now the village greengrocer to enable the five Stones to avail themselves of some Castlemartyr refreshment. While the two older band members, Charlie Watts and Bill Wyman, headed for tea at Mrs Farrell's eating house, Mick Jagger, Keith Richard and Brian Jones made for a winter warmer or two at Barry's Bar. The village is little changed since their visit, a fact proved by a brief scene in Charlie Is My Darling, the Stones' cult movie of their riotously received three-day Irish tour.

LOCATION 645: one of two villages in County Cork with this name, the Castlemartyr the Stones visited is about 25 miles east of Cork on the N25. The bridge end of Main Street is where they stopped. Barry's Bar is now Pat Shortt's, owned by the Irish celebrity of that name, but Mrs Farrell's establishment is long gone

BOHERLAHEN HORSLIPS' HAUNTED HOUSE OF BALES

Set in a "rural hinterland" according to the local property agents, Longfield House was the base for the recordings of Celtic rockers Horslips' debut album Happy To Meet ... Sorry To Part in autumn 1972. Hiring The Rolling Stones' mobile unit, the band booked the 18th century County Tipperary house, recording in the drawing room, cellar and library. Perfecting the old house's acoustics proved a problem. Improvising, they used the neighbouring farm's hay bales and loaned the stage curtains from Trinity College Players Theatre in Dublin as sound baffles. All remote old houses rented for get-away-from-it-all rock music recordings are reportedly haunted and Longfield House was no exception; although the band were probably more materially irritated by the vast numbers of insects that plagued the place once they had escaped from the imported infested farm hay bales.

LOCATION 646: in the centre of the lush Golden Vale, near the village of Boherlahen, five miles north of Cashel, off the R660, in County Tipperary

CLANE RONNIE WOOD'S HOME FROM HOME AT SANDYMOUNT

A good pint of Guinness and a decent snooker table were always essentials in the Ronnie Wood lifestyle. Two good reasons why the former Faces guitarist made Sandymount House his rural home when the money rolled in from The Rolling Stones' lucrative Steel Wheels tour in 1989/90. He converted the property's outbuildings into an art studio, a film and tape archive and his own pub (Yer Father's Yacht) and set about breeding racehorses. Outside a statue of Elvis Presley greets house guests, which have included Slash, David Bowie, Bob Dylan, Jerry Lee Lewis and the remaining Stones, who all convened here for early work on 1994 album Voodoo Lounge. Wood's sanctuary in the lush County Kildare countryside is bordered by the Grand Canal and was a real home from home for the musician and talented painter, who as a child grew up on the banks of the Grand Union Canal, at Yiewsley, in north-west London.

LOCATION 647: two miles north of the M8 and two miles south of Clane, Sandymount House is at the 16th lock and bridge on the Grand Canal, County Kildare

CLONAKILTY
ENGLISH ROCK AND FOLK LEGENDS AT DE BARRA

A very musical town and nicknamed 'Bohemia by the sea' by The Irish Times, Clonakilty has a number of hostelries doubling as rock and folk venues. The atmospheric De Barra has the highest profile due to English singer songwriter Roy Harper's 2004 DVD Beyond The Door being recorded there and, until his death in 2003, legendary Jimi Hendrix Experience bass guitarist Noel Redding's regular Friday night performances. Both musicians moved to this south coast region to set up home and The Noel Redding Band's 1975 debut album was affectionately titled Clonakilty Cowboys. Among the music memorabilia on display is Noel's signature Fender bass, photos, letters, gold discs, a number of traditional Irish folk instruments and Roy Harper's Mojo magazine Hero award. There is a plaque commemorating Noel Redding's life outside the front door of De Barra and every May since he died the place hosts the Noel Redding Experience festival, celebrating all things Noel. Shanley's, Mick Finns, O'Donovan's Hotel, Scannells Beer Garden and The Back Door are just some of the venues which also contribute to the town's commendable musical heritage, which includes the international guitar festival.

❛ Mitch Mitchell performed in the folk club with Noel [Redding], which was as close as many of us here ever got to seeing the legendary Hendrix Experience. ❜
Ray Blackwell, De Barra's manager

LOCATION 648: Clonakilty is on the N71 in West Cork. De Barra is on the R588 in the town centre at 55 Pearse Street

CASHEL ALBUM TITLE SNAPPED BY SEBADOH

American band Sebadoh visually adopted this town in County Tipperary when the cover of their 1996 album Harmacy pictured a pharmacy in Cashel's Main Street. While on tour in Ireland, the band's multi-instrumentalist Jason Loewenstein snapped a number of photos on the road.

❛ We did a little tour of Ireland and Jason took this picture of this totally run-down pharmacy from the van window and the pharmacy was just run down to the point where the 'P' had actually fallen off – really big letters, too, and when we were looking for pictures for the album he had a lot of pictures that he had taken and we chose three of his photographs for the album. And when we saw the pharmacy picture we're like, 'That's it, that's the ******* title right there!' ❜
Lou Barlow of Sebadoh talking to Michael Stutz in 2008

LOCATION 649: O'Dwyer's Pharmacy, 34 Main Street. Cashel is off the M8 Dublin to Cork motorway

Diarmiud O'Sullivan

The Elephant Family charity makes an impact on this De Barra regular

Republic of Ireland

CORK THE RORY GALLAGHER TOUR

The town where Rory Gallagher grew up has a number of significant locations connected to the Irish guitar hero. A Gallagher tour of the city would best start chronologically at Crowley's Music Centre, the shop where the budding guitarist purchased his first Fender Stratocaster in 1963 and where a wall plaque informs visitors that Rory once lived on the same street. Then head for the Long Valley Bar where his band Taste were said to have formed, and shop at Leaders where Gallagher bought his trademark check shirts. A Rory Gallagher sculpture by his childhood friend Geraldine Creedon was unveiled in 1997 in what is now Rory Gallagher Place (formerly Paul Street Plaza) and a café named Taste! complete with replica Stratocaster is a good place to pause before continuing your tour at the Cork Library's Rory Gallagher Music Room, which displays memorabilia from the man's short career and opened in the same year as the café, in 2004. He also once played at the still elegant building that housed the Savoy Theatre and may well have been one of the lucky fans who squeezed into the venue for the legendary Rolling Stones' two shows on January 8th 1965.

LOCATIONS 650, 651, 652, 653, 654, 655 and 656: all within walking distance and with the northernmost first. Crowley's Music Centre is north over the river at 29 MacCurtain Street. Then head back west to Leaders at 76-77 North Main Street. Next stop is back east to Rory Gallagher Place and then south to the Savoy Theatre at 108 St Patrick's Street. Then head south to the Long Valley bar at 10 Winthrop Street and continue south across the southern section of the River Lee to the Taste! café at 4 Union Quay. End your tour by heading west again over the river to the Cork Library on Grand Parade

Left: Rory Gallagher's first Stratocaster was bought at Crowley's Music Centre on the street where he lived
Above: The MacCurtain Street plaque
Bottom left: Rory Gallagher Place: the setting for a tribute sculpture to the guitarist by Geraldine Creedon
Bottom right: The Savoy Theatre is still operating as a live music venue. Where once The Rolling Stones famously trod this stage, now the likes of the Wu-Tang Clan and Mumford & Sons attract the famously enthusiastic Cork music fans

DORINISH ISLAND LENNON'S "ISLAND OFF IRELAND"

After spotting a newspaper "for sale" headline advertising "An Island off Ireland", John Lennon purchased Dorinish Island in Clew Bay off the west coast in 1967 for £1,700. On instructions from Lennon, The Beatles' "Mr Fixit", Alistair Taylor, travelled to Ireland and outbid a crowd of more than 30 locals to secure the place for Lennon. The then uninhabited island was visited by Lennon, who shipped a psychedelically painted caravan to the 19-acre plot of land for him, wife Cynthia and son Julian to sleep in. A year later, he visited again with new partner Yoko Ono and the couple looked forward to building a cottage and spending holidays in their off-shore Irish bolt-hole. But time ran out on a planning permission option and, after Lennon's death, Yoko sold Dorinish in 1984 to a local farmer who now grazes his sheep on it. When in the area to visit the island, John and Yoko stayed at the Mulranny Park Hotel, with views of the Atlantic Ocean over Clew Bay. This grand 81-bedroom Victorian hotel has appropriately themed the room the couple once used (now offered as the John Lennon Suite), in a tribute to the Beatle who so loved this quiet Irish outpost.

The John Lennon Suite
at the Mulranny Park Hotel

❝ The most peaceful place on earth. ❞
John Lennon's description of Dorinish Island

LOCATION 657:
a 20-minute boat ride from the mainland at Westport, Dorinish is one of 365 islands in Clew Bay off the west coast of County Mayo. The Mulranny Park Hotel is at 1 Mulranny Road, off the N59, County Mayo. Website: www.mulrannyparkhotel.ie

DUBLIN 1 THE BEATLES ESCAPE TO THE GRESHAM HOTEL

The venue for The Beatles' only performances in the Republic of Ireland, the now demolished Adelphi Cinema, may be long gone but Dublin's Gresham Hotel where the Fab Four stayed continues to thrive. Their visit coincided with the release of No.1 EP, featuring the tracks 'I Saw Her Standing There', 'Misery', 'Anna' and 'Chains'. Arriving at Dublin Airport shortly after midday on November 7th 1963, John, Paul, George and Ringo were driven away to the Gresham before heading to the Adelphi for a press conference ahead of two sold-out concerts at 6.30 and 9pm at the 2,304 capacity cinema. Their relatively sedate journey to the hotel from the airport was in stark contrast to the manner in which they found themselves transported back to the Gresham after the concert curtain came down at 11pm. All four Beatles exited the Adelphi via the back entrance in Prussia Street, where a waiting Evening Herald newspaper van whisked them back to their hotel in the wake of scenes approaching riot status. The mayhem had begun earlier when fans attending the first evening performance clashed with those pushing their way enthusiastically in for the second show of the night. In the chaos that followed, windows were smashed, at least one car in the streets outside was set ablaze and others were overturned.

LOCATION 658 and **659:** The Adelphi Cinema (now demolished and replaced with a car park for Arnotts department store) was at 98-101 Middle Abbey Street. The Gresham Hotel is at 23 Upper O'Connell, Dublin 1

❝I have real tangible sight and sound and smell memories of things like The Beatles: very heavy velvet draped curtains, a leather pointed boot sticking out under the curtain and the place going ballistic. ❞
Bob Geldof recalls his experience as a 12-year-old at the Adelphi

❝ When The Beatles came on I remember what I thought. I said 'That there actually is John Lennon – actually right there in front of me.' ❞
Bob Geldof, present at the Adelphi in November 1963

Republic of Ireland

Thin Lizzy, variously advertised as The Tin Lizzie and Thin Lizzie and promoted as a new supergroup featuring former members of Them, The Dreams, Skid Row, Orphanage, Sugarshack and The Trixons, played their first gigs in and around Dublin in 1970. Early venues St Anthony's, Liberty and St Aidan's Halls, Glasnevin Tennis Club and The Town and Country and Countdown Clubs helped propel the band to the world stage after the release of their breakthrough hit 'Whiskey In The Jar'. The English-born Lizzy frontman, bass guitarist and solo star Phil Lynott died aged just 36 in 1986 but is rock royalty to Dublin's music fans, where his statue stands close to two of his favourite haunts, the Zodiac Club and The Bailey pub in Upper Duke Street. Unveiled in 2005 by his mother Philomena, the statue was created by Paul Daly and cast in bronze by Leo Higgins. Lynott, who grew up on Leighlin Road, Crumlin, used his beloved Dublin as the backdrop to the video for his solo single 'Old Town' in 1982.

LOCATION 660: the statue stands just north of St Stephen's Green, outside Bruxelles bar on Harry Street, Dublin 2

West Bromwich-born, Irish to the core and immortalised in bronze: Phil Lynott

Stephen Wallis Photography · stephenwallis.ie

DUBLIN 2
ROCK TREASURES AT THE HARD ROCK CAFÉ

Fittingly dominated by U2 memorabilia, Dublin's Hard Rock Café includes an original U2 Zoo TV Tour Trabant car suspended from the restaurant ceiling. A shirt worn by Elvis in the 50s, a Madonna jacket and Paul McCartney's Beatle boots are just some of the treasures on display.

LOCATION 661: 12 Fleet Street in the heart of the Temple Bar area, Dublin 2

U2 suspension at the Hard Rock Dublin: a Trabant car stage prop from the band's 1992-93 arena and stadium tour

DUBLIN 1
THE CITY'S BIGGEST ROCK VENUE AND EUROVISION LANDMARK

The city's largest venue is the 13,000 capacity O2 Arena. Before the site's 2007 refurbishment and renaming it was as The Point that it had built a reputation in the Nineties as the country's foremost music venue, hosting the Eurovision Song Contest three times and the MTV Europe awards. The former dockside train depot has attracted worldwide talent of the calibre of Bob Dylan, David Bowie, Bruce Springsteen, Oasis, R.E.M., Nirvana, U2, Coldplay, Def Leppard, Beyoncé and Kings of Leon, with local boys Westlife hitting the headlines with 12 sold-out shows in 2007.

LOCATION 662: north side of the River Liffey at the end of North Wall Quay, Dublin 1

DUBLIN 2
IRISH TOP 12 HONOURED ON THE WALL OF FAME

The Wall of Fame was launched in 2005 when music broadcaster Dave Fanning flicked a switch to light up the images of a dozen Irish music legends on a unique tribute in Dublin's cultural quarter, Temple Bar. The wall is made up of a permanent exhibition of illuminated photographs illustrating 12 of Ireland's greatest musicians. Not a definitive list, say the organisers, those currently selected for their commercial success, pioneering and influential contributions are Christy Moore, Paul Brady, Luke Kelly, Phil Lynott, Rory Gallagher, Dolores O'Riordan, Bob Geldof, Shane MacGowan, Sinéad O'Connor, The Undertones, Van Morrison and U2.

LOCATION 663: in the popular Temple Bar area at the junction of Curved Street and Temple Lane South, Dublin 2. Website: www.walloffame.ie

DUBLIN 2 THE RORY GALLAGHER STRAT SCULPTURE

A detailed and realistic replica of blues man Rory Gallagher's iconic, battered 1961 Fender Stratocaster guitar is fixed to the wall that bears his name in one of Dublin's busiest spots. The actual-size bronze cast sculpture at Rory Gallagher Corner was unveiled as a tribute to the guitarist in 2007, a ceremony attended by Dublin Mayor Catherine Byrne and a rock God in the form of U2 guitarist The Edge. Rory's guitar was said to be the first Fender Stratocaster purchased in Ireland. As a measure of his enduring popularity, Rory's DVD, Live At Montreux, was top of the Irish chart at the time of the Strat's unveiling.

❢ I always admired Rory as a musician and was later lucky enough to call him a friend. His legacy will live on in hundreds of bands in this country. ❢
The Edge remembers Rory Gallagher at the unveiling of the Stratocaster in Temple Bar

The realistic battered replica guitar in its elevated wall position in Temple Bar

LOCATION 664: the Strat sculpture is at Rory Gallagher Corner on East Essex Street, just beside Meeting House Square, Temple Bar, Dublin 2

Republic of Ireland

DUBLIN 2 THE SCRIPT 'BREAKEVEN' AT WHELAN'S

Since 1989, when Whelan's morphed into a music venue, Bloc Party, Nick Cave, Arctic Monkeys, The Magic Numbers and Jeff Buckley have all played the place where a pub has stood since 1771. Dubliners The Script shot the video for their 2008 single 'Breakeven' at Whelan's and out and about in Dublin. Script band members Danny O'Donoghue and Mark Sheehan met in The Liberties area of the city and songs like their first single, the anthemic 'We Cry', were inspired by the people and streets of their home city.

LOCATION 665: 25 Wexford Street, Dublin 2

Bloc Party rock the convivial Whelan's pub on Wexford Street

DUBLIN 2 HORSLIPS' CELTIC ROCK ON CROW STREET

An art gallery in Crow Street was the beginning of the story for Ireland's innovative folk rockers Horslips. In the early seventies they rehearsed and played their first gigs at Galerie Langlois, a gallery owned by Brendan Langlois-Kennedy, an artist friend of the band. The building is now part of the music, food, fashion and arts community of shops at Crow Street Bazaar.

LOCATION 666: at 7 Crow Street, Temple Bar, Dublin 2

DUBLIN 2 BONO'S FITZWILLIAM STREETS' VIDEO APOLOGY

The U2 video for 1998 hit 'Sweetest Thing' was filmed entirely in Fitzwilliam Place and north-east on Upper Fitzwilliam Street and Lower Fitzwilliam Street. Bono's personal apology in song to his wife Ali, whose birthday he had forgotten, is delivered with a good deal of humour in one take in the Kevin Godley-directed film on a carriage ride through Dublin 2. The contrite husband and U2 frontman is joined, at various points, by the rest of the band, Boyzone, gyrating, fire-fighting Chippendales and an elephant.

LOCATION 668: take your own carriage ride in the area between St Stephen's Green, Fitzwilliam Place and Upper and Lower Fitzwilliam Streets, Dublin 2

DUBLIN 2 THE DUBLINERS START AT O'DONOGHUES

The Dubliners were formed at O'Donoghues Bar on Merrion Row and have returned to this shrine to Irish music regularly. Also associated closely with O'Donoghues are those other Irish folk favourites The Fureys, who hailed from Ballyfermot to the west of the city.

LOCATION 667: 15 Merrion Row is near the north-east corner of St Stephen's Green

An appropriate way for the Rock Atlas tourist to write home with The Dubliners adorning your postcard

ÉIRE 48c

THE DUBLINERS

2006

DUBLIN 2 U2'S 'BEAUTIFUL DAY' ON THE ROOF

The Clarence Hotel was famously purchased by U2's Bono and The Edge in 1992. The pair are regular visitors and famously used the hotel's rooftop as the stage when the band previewed new tracks 'Elevation' and 'Beautiful Day' for broadcast on BBC TV's Top Of The Pops in 2000. By the time the quartet arrived to perform on September 27th at 3pm, the wind and rain that had failed to deter thousands of fans lining the surrounding streets and bridges was replaced, appropriately, by a beautiful day's sunshine.

LOCATION 669: in the west end of the city's cultural quarter Temple Bar, south side of the River Liffey on Wellington Quay, Dublin 2

DUBLIN 2 & 4
U2 RECORDING STUDIOS AND MESSAGE WALLS

Two districts of Dublin with a history of inspirational work where some of rock's greatest ever recording moments were committed to tape. Hanover Quay Studios has been the most used of U2's recording bases this century. Situated by the still waters of the Grand Canal Dock since 1994, the band's creative hub may face relocation soon as redevelopment of the old South Docks has been gathering pace over recent years. A wall of graffiti messages from visiting fans wanting to leave their mark is situated between the studio and the neighbouring concrete works. Years earlier, Windmill Lane Recording Studios was where the first three U2 albums were recorded in their entirety. They were the first rock band to record at the Irish traditional music set-up subsequently used by Kate Bush and the Spice Girls and purchased by Van Morrison in 2006. Although U2 no longer frequent these studios, now mostly used for TV and multimedia work, the original graffiti walls with thousands of messages still remain. In 1989, Windmill Lane Studios moved from Windmill Lane to Ringsend Road where the band continued recording and mixing their albums. Also used by U2 for recordings and tour rehearsals is The Factory on Barrow Street. In 1994, Windmill Lane Studios was the battleground for one of Mick Jagger and Keith Richards' most notorious rows during tense recordings for The Rolling Stones' Voodoo Lounge album. Appropriately, their festering animosity was brought to a head during the development of 'I Go Wild', a song that would end up as one of the album's single releases.

LOCATIONS 670, 671, 672 and 673: all within a short distance of each other, the original site for Windmill Studios is south side of the River Liffey at 4 Windmill Lane, Dublin 2, and later a few streets east at 20 Ringsend Road, Dublin 4. The Factory is in the next road at 35a Barrow Street, Dublin 4, and Hanover Studios is over the canal at Hanover Quay, Dublin 4

DUBLIN 5 LARRY MULLEN, JR'S CHILDHOOD HOME

U2 drummer Larry Mullen, Jr's home was at 60 Rosemount Avenue, Artane. This was the venue for a band meeting after the 14-year-old Mullen advertised for musicians on the Mount Temple Comprehensive School notice board in 1976, leading to the formation of U2.

LOCATION 674: 60 Rosemount Avenue, Artane, is a private residence about five miles north-east of the city centre, between the R107 and R105

DUBLIN 10
CLADDAGH ROAD BEGINNINGS FOR THE FUREYS

World famous Irish band of brothers The Fureys came from a family of travelling people who settled in Claddagh Road, which provided the folk group with the title of their 1994 album, the last recorded with Finbar Furey.

❝ My father played the fiddle and the pipes; my mother played melodeon and five-string banjo. She was a wonderful singer as well... I can remember when we moved into our new house in Ballyfermot. My father singing in the empty rooms. We lived and breathed music. ❞
Finbar Furey

LOCATION 675: Claddagh Road is about six miles west of Dublin city centre at Balleyfermot, Dublin 10

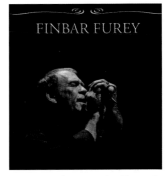

FINBAR FUREY

Releasing solo albums in the 21st century, this young Furey's musical upbringing on Claddagh Road led to him enthusiastically busking age nine before becoming the junior All-Ireland Uillean Pipe Champion at 15

Republic of Ireland

HOWTH VAN'S VEEDON FLEECE BACKDROP

The grassy landscape depicted on the cover of Van Morrison's 1974 LP Veedon Fleece is in the grounds of Sutton House Hotel. The mansion is now a private residence and was the place overlooking Dublin Bay where Van Morrison holidayed when he first arrived back in Ireland after a gruelling 1973 tour. His three-week vacation, with fiance Carol Guida in October, led to a wave of song-writing that culminated in the release of Veedon Fleece a year later.

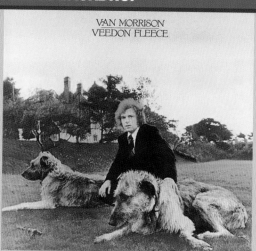

LOCATION 676: eight miles north-east of Dublin city centre, Sutton House, Shielmartin Road, Howth, north shore of Dublin Bay, County Fingal

An uneasy-looking Van Morrison and Irish wolfhounds on the lawns at Sutton House, former home of the Jameson Irish Whiskey family

DUBLIN 11
BONO'S GLASNEVIN CHILDHOOD HOME

The house where young Paul Hewson changed into U2 frontman Bono (he had the box room bedroom). After Mum and Dad Hewson sold the place in 1986, the new owners were enjoying their first Christmas in the house when a concerned Bono is said to have turned up and enquired how they were coping with U2 fans making a pilgrimage to the place. In the U2 video for the 2005 chart-topping single 'Sometimes You Can't Make It On Your Own', a hooded Bono is filmed walking down Cedarwood Road vocalising an emotional tribute to his late father. Across the road is the house where the Rowan family lived. Bono's childhood friend Derek Rowan and his kid brother Peter also made their own unique mark on rock history. Peter was the blonde youngster pictured on U2 album covers Boy (1981) and War (1983) and Derek (aka Guggi), along with Bono and Gavin Friday, formed Irish punk band Virgin Prunes in 1977.

LOCATION 677: a private residence, 10 Cedarwood Road is four miles north of the centre of Dublin, found by taking the N2 out of the city, then right at the R103, then left onto Grove Park Road. Turn right and then left into Cedarwood Road

Bono's young Cedarwood Road neighbour, Peter Rowan, was paid in Mars Bars for this modelling assignment

DUBLIN 8 MADE IN CORK - NAMED AFTER DUBLIN'S FATIMA MANSIONS

The Fatima Mansions are actual mansions! Built shortly after World War II, these 15 four-storey blocks of flats were demolished in 2006. Perceived as luxury dwellings when built but in decline and progressive decay by the 1970s, the community provided the name of nineties chart band The Fatima Mansions, whose frontman Cathal Coughlan was actually from Cork. The area has recently undergone a second upmarket regeneration.

LOCATION 678: beside the Grand Canal, Rialto, a mile or so west of the city centre at Dublin 8

LISLARKIN DUSTY SPRINGFIELD'S CLIFFTOP MEMORIAL

The dramatic Atlantic coastal Cliffs of Moher is the spot where Tom Springfield scattered his sister Dusty's ashes in 2007, more than seven years after her death. This very dramatic location is said to have been a favourite of the iconic pop star, whose family roots were in Tralee, County Kerry, where her mother grew up.

LOCATION 679: take the R478 about 30 miles south-west of Galway on the west coast and head for Lislarkin in County Clare

HOWTH PHIL LYNOTT'S SEASIDE HOMES AND RESTING PLACE

The peaceful seaside peninsula north-east of Dublin is where Phil Lynott once lived and is now buried at the local cemetery, St Fintan's, which is much visited by fans. A short stroll up the coast brings you to the home, White Horses, he bought for his mother Philomena, who acts as curator of a good deal of memorabilia and enthusiastic and hard-working secretary of the Phil Lynott fanclub. A Dublin tourism plaque is positioned above the front door of the house describing "Philip Parris Lynott" as "singer, songwriter, musician and poet." Back towards the north of the peninsula is Glen Corr, the home that the Thin Lizzy frontman purchased with the proceeds from the band's great commercial success in the 70s and 80s.

LOCATIONS 680 and **681:** situated on the east coast peninsula near Howth at County Fingal, eight miles north-east of Dublin. For Glen Corr, head left at the R105 and R106 crossroads on to Howth Road, then left on to Claremount Road to the green pillared entrance to Glen Cross, which is a private residence. St Fintan's Cemetery is on the right on Carrickbrack Road, a mile or so from the R105 and R106 crossroads. Phil Lynott is buried on the far side from the first entrance gate in Row 1, Plot 13. White Horses faces the beach on Strand Road, opposite the Sutton Dinghy Club

KILLINEY BONO AND ENYA IN 'BEL EIRE'

Around ten miles south east of Dublin is Ireland's own Laurel Canyon-like scattering of rock and pop star properties nicknamed Bel Eire. Bono's elevated estate hugs the coast, while fellow U2 band mate The Edge has a property at nearby Killiney Hill Road. Other musicians in love with the area include current property owners Van Morrison and Lisa Stansfield and former residents Jim Kerr and Chris de Burgh. Most spectacular of the Bel Eire rock pads is Ayesha Castle, renamed Manderley by its owner Enya due to the singer's love of the Daphne du Maurier book Rebecca, in which the house played a central role. These rock star pads are very private places and you will not gain access unless you are a family member or (in Bono's case) a world leader!

❝ It's not an intimidating castle, it's not full of huge ballrooms. It's very cosy. ❞
Enya talking to RTE Guide

LOCATIONS 682 and **683** in County Dublin where Bono's private estate is ten miles south of the city of Dublin on the R119 coastal Vico Road, at the junction with Strathmore Road. The property is best viewed from the beach as Bono's privacy is protected by large gates. Enya's similarly private Ayesha castle is on nearby Victoria Road

LIMERICK FRANZ FERDINAND WARM-UP DOLANS

Anyone wanting to sample second hand the atmosphere at Dolans could do worse than check out the DVD recorded at the venue by accordion maestro Sharon Shannon and her Big Band. Dolans boasts a pub, a restaurant and most famously The Warehouse music venue which, in addition to showcasing all that is good about traditional Irish music, has hosted top quality acts from farther afield including The Magic Numbers, Biffy Clyro, Kasabian, Alabama 3 and Scouting For Girls. Most impressive of all, Franz Ferdinand chose Dolans as a 300 capacity warm-up venue for their 2009 European tour.

LOCATION 684: 3/4 Dock Road on the south side of the River Shannon, west of the city centre. Website: www.dolanspub.com

Tonight let's have a big Dolans hand for Franz Ferdinand

County Clare girl Sharon Shannon brings the Dolans atmosphere to DVD in 2007

Republic of Ireland

SLANE IRELAND'S PREMIER OUTDOOR MUSIC VENUE AT SLANE CASTLE

Home to the Eighth Marquess Conyngham, Lord Henry Mount Charles and, for a short while, U2 when recording their album The Unforgettable Fire in 1984, Slane Castle is Ireland's premier outdoor concert venue, attracting the world's biggest rock bands. Few venues can match a history of concert headliners that have included Neil Young (1993), The Rolling Stones (1982 and 2007), U2 (1983 and 2001), Bob Dylan (1984), Bruce Springsteen (1985), Queen (1986), David Bowie (1987), Guns n' Roses (1992), R.E.M. (1995), The Verve (1998), Robbie Williams (1999), Bryan Adams (2000), Stereophonics (2002), Red Hot Chili Peppers (2003), Madonna (2004) and Oasis (2009). It all began with headliners Thin Lizzy in 1981.

❛ **Their musical journey is special. They have openly admitted that Thin Lizzy was one of their primary influences and they opened the first Slane in 1981. Thirty years later that had a poignancy to me.** ❜
Lord Henry Mount Charles announces Kings of Leon as 2011 Slane Castle headliners

LOCATION 685: about 30 miles north of Dublin where the N2 meets the N51, Slane Castle is just over half a mile from the village of Slane in County Meath. From Slane, head up the hill towards Navan. The castle is on the left. Website: www.slanecastle.ie

Ireland's largest rock venue, Slane Castle, on the banks of the River Boyne, attracts crowds of up to 80,000 fans

SPIDDAL 'SPRING COMES TO SPIDDAL' FOR THE WATERBOYS

Spiddal House, in the village of Spiddal, forms the backdrop to the group photo on the cover of The Waterboys' 1988 album Fisherman's Blues. Spiddal House was discovered by the band's Mike Scott and rented as a perfect location for completing work on what would turn out to be the Celtic rockers' best-selling album. The cover photo was taken towards the end of recording in May that year and features the band members and recording personnel involved during an idyllic couple of months spent by the band in this seaside spot overlooking Galway Bay. Jam sessions, including at least one fair weather appearance on the house's flat roof, games of football and regular appearances at local watering hole Hughes' and the Quays bar (where new-found friends The Saw Doctors were playing every Tuesday) provided the happy atmosphere that enabled the band to complete Fisherman's Blues. Eager to draw on the magical surroundings again, The Waterboys returned to record all of the follow-up Room To Roam, which namechecks the location on the album's track 'Spring Comes To Spiddal'.

❛ The six or seven weeks of Waterboys recording sessions at Spiddal House in Spring 1988 passed like a dream, and they form an enchanted but imprecise memory in my mind; a memory filled with sea, sky, music and old stone masonry. ❜
Mike Scott

LOCATION 686: Spiddal is on the R336 12 miles west of Galway on the coast of Galway Bay. Spiddal House is up the Moycullen Road

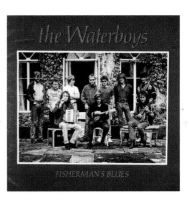

The Spiddal House base for the completion of work on The Waterboys' best-selling album

Slane Castle Ltd

Republic of Ireland

MULLINGAR THE JOE DOLAN BRIDGE AND STATUE

One of Ireland's most successful pop stars, Joe Dolan, was born and based in Mullingar, where the cover of his debut album was photographed. The Answer To Everything (1964) cover depicts Joe and The Drifters Showband in the grounds of Belvedere House, a Georgian mansion and 160-acre estate on the shores of Lough Ennel. After his death, Dolan was buried at Walshestown Cemetery near Mullingar and honoured with a statue in the centre of the town, which drew 6,000 fans at its unveiling in 2008. Local fondness for the entertainer didn't stop there: the final link in the Mullingar

ring road was named after him when the 540-metre Joe Dolan Bridge was opened in 2010.

LOCATIONS 687, 688 and 689: the statue is on the square just at the corner of Pearse Street and Mount Street, in front of Canton Casey's pub and the tourist information office in Mullingar. Belvedere House, gardens and park are open to the public (website: www.belvedere-house.ie), best accessed by taking Lynn Road south out of Mullingar for approximately six miles. The Joe Dolan Bridge links the Clonmore Business

Born in the Republic of Ireland

Leo Barnes, saxophone, Hothouse Flowers (b. 5 Oct 1965, Dublin)
Mary Black (b. 22 May 1955, Dublin)
Bono, U2 (b. 10 May 1960, Dublin)
Tim Booth, vocals/guitar, Dr Strangely Strange (b. 6 Sep 1943, Co. Kildare)
Ciarán Bourke, The Dubliners (b. 18 Feb 1935, Dublin, d. 10 May 1988)
Brendan Bowyer, vocals, The Royal Showband (b. 12 Oct 1938, Waterford)
Paul Brady (b. 19 May 1947, Strabane, Co. Tyrone)
Ciarán Brennan, Clannad (b. 4 Mar 1954, Gweedore)
Maire Brennan, Clannad (b. 4 Aug 1952, Gweedore)
Pete Briquette, bass, The Boomtown Rats (b. 2 Jul 1954, Dublin)
Nicky Byrne, Westlife (b. 9 Oct 1978, Dublin)
Eamonn Campbell, The Dubliners (b. 29 Nov 1946, Drogheda)
Seán Cannon, The Dubliners (b. 29 Nov 1940, Galway)
Eamon Carr, Horslips (b. 12 Nov 1948, Kells, Co. Meath)
Davy Carton, vocals, The Saw Doctors (b. 10 Apr 1959, Tuam, Co. Galway)
Philip Chevron, guitar, The Pogues (b. 17 Jun 1957, Dublin)
Con Cluskey, The Bachelors (b. 18 Nov 1941, Dublin)

Dec Cluskey, The Bachelors (b. 23 Dec 1942, Dublin)
Sonny Condell, Tír Na Nóg/Scullion (b. 1 Jul 1949, Newtownmountkennedy)
Kevin Conneff, The Chieftains (b. 8 Jan 1945, Donore, Co. Meath)
Andrea Corr, vocals/tin whistle, The Corrs (b. 17 May 1974, Dundalk)
Caroline Corr, drums/vocals, The Corrs (b. 17 Mar 1973, Dundalk)
Jim Corr, keyboards, The Corrs (b. 31 Jul 1964, Dundalk)
Sharon Corr, vocals/violin, The Corrs (b. 24 Mar 1970, Dundalk)
Gerry Cott, guitar, The Boomtown Rats (b. 15 Oct 1954, Dublin)
Cathal Coughlan, The Fatima Mansions (b. Cork)
Mary Coughlan (b. 5 May 1956, Co. Galway)
Simon Crowe, drums, The Boomtown Rats (b. 14 Apr 1955, Dublin)
Conor Deasy, vocals, The Thrills (b. 31 Dec 1969, Dublin)
Barry Devlin, Horslips (b. 27 Nov 1946, Newry, Co. Down)
Joe Dolan (b. 16 Oct 1939, Mullingar, d. 26 Dec 2007)
Val Doonican (b. 3 Feb 1927, Waterford)
Brian Downey, drums, Thin Lizzy (b. 27 Jan 1951, Dublin)
Ronnie Drew, The Dubliners (b. 16 Sep

1934, Dún Laoghaire, d. 16 Aug 2008)
Keith Duffy, vocals, Boyzone (b. 1 Oct 1974, Dublin)
Noel Duggan, guitar/vocals, Clannad (b. 23 Jan 1949, Gweedore)
Pádraig Duggan, mandolin/vocals, Clannad (b. 23 Jan 1949, Gweedore)
Kian Egan, Westlife (b. 29 Apr 1980, Sligo)
Enya (b. 17 May 1961, Gweedore, Co. Donegal)
Siobhan Fahey, Shakespears Sister/Bananarama (b. 10 Sep 1958, Dunshaughlin, Co. Meath)
Johnny Fean, Horslips (b. 17 Nov 1951, Dublin)
Mark Feehily, Westlife (b. 28 May 1980, Sligo)
Jerry Fehily, drums, Hothouse Flowers (b. 28 Aug 1963, Bishopstown, Cork)
Shane Filan, Westlife (b. 5 Jul 1979, Sligo)
Johnnie Fingers, keyboards, The Boomtown Rats (b. John Moylett, 10 Sep 1956, Dublin)
Gavin Friday (b. 8 Oct 1959, Dublin)
Eddie Furey, The Fureys (b. 23 Dec 1944, Dublin)
Finbar Furey, The Fureys (b. 28 Sep 1946, Dublin)
George Furey, The Fureys (b. 11 Jun 1951, Dublin)
Paul Furey, The Fureys (b. 6 May 1948, Dublin)

Park to the Lynn Roundabout on Tullamore Road and spans the flood plains of the River Brosna and Lacy's Canal

Artist Carl Payne's statue of Joe Dolan proved so popular, and so many fans clambered on it, that it had to be returned to a foundry for re-enforcing in 2010

Rory Gallagher (b. 2 Mar 1948, Ballyshannon, d. 14 Jun 1995)

Stephen Gately, vocals, Boyzone (b. 17 Mar 1976, Dublin, d. 10 Oct 2009)

Bob Geldof, vocals, The Boomtown Rats (b. 5 Oct 1951, Dublin)

Liam Genockey, drums, Steeleye Span (b. 12 Aug 1948, Dublin)

Tim Goulding, Dr Strangely Strange (b. 15 May 1945, Dublin)

Mikey Graham, vocals, Boyzone (b. 15 Aug 1972, Dublin)

Michael Hogan, bass, The Cranberries (b. 29 Apr 1973, Moyross)

Noel Hogan, guitar, The Cranberries (b. 25 Dec 1971, Moyross)

Graham Hopkins, drums, Therapy? (b. 20 Dec 1975, Dublin)

Richard James, aka Aphex Twin (b. 18 Aug 1971, Limerick)

Seán Keane, The Chieftains (b. 12 Jul 1946, Dublin)

Ronan Keating, Boyzone (b. 3 Mar 1977, Dublin)

Luke Kelly, The Dubliners (b. 17 Nov 1940, Dublin, d. 30 Jan 1984)

Mark Kelly, keyboards, Marillion (b. 9 Apr 1961, Dublin)

Fergal Lawler, drums, The Cranberries (b. 4 Mar 1971, Limerick)

Jim Lockhart, Horslips (b. 3 Feb 1948, Dublin)

Bob Lynch, The Dubliners (b. 18 May 1935, Dublin, d. 2 Oct 1982)

Shane Lynch, Boyzone (b. 3 Jul 1976, Dublin)

Drew McConnell, bass, Babyshambles (b. 10 Nov 1978, Dublin)

Brian McFadden, Westlife (b. 12 Apr 1980, Dublin)

Barney McKenna, banjo, The Dubliners (b. 16 Dec 1939, Dublin)

Paddy Moloney, The Chieftains (b. 1 Aug 1938, Dublin)

Imelda May (b. 10 Jul 1974, Dublin)

Matt Molloy, The Bothy Band/The Dubliners/Planxty (b. 12 Jan 1947, Ballaghaderreen, Co. Roscommon)

Christy Moore (b. 7 May 1945, Dublin)

Leo Moran, guitar, The Saw Doctors (b. 9 Nov 1964, Tuam, Co. Galway)

Larry Mullen, Jr, drums, U2 (b. 31 Oct 1961, Artane, Dublin)

Tony Murray, guitar, The Troggs (b. 26 Apr 1943, Dublin)

Fiachna Ó Braonáin, guitar, Hothouse Flowers (b. 27 Nov 1965, Dublin)

Colm Ó Cíosóig, drums/keyboards, My Bloody Valentine (b. 31 Oct 1964, Dublin)

Sinéad O'Connor (b. 8 Dec 1966, Glenageary, Co. Dublin)

Daniel O'Donnell (b. 12 Dec 1961, Kincasslagh, Co. Donegal)

Danny O'Donoghue, vocals, The Script (b. 3 Oct 1980, Dublin)

Leo O'Kelly, Tír Na Nóg (b. 27 Nov 1949, Carlow)

Liam Ó Maonlaí, vocals/keyboards, Hothouse Flowers (b. 7 Nov 1964, Monkstown)

Dolores O'Riordan, vocals, The Cranberries (b. 6 Sep 1971, Limerick)

Gilbert O'Sullivan (b. 1 Dec 1946, Waterford)

Peter O'Toole, bass, Hothouse Flowers (b. 1 Apr 1965, Dublin)

Paddy Reilly, The Dubliners (b. 18 Oct 1939, Rathcoole, South Dublin Co.)

Damien Rice (b. 7 Dec 1973, Celbridge, Co. Kildare)

Gary Roberts, guitar, The Boomtown Rats (b. 16 Jun 1954, Dublin)

Sharon Shannon (b. 12 Nov 1968, Ruan, Co. Clare)

John Sheahan, The Dubliners (b. 19 May 1939, Dublin)

Mark Sheehan, vocals/bass, The Script (b. 29 Oct 1981, Dublin)

John Stokes, The Bachelors (b. 13 Aug 1940, Dublin)

Louis Walsh, manager, talent show judge (b. 5 Aug 1952, Kiltimagh, Co. Mayo)

Terry Woods, mandolin/guitar, The Pogues (b. 4 Dec 1947, Dublin)

CLARKSDALE

meet you
at the crossroads

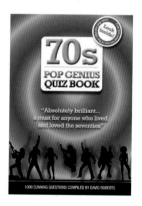

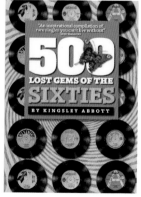

www.clarksdalebooks.co.uk
clarksdale@ovolobooks.co.uk